T0207298

Communications
in Computer and Information Science 2142

Editorial Board Members

Rationale

The CCIS series is devoted to the publication of proceedings of computer science conferences. Its aim is to efficiently disseminate original research results in informatics in printed and electronic form. While the focus is on publication of peer-reviewed full papers presenting mature work, inclusion of reviewed short papers reporting on work in progress is welcome, too. Besides globally relevant meetings with internationally representative program committees guaranteeing a strict peer-reviewing and paper selection process, conferences run by societies or of high regional or national relevance are also considered for publication.

Topics

The topical scope of CCIS spans the entire spectrum of informatics ranging from foundational topics in the theory of computing to information and communications science and technology and a broad variety of interdisciplinary application fields.

Information for Volume Editors and Authors

Publication in CCIS is free of charge. No royalties are paid, however, we offer registered conference participants temporary free access to the online version of the conference proceedings on SpringerLink (http://link.springer.com) by means of an http referrer from the conference website and/or a number of complimentary printed copies, as specified in the official acceptance email of the event.

CCIS proceedings can be published in time for distribution at conferences or as post-proceedings, and delivered in the form of printed books and/or electronically as USBs and/or e-content licenses for accessing proceedings at SpringerLink. Furthermore, CCIS proceedings are included in the CCIS electronic book series hosted in the SpringerLink digital library at http://link.springer.com/bookseries/7899. Conferences publishing in CCIS are allowed to use Online Conference Service (OCS) for managing the whole proceedings lifecycle (from submission and reviewing to preparing for publication) free of charge.

Publication process

The language of publication is exclusively English. Authors publishing in CCIS have to sign the Springer CCIS copyright transfer form, however, they are free to use their material published in CCIS for substantially changed, more elaborate subsequent publications elsewhere. For the preparation of the camera-ready papers/files, authors have to strictly adhere to the Springer CCIS Authors' Instructions and are strongly encouraged to use the CCIS LaTeX style files or templates.

Abstracting/Indexing

CCIS is abstracted/indexed in DBLP, Google Scholar, EI-Compendex, Mathematical Reviews, SCImago, Scopus. CCIS volumes are also submitted for the inclusion in ISI Proceedings.

How to start

To start the evaluation of your proposal for inclusion in the CCIS series, please send an e-mail to ccis@springer.com.

Juan Antonio Lossio-Ventura ·
Eduardo Ceh-Varela · Genoveva Vargas-Solar ·
Ricardo Marcacini · Claude Tadonki ·
Hiram Calvo · Hugo Alatrista-Salas
Editors

Information Management and Big Data

10th Annual International Conference, SIMBig 2023
Mexico City, Mexico, December 13–15, 2023
Proceedings

Springer

Editors
Juan Antonio Lossio-Ventura ⓘ
National Institutes of Health (NIH)
Bethesda, MD, USA

Eduardo Ceh-Varela ⓘ
Eastern New Mexico University
Portales, NM, USA

Genoveva Vargas-Solar ⓘ
CNRS, LIRIS
Lyon, France

Ricardo Marcacini ⓘ
University of São Paulo
São Paulo, Brazil

Claude Tadonki ⓘ
Mines ParisTech
Paris, France

Hiram Calvo ⓘ
Instituto Politecnico Nacional
Mexico City, Mexico

Hugo Alatrista-Salas ⓘ
Léonard de Vinci Pôle Universitaire
Paris, France

ISSN 1865-0929   ISSN 1865-0937 (electronic)
Communications in Computer and Information Science
ISBN 978-3-031-63615-8   ISBN 978-3-031-63616-5 (eBook)
https://doi.org/10.1007/978-3-031-63616-5

This Springer imprint is published by the registered company Springer Nature Switzerland AG
The registered company address is: Gewerbestrasse 11, 6330 Cham, Switzerland

If disposing of this product, please recycle the paper.

Preface

SIMBig 2023[1], the 10th edition of the International Conference on Information Management and Big Data, was held between December 13–15, 2023 at the Centro de Investigación en Computación (CIC)[2], of the Instituto Politécnico Nacional (IPN)[3], Mexico City, Mexico. SIMBig 2023 introduced innovative approaches for analyzing and handling datasets as well as new methods based on Artificial Intelligence (AI), Data Science, Machine Learning, Natural Language Processing, Semantic Web, Data-driven Software Engineering, Health Informatics, and more.

The SIMBig conference series aims to promote cooperation between national and international researchers to improve data-driven decision-making by using new technologies dedicated to analyzing data. SIMBig is a convivial place where participants present their scientific contributions in the form of full and short papers. This book contains the proceedings of the papers presented at the tenth edition of SIMBig. In this edition, 19 long papers and 6 short papers were selected for publication.

Dr. Marc Najork, from Google, USA, discussed the historical paradigm of information retrieval systems, emphasizing their limitations in integrating information from multiple documents into a direct answer. He noted that the advent of large language models (LLMs), empowered by deep neural networks, had challenged this paradigm by enabling models to memorize facts and relations. Dr. Najork outlined the emergence of generative information retrieval systems, addressing challenges such as grounding answers, attributing passages to primary sources, providing nuanced responses, avoiding bias, and navigating the evolving content ecosystem influenced by LLMs. This raised questions about the treatment of generated content, differentiation from human-authored content, and the impact on business models.

Dr. Stefano Ermon, from Stanford University, USA, talked about generative models that are typically based on explicit representations of probability distributions (e.g., autoregressive) or implicit sampling procedures (e.g., GANs). Dr. Ermon presented an alternative approach based on modeling directly the vector field of gradients of the data distribution (scores) which underlies recent score-based diffusion models. This framework allowed flexible architectures, required no sampling during training or the use of adversarial training methods. Additionally, score-based diffusion generative models enabled exact likelihood evaluation through connections with neural ODEs, achieving state-of-the-art sample quality and excellent likelihoods on image datasets. Dr. Ermon also discussed numerical and distillation methods to accelerate sampling and their application to inverse problem solving.

Dr. Huan Liu, from Arizona State University, USA, titled his presentation "Social Media Mining - A Bountiful Frontier in AI and Data Science". Dr. Liu highlighted unprecedented research opportunities that emerged in AI and Data Science through the

---

[1] https://simbig.org/SIMBig2023/.

[2] https://www.cic.ipn.mx/.

[3] https://www.ipn.mx/.

lens of social media data. Dr. Liu presented his research which contemplated the role of social media mining in the rapid development of AI and Big Data, emphasizing its potential for understanding human behavior, predicting trends, and informing decision-making processes across various domains.

Dr. Yan Liu, from the University of Southern California, USA, titled her presentation "Frontiers of Foundation Models for Time Series Modeling and Analysis". Dr. Liu delved into the recent developments in deep learning that have catalyzed research progress in time series modeling and analysis, highlighting the transformative potential these advancements hold across various domains. Dr. Liu discussed how practical applications of time series data pose a series of new challenges, including but not limited to multi-resolution, multimodal, missing values, distributing, and interpretability issues. Throughout her presentation, Dr. Liu provided insights into potential approaches towards establishing foundation models for time series data, exploring methodologies that address these challenges and proposing future directions to advance the field of time series research.

Dr. Mona Diab, from Carnegie Mellon University, USA, titled her presentation "Responsible Thinking: Laying the Operational Foundation". In her presentation, Dr. Diab outlined a practical and operational foundation for what she coined responsible thinking. She emphasized the critical importance of this approach for developing modern technologies that reside at the intersection of AI and society

Dr. Wen Yu, from CINVESTAV-IPN, Mexico, discussed how deep learning has demonstrated remarkable success in image and speech recognition, natural language processing, and various other domains. However, it had not yet been extensively utilized in modeling complex nonlinear systems. In his talk, Dr. Yu explored several deep learning methods for nonlinear system identification. These methods included the use of long short-term memory networks (LSTMs) for modeling dynamic behaviors, convolutional neural networks (CNNs) for addressing spatial dependencies in nonlinear modeling, and transfer learning to handle limited data for specific nonlinear systems. Additionally, Dr. Yu discussed their application in time series prediction. The efficacy of these deep learning methods was validated through several benchmark examples.

Dr. Xiaoou Li, from CINVESTAV-IPN, Mexico, talked about machine learning and big data analytics for sustainable Food-Energy-Water (FEW) nexus. These critical resources are pivotal for human survival and align with the United Nations' Sustainable Development Goals for 2030. Technological advancements have generated vast FEW-related data, attracting data scientists to address challenges such as predicting wind energy production, analyzing land irrigation efficiency, and monitoring water quality. Machine learning techniques and Big Data analytics offer solutions to these challenges, including handling high-dimensional data and integrating disparate data sets through data fusion strategies. The presentation explored FEW systems and associated data science challenges, sharing preliminary findings on long-term prediction of time series within wind energy systems, even in the presence of missing data points.

April 2024

Juan Antonio Lossio-Ventura
Eduardo Ceh-Varela
Genoveva Vargas-Solar
Ricardo Marcacini
Claude Tadonki
Hiram Calvo
Hugo Alatrista-Salas

Organization

Organizing Committee

General Organizers

Juan Antonio Lossio-Ventura   National Institutes of Health, USA
Hugo Alatrista-Salas   Léonard de Vinci Pôle Universitaire, Research
                                   Center, Paris La Défense, France

Local Organizers

Hiram Calvo   Instituto Politécnico Nacional, Mexico
Grigori Sidorov   Instituto Politécnico Nacional, Mexico

DISE Track Organizers

Eduardo Díaz   Universidad Peruana de Ciencias Aplicadas, Peru
Eduardo Ceh-Varela   Eastern New Mexico University, USA

ANLP Track Organizers

Lilian Berton   Federal University of São Paulo, Brazil
Pedro Shiguihara   Universidad San Ignacio de Loyola, Peru
Ricardo Marcacini   University of São Paulo, Brazil

EE-AI-HPC Track Organizers

David Balderas Silva   Tecnológico de Monterrey, Mexico
Claude Tadonki   MINES Paris, France
Sergio Ruiz Loza   Tecnológico de Monterrey, Mexico

D&I Track Organizers

Barbara Catania   Università degli Studi di Genova, Italy
Genoveva Vargas-Solar   CNRS, France
Ester Zumpano   University of Calabria, Italy

SNMAM Track Organizers

Jorge Valverde-Rebaza   Tecnológico de Monterrey, Mexico
Alan Demétrius Baria Valejo   Federal University of São Carlos, Brazil
Fabiana Rodrigues de Góes   Visibilia, Brazil
Thiago de Paulo Faleiro   University of Brasilia, Brazil

Program Committee

Main Track Program Committee

Nathalie Abadie   COGIT IGN, France
Pedro Marco Achanccaray Diaz   Pontifical Catholic University of Rio de Janeiro,
                                       Brazil
Marco Alvarez   University of Rhode Island, USA
Alexandre Alves   Université Paris 1 Panthéon-Sorbonne, France
Francesco Amigoni   Politecnico di Milano, Italy
Yuan An   Drexel University, USA
Sophia Ananiadou   University of Manchester, UK
Erick Antezana   Norwegian University of Science and Technology,
                                       Norway
Smith Washington Arauco   Pontifical Catholic University of Rio de Janeiro,
  Canchumuni   Brazil
John Atkinson   Universidad Adolfo Ibañez, Chile
Imon Banerjee   Mayo Clinic, USA
Guissela Bejarano Nicho   Universidad Peruana Cayetano Heredia, Peru
Patrice Bellot   Aix-Marseille Université, France
Serge Belongie   University of Copenhagen, Denmark
Giacomo Bergami   Newcastle University, UK
Jose Bermudez Castro   Pontifical Catholic University of Rio de Janeiro,
                                       Brazil
Jiang Bian   University of Florida, USA
Albert Bifet   Telecom ParisTech, France
Fernando Birra   New University of Lisbon, Portugal
Carmen Brando   École des Hautes Études en Sciences Sociales,
                                       France
Andrei Broder   Google, USA
Jean-Paul Calbimonte Pérez   University of Applied Sciences and Arts Western
                                       Switzerland, Switzerland
Ricardo Campos   Polytechnic Institute of Tomar/LIAAD INESC
                                       TEC, Portugal

Sanjay Madria	Missouri University of Science and Technology, USA
Bruno Martins	INESC-ID and Instituto Superior Técnico, University of Lisbon, Portugal
Patrick McClure	National Institutes of Health (NIMH/NIH), USA
Florent Masseglia	Inria, France
Rosario Medina Rodriguez	Pontificia Universidad Católica del Perú, Peru
Guillaume Metzler	ERIC, Université Lumière Lyon 2, France
Avdesh Mishra	Texas A&M University-Kingsville, USA
Giovanni Montana	Imperial College London, UK
Regina Motz	Universidad de la República, Uruguay
Pritam Mukherjee	National Institutes of Health (NLM/NIH), USA
Behzad Naderalvojoud	Stanford University, USA
Mark Musen	Stanford University, USA
Behzad Naderalvojoud	Stanford University, USA
Jordi Nin	Universitat Ramon Llull, ESADE, Spain
Nhung Nguyen	University of Manchester, UK
Miguel Nuñez-del-Prado-Cortéz	World Bank, USA
Maciej Ogrodnicz	Institute of Computer Science of the Polish Academy of Sciences, Poland
Fernando Ortiz-Rodriguez	Universidad Autonoma de Tamaulipas, Mexico
Matilde Pato	Instituto Superior de Engenharia de Lisboa - ISEL, Portugal
Evelyn Perez-Cervantes	Oracle, Brazil
Jessica Pinaire	Kalya, France
Pascal Poncelet	University of Montpellier, France
Mattia Prosperi	University of Florida, USA
Marcos Quiles	Federal University of São Paulo, Brazil
José Fabián Reyes Román	Universitat Politècnica de València, Spain
Justine Reynaud	University of Normandie, France
Edgar Rios	Genentech, USA
Mathieu Roche	CIRAD, France
Nancy Rodriguez	University of Montpellier, France
Alejandro Rodríguez-Gonzales	Universidad Politècnica de Madrid, Spain
Edelweis Rohrer	Universidad de la República, Uruguay
Silvia Rueda Pascual	University of Valencia, Spain
Arnaud Sallaberry	Paul Valéry University, France
Christian Sallaberry	Université de Pau et des Pays de l'Adour - UPPA, France
Julio Sandobalin	Escuela Politècnica Nacional, Peru
Shengtian Sang	Stanford University, USA
Edgar Sarmiento-Calisaya	Universidad Nacional de San Agustín, Peru

José Segovia-Juárez	Instituto Nacional de Innovación Agraria - INIA, Peru
Nazha Selmaoui-Folcher	University of New Caledonia, New Caledonia
Selja Seppälä	University College Cork, Ireland
Muhammad Shafiq	Guangzhou University, China
Matthew Shardlow	University of Manchester, UK
Diego Silva	Universidade Federal de São Carlos, Brazil
Thiago Silva	Federal University of Technology - UTFPR, Nigeria
Wenyu Song	Harvard University, USA
Madhumita Sushil	University of California, San Francisco, USA
Claude Tadonki	MINES ParisTech, France
Maguelonne Teisseire	INRAE, France
Sanju Tiwari	Universidad Autonoma de Tamaulipas, Mexico
Andrew Tomkins	Google, USA
Juan-Manuel Torres-Moreno	University of Avignon, France
Nicolas Travers	Léonard de Vinci Pôle Universitaire Research Center, France
Willy Ugarte	Universidad Peruana de Ciencias Aplicadas, Peru
Alan Valejo	University of São Paulo, Brazil
Carlos Vazquez	École de Technologie Supérieure, Canada
Maria-Esther Vidal	Universidad Simón Bolívar, Venezuela
Edwin Villanueva Talavera	Pontificia Universidad Católica del Perú, Peru
Sebastian Walter	Semalytix GmbH, Germany
Lana Yeganova	National Institutes of Health (NLM/NIH), USA
Yuan Zhao	National Institutes of Health (NIMH/NIH), USA
Charles Zheng	National Institutes of Health (NIMH/NIH), USA
Chryssa Zerva	Instituto de Telecomunicações, Portugal
Pierre Zweigenbaum	Université Paris-Saclay, CNRS, LISN, France
Ivan Dimitry Zyrianoff	University of Bologna, Italy

EE-AI-HPC Program Committee

Corinne Ancourt	MINES Paris - PSL, France
Diego Leonel Cadette Dutra	LCP/PESC/COPPE/UFRJ, Brazil
Maria Clicia Castro	State University of Rio de Janeiro, Brazil
Petr Dokladal	MINES Paris - PSL, France
Henrique Freitas	PUC Minas, Brazil
Khaled Ibrahim Lawrence	Berkeley National Lab, USA
Gabriele Mencagli	University of Pisa, Italy
Marcin Paprzycki	IBS PAN and WSM, Poland
Hermes Senger	UFSCAR, Brazil

Georges-Andre Silber   MINES Paris - PSL, France
Miwako Tsuji   RIKEN R-CCS, Japan

SNMAM Program Committee

Francesco Bailo   University of Sydney, Australia
César Beltrán   Pontificia Universidad Catolica del Perú, Peru
Renan de Padua   iFood, Brazil
Rafael Delalibera Rodrigues   University of São Paulo, Brazil
Alexandre Donizeti   Federal University of ABC, Brazil
Brett Drury   Liverpool Hope University, UK
Luis Paulo Faina Garcia   University of Brasilia, Brazil
Maria Cristina Ferreira de Oliveira University of São Paulo, Brazil
Cristian Gawron   South Westphalia University of Applied Sciences,
                                       Germany
Sabrine Mallek   ICN Business School, France
Katarzyna Musial   University of Technology Sydney, Australia
Murilo Naldi   Federal University of São Carlos, USA
Ankur Singh Bist   Graphic Era Hill University, India
Aurea Rossy Soriano Vargas   State University of Campinas, Brazil
Rafael Santos   Brazilian National Institute for Space Research
                                       (INPE), Brazil
Fabiola Souza Fernandes Pereira   Federal University of Uberlandia, Brazil
Newton Spolaor   Western Parana State University, Brazil
Victor Stroele   Federal University of Juiz de Fora, Brazil
Edwin Villanueva Talavera   Pontificia Universidad Católica del Perú, Peru

DISE Program Committee

Carlos Gavidia Calderon   The Alan Turing Institute, UK
Gandhi Samuel Hernandez Chan   CentroGeo - CONACYT, Mexico
Essa Imhmed   Eastern New Mexico University, USA
Carlos Efraín Iñiguez Jarrín   Escuela Politécnica Nacional, Ecuador
Denisse Muñante Arzapalo   ENSIIE & Samovar, France
Jose Ignacio Panach Navarrete   Universitat de València, Spain
Otto Parra   Universidad de Cuenca, Ecuador
Gonzalo Peraza Mues   Tecnologico de Monterrey, Mexico
Jose Fabián Reyes-Román   Universitat Politècnica de València, Spain
Silvia Rueda Pascual   Universitat de València, Spain
Sarbagya Shakya   Eastern New Mexico University, USA

ANLP Program Committee

Diego Amancio	University of São Paulo, Brazil
Evelin Amorim	Institute for Systems and Computer Engineering, Technology and Science, Portugal
Honorio Apaza	Universidad Nacional de Moquegua, Peru
Marcio Basgalupp	Federal University of São Paulo, Brazil
Hugo Calderón-Vilca	Universidad Nacional Mayor de San Marcos, Peru
Juan Gutierrez	Universidad de Lima, Peru
Nils Murrugarra-Llerena	Weber State University, USA
Dennis Núñez-Fernández	Université Paris Cité, France
Luis Pereira	Federal University of São Paulo, Brazil
Thiago Paulo	University of Brasilia, Brazil
Efstathios Stamatatos	University of the Aegean, Greece

Organizing Institutions and Sponsors

Organizing Institutions

Instituto Politécnico Nacional, Mexico[4]
Centro de Investigación en Computación, Mexico[5]

Collaborating Institutions

Sociedad Mexicana de Inteligencia Artificial, Mexico[6]
The North American Chapter of the Association for Computational Linguistics NAACL, USA[7]

---

[4] https://www.gob.mx/segob/en.
[5] https://www.cic.ipn.mx/.
[6] https://smia.mx/.
[7] http://naacl.org/.

Contents

Parallel-EvoCluster: An Open-Source Parallel Nature-Inspired Optimization Clustering

Edwin Alvarez-Mamani[1]($\boxtimes$) (iD), Milagros Yarahuaman-Rojas[2] (iD),
and Raul Huillca-Huallparimachi[3] (iD)

[1] Engineering Department, Pontificia Universidad Católica del Perú, Lima, Peru
edwin.alvarez@pucp.edu.pe
[2] Department of Informatics, Universidad Nacional de San Antonio Abad del Cusco,
Cusco, Peru
171071@unsaac.edu.pe
[3] Faculty of Systems Engineering and Informatics, Universidad Nacional Mayor de
San Marcos, Lima, Peru
raul.huillca@unmsm.edu.pe

Abstract. Bio-inspired algorithms are a branch of Artificial Intelligence
in which the behavior of natural systems is emulated to design non-
deterministic heuristic methods for search, clustering, optimization, and
simulation. Clustering algorithms search for patterns in the data and
identify groups into clusters having similar features. The objective of this
research is to improve the execution times of ten bio-inspired serial algorithms to solve clustering problems. To achieve our objective, we use parallelization techniques to reduce execution time by utilizing all processing
resources. We proposed `Parallel-EvoCluster` to parallelize ten algorithms through two parallelization approaches, such as shared-memory
and distributed-memory architecture using Open Multi-Processing and
Message Passing Interface APIs respectively. Both approaches were performed using 24 CPU cores. The results show a significant improvement
in runtimes of the parallel algorithms, parallelization with MPI on average is 10.14x times faster and the average parallelization with OMP
is 9.05x times faster than the serial versions. The code is available at:
https://github.com/win7/Parallel_EvoCluster.

Keywords: Clustering · Parallel computer · Bio-inspired · Model
island · MPI · OMP

1 Introduction

There are bio-inspired serial algorithms for clustering problems that, due to their
nature, have a very high computational cost. On the other hand, these algorithms
are parallelized to improve their runtimes. As a consequence of the above, the
objective of this research is to improve the runtimes of ten bio-inspired serial

J. A. Lossio-Ventura et al. (Eds.): SIMBig 2023, CCIS 2142, pp. 1–16, 2024.
https://doi.org/10.1007/978-3-031-63616-5_1

algorithms found and cited in the literature. For this purpose, these bio-inspired serial algorithms were parallelized using the APIs Open Multi-Processing (OMP) and Message Passing Interface (MPI).

We start by analyzing the research problem. Then, parallel versions of the bio-inspired serial algorithms are implemented and subjected to experiments. Finally, the algorithms with the best performance in terms of runtimes and quality of results are identified. The proposal of this research is the parallel implementation of ten bio-inspired serial algorithms called `Parallel-EvoCluster`.

The approach taken by bio-inspired algorithms is characterized by variables in mathematical models for optimization problems. In [1], they implement ten serial bio-inspired algorithms to solve clustering problems, which we cite below: Genetic Algorithm (GA) [2], Particle Swarm Optimization (PSO) [3,4], Salp Swarm Algorithm (SSA) [5], Firefly Algorithm (FFA) [6], Gray Wolf Optimizer (GWO) [7], Whale Optimization Algorithm (WOA) [8], Multi-Verse Optimizer (MVO) [9], Moth-Flame Optimizer (MFO) [10], Bat Algorithm (BAT) [11] and Cuckoo Search Algorithm (CS) [12].

This research paper is organized as follows. A literature review of bio-inspired parallel algorithms is given in Sect. 2. In Sect. 3, the bio-inspired parallel algorithms are defined. In Sect. 4 the experiments and results are analyzed. In Sect. 5 the results concerning the previous section are discussed. Finally, Sect. 6 contains the conclusions.

2   Related Works

In [13], a Parallel Distributed System for Gene Expression Profiling (PDS-GEF) is proposed, based on two main techniques: Generalized Island Model (GIM) and clustering set, used to generate good quality clusters. These techniques work on three-by-three ensembles, exchanging the subset of solutions through asynchronous communication. In turn, an approach called Evidence ACcumulation (EAC) is used. The experimentation generated good-quality cluster solutions that combine to obtain high-quality clustering by exploiting the EAC consensus function.

A technique to optimize PSO was proposed in [14], the Parallel Boundary Search Particle Swarm Optimization (PBSPSO) algorithm is defined to moderate the complex course of parameter setting in traditionally constrained PSO methods. Its cooperative mechanism increases the possibility of finding globally optimal solutions, which is suitable for practical optimization problems with engineering constraints.

Parallel Conical Area Community Detection Algorithm (PCACD) [15] is proposed to solve a Multi-objective Optimization Problem (MOP) effectively and efficiently. To reduce the runtimes, PCACD applies a global island model and a directed elitist migration policy to parallelize the Conical Area Evolutionary Algorithm (CAEA). This global island model preserves a complete population on each island to implement global selection and updates, while each island handles the optimization of only a portion of the subproblems. PCACD achieves high-quality community structures with satisfactory speed-up by the global island model and directed elitist migration policies.

A node localization algorithm based on Received Signal Strength (RSS) measurements and Parallel Firefly Algorithm (PFA), in Wireless Sensor Network (WSN) is proposed in [16]. These parallel optimization algorithms share the computational workload among multiple processors and get the populations to cooperate in the optimization algorithms. As each subpopulation runs in parallel, the worst fireflies in the subgroups will be replaced by new better fireflies from neighboring subgroups, thus improving result accuracy. Experimental results show that the proposed method can achieve better results than those obtained with PSO, GA, and the original methods in terms of accuracy.

A method for analyzing Multi-Objective Problems (MOP) that are related to high volumes of data was developed by Mohamed et al. [17]. The method uses Pareto Optimization (PO) ensuring that all applicable solutions in the MOPs are obtained and Swarm Intelligence (SI) to speed up the proposed algorithm. The method is adapted to run on big data and online frameworks, such as Hadoop Distributed File System (HDFS), MapReduce, and AS. These facilitate storing and analyzing Big Data in computational clusters. The research presents how SI methods can be parallelized to run on distributed computing nodes. In [18], a similar approach was taken by optimizing a multi-objective function to minimize the cost of center-based clustering problems. Feature Selection Method of Parallel Binary Gray Wolf Optimization Algorithm (SPBGWO) is proposed in [19], for the Parallel Binary Grey Wolf Optimization of the AS distributed platform. The Binary Gray Wolf Optimization algorithm (BGWO), requires multiple iterations to obtain the optimal solution, where each wolf has its fitness and each iteration of the wolves searches for the solution by updating its position. Consequently, for multiple queries, the AS platform is used, and the best solution is found in less time. Experiments with SPBGWO stop the algorithm from falling into a local optimum and improve solution accuracy, classification performance, dimensionality reduction, runtime, and scalability.

Parallel Whale Optimization Algorithm (PWOA) [20], proposes two inter-population communication strategies and a Distance vector-Hop (Dv-Hop) method to solve the localization problem in Wireless Sensor Networks (WSN). The first strategy is to merge groups to achieve information communication and properly exploit the promising area. The second strategy introduces the influence of the average position of the whole population. This improves the overall search capability and diversity of the WOA population. In conclusion, PWOA achieves better results than the WOA and PSO algorithms.

Another variant of BAT is proposed in [21], called the Parallel Distributed Bat Algorithm (PDBA). The parallelization is performed using the C programming language and the MPI API, through a cluster of computers with the master-worker model. The master can be used in exploration and the workers mainly in the exploitation of the search space. The results show the effectiveness of the algorithm for optimization problems with a large population size and a vast search space, it is also observed that in PDBA the convergence rate and speed increase as the size of the computer cluster increases.

Pei-Cheng et al. [22] propose a Parallel Compact Cuckoo Search Algorithm (pcCS) based on compact and parallel techniques for three-dimensional path planning problems. This paper implements the Compac Cucko Search (cCS) algorithm and then, proposes a new parallel communication strategy. This strategy achieves faster convergence and can find better solutions more quickly, it also prevents the algorithm from being trapped in local optima. The proposed algorithm provides more competitive results and achieves more efficient execution.

Finally, in [23] a parallel subpopulation-based CS search algorithm using the OMP API is proposed for TSP. The behaviors of cuckoo parasitism and CS mapping are explored to design the parallelization on the fork-join model of OMP. Pseudo Random Number Generator (PRNG) is also used to generate different random seeds per thread during program initialization, consequently generating unique solutions and avoiding falling into local optima. The results demonstrate that multithreaded parallelism is effective in achieving speed-up of population-based evolutionary algorithms. This efficiency is achieved by dividing the main population into subpopulations, which increases the diversity in solution exploration compared to serial CS. The approach leads to reduced run time and higher solution quality.

3   Parallel Nature-Inspired Metaheuristics

The process to parallelize a serial algorithm can be performed by two parallelization approaches, such as shared memory and distributed memory architecture using the Open Multi-Processing (OMP) and Message Passing Interface (MPI) APIs respectively [24].

In this work we used both approaches, to implement the parallel version of ten bio-inspired algorithms for solving clustering problems, previously implemented in [1]. `Parallel-EvoCluster` is the name given to the parallel implementation of these algorithms.

3.1   Bio-inspired Algorithm

Bio-inspired algorithms are a branch of Artificial Intelligence in which the behavior of natural systems is emulated to design non-deterministic heuristic methods for search, optimization, learning, recognition, simulation, and characterization [25].

In the research field of nature-inspired metaheuristic algorithms, swarm intelligence has taken importance for solving combinatorial optimization problems, since they are efficient and versatile for solving real-world problems [26].

Among the characteristics of bio-inspired algorithms, we can mention that: they are population-based and can simultaneously process a complete collection of individuals. They use recombination to mix the information of several candidate solutions and obtain a new best-fit solution [27].

The serial versions of all these algorithms were implemented in [1], using the programming language Python. The parallel implementation of the algorithms using MPI are named as follows: SSA_{mpi}, PSO_{mpi}, GA_{mpi}, BAT_{mpi}, FFA_{mpi}, GWO_{mpi}, WOA_{mpi}, MVO_{mpi}, MFO_{mpi}, CS_{mpi}. Otherwise, the implementation of the algorithms using OMP are called as follows: SSA_{mp}, PSO_{mp}, GA_{mp}, BAT_{mp}, FFA_{mp}, GWO_{mp}, WOA_{mp}, MVO_{mp}, MFO_{mp}, CS_{mp}.

3.2 Message Passing Interface (MPI)

The message-passing interface API has several processes and each one of them has its own memory space. The communication between them is done through the exchange of information with send-and-receive primitives. Likewise, this model makes use of function libraries, where sending and receiving operations are added to the program. MPI builds a process from basic statements through the use of composition operations that include sequence, condition, and cycle.

MPI uses a distributed memory model, which consists of a set of independent *processes* with local memory that can communicate with other processes by sending and receiving messages, the distributed memory architecture is shown in Fig. 1(a).

The parallel implementation in distributed memory is performed using the MPI application programming interface, where messages can be sent and received between the connected nodes (cores). The process of sending and receiving is done considering migration policies, which were used in similar works [28–31]. Migration policies increase the diversity of the population and help to achieve better results. These migration policies contemplate the following parameters:

- **Number of islands:** number of instances of an algorithm.
- **Migration topology:** defines how islands are connected to establish communication. Communication on such topologies may be *static* or *dynamic*.
- **Type of emigrant:** represent the individuals selected to be sent from a local island to other islands. Emigrants are classified as *better*, *worse*, or *random*.
- **Type of immigrant:** defines the individuals selected on a local island to be replaced by the immigrants from other islands. These individuals can be *better*, *worse*, or *random*.
- **Emigration policy:** indicates whether emigrants will be *cloned* or *removed*.
- **Immigration policy:** indicates if immigrants will *replace* or not individuals from the local island. If the emigration policy *remove* is chosen then the immigrants replace the existing free spaces on the local island. Otherwise, if the emigration policy *clone* is chosen then immigrants replace individuals on the local island according to the type of immigrant individual.
- **Number of emigrants/immigrants:** refers to the number of individuals that can be sent and received from one population to another.
- **Migration interval:** defines the migration frequency with which an exchange of individuals between the islands is done, taking into account the emigration and immigration policy.

Parameters of the migration policies used in this work are described in Table 1. The implementation of the migration policies was done according to the work of [31]. This implementation is similar to the ten parallel algorithms we implemented in this work, for this reason in Algorithm 1 only the pseudocode of the BAT_{mpi} algorithm is shown.

Table 1. Estimated parameters for MPI algorithms.

Parameters	Estimated values
(a) Number of islands	24
(b) Migration topology	unidirectional ring (0), tree (1), net-A (2), net-B (3), torus (4), complete graph (5), between similar (6), between good and bad (7), between random (8)
(c) Emigration policy	clone (0), remove (1)
(d) Immigration policy	replace (0), restore (1)
(e) Type of migrant individual	better (0), worse (1), random (2)
(f) Type of immigrant individual	better (0), worse (1), random (2)
(g) Number of emigrants/immigrants	1, 2, 3, 4, 5
(h) Migration interval	1, 2, 4, 6, 8, 10

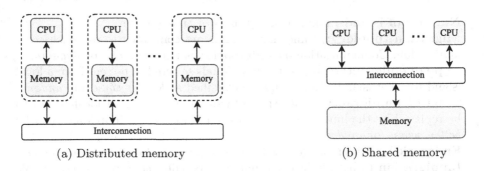

(a) Distributed memory   (b) Shared memory

Fig. 1. Distributed and shared memory.

3.3 Open Multi-Processing (OMP)

OMP is used for parallel programming on shared memory architectures. A program in OMP is executed by a group of cooperating threads [32]. OMP implements a parallelism model *fork-join* which is a way to configure and execute programs in parallel, the program starts with a single thread in the execution,

---

Algorithm 1: BAT_{mpi}

Input: *objective_function, population_size, iterations, num_clusters*, array *points* of individuals, *metric*, migration *policy, population*.

Output: Metric $\mathcal{M}$ of the clusters found and *labels*.

1   MPI_Init
2   *rank* ← MPI_Comm_rank get process id
3   *size* ← MPI_Comm_size get the number of processes
4   Read initial *population*
5   Evaluate initial random solutions
6   **for** $i \leftarrow 0$ **to** *population_size* **do**
7 | $\mathcal{M}$, *labels* ← *objective_function* (*points, num_clusters, metric*)

8   Find the initial best solution
9   **for** $i \leftarrow 0$ **to** *iterations* **do**
10 | **for** $j \leftarrow 0$ **to** *population_size* **do**
11 | | Calculate the frequencies, velocity
12 | | Update the pulse rate
13 | | Evaluate new solutions
14 | | $\mathcal{M}$, *labels* ← *objective_function*(*points, num_clusters, metric*)
15 | | Evaluate and update if the solution improves
16 | | Evaluate and update the current best solution

    | // Migrations
17 | **if** i **mod** *policy.migration_interval* $= 0$ **then**
18 | | Run migration according to *policy* (Based on [31])

19   **if** *rank* $= 0$ **then**
20 | **for** $i \leftarrow 1$ **to** *size - 1* **do**
21 | | MPI_Recv the metric $\mathcal{M}$, *labels* from process i and keep the best solution

22   **else**
23 | MPI_Send the best metric $\mathcal{M}$, *labels* to process 0
24   MPI_Finalize
25   **return** $\mathcal{M}$ *and labels*

---

so that in the region where you want to parallelize it forks and generates a set of threads which work in parallel to join at a later point and resume execution in serial [33].

In addition, OMP is based on a shared memory model, which means that all threads can access the available memory and interact with other threads through shared variables, the shared memory architecture [34] is shown in Fig. 1(b).

To implement the parallel version using OMP, it was necessary to find the bottlenecks for each of the ten algorithms, which was possible thanks to the "profile" command of the Python programming language to run a program. Algorithm 2 shows the BAT_{mp} pseudocode implemented using the OMP approach.

Algorithm 2: BAT_{mp}

Input: *objective_function, population_size, iterations, num_clusters,*
        points, metric, population, cores.
Output: Metric $\mathcal{M}$ of the clusters found and *labels*.

1 Read initial *population*
2 Evaluate initial random solutions
3 **with parallel** *(cores)*:
4   **for** $i \leftarrow 0$ **to** *cores.range(population_size)* **do**
5         $\mathcal{M}$, *labels* $\leftarrow$ *objective_function(points, num_clusters, metric)*

6 Find the initial best solution
7 **for** $i \leftarrow 0$ **to** *iterations* **do**
8   **with parallel** *(cores)*:
9   **for** j in *cores.range(population_size)* **do**
10   Calculate the frequencies, velocity
11   Update the pulse rate
12   Evaluate new solutions
13           $\mathcal{M}$, *labels* $\leftarrow$ *objective_function(points, num_clusters, metric)*
14   **with parallel** *(cores.lock)*:
15   Evaluate and update if the solution improves
16   Evaluate and update the current best solution

17 **return** $\mathcal{M}$ *and labels*

3.4 Objetive Functions and Evaluation

The objective functions [1] are used to optimize the individuals at each iteration: Sum of Squared Error (SSE), Total Within Cluster Variance (TWCV), Silhouette Coefcient (SC), Davies-Bouldin index (DB), Dunn Index (DI). On the other hand, the evaluation of the results used the metrics Purity (P), Entropy (E), Homogeneity score (HS), Completeness score (CS), V-measure (VM), Adjusted Mutual Information (AMI), Adjusted Rand Index (ARI). In the experiments of Sect. 4, the objective function SSE was used to obtain the value of fitness according to Euclidean distance.

4 Experiments and Results

The experiments were run on a computer with two Intel Xeon Gold 6134s (-MT-MCP-SMP-) processors, each processor with 8 cores with *hyper-threading*, with a maximum clock speed of 3.7 GHz and 128 GB of RAM. The implementation was done in Python, using the APIs MPI, OMP, and the libraries mpi4py, pymp. The source code is available at https://github.com/win7/Parallel_EvoCluster.

To compare the implemented algorithms, we first ran previous experiments to determine the best parameters of the implemented algorithms using MPI.

For this, 24 cores were used, and each algorithm was run five times, with 100 generations (iterations) and a population of 30 individuals per core. The datasets used in these experiments were d1, d2, d3, d4, d5, d6 (shown in the Table 2). The best parameters can be found in Table 3.

Serial algorithms, algorithms using MPI, and algorithms using OMP were run to determine the best metrics and runtimes. Each algorithm was run ten times on the datasets d7, d8, d9, and d10 described in Table 2, with a total population of 720 individuals and using 24 cores. In addition, the algorithms implemented using MPI were run using the best parameters from Table 3 and a population of 30 individuals for each core.

Table 2. Dataset information for experiments.

Id	Dataset	Size	Num. classes	Features
d1	Balance	625	3	4
d2	Blood	748	2	4
d3	Pathbased	300	3	2
d4	Smiley	500	4	2
d5	Vary density	150	3	2
d6	Wine	178	3	13
d7	Aniso	1500	3	2
d8	Banknote	1372	2	4
d9	Blobs	1500	3	2
d10	Ecoli	327	5	7

Table 3. Parameter settings for MPI algorithms.

Param.	SSA_{mpi}	PSO_{mpi}	GA_{mpi}	BAT_{mpi}	FFA_{mpi}	GWO_{mpi}	WOA_{mpi}	MVO_{mpi}	MFO_{mpi}	CS_{mpi}
(b)	2	3	2	3	2	5	3	5	5	1
(c)	0	0	0	1	0	0	1	0	0	0
(d)	0	0	0	1	0	0	1	0	0	0
(e)	1	1	0	1	1	2	0	2	0	2
(f)	0	1	0	0	2	2	2	2	2	0
(g)	5	5	4	3	5	3	4	1	2	2
(h)	1	1	1	8	2	2	1	1	10	2

Tables 4, 5, 6 and 7 show the best fitness for each serial and parallel algorithm (MPI, OMP). The best values for fitness are highlighted in bold. Fitness reports that serial algorithms compared to parallel versions using OMP do not differ because the threads execute the same algorithm. On the other hand, parallel versions using MPI do differ because they share individuals according to migration policies. Based on runtime, these values are shown in the Tables 8, 9, 10 and 11, where the bold values correspond to the lowest runtimes. Tables 12 and 13 show the speed-up values for the algorithms implemented using MPI and OMP. The average values of speed-up are ordered from best to worst.

Table 4. Fitness (SSE) of experiments for dataset (d7).

Alg.	Serial	MPI	OMP
SSA	331.96	331.96	331.96
PSO	331.96	331.96	331.96
GA	349.24	334.87	344.7
BAT	**53.42**	54.89	**53.66**
FFA	60.54	**53.42**	60.54
GWO	331.96	331.97	331.96
WOA	331.96	331.96	331.96
MVO	331.96	331.96	331.96
MFO	331.96	331.96	331.96
CS	72.25	71.32	68.38

Table 5. Fitness (SSE) of experiments for dataset (d8).

Alg.	Serial	MPI	OMP
SSA	477.94	477.94	477.94
PSO	477.94	477.94	477.94
GA	524.65	481.63	530.85
BAT	408.32	405.67	408.39
FFA	**405.8**	**404.11**	**405.8**
GWO	477.97	478.09	477.99
WOA	477.94	477.94	477.94
MVO	477.94	477.94	477.94
MFO	477.94	477.94	477.94
CS	423.63	432.39	421.75

Table 6. Fitness (SSE) of experiments for dataset (d9).

Alg.	Serial	MPI	OMP
SSA	409.5	409.5	409.5
PSO	409.5	409.5	409.5
GA	423.03	412.25	425.79
BAT	**21.41**	**21.41**	**21.41**
FFA	**21.41**	**21.41**	**21.41**
GWO	409.76	409.62	409.64
WOA	409.5	409.5	409.5
MVO	409.5	409.5	409.5
MFO	409.5	409.5	409.5
CS	43.66	323.72	39.47

Table 7. Fitness (SSE) of experiments for dataset (d10).

Alg.	Serial	MPI	OMP
SSA	22.23	21.32	21.89
PSO	31.99	30.96	27.31
GA	48.66	22.97	47.15
BAT	**21.04**	22.99	**21.57**
FFA	31.96	21.78	31.96
GWO	23.15	**20.71**	23.6
WOA	24.62	24.08	24.7
MVO	22.69	21.15	23.66
MFO	32.87	26.07	35.49
CS	47.7	51.03	45.83

Table 8. Runtimes (second) of experiments for dataset (d7).

Alg.	Serial	MPI	OMP
SSA	937.91	104.64	87.95
PSO	1017.24	103.77	90.02
GA	**838.53**	102.52	90.19
BAT	895.11	**101.28**	**81.71**
FFA	1477.69	107.52	553.97
GWO	1025.65	109.47	93.86
WOA	1027.81	108.19	95.2
MVO	1020.45	109.91	94.2
MFO	1011.59	108.26	95.76
CS	2023.43	207.39	194.48

Table 9. Runtimes (second) of experiments for dataset (d8)

Alg.	Serial	MPI	OMP
SSA	1026.87	109.81	94.86
PSO	1011.58	**104.4**	93.6
GA	1025.11	107.69	104.42
BAT	**942.06**	104.61	**85.37**
FFA	1492.82	109.93	567.96
GWO	1023.99	107.72	93.94
WOA	1023.11	110.51	93.19
MVO	1043.57	111.37	93.2
MFO	1028.68	113.08	96.43
CS	2136.21	216.97	205.53

Table 10. Runtimes (second) of experiments for dataset (d9)

Algo.	Serial	MPI	OMP
SSA	1025.7	105.98	93.09
PSO	1007.39	105.76	92.19
GA	1055.96	105.37	104.61
BAT	**905.99**	**93.67**	**82.48**
FFA	1467.47	104.15	554.3
GWO	1015.7	107.28	92.27
WOA	1003.48	103.13	92.2
MVO	1026.28	106.35	91.43
MFO	1055.59	106.2	95.41
CS	2058.8	205.81	195.5

Table 11. Runtimes (second) of experiments for dataset (d10)

Algorithm	Serial	MPI	OMP
SSA	230.67	23.44	30.05
PSO	215.16	**22.52**	32.51
GA	225.59	23.52	37.37
BAT	**208.35**	22.74	**27.16**
FFA	633.51	25.77	455.91
GWO	225.61	24.57	34.5
WOA	221.62	23.93	31.2
MVO	222.16	23.81	30.54
MFO	212.47	23.55	31.89
CS	429.1	46.54	59.39

Table 12. Speed-up for MPI algorithms

Alg.	d7	d8	d9	d10	Avg.
FFA_{mpi}	8.96	9.35	9.68	9.84	9.46
CS_{mpi}	9.8	9.69	9.53	9.55	9.64
SSA_{mpi}	8.18	9.52	10.02	9.59	9.33
WOA_{mpi}	8.84	9.01	9.67	9.16	9.17
GWO_{mpi}	13.74	13.58	14.09	24.58	16.5
MFO_{mpi}	9.37	9.51	9.47	9.18	9.38
GA_{mpi}	9.50	9.26	9.73	9.26	9.44
PSO_{mpi}	9.28	9.37	9.65	9.33	9.41
BAT_{mpi}	9.34	9.1	9.94	9.02	9.35
MVO_{mpi}	9.76	9.85	10.0	9.22	9.71

Table 13. Speed-up for OMP algorithms

Alg.	d7	d8	d9	d10	Avg.
BAT_{mp}	10.95	11.04	10.98	7.67	10.16
MVO_{mp}	10.83	11.2	11.22	7.27	10.13
SSA_{mp}	10.66	10.83	11.02	7.68	10.05
WOA_{mp}	10.8	10.98	10.88	7.1	9.94
PSO_{mp}	11.3	10.81	10.93	6.62	9.91
GWO_{mp}	10.93	10.9	11.01	6.54	9.84
MFO_{mp}	10.56	10.67	11.06	6.66	9.74
CS_{mp}	10.4	10.3	10.53	7.23	9.62
GA_{mp}	9.3	9.82	10.09	6.04	8.81
FFA_{mp}	2.67	2.63	2.65	1.39	2.34

Table 14. Ranking of the algorithm's fitness.

Num.	Min-max normalization	Maximum absolute scaler
1	FFA_{mpi}	BAT
2	BAT	FFA_{mpi}
3	BAT_{mp}	BAT_{mp}
4	BAT_{mpi}	BAT_{mpi}
5	FFA	FFA
6	FFA_{mp}	FFA_{mp}
7	CS_{mp}	CS_{mp}
8	CS	CS
9	CS_{mpi}	CS_{mpi}
10	GWO_{mpi}	GWO_{mpi}
11	MVO_{mpi}	MVO_{mpi}
12	SSA_{mpi}	SSA_{mpi}
13	SSA_{mp}	SSA_{mp}
14	SSA	SSA
15	MVO	MVO
16	GWO	GWO
17	GWO_{mp}	GWO_{mp}
18	MVO_{mp}	MVO_{mp}
19	WOA_{mpi}	GA_{mpi}
20	GA_{mpi}	WOA_{mpi}
21	WOA	WOA
22	WOA_{mp}	WOA_{mp}
23	MFO_{mpi}	MFO_{mpi}
24	PSO_{mp}	PSO_{mp}
25	PSO_{mpi}	PSO_{mpi}
26	PSO	PSO
27	MFO	MFO
28	MFO_{mp}	MFO_{mp}
29	GA_{mp}	GA_{mp}
30	GA	GA

Table 15. Ranking of the algorithm's runtime.

Num.	Min-max normalization	Maximum absolute scaler
1	BAT_{mp}	BAT_{mp}
2	BAT_{mpi}	BAT_{mpi}
3	SSA_{mp}	SSA_{mp}
4	MVO_{mp}	MVO_{mp}
5	PSO_{mp}	PSO_{mp}
6	WOA_{mp}	WOA_{mp}
7	PSO_{mpi}	PSO_{mpi}
8	MFO_{mp}	MFO_{mp}
9	GA_{mpi}	GA_{mpi}
10	GWO_{mp}	GWO_{mp}
11	SSA_{mpi}	SSA_{mpi}
12	WOA_{mpi}	WOA_{mpi}
13	MFO_{mpi}	MFO_{mpi}
14	GWO_{mpi}	GWO_{mpi}
15	MVO_{mpi}	MVO_{mpi}
16	FFA_{mpi}	FFA_{mpi}
17	GA_{mp}	GA_{mp}
18	CS_{mpi}	CS_{mpi}
19	CS_{mp}	CS_{mp}
20	FFA_{mp}	FFA_{mp}
21	BAT	BAT
22	GA	GA
23	PSO	PSO
24	SSA	SSA
25	WOA	WOA
26	MFO	MFO
27	GWO	GWO
28	MVO	MVO
29	FFA	FFA
30	CS	CS

5   Discussion

The proposal shows a significant improvement in the runtimes and speed-up of the parallel versions concerning their serial versions. To obtain the best algorithms, the runtimes and fitness were compared through a ranking, which was obtained by calculating the average of the normalized data of the fitness (Tables 4, 5, 6, and 7) and runtime (Tables 8, 9, 10, 11), using transformation techniques Maximum absolute scaler and Min-max normalization.

Regarding speed-up, parallelization with MPI (Table 12), on average is 10.14x times faster compared to its serial versions. On the other hand, the result of parallelization with OMP (Table 13), on average is 9.05x times faster. For both calculations, we excluded the values of the speed-up values of FFA_{mpi} and FFA_{mp} due to the atypical nature of their averages.

Table 14 shows algorithm rankings according to fitness. The fitnesses of the serial and parallel algorithms are similar, which means that both algorithms perform well. The convergence of all algorithms is shown in the Fig. 2, specifically the FFA_{mpi} algorithm converged to the optimal solutions gradually in Figs. 2, 2(b), 2(c), and 2(d), the number of iterations to obtain required optimal solutions was lower than the sequential FFA as well as in the [35].

Table 15 shows the ranking of the algorithm's runtime, where the five best algorithms are: BAT_{mp}, BAT_{mpi}, SSA_{mp}, MVO_{mp} and PSO_{mp}. Although the best algorithms belong to the OMP approach, on average the MPI approach performs better because the experiments were run on a computer with distributed memory; a similar result is found in [21], where the BAT_{mpi} algorithm requires less runtime. Finally, in the Fig. 3 and Table 15 displays the runtimes, with the BAT_{mp} and BAT_{mpi} being the most relevant algorithms.

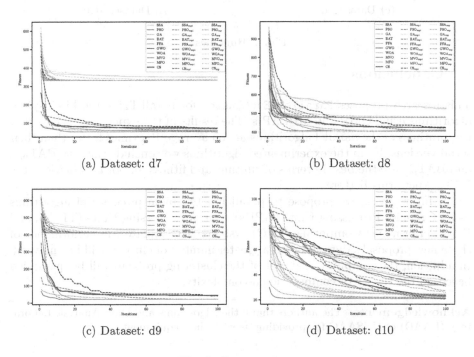

(a) Dataset: d7

(b) Dataset: d8

(c) Dataset: d9

(d) Dataset: d10

Fig. 2. Convergences.

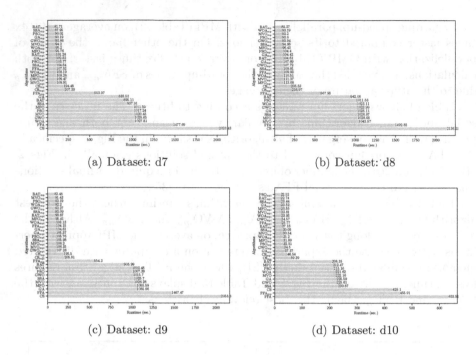

(a) Dataset: d7

(b) Dataset: d8

(c) Dataset: d9

(d) Dataset: d10

Fig. 3. Runtimes.

6 Conclusions

This research proposes `Parallel-EvoCluster` for parallelizing ten bio-inspired algorithms using OMP and MPI APIs. The results of the experiments show that the runtimes of the parallel algorithms are on average 10x times faster than their serial versions. From the experimented algorithms we conclude that the BAT_{mpi} and BAT_{mp} are the best in terms of runtime and fitness, in both evaluations the BAT_{mp} performs better.

In future work, we propose to parallelize ten bioinspired serial algorithms using Graphics Processing Units (GPUs), Tensor Processing Units (TPUs), and High-Performance Computing (HPC) systems. To evaluate the performance of these new proposals, datasets with a greater number of clusters will be analyzed. In addition, the computational cost of the clustering problem will be quantified based on the theory of computational complexity.

Acknowledgements. The authors thank the Algorithms and Data Analysis Laboratory (LAAD) of UNSAAC for providing us with their equipment.

References

1. Qaddoura, R., Faris, H., Aljarah, I., Castillo, P.A.: Evocluster: an open-source nature-inspired optimization clustering framework. SN Comput. Sci. 2(3), 1–12 (2021)

2. Rosenberg, A., Hirschberg, J.: V-measure: a conditional entropy-based external cluster evaluation measure. In: Proceedings of the 2007 Joint Conference on Empirical Methods in Natural Language Processing and Computational Natural Language Learning (EMNLP-CoNLL), pp. 410–420 (2007)

3. Khurma, R.A., Aljarah, I., Sharieh, A., Mirjalili, S.: EvoloPy-FS: an open-source nature-inspired optimization framework in python for feature selection. In: Mirjalili, S., Faris, H., Aljarah, I. (eds.) Evolutionary Machine Learning Techniques. AIS, pp. 131–173. Springer, Singapore (2020). https://doi.org/10.1007/978-981-32-9990-0_8

4. Shi, Y., Eberhart, R.: A modified particle swarm optimizer. In: 1998 IEEE International Conference on Evolutionary Computation Proceedings. IEEE World congress on Computational Intelligence (Cat. No. 98TH8360), pp. 69–73. IEEE (1998)

5. Mirjalili, S., Gandomi, A.H., Mirjalili, S.Z., Saremi, S., Faris, H., Mirjalili, S.M.: Salp swarm algorithm: a bio-inspired optimizer for engineering design problems. Adv. Eng. Softw. **114**, 163–191 (2017)

6. Yang, X.-S.: Firefly algorithm, stochastic test functions and design optimisation. arXiv preprint arXiv:1003.1409 (2010)

7. Aljarah, I., Mafarja, M., Heidari, A.A., Faris, H., Mirjalili, S.: Clustering analysis using a novel locality-informed grey wolf-inspired clustering approach. Knowl. Inf. Syst. **62**(2), 507–539 (2020)

8. Mirjalili, S., Lewis, A.: The whale optimization algorithm. Adv. Eng. Softw. **95**, 51–67 (2016)

9. Aljarah, I., Mafarja, M., Heidari, A.A., Faris, H., Mirjalili, S.: Multi-verse optimizer: theory, literature review, and application in data clustering. Nature-inspired Optimizers, pp. 123–141 (2020)

10. Mirjalili, S.: Moth-flame optimization algorithm: a novel nature-inspired heuristic paradigm. Knowl.-Based Syst. **89**, 228–249 (2015)

11. Yang, X.-S.: A new metaheuristic bat-inspired algorithm. In: Nature Inspired Cooperative Strategies for Optimization (NICSO 2010), pp. 65–74. Springer (2010). https://doi.org/10.1007/978-3-642-12538-6_6

12. Yang, X.-S., Deb, S.: Cuckoo search via lévy flights. In: 2009 World Congress on Nature & Biologically Inspired Computing (NaBIC), pp. 210–214. IEEE (2009)

13. Benmounah, Z., Batouche, M.: A parallel distributed system for gene expression profiling based on clustering ensemble and distributed optimization. In: Kołodziej, J., Di Martino, B., Talia, D., Xiong, K. (eds.) ICA3PP 2013. LNCS, vol. 8285, pp. 176–185. Springer, Cham (2013). https://doi.org/10.1007/978-3-319-03859-9_14

14. Liu, Z., Li, Z., Zhu, P., Chen, W.: A parallel boundary search particle swarm optimization algorithm for constrained optimization problems. Struct. Multidiscip. Optim. **58**(4), 1505–1522 (2018)

15. Ying, W., Jalil, H., Bingshen, W., Yu, W., Ying, Z., Luo, Y., Wang, Z.: Parallel conical area community detection using evolutionary multi-objective optimization. Processes **7**(2), 111 (2019)

16. Sai, V.-O., Shieh, C.-S., Nguyen, T.-T., Lin, Y.-C., Horng, M.-F., Le, Q.-D.: Parallel firefly algorithm for localization algorithm in wireless sensor network. In: 2015 Third International Conference on Robot, Vision and Signal Processing (RVSP), pp. 300–305. IEEE (2015)

17. AbdelAziz, A.M., Ghany, K.K.A., Soliman, T.H.A., El-Magd Sewisy, A.A.: A parallel multi-objective swarm intelligence framework for big data analysis. Int. J. Comput. Appl. Technol. **63**(3), 200–212 (2020)

18. León, J., Chullo-Llave, B., Enciso-Rodas, L., Soncco-Álvarez, J.L.: A multi-objective optimization algorithm for center-based clustering. Electron. Notes Theor. Comput. Sci. **349**, 49–67 (2020)
19. Chen, H., et al.: A feature selection method of parallel grey wolf optimization algorithm based on spark. In: 2019 10th IEEE International Conference on Intelligent Data Acquisition and Advanced Computing Systems: Technology and Applications (IDAACS), vol. 1, pp. 81–85. IEEE (2019)
20. Chai, Q., Chu, S.-C., Pan, J.-S., Pei, H., Zheng, W.: A parallel woa with two communication strategies applied in dv-hop localization method. EURASIP J. Wirel. Commun. Netw. **2020**(1), 1–10 (2020)
21. Noor, F., Ibrahim, A., AlKhattab, M.M.: Performance of parallel distributed bat algorithm using mpi on a pc cluster. Annals of Emerging Technologies in Computing (AETiC), Print ISSN, pp. 2516–0281 (2020)
22. Song, P.-C., Pan, J.-S., Chu, S.-C.: A parallel compact cuckoo search algorithm for three-dimensional path planning. Appl. Soft Comput. **94**, 106443 (2020)
23. Tzy-Luen, N., Keat, Y.T., Abdullah, R.: Parallel cuckoo search algorithm on openmp for traveling salesman problem. In: 2016 3rd International Conference on Computer and Information Sciences (ICCOINS), pp. 380–385. IEEE (2016)
24. Basloom, H.S., et al.: . Errors classification and static detection techniques for dual-programming model (openmp and openacc). IEEE Access **10**, 117808–117826 (2022)
25. Cárdenas Cardona, A.: Inteligencia artificial, métodos bio-inspirados: un enfoque funcional para las ciencias de la computación (2012)
26. Yang, X.-S., Karamanoglu, M.: Swarm intelligence and bio-inspired computation: an overview. Swarm Intelligence and Bio-Inspired Computation, pp. 3–23 (2013)
27. López Gómez, J.A.: Algoritmos bioinspirados aplicados al control de formaciones de múltiples nanorobots móviles (2015)
28. da Silveira, L.Â., Soncco-Álvarez, J.L., de Barros, J., Llanos, C.H., Ayala-Rincón, M.: On the behavior of parallel island models. Universidade de Brasília, Tech. Rep (2019)
29. da Silveira, L. Â., Soncco-Álvarez, J.L., de Lima, T.A., Ayala-Rincón, M.: Parallel Island model genetic algorithms applied in NP-Hard problems. In: 2019 IEEE Congress on Evolutionary Computation (CEC), pp. 3262–3269. IEEE (2019)
30. da Silveira, LÂ., Soncco-Álvarez, J.L., de Lima, T.A., Ayala-Rincón, M.: Behavior of bioinspired algorithms in parallel Island models. In 2020 IEEE Congress on Evolutionary Computation (CEC). IEEE (2020)
31. Alvarez-Mamani, E., Enciso-Rodas, L., Ayala-Rincón, M., Soncco-Álvarez, J.L.: Parallel social spider optimization algorithms with Island model for the clustering problem. In: Lossio-Ventura, J.A., Valverde-Rebaza, J.C., Díaz, E., Alatrista-Salas, H. (eds.) SIMBig 2020. CCIS, vol. 1410, pp. 122–138. Springer, Cham (2021). https://doi.org/10.1007/978-3-030-76228-5_9
32. Kwedlo, W., Czochanski, P.J.: A hybrid mpi/openmp parallelization of k-means algorithms accelerated using the triangle inequality. IEEE Access **7**, 42280–42297 (2019)
33. Duran Gonzalez, J.A., del Valle Gallegos, E., Gómez Torres, A.M.: Aplicación de memoria compartida en el código aztran usando openmp. XXIV Reunión Nacional Académica de Física y Matemáticas. Ciudad de México, México (2019)
34. Duran Gonzalez, J.A., Del Valle Gallegos, E., Gomez Torres, A.M.: Hybrid parallelization (mpi-openmp) in aztran transport code (2020)
35. Mathew, J., Vijayakumar, R.: Scalable parallel clustering approach for large data using parallel k means and firefly algorithms. In: 2014 International Conference on High Performance Computing and Applications (ICHPCA), pp. 1–8. IEEE (2014)

Expanding Chemical Representation with k-mers and Fragment-Based Fingerprints for Molecular Fingerprinting

Sarwan Ali$^{(\boxtimes)}$, Prakash Chourasia, and Murray Patterson

Georgia State University, Atlanta, GA 30303, USA
{sali85,pchourasia1}@student.gsu.edu, mpatterson30@gsu.edu

Abstract. This study introduces a novel approach, combining substruct counting, k-mers, and Daylight-like fingerprints, to expand the representation of chemical structures in SMILES strings. The integrated method generates comprehensive molecular embeddings that enhance discriminative power and information content. Experimental evaluations demonstrate its superiority over traditional Morgan fingerprinting, MACCS, and Daylight fingerprint alone, improving chemoinformatics tasks such as drug classification. The proposed method offers a more informative representation of chemical structures, advancing molecular similarity analysis and facilitating applications in molecular design and drug discovery. It presents a promising avenue for molecular structure analysis and design, with significant potential for practical implementation.

Keywords: Molecular fingerprinting · k-mers · Cheminformatics · Chemical structure representation · Molecular descriptors

1 Introduction

Molecular structure analysis is a vital endeavor in drug discovery and molecular design [24]. Due to their simplicity and usability, Simplified Molecular Input Line Entry System (SMILES) strings have become more popular as a preferred way for encoding molecular structure data [23] (see Fig. 1 for an example of a SMILES string). However, modeling and analyzing molecular structures expressed as SMILES strings present several difficulties [13]. These difficulties include managing the enormous complexity of the data and comprehending the intricate non-linear interactions between the structures. Applications in machine learning rely primarily on numerical representations of the data [9]. The conversion of SMILES strings into machine-readable numerical representations is a complex task that demands sophisticated techniques.

The analysis of SMILES strings has gained significant importance in the field of drug discovery and cheminformatics [3]. SMILES strings are a well-liked method for encoding molecular information in machine learning models because they offer a succinct description of a molecule's structure [29, 30]. These models

J. A. Lossio-Ventura et al. (Eds.): SIMBig 2023, CCIS 2142, pp. 17–29, 2024.
https://doi.org/10.1007/978-3-031-63616-5_2

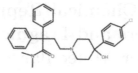

Fig. 1. Molecular structure for the drug named "Loperamide", with solubility AlogPS (Aqueous solubility and Octanol/Water partition coefficient) value of 0.00086, and the following SMILES string: `CN(C)C(=O)C(CCN1CCC(O)(CC1)C1=CC=C(Cl)C=C1)(C1=CC=CC=C1)C1=CC=CC=C1`

are used for several tasks, including subtype prediction [4] and drug solubility prediction [7]. By comparing the effectiveness of various embedding techniques and ML models for classification tasks using SMILES strings as input, this research intends to close this knowledge gap. The project also suggests a fresh approach to SMILES string analysis. The results of this study may have important ramifications for drug discovery and aid in determining the best techniques for predicting molecular characteristics.

The proposed approach addresses challenges in modeling and analyzing chemical structures represented as SMILES strings. It incorporates various fingerprinting methodologies to capture intricate non-linear interactions and overcome high-dimensional data. Using the RDKit library, we transform SMILES strings into molecular structures and generate feature vectors. To gather more information, we combine the Morgan fingerprint with k-mers extracted from the SMILES string. Which helps to capture local and variable-length substructs, revealing structural relationships and functional groups. The effectiveness of the proposed fingerprint embeddings is evaluated in drug subcategory prediction tasks.

The proposed method has a wide variety of potential applications, including drug discovery, and molecular design. It offers the opportunity to quickly search through vast datasets of chemical structures in search of compounds with desirable properties. By creating low-dimensional embeddings and using them to find molecules with related qualities, the approach makes it possible to construct unique compounds with certain properties. Overall, this signifies a promising avenue for molecular structure analysis, employing kernel methods to unlock new possibilities. Following are our contributions:

1. We propose a novel method for embedding generation for SMILES strings, which can be used for underlying supervised analysis such as classification. Our approach is predicated on the notion of first turning SMILES strings into molecular graphs, and computing fingerprints while incorporating k-mers.
2. We show that the proposed method preserves both the structural and contextual information better when compared to the baselines.
3. Using extensive experimentation, we demonstrated that the proposed method can achieve higher predictive performance on the benchmark SMILES string dataset.

The remainder of the paper is structured as: Sect. 2 reviews related work, Sect. 3 presents our proposed approach, Sect. 4 describes the dataset and experimental setup, Sect. 5 presents the outcomes of the proposed and baseline methods, and Sect. 6 concludes the paper.

2 Related Work

Molecular fingerprints are popular and widely used for encoding structural information in molecules [18, 29, 30]. They have been successfully applied in drug solubility prediction [16], with random forest regression and support vector regression showing superior performance [2]. Graph convolutional neural networks have also achieved promising results [20, 32]. Further research is needed to explore different embeddings, classification, and regression models for solubility and drug subtype prediction. Kernel methods, such as kernel ridge regression (KRR) [6, 26] and support vector machine (SVM) [27, 28], are commonly used for molecular data analysis. To find similarities using molecular fingerprints, several works propose to combine various methods using data fusion [21], either by combining different fingerprints [1, 22, 31] or by combining fingerprints with other methods, especially structure-based methods [15]. The several combinations help to capture various chemical information, making them more relevant and making it better compared to what a single approach would introduce. Kernel principal component analysis (PCA) effectively reduces dimensionality and feature extraction [8, 19]. It has been successfully used in molecular property prediction and activity classification [8]. However, these methods have limitations, such as computational complexity and potential overfitting, especially for large datasets.

3 Proposed Approach

In this section, we discuss the main idea of the Morgan Fingerprint followed by the integration of k-mers in the Morgan Fingerprint.

The Morgan Fingerprint algorithm [16], as shown in Algorithm 1, is designed to generate a fingerprint representation for a given SMILES string. The fingerprint captures the occurrence of substructs within the SMILES string, which is defined by a specified radius. The algorithm starts by initializing an empty dictionary, substructCnt, to store the occurrence count of each substruct. It then iterates over the specified radius, and for each radius, iterates over the SMILES string to extract substructs of that radius. If a substruct is already present in substructCnt, its count is incremented; otherwise, it is added to substructCnt with an initial count of 1. Once all substructs have been counted, they are sorted alphabetically to create the list sortedSubstruct. Next, the algorithm constructs the binary fingerprint representation. It initializes an empty list, fingerprint, and iterates over the sorted substructs. For each substruct, its occurrence count is converted into a binary representation using 32 bits, where each bit corresponds to whether the count has a value of 0 or 1. These binary representations are appended to fingerprint. After constructing the fingerprint, the algorithm checks if the length of the fingerprint is greater than or equal to the desired number of bits, nBits. If it is, the fingerprint is truncated to the first nBits elements. Otherwise, it is padded with zeros ([0]) to reach the desired length. Finally, the generated fingerprint is returned as the output of the Generate-MorganFingerprint function. Figure 2a shows the process we use for generating Morgan fingerprints.

Algorithm 1. Morgan Fingerprint

```
1:  function GENERATEMORGANFINGERPRINT(smiles, radius=2, nBits=2048)
2:      substructCnt ← []
3:      for i ← 1 to radius do
4:          for j ← 0 to len(smiles)-i do
5:              substruct ← smiles[j:j+i]
6:              if substruct ∈ substructCnt then
7:                  substructCnt[substruct] + = 1
8:              else
9:                  substructCnt[substruct] ← 1
10:             end if
11:         end for
12:     end for
13:     sortedSubstruct ← sort(substructCnt.keys())
14:     fingerprint ← []
15:     for substruct ∈ sortedSubstruct do
16:         substructBinary ← [int(bit) for bit in bin(substructCnt[substruct])[2:].zfill(32)]
17:         fingerprint.extend(substructBinary)
18:     end for
19:     if len(fingerprint) ≥ nBits then
20:         fingerprint ← fingerprint[:nBits]
21:     else
22:         fingerprint ← fingerprint + [0] × (nBits - len(fingerprint))
23:     end if
24:     return fingerprint
25: end function
```

3.1 Integration of *k*-mers in Morgan Fingerprint

The "Morgan Fingerprint with k-mers" algorithm, as depicted in Algorithm 2, generates a fingerprint representation for a given SMILES string. The function GenerateMorganFingerprintKmers takes the SMILES string as input along with optional parameters such as the radius (default value of 2), *k*-mer length (default value of 3), and desired number of bits for the fingerprint (default value of 2048). The algorithm starts by initializing an empty list, substructure count (substructCnt), to store the counts of substructs. It then iterates through each possible radius value from 1 to the specified radius. Within this loop, it further iterates through the characters of the SMILES string to extract substructs of the given radius. The substruct is checked for existence in substructCnt, and if present, its count is incremented; otherwise, a new entry is added with an initial count of 1. Next, another loop is executed to generate k-mers from the

SMILES string. Similar to the previous loop, it extracts substructs of length k from the string and updates their counts in substructCnt. The algorithm then sorts the substructs in substructure alphabetically to ensure consistent ordering. It initializes an empty list, fingerprint, to store the binary representation of the substruct counts. For each substruct in the sorted order, it converts the corresponding count to a binary representation of length 32 and appends each bit to the fingerprint. After generating the fingerprint, the algorithm checks if the length of the fingerprint is greater than or equal to the desired number of bits. If it exceeds, the fingerprint is truncated to the desired length; otherwise, it is padded with additional zeros to match the desired length. Finally, the algorithm returns the generated fingerprint as the output of the function.

Algorithm 2. Morgan Fingerprint with k-mers

```
 1: function GENERATEMORGANFINGERPRINTKMERS(smiles, radius=2, k=3, nBits=2048)
 2:     substructCnt ← []
 3:     for i ← 1 to radius do
 4:         for j ← 0 to len(smiles) - i do
 5:             substruct ← smiles[j:j+i]
 6:             if substruct ∈ substructCnt then
 7:                 substructCnt[substruct] += 1
 8:             else
 9:                 substructCnt[substruct] ← 1
10:             end if
11:         end for
12:     end for
13:     for j ← 0 to len(smiles) - k do
14:         substruct ← smiles[j:j+k]
15:         if substruct ∈ substructCnt then
16:             substructCnt[substruct] += 1
17:         else
18:             substructCnt[substruct] ← 1
19:         end if
20:     end for
21:     sortedSubstruct ← sort(substructCnt.keys())
22:     fingerprint ← []
23:     for substruct ∈ sortedSubstruct do
24:         substructBinary ← [int(bit) for bit in bin(substructCnt[substruct])[2:].zfill(32)]
25:         fingerprint.extend(substructBinary)
26:     end for
27:     if len(fingerprint) ≥ nBits then
28:         fingerprint ← fingerprint[:nBits]
29:     else
30:         fingerprint ← fingerprint + [0] × (nBits - len(fingerprint))
31:     end if
32:     return fingerprint
33: end function
```

3.2 Daylight Fingerprint

The "Daylight Fingerprint" algorithm [10], as given in Algorithm 3, generates a binary fingerprint for a given SMILES string. It extracts atom pairs and bond types from the string, incrementing their counts in a dictionary. The counts are then converted to a binary representation, forming the fingerprint. The finger-print is truncated or padded to the desired length. This unique binary repre-sentation captures the substructs present in the SMILES string. Figure 2c shows the process for generating the proposed Feature Vector. Figure 2c shows the pro-cess we use for generating the proposed Feature Vector which includes Morgan fingerprint with k-mer inclusion and Daylight fingerprint.

Algorithm 3. Daylight Fingerprint

```
 1: function GENERATEDAYLIGHTFINGERPRINT(smiles, nBits=2048)
 2:     substructCnt ←
 3:     for i ← 0 to len(smiles) - 2 do
 4:         atom_pair ← smiles[i:i+2]
 5:         bond_type ← smiles[i+1:i+2]
 6:         substruct ← atom_pair + bond_type
 7:         if substruct ∈ substructCnt then
 8:             substructCnt[substruct] += 1
 9:         else
10:             substructCnt[substruct] ← 1
11:         end if
12:     end for
13:     sortedSubstruct ← sort(substructCnt.keys())
14:     fingerprint ← []
15:     for substruct ∈ sortedSubstruct do
16:         substructBinary ← [int(bit) for bit in bin(substructCnt[substruct])[2:].zfill(32)]
17:         fingerprint.extend(substructBinary)
18:     end for
19:     if len(fingerprint) ≥ nBits then
20:         fingerprint ← fingerprint[:nBits]
21:     else
22:         fingerprint ← fingerprint + [0] × (nBits - len(fingerprint))
23:     end if
24:     return fingerprint
25: end function
```

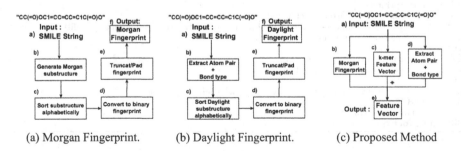

(a) Morgan Fingerprint.   (b) Daylight Fingerprint.   (c) Proposed Method

Fig. 2. Different methods for Feature Vector generation using SMILE String

4   Experimental Setup

In this section, we report the dataset statistics. The detail regarding experimen-tation, including classifiers description along with evaluation metrics is reported in Sect. 4.2. Moreover, the detail regarding the baseline models is also given in Sect. 4.1. We obtained a dataset consisting of 6897 SMILES strings from the benchmark DrugBank dataset [25]. The objective is to classify drugs based on their subtypes, with a total of 188 distinct subcategories being assigned as target labels. The top 10 drug subcategories, obtained from the Food and Drug Administration (FDA) website[1], are provided in Table 1. To illustrate, Table 2 presents an example of a SMILES string along with its corresponding attributes. We also performed t-SNE-based visualization of different embeddings as shown in Sect. 4.3.

Table 1. Drug subtypes (Top 10) extracted from FDA website. EPC => "Established Pharmacologic Class".

Drug Subcategory		String Length Statistics		
	Count	Min.	Max.	Avg.
Others	6299	2	569	55.4448
Barbiturate [EPC]	54	16	136	51.2407
Amide Local Anesthetic [EPC]	53	9	149	39.1886
Non-Standardized Plant Allergenic Extract [EPC]	30	10	255	66.8965
Sulfonylurea [EPC]	17	22	148	59.7647
Corticosteroid [EPC]	16	57	123	95.4375
Nonsteroidal Anti-inflammatory Drug [EPC]	15	29	169	53.6000
Nucleoside Metabolic Inhibitor [EPC]	11	16	145	59.9090
Nitroimidazole Antimicrobial [EPC]	10	27	147	103.800
Muscle Relaxant [EPC]	10	9	82	49.8000

4.1   Baseline Models

In this section, we discuss various baseline techniques that were utilized to compare the outcomes with the proposed method.

MACCS Fingerprint. The binary fingerprint known as the MACCS fingerprint [5,12] makes use of predetermined substructs based on functional groups and ring systems typically present in organic compounds. The existence or absence of each substruct is encoded in the resulting binary vector.

k-mers. In the SMILES string, this approach uses a sequence-based embedding to express the frequencies of overlapping sub-sequences [11] of length k. The

---

[1] https://www.fda.gov/.

SMILES string is broken up into overlapping sub-sequences of length k using a sliding window, and the frequency of each sub-sequence is used to create an embedding. For our experiments, we use k = 3. The frequency count for each k-mer is then taken to use for generating the feature vector.

Weighted k-mers. In order to improve the quality of the k-mers-based embedding, we adopt a weighted variant that uses Inverse Document Frequency (IDF) to give each k-mer in the embedding [17] a weight. Rare k-mers that exist in only a small number of SMILES strings are more informative than frequent k-mers that frequently appear in those strings. The frequency of each k-mer is therefore down-weighted using IDF based on the number of SMILES strings in which it appears. A weighted k-mers-based embedding that better reflects the distinctive characteristics of each SMILES string is the consequence of this. For our studies, $k = 3$, and the Algorithm 4 provides the pseudocode for determining the weights for k-mers using IDF.

Algorithm 4. Weighted k-mers Generation Using IDF

1: **function** WEIGHTEDKMERS($kMersLst$)
2:     $totSamples \leftarrow |kMersLst|$ ▷ $kMersLst$: list of all k-mers
3:     $weightsIDF \leftarrow \{\}$ ▷ Dictionary for set of k-mers
4:     **for** $kmers$ in $kMersLst$ **do**
5:         **for** $kVal$ **in** set($kmers$) **do**
6:             **if** $kVal$ not in $weightsIDF$ **then**
7:                 $weightsIDF[kVal] \leftarrow 0$ ▷ add new unique k-mers to dictionary
8:             **end if**
9:             $weightsIDF[kVal] + +$ ▷ increment corresponding k-mer count
10:        **end for**
11:    **end for**
12:    **for** $kVal, ToT$ in $weightsIDF$ **do**
13:        $weightsIDF[kVal] \leftarrow \log(\frac{totSamples}{ToT})$ ▷ log for # of samples over k-mers count
14:    **end for**
        return $weightsIDF$
15: **end function**

4.2   Evaluation Metrics

For our classification task, we employ a range of linear and non-linear classifiers, including SVM, Naive Bayes (NB), Multi-Layer Perceptron (MLP), K Nearest Neighbors (KNN), Random Forest (RF), Logistic Regression (LR), and Decision Tree (DT). Our evaluation metrics encompass average accuracy, precision, recall, weighted F1, macro F1, ROC-AUC, and classifier training runtime. To establish training and test sets, we randomly split our data with a $70 - 30\%$ distribution, and we conduct our experiments five times to obtain average outcomes. For hyperparameter tuning, we allocate 10% of the training data as a validation set. To ensure reproducibility, we provide online access to our code and pre-processed dataset[2].

---

[2] Available in the published version.

Table 2. Randomly selected SMILES string example along with its drug name, drug subcategory, and Solubility AlogPS values.

SMILE String	Drug Name	Drug Subcategory	Solubility AlogPS
[Ca++].CC([O-])=O.CC([O-])=O	Calcium Acetate	Non-Standardized Plant Allergenic Extract [EPC]	147.0 g/l

4.3 Data Visualization

We use the t-distributed Stochastic Neighbour Embedding (t-SNE) algorithm to create 2-dimensional representations of the different embeddings [14]. To have a visual inspection and determine whether different embedding strategies are keeping the structure of the data the t-SNE plots are generated. Figure 3 shows the scatter plots produced by t-SNE for various embedding techniques. The MACCS fingerprint displays some clustering overall, which is similar for k-mers and weighted k-mer. On the other hand Morgan Fingerprint daylight are giving different scattered patterns. We can see the merged pattern with heavy inheritance from daylight when merged with Morga. The proposed MERGE displays a mix of all in Fig. 3(h), which is inherited clearly from Fig. 3(f) and Fig. 3(g).

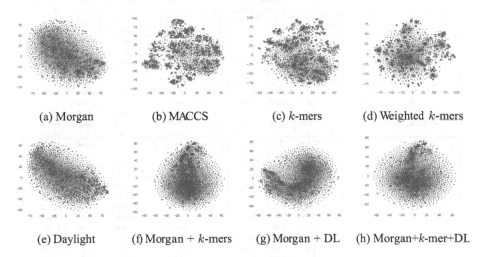

(a) Morgan   (b) MACCS   (c) k-mers   (d) Weighted k-mers

(e) Daylight   (f) Morgan + k-mers   (g) Morgan + DL   (h) Morgan+k-mer+DL

Fig. 3. The t-SNE plots for different feature embedding methods. The DL stands for Daylight.

5   Results and Discussion

Table 3 presents the average classification results obtained from various methods and datasets, along with different evaluation metrics. We can observe that the proposed "Morgan + k-mers" method stands out with the highest accuracy (0.9162), precision (0.8541), recall (0.9162), and F1 score (0.8779). It also

Table 3. Average Classification results (of 5 runs) for different methods and datasets using different evaluation metrics. The best values are shown in bold.

Embedding	Algo.	Acc. ↑	Prec. ↑	Recall ↑	F1 (Weig.) ↑	F1 (Macro) ↑	ROC-AUC ↑	Train Time (Sec.) ↓
MACCS Fingerprint [5,12]	SVM	0.8705	0.8539	0.8705	0.8613	0.0520	0.5441	3.1812
	NB	0.2458	0.8473	0.2458	0.3698	0.0359	0.5224	0.5048
	MLP	0.8659	0.8444	0.8659	0.8547	0.0220	0.5175	21.0636
	KNN	0.9076	0.8447	0.9076	0.8741	0.0305	0.5107	0.0903
	RF	0.9057	0.8499	0.9057	0.8749	0.0344	0.5149	1.1254
	LR	0.9126	0.8331	0.9126	0.8710	0.0100	0.5000	3.2345
	DT	0.8227	0.8522	0.8227	0.8363	0.0457	0.5436	**0.1100**
k-mers [11]	SVM	0.8190	0.8514	0.8190	0.8341	0.0413	0.5487	11640.03
	NB	0.7325	0.8425	0.7325	0.7816	0.0247	0.5149	2348.88
	MLP	0.8397	0.8465	0.8397	0.8426	0.0270	0.5311	7092.26
	KNN	0.9101	0.8480	0.9101	0.8766	0.0429	0.5167	68.50
	RF	0.9098	0.8449	0.9098	0.8740	0.0265	0.5075	655.47
	LR	0.8885	0.8423	0.8885	0.8642	0.0461	0.5286	1995.11
	DT	0.8429	0.8490	0.8429	0.8455	0.0397	0.5361	211.38
Weighted k-mers [17]	SVM	0.8219	0.8355	0.8219	0.8368	0.0451	0.5490	9926.76
	NB	0.7490	0.8475	0.7490	0.7931	0.0360	0.5221	2564.96
	MLP	0.8288	0.8511	0.8288	0.8392	0.0270	0.5345	7306.79
	KNN	0.9122	0.8473	0.9122	0.8728	0.0307	0.5091	53.06
	RF	0.9135	0.8455	0.9135	0.8758	0.0245	0.5067	619.65
	LR	0.8928	0.8492	0.8928	0.8697	**0.0595**	0.5293	1788.37
	DT	0.8420	0.8518	0.8420	0.8461	0.0445	0.5347	147.47
2.1cmDaylight Fingerprint [10]	SVM	0.8562	0.8398	0.8562	0.8476	0.0165	0.5065	90.3683
	NB	0.1591	0.8123	0.1591	0.2612	0.0058	0.5010	10.9286
	MLP	0.8559	0.8371	0.8559	0.8462	0.0101	0.5041	53.3854
	KNN	0.9115	0.8384	0.9115	0.8725	0.0120	0.5007	37.1265
	RF	0.9112	0.8414	0.9112	0.8723	0.0138	0.5007	3.0294
	LR	0.9129	0.8348	0.9129	0.8720	0.0134	0.5011	2.5398
	DT	0.7958	0.8374	0.7958	0.8160	0.0111	0.5050	0.4753
Morgan Fingerprint [10]	SVM	0.8564	0.8394	0.8564	0.8474	0.0245	0.5065	87.6153
	NB	0.2792	0.8273	0.2792	0.4122	0.0089	0.5004	10.4096
	MLP	0.8412	0.8373	0.8412	0.8391	0.0091	0.5065	42.6769
	KNN	0.9094	0.8363	0.9094	0.8705	0.0120	0.5007	35.5932
	RF	0.9105	0.8361	0.9105	0.8709	0.0131	0.5009	2.8328
	LR	0.9117	0.8356	0.9117	0.8714	0.0159	0.5019	3.8399
	DT	0.7934	0.8381	0.7934	0.8148	0.0163	0.5073	0.6120
2.1cmMorgan + k-mers (Ours)	SVM	0.8593	0.8459	0.8593	0.8522	0.0216	0.5088	97.1471
	NB	0.4217	0.8413	0.4217	0.5573	0.0085	0.5011	10.3967
	MLP	0.8249	0.8440	0.8249	0.8342	0.0096	0.5086	41.2894
	KNN	0.9156	0.8460	0.9156	0.8778	0.0167	0.5026	35.3930
	RF	0.9150	0.8453	0.9150	0.8772	0.0152	0.5017	2.6111
	LR	**0.9162**	**0.8541**	**0.9162**	**0.8779**	0.0135	0.5010	5.6350
	DT	0.8086	0.8449	0.8086	0.8262	0.0126	0.5066	0.6623
2.1cmMorgan + Daylight Fingerprint (Ours)	SVM	0.8593	0.8425	0.8593	0.8504	0.0247	0.5106	97.5363
	NB	0.3472	0.8356	0.3472	0.4848	0.0084	0.5086	11.6528
	MLP	0.8233	0.8389	0.8233	0.8309	0.0095	0.5081	46.4655
	KNN	0.9131	0.8421	0.9131	0.8747	0.0136	0.5009	37.6461
	RF	0.9126	0.8420	0.9126	0.8743	0.0188	0.5027	2.6711
	LR	0.9140	0.8412	0.9140	0.8749	0.0153	0.5015	5.8494
	DT	0.7958	0.8407	0.7958	0.8173	0.0117	0.5059	0.7014
Morgan + k-mers + Daylight Fingerprint (Ours)	SVM	0.8521	0.8326	0.8521	0.8416	0.0216	0.5048	98.6409
	NB	0.4354	0.8304	0.4354	0.5650	0.0087	0.5027	10.3506
	MLP	0.8150	0.8326	0.8150	0.8236	0.0117	0.5120	41.1420
	KNN	0.9093	0.8342	0.9093	0.8687	0.0176	0.5032	36.9900
	RF	0.9088	0.8353	0.9088	0.8680	0.0129	0.5007	2.7349
	LR	0.9101	0.8363	0.9101	0.8692	0.0152	0.5017	5.8551
	DT	0.8114	0.8353	0.8114	0.8229	0.0152	**0.5492**	0.6160

achieves a relatively low training time of 5.6350 s compared to other baselines. These results demonstrate its effectiveness in accurately classifying the datasets. Although the F1 (Macro) score is relatively low compared to some baselines, its overall performance is better, considering its high accuracy, precision, and recall. Furthermore, the proposed method exhibits competitive performance in terms of ROC-AUC, indicating its ability to discriminate between positive and negative instances. Our Morgan Fingerprint + k-mers + Daylight Fingerprint performs the best in terms of ROC-AUC.

5.1 Statistical Significance

To address concerns regarding the statistical significance of our results, we employed the student t-test. We calculated p-values using the averages and standard deviations (SD) from five runs, where each run involved different random data splits. It is worth noting that the SD values for all metrics were very small, typically below 0.002. As a result, we found that the p-values were less than 0.05, indicating statistical significance.

6 Conclusion

In conclusion, In conclusion, we have presented a method for chemical representation with k-mers and fragment-based fingerprints for molecular fingerprinting, which is a novel method for generating molecular embeddings from SMILES strings. By combining the strengths of substruct counting, k-mers, and Daylight-like fingerprints, our method offers a more informative representation of chemical structures. Our experimental evaluations demonstrate the superiority of the proposed method over traditional methods, such as Morgan fingerprinting alone, in various cheminformatics tasks, including drug classification and solubility prediction. The integration of k-mers and Daylight-like fingerprints improves supervised analysis, making our method promising for molecular design and drug discovery. It advances the field of cheminformatics, offering new possibilities for molecular structure analysis and design.

References

1. Awale, M., Reymond, J.L.: A multi-fingerprint browser for the zinc database. Nucleic Acids Res. **42**(W1), W234–W239 (2014)
2. Chen, H., Engkvist, O., Wang, Y., Olivecrona, M., Blaschke, T.: The rise of deep learning in drug discovery. Drug Discovery Today **23**(6), 1241–1250 (2018)
3. Chen, H., Kogej, T., Engkvist, O.: Cheminformatics in drug discovery, an industrial perspective. Mol. Inf. **37**(9–10), 1800041 (2018)
4. Choi, Y., Shin, et al.: Target-centered drug repurposing predictions of human angiotensin-converting enzyme 2 (ace2) and transmembrane protease serine subtype 2 (tmprss2) interacting approved drugs for coronavirus disease 2019 (covid-19) treatment through a drug-target interaction deep learning model. Viruses **12**(11), 1325 (2020)
5. Durant, J.L., Leland, B.A., Henry, D.R., Nourse, J.G.: Reoptimization of mdl keys for use in drug discovery. J. Chem. Inf. Comput. Sci. **42**(6), 1273–1280 (2002)

6. Fabregat, R., van Gerwen, P., Haeberle, M., Eisenbrand, F., Corminboeuf, C.: Metric learning for kernel ridge regression: assessment of molecular similarity. Mach. Learn. Sci. Technol. **3**(3), 035015 (2022)
7. Francoeur, P.G., Koes, D.R.: Soltrannet-a machine learning tool for fast aqueous solubility prediction. J. Chem. Inf. Model. **61**(6), 2530–2536 (2021)
8. Fu, G.H., Cao, D.S., Xu, Q.S., Li, H.D., Liang, Y.Z.: Combination of kernel pca and linear support vector machine for modeling a nonlinear relationship between bioactivity and molecular descriptors. J. Chemom. **25**(2), 92–99 (2011)
9. Glorot, X., Bordes, A., Bengio, Y.: Domain adaptation for large-scale sentiment classification: a deep learning approach. In: Proceedings of the 28th International Conference on Machine Learning (ICML-11), pp. 513–520 (2011)
10. James, C., Weininger, D., Delany, J.: Daylight theory manual. daylight chemical information systems. Inc., Irvine, CA (1995)
11. Kang, J.L., Chiu, C.T., Huang, J.S., Wong, D.S.H.: A surrogate model of sigma profile and cosmosac activity coefficient predictions of using transformer with smiles input. Digital Chem. Eng. **2**, 100016 (2022)
12. Keys, M.S.: Mdl information systems inc. San Leandro, CA (2005)
13. Krenn, M., Häse, F., Nigam, A., Friederich, P., Aspuru-Guzik, A.: Self-referencing embedded strings (selfies): a 100% robust molecular string representation. Mach. Learn. Sci. Technol. **1**(4), 045024 (2020)
14. Van der Maaten, L., Hinton, G.: Visualizing data using t-sne. Journal of machine learning research **9**(11) (2008)
15. Muegge, I., Mukherjee, P.: An overview of molecular fingerprint similarity search in virtual screening. Expert Opin. Drug Discov. **11**(2), 137–148 (2016)
16. Nakajima, M., Nemoto, T.: Machine learning enabling prediction of the bond dissociation enthalpy of hypervalent iodine from smiles. Sci. Rep. **11**(1), 20207 (2021)
17. Öztürk, H., Özgür, A., Schwaller, P., Laino, T., Ozkirimli, E.: Exploring chemical space using natural language processing methodologies for drug discovery. Drug Discovery Today **25**(4), 689–705 (2020)
18. Probst, D., Reymond, J.L.: A probabilistic molecular fingerprint for big data settings. J. Cheminformatics **10**, 1–12 (2018)
19. Rensi, S., Altman, R.B.: Flexible analog search with kernel pca embedded molecule vectors. Comput. Struct. Biotechnol. J. **15**, 320–327 (2017)
20. Rupp, M., Tkatchenko, A., Müller, K.R., Von Lilienfeld, O.A.: Fast and accurate modeling of molecular atomization energies with machine learning. Phys. Rev. Lett. **108**(5), 058301 (2012)
21. Salim, N., Holliday, J., Willett, P.: Combination of fingerprint-based similarity coefficients using data fusion. J. Chem. Inf. Comput. Sci. **43**(2), 435–442 (2003)
22. Sastry, G.M., Inakollu, V.S., Sherman, W.: Boosting virtual screening enrichments with data fusion: coalescing hits from two-dimensional fingerprints, shape, and docking. J. Chem. Inf. Model. **53**(7), 1531–1542 (2013)
23. Schwaller, P., Vaucher, A.C., Laplaza, R., Bunne, C., Krause, A., Corminboeuf, C., Laino, T.: Machine intelligence for chemical reaction space. Wiley Interdisciplinary Rev. Comput. Molecular Sci. **12**(5), e1604 (2022)
24. Sellwood, M.A., Ahmed, M., Segler, M.H., Brown, N.: Artificial intelligence in drug discovery (2018)
25. Shamay, Y., et al.: Quantitative self-assembly prediction yields targeted nanomedicines. Nat. Mater. **17**(4), 361–368 (2018)
26. Stuke, A., et al.: Chemical diversity in molecular orbital energy predictions with kernel ridge regression. J. Chem. Phys. **150**(20), 204121 (2019)

27. Thomas, J., Sael, L.: Multi-kernel ls-svm based integration bio-clinical data analysis and application to ovarian cancer. Int. J. Data Min. Bioinform. **19**(2), 150–167 (2017)
28. Tkachev, V., Sorokin, M., Mescheryakov, A., Simonov, A., Garazha, A., Buzdin, A., Muchnik, I., Borisov, N.: Floating-window projective separator (flowps): a data trimming tool for support vector machines (svm) to improve robustness of the classifier. Front. Genet. **9**, 717 (2019)
29. Ucak, U.V., Ashyrmamatov, I., Lee, J.: Reconstruction of lossless molecular representations from fingerprints. J. Cheminformatics **15**(1), 1–11 (2023)
30. Wigh, D.S., Goodman, J.M., Lapkin, A.A.: A review of molecular representation in the age of machine learning. Wiley Interdisciplinary Rev. Comput. Molecular Sci. **12**(5), e1603 (2022)
31. Willett, P.: Fusing similarity rankings in ligand-based virtual screening. Comput. Struct. Biotechnol. J. **5**(6), e201302002 (2013)
32. Zhang, Y., et al.: Automatic term name generation for gene ontology: task and dataset. In: Findings of the Association for Computational Linguistics: EMNLP 2020, pp. 4705–4710 (2020)

Beyond Accuracy: Measuring Representation Capacity of Embeddings to Preserve Structural and Contextual Information

Sarwan Ali[✉]

Georgia State University, Atlanta, GA 30303, USA
sali85@student.gsu.edu

Abstract. Effective representation of data is crucial in various machine learning tasks, as it captures the underlying structure and context of the data. Embeddings have emerged as a powerful technique for data representation, but evaluating their quality and capacity to preserve structural and contextual information remains a challenge. In this paper, we address this need by proposing a method to measure the *representation capacity* of embeddings. The motivation behind this work stems from the importance of understanding the strengths and limitations of embeddings, enabling researchers and practitioners to make informed decisions in selecting appropriate embedding models for their specific applications. By combining extrinsic evaluation methods, such as classification and clustering, with t-SNE-based neighborhood analysis, such as neighborhood agreement and trustworthiness, we provide a comprehensive assessment of the representation capacity. Additionally, the use of optimization techniques (bayesian optimization) for weight optimization (for classification, clustering, neighborhood agreement, and trustworthiness) ensures an objective and data-driven approach in selecting the optimal combination of metrics. The proposed method not only contributes to advancing the field of embedding evaluation but also empowers researchers and practitioners with a quantitative measure to assess the effectiveness of embeddings in capturing structural and contextual information. For the evaluation, we use 3 real-world biological sequence (proteins and nucleotide) datasets and performed representation capacity analysis of 4 embedding methods from the literature, namely Spike2Vec, Spaced k-mers, PWM2Vec, and AutoEncoder. Experimental results demonstrate the Spaced k-mers-based embedding shows better representation capacity on 2 out of three datasets. From the weights computed through optimization, we observed that classification, clustering, and trustworthiness hold the maximum weights while neighborhood agreement weight share towards the representation capacity score is very small. The first of its kind study in the domain of bioinformatics (to the best of our knowledge), the efficacy of the proposed method in accurately measuring the representation capacity of embeddings will lead to improved decision-making and performance in various machine-learning applications in healthcare.

Keywords: Embeddings · Data representation · Representation capacity · t-SNE · Optimization

J. A. Lossio-Ventura et al. (Eds.): SIMBig 2023, CCIS 2142, pp. 30–45, 2024.
https://doi.org/10.1007/978-3-031-63616-5_3

1 Introduction

Effective data representation is vital in various machine learning tasks as it captures the underlying structure and context of the data [1]. It enables accurate modeling and decision-making [2]. Embeddings, as low-dimensional vector representations, have gained prominence for data representation due to their ability to capture meaningful relationships and semantic information in the data [3].

While embeddings are widely used, assessing their quality and capacity to preserve structural and contextual information is challenging. Existing evaluation methods often focus on specific aspects and fail to provide a comprehensive assessment of representation capacity. Current evaluation methods may lack holistic evaluation criteria, focusing on individual tasks or aspects of embeddings. This leads to a limited understanding of their overall effectiveness. Knowing the strengths and limitations of embeddings is crucial for selecting appropriate models, improving performance, and avoiding unintended biases or inaccuracies in downstream applications [4]. The quality of embeddings directly affects the performance and reliability of machine learning systems, making it essential to have reliable metrics to assess representation capacity [5].

The primary objective of this research is to develop a robust and comprehensive evaluation framework to measure the representation capacity of embeddings. The proposed framework combines extrinsic evaluation methods, such as classification and clustering, with neighborhood analysis [6] and trustworthiness [7] using t-SNE to provide a holistic assessment. By integrating classification and clustering tasks with t-SNE-based neighborhood analysis and trustworthiness, we capture both functional and structural aspects of the embeddings. Prior research has proposed various evaluation techniques, including intrinsic evaluation measures like word similarity and analogy tasks [7], as well as extrinsic evaluation through downstream tasks [8,9]. However, current evaluation methods often lack a comprehensive evaluation framework that combines multiple metrics and fails to address the full representation capacity of embeddings. The proposed method overcomes the limitations of existing approaches by providing a comprehensive assessment of representation capacity, considering both functional and structural aspects.

An alternative approach to embedding design in sequence classification is the utilization of a kernel (gram) matrix. Kernel-based machine learning classifiers, such as Support Vector Machines (SVM) [10], can leverage kernel matrices for effective classification. These methods have shown promising results compared to feature engineering-based techniques [8]. In this approach, the kernel matrix is computed by evaluating the similarity (kernel) values between sequences based on the number of matches and mismatches between k-mers [11]. The resulting kernel matrix can be employed not only with kernel-based classifiers like SVM but also with non-kernel-based classifiers such as decision trees using kernel Principal Component Analysis (PCA) [12]. However, the kernel-based approach faces two main challenges:

– **Computation of Pairwise Sequence Similarity:** Computing the pairwise sequence similarity required for constructing the kernel matrix can be computationally expensive. As the number of sequences increases, the computational cost grows significantly, limiting the scalability of the kernel-based method.

- **Memory Storage of Large Kernel Matrices:** Storing a kernel matrix of dimensions $n \times n$, where n represents the number of sequences, can be challenging, especially when n is very large. The memory requirements for such matrices can become prohibitive, making it difficult to scale the kernel-based method to handle a large number of sequences effectively.

Due to the problems discussed above for kernel-based methods, feature engineering and deep learning-based methods for embedding design are more popular among researchers. For this purpose, we only focus on those types of embeddings in this paper. The proposed evaluation framework incorporates classification tasks to assess the discriminative power of embeddings and clustering analysis to evaluate their ability to capture inherent data clusters. The neighborhood structures of embeddings in high-dimensional and low-dimensional spaces are compared using t-SNE to evaluate the preservation of local relationships. The Bayesian optimization approach is employed to optimize the weights assigned to different evaluation metrics including classification, clustering, neighborhood agreement, and trustworthiness, ensuring a balanced assessment of representation capacity. The proposed method offers a comprehensive and holistic understanding of embedding quality. The incorporation of an optimization approach, which allows for the automatic selection of weights, ensures an objective and data-driven approach to measuring the importance of different evaluation metrics. The proposed method equips researchers and practitioners with a robust and quantifiable measure to assess the effectiveness of embeddings in preserving structural and contextual information, enabling informed decision-making in selecting appropriate embedding models. Our contributions to this paper are summarized as follows:

1. **Development of a Comprehensive Evaluation Framework:** We propose a novel evaluation framework to measure the representation capacity of embeddings. Unlike existing methods that focus on specific aspects, our framework integrates classification, clustering, t-SNE-based neighborhood analysis, and trustworthiness to provide a holistic assessment. This comprehensive approach enables a thorough understanding of the effectiveness of embeddings in preserving structural and contextual information.
2. **Incorporation of Optimization Technique:** To ensure an objective and data-driven evaluation, we employ Bayesian optimization for weight optimization. This approach automatically selects optimal weights for different evaluation metrics, including classification, clustering, neighborhood agreement, and trustworthiness. By optimizing the weights, we achieve a balanced assessment of representation capacity, considering the relative importance of each metric.
3. **Application to Real-World Biological Sequence Datasets:** We apply our evaluation framework to three real-world biological sequence datasets, including proteins and nucleotides. By analyzing the representation capacity

of four embedding methods from the literature (Spike2Vec, Spaced k-mers, PWM2Vec, and AutoEncoder), we demonstrate the practicality and effectiveness of our approach in assessing different embedding models.

4. **Identification of Embedding Strengths and Weaknesses:** Through the evaluation process, we identify the strengths and weaknesses of the evaluated embedding methods. Specifically, we observe that Spaced k-mers-based embedding shows superior representation capacity on two out of three datasets. This insight provides valuable guidance for researchers and practitioners in selecting the most suitable embedding models for specific tasks.

5. **Novelty in the Domain of Bioinformatics:** To the best of our knowledge, this study represents the first comprehensive evaluation of representation capacity in the domain of bioinformatics. By quantitatively measuring the quality of embeddings, our research contributes to improved decision-making and performance in various machine learning applications in healthcare.

The rest of the paper is organized as follows. The discussion of existing related studies is given in Sect. 2. The proposed method to compute the representation capacity score is given in Sect. 3. The detail regarding the experimental setup and dataset is reported in Sect. 4. We report the findings from our research in Sect. 5. Finally, the paper is concluded in Sect. 6.

2 Related Work

Various evaluation methods have been proposed to assess the quality and effectiveness of embeddings in capturing data semantics and relationships [13–15]. Intrinsic evaluation measures, such as word similarity [16] and analogy tasks [17], evaluate embeddings based on their ability to capture linguistic properties and semantic similarities [18]. These measures provide insights into the semantic representation capabilities of embeddings [18,19].

Extrinsic evaluation approaches assess the performance of embeddings in downstream tasks, such as sentiment analysis [20], named entity recognition [21], and machine translation [22]. These evaluations measure the impact of embeddings on task-specific performance, providing a practical evaluation of their usefulness in real-world applications [23–25].

Existing evaluation methods for embeddings suffer from several limitations and gaps that hinder a comprehensive assessment of their representation capacity [26]. Firstly, many methods focus on specific aspects of embeddings, such as semantic similarity [27] or performance on individual tasks [28,29], without considering the broader context of representation capacity.

Secondly, the evaluation metrics often lack a holistic approach, failing to capture the full spectrum of functional and structural aspects of embeddings [30, 31]. This limited perspective can lead to incomplete assessments and overlook potential weaknesses or biases in the embeddings.

Several authors proposed feature engineering [8,32,33] and deep learning-based methods [34] to design embeddings for different downstream tasks, such as classification and clustering [35]. Authors in [36] use the ResNet model to perform classification. However, in the case of tabular data, the deep learning models show suboptimal results [37]. Authors in [38,39] convert the biological sequences to images, which can then be applied for classification using deep learning image classifiers. However, transforming a biological sequence into an image without loss of information is still a challenging task. Moreover, it is not known how much information is preserved in the images.

The proposed method fills the gaps in current evaluation approaches by providing a comprehensive assessment of representation capacity. By combining multiple evaluation metrics, including classification, clustering, and neighborhood analysis, the proposed framework captures both the discriminative power and the preservation of structural and contextual information.

3   Proposed Approach

In this section, we present our proposed methodology for evaluating the representation capacity of embeddings. Our approach combines classification and clustering evaluation with neighborhood analysis using t-SNE and leverages Bayesian optimization approach for weight optimization.

3.1   Embedding Generation

Given the biological sequences as input, the first step is to generate fixed-length numerical representation from variable-length sequences. For this purpose, we use the idea of an embedding method, called Spike2Vec, proposed in [9].

Spike2Vec. Given a biological sequence s as input, this method first generates substrings (called mers) of length k (hence k-mers). For example, if the sequence is "ATCGGCA" and k = 3, the k-mers would be "ATC", "TCG", "CGG", "GGC", "GCA". We generate all possible k-mers for the entire sequence. The total number of k-mers that can be generated from a given sequence are:

$$|k - mers| = |s| - k + 1 \qquad (1)$$

where $|s|$ is the length of the biological sequence. Generating k-mers basically means breaking down the original sequence into overlapping k-mers. Note that the value of k is a tunable parameter, which is selected using the standard validation set approach [40].

The next step is to count the frequency of occurrence for each k-mer in the sequence. This will create a k-mer spectrum, which represents the distribution of k-mers in the sequence. The length of the k-mer spectrum equals all possible k-mers within a sequence. Formally, given the alphabet Σ (where Σ corresponds to an alphabet comprised of all possible characters within a biological sequence $ACDEFGHIKLMNPQRSTVWXY$), the length of a spectrum is $|\Sigma|^k$, which contains the count of k-mers within a sequence. For this method, we took $k = 3$. We then normalize the k-mer spectrum to account for variations in sequence length. For this purpose, we divide the count of each k-mer by the total number of k-mers to obtain the normalized frequency, which we call Spike2Vec, which captures the information about the distribution and frequency of k-mers in the sequence.

Spaced k-mers. The feature vectors generated based on the frequencies of k-mers in sequences tend to be large and sparse, which can have a detrimental effect on sequence classification performance. To mitigate this issue, the concept of spaced k-mers was introduced [41], aiming to generate compact feature vectors with reduced sparsity and size. Spaced k-mers involve using non-contiguous length k subsequences, referred to as g-mers. Given a biological sequence as input, the algorithm first computes g-mers and then derives k-mers from those g-mers, where the value of k is less than g. In our experiments, we specifically used $k = 4$ and $g = 9$. The size of the gap between consecutive k-mers is determined by $g - k$. The resultant k-mers are then used to compute the spectrum of length $|\Sigma|^k$ as done in the case of Spike2Vec.

PWM2Vec. The Spike2Vec method yields frequency vectors that are relatively low-dimensional but still maintain a high-dimensional representation. However, the process of matching k-mers to their corresponding location/bin in the vector (bin matching) can be computationally intensive. To address these challenges, PWM2Vec [32] has been introduced as a potential solution. PWM2Vec leverages the concept of position-weight matrices (PWMs) to generate a fixed-length numerical feature vector. By constructing a PWM from the k-mers in the sequence, PWM2Vec assigns a score to each k-mer in the PWM and incorporates both localization information and the significance of each amino acid's position in the sequence. This approach allows for the creation of a concise and comprehensive feature embedding that can be applied to various machine learning tasks downstream. PWM2Vec offers a more efficient and effective alternative to the computation of k-mer frequency vectors, combining important information in a compact manner.

AutoEncoder. The AutoEncoder-based approach [42] uses a deep neural network to learn a compact feature representation of the input data. This is achieved by employing a non-linear mapping technique that transforms the data space X into a lower-dimensional feature space Z. Given one-hot encoding-based vectors as input, this approach iteratively optimizes an objective function to refine the feature representation. In our experiments, we employed a two-layered neural network with an ADAM optimizer and Mean Squared Error (MSE) loss function. The sequences serve as the input to the network, and through the training process, the network learns to extract meaningful and discriminative features from the data.

3.2   Classification and Clustering Evaluation

To assess the discriminative power and clustering ability of embeddings, we perform both classification and clustering tasks.

Classification Evaluation. We train a classification model, called logistic regression classifier, using the Spike2Vec embedding as input features. The classification accuracy, denoted as Acc_{class}, measures the model's ability to correctly classify instances based on the embeddings.

Clustering Evaluation. We apply clustering algorithms, called k-means to group instances based on the embeddings. The number of clusters selected for each dataset equals the number of classes within the dataset (as tager labels are available in the datasets used for experimentation). We evaluate the quality of clustering using the silhouette score, denoted as $Score_{clust}$. A higher $Score_{clust}$ indicates better clustering performance.

Silhouette Score. The silhouette score is a measure of how well each data point in a cluster is separated from points in other clusters. It takes into account both the average distance between points within a cluster (cohesion) and the average distance between points in different clusters (separation). The silhouette score for a data point i can be calculated using the following equation:

$$Score_{clust}(i) = \frac{b(i) - a(i)}{max(a(i), b(i))} \tag{2}$$

where $Score_{clust}(i)$ is the silhouette score for data point i, the $a(i)$ is the average distance between data point i and all other points within the same cluster, and $b(i)$ is the average distance between data point i and all points in the nearest neighboring cluster (the cluster that gives the smallest value of b(i)). The silhouette score ranges from -1 to $+1$, where a higher value indicates that the data point is well-matched to its own cluster and poorly matched to neighboring clusters. A score close to 1 implies a well-clustered data point, while a score close to -1 suggests that the data point may be assigned to the wrong cluster. A score around 0 indicates that the data point is on or very close to the decision boundary between two neighboring clusters. The average silhouette score for all data points in a clustering solution provides an overall measure of the quality of the clustering result.

3.3   Neighborhood Analysis Using T-SNE

To analyze the preservation of neighborhood structures in the embeddings, we employ t-stochastic neighborhood embedding (t-SNE) [43], a dimensionality reduction technique that maps high-dimensional embeddings to a low-dimensional space while preserving local relationships. The pseudocode to compute t-SNE is given in Algorithm 1.

Algorithm 1 t-SNE Computation

Require: High-dimensional data points X, perplexity $Perp$, number of iterations $Iter$
 1: Compute pairwise Euclidean distances D between data points
 2: Initialize low-dimensional embedding Y randomly
 3: **for** $t = 1$ **to** $Iter$ **do**
 4:     Compute similarity matrix P using the Gaussian kernel with adaptive perplexity
 5:     Compute perplexity-based probabilities Q using binary search
 6:     Compute gradient $\frac{\partial C}{\partial Y}$ using Eq. 3
 7:     Update low-dimensional embedding Y using gradient descent with momentum
 8: **end for**
 9: **return** Low-dimensional embedding Y

Compute Gradient. An important step in t-SNE is the computation of gradient. The gradient $\frac{\partial C}{\partial Y}$ in the t-SNE algorithm is computed to optimize the embedding space. It represents the direction and magnitude of the change that needs to be made to the embedding coordinates in order to minimize the cost function C. The equation for computing the gradient is as follows:

$$\frac{\partial C}{\partial Y} = 4 \sum_{i=1}^{N} \left(\sum_{j=1}^{N} P_{ij} - Q_{ij} \right) (Y_i - Y_j) \tag{3}$$

where N is the number of data points, P_{ij} is the similarity between points i and j based on the gaussian kernel, Q_{ij} is the perplexity-based probability between points i and j, and Y_i and Y_j are the low-dimensional coordinates of points i and j. By computing the gradient using Eq. 3 and updating the embedding coordinates accordingly, the t-SNE algorithm optimizes the embedding space to better represent the underlying structure of the high-dimensional data.

Given the original high-dimensional embeddings X and the corresponding t-SNE embeddings Y, we calculate the pairwise Euclidean distances between instances in both spaces as D_X and D_Y, respectively. The neighborhood agreement, denoted as $Agree_{neighbor}$, is computed using the K-nearest neighbors (KNN) approach:

$$Agree_{neighbor} = \frac{1}{N} \sum_{i=1}^{N} \frac{1}{K} \sum_{j \in KNN_i} \delta(||X_i - X_j|| - ||Y_i - Y_j||) \tag{4}$$

where N is the total number of instances, K is the number of nearest neighbors considered, and $\delta(\cdot)$ is the indicator function that returns 1 if the argument is true and 0 otherwise. The value for $Agree_{neighbor}$ ranges from 0 to 100, where the maximum value is better. We measure the neighborhood agreement from $K = 1$ until $K = 100$, normalize them between 0 and 1 (using min-max normalization), and take the average to get a scaler value.

3.4 Trustworthiness Analysis Using T-SNE

To perform a further evaluation using t-SNE, we use trustworthiness, which is a measure that quantifies the extent to which the local relationships among data points are preserved in the embedding space produced by t-SNE. It is computed by comparing the distances between data points in the original high-dimensional space with the distances between the corresponding points in the t-SNE embedding space. The trustworthiness for a given value of K (i.e. number of nearest neighbors), denoted as $Trust(K)$, is calculated using the following equation:

$$Trust(K) = 1 - (\frac{2}{n \times (n-1)}) \times \sum_{i=1}^{n} \sum_{j=1}^{K} (rank(i,j) - K) \qquad (5)$$

where n is the total number of data points, $rank(i,j)$ represents the rank of the $j-th$ nearest neighbor of the $i-th$ data point in the original high-dimensional space, and K is the number of nearest neighbors used for the comparison. This process is repeated for different values of K from 1 to 100 to get $Trust_{neighbor}$.

The trustworthiness calculation involves computing the rank of each data point's neighbors in the original space and comparing it with the ranks of the corresponding points' neighbors in the t-SNE embedding space. A lower rank indicates that the corresponding points in the embedding space are closer to each other, implying a higher level of trustworthiness.

By evaluating trustworthiness for various values of K (i.e. various numbers of neighbors ranging from 1 to 100), it is possible to analyze how well the t-SNE algorithm preserves the local relationships of the data (its value ranges from 0 to 1). Higher values of Trust(K) indicate that the local structures are well-maintained, implying higher trustworthiness of the t-SNE embedding. This measure is valuable for assessing the reliability and quality of the t-SNE visualization or clustering results. We measured the trustworthiness from $K = 1$ until $K = 100$ and took the average to get a scaler value.

3.5 Weight Optimization

After computing Acc_{class}, $Score_{clust}$, $Agree_{neighbor}$, and $Trust_{neighbor}$, the final step is to combine these 4 values to get the representation capacity score. To obtain a balanced evaluation and ensure each metric contributes appropriately to the final representation capacity score, we employ an automatic approach for weight optimization. We aim to find optimal weights for each metric that maximize the overall evaluation performance.

We define the weights as follows: w_{class}, w_{clust}, w_{neighb}, and w_{trust}. These weights determine the importance assigned to each metric.

The representation capacity score, denoted as RC, is calculated as follows:

$$RC = \left[w_{class} \times \frac{Acc_{class}}{max(Acc_{class})} + w_{clust} \times \frac{Score_{clust}}{max(Score_{clust})} \right] - \left[w_{neighb} \times \frac{Agree_{neighbor}}{max(Agree_{neighbor})} + w_{trust} \times \frac{Trust_{neighbor}}{max(Trust_{neighbor})} \right] \tag{6}$$

where $max(\cdot)$ represents the maximum value obtained in each metric.

We employ a Bayesian optimization approach to iteratively search for the optimal weights that maximize the representation capacity score. The optimization process is performed using the Optuna framework[1]. Optuna is a library for hyperparameter optimization that utilizes Bayesian optimization as its underlying algorithm. Bayesian optimization is a sequential model-based optimization technique that aims to find the global optimum of an objective function by iteratively exploring the search space and updating a probabilistic model of the objective function.

The key idea behind Bayesian optimization is to model the unknown objective function using a surrogate model. This surrogate model approximates the true objective function and provides estimates of its values at unexplored points in the search space. The surrogate model is often a probabilistic model such as a Gaussian Process (GP) or a Tree-structured Parzen Estimator (TPE).

The Bayesian optimization process consists of several steps. Initially, a set of hyperparameter configurations is randomly sampled from the search space and evaluated using the objective function. This initial data is used to train the surrogate model.

Next, an acquisition function is defined to guide the search for the next promising hyperparameter configuration. The acquisition function balances exploration and exploitation by considering both the surrogate model's predictions and its uncertainty. Commonly used acquisition functions include Expected Improvement (EI), Probability of Improvement (PI), and Upper Confidence Bound (UCB).

The acquisition function is optimized to find the hyperparameter configuration that maximizes its value. This configuration is then evaluated using the objective function, and the resulting data is used to update the surrogate model. The process iterates, with the surrogate model and acquisition function being updated based on the new data.

The optimization process continues until a stopping criterion is met, such as reaching a maximum number of iterations or the objective function converging to a satisfactory value. In our case, we use the 1000 number of iterations as the stopping criteria. The algorithm aims to iteratively explore promising regions of the search space and focus on areas that are likely to yield better results.

---

[1] https://optuna.org/.

In summary, Optuna utilizes Bayesian optimization to efficiently search the hyperparameter space by iteratively updating a surrogate model and selecting promising hyperparameter configurations using an acquisition function. This approach allows for an adaptive and data-driven exploration of the search space, leading to improved performance in hyperparameter optimization tasks.

4 Experimental Setup

This section presents the dataset utilized in our experiments along with experimental setting details. The experiments were conducted on a system featuring an Intel Core i5 processor running at 2.40 GHz, coupled with 32 GB of memory, and operated on the Windows operating system.

4.1 Dataset Statistics

We use 3 different biological datasets in this study to compute the embeddings and evaluate their representation capacity. The detail of each dataset is described below.

Spike7k Dataset. The Spike7k dataset consists of aligned spike protein sequences obtained from the GISAID database[2]. The dataset comprises a total of 7000 sequences, which represent 22 different lineages of coronaviruses (class labels). Each sequence in the dataset has a length of 1274 amino acids. The distribution of lineages (class labels) in the Spike7k dataset is the following: B.1.1.7 (3369), B.1.617.2 (875), AY.4 (593), B.1.2 (333), B.1 (292), B.1.177 (243), P.1 (194), B.1.1 (163), B.1.429 (107), B.1.526 (104), AY.12 (101), B.1.160 (92), B.1.351 (81), B.1.427 (65), B.1.1.214 (64), B.1.1.519 (56), D.2 (55), B.1.221 (52), B.1.177.21 (47), B.1.258 (46), B.1.243 (36), R.1 (32).

Protein Subcellular. The Protein Subcellular dataset [44] comprises unaligned protein sequences annotated with information on 11 distinct subcellular locations, which are used as class labels for classification tasks. The dataset contains a total of 5959 sequences. The classes along with their counts in this dataset are the following: Cytoplasm (1411), Plasma Membrane (1238), Extracellular Space (843), Nucleus (837), Mitochondrion (510), Chloroplast (449), Endoplasmic Reticulum (198), Peroxisome (157), Golgi Apparatus (150), Lysosomal (103), Vacuole (63).

Human DNA. This data comprised a collection of unaligned Human DNA nucleotide sequences, comprising a total of 4,380 sequences [45]. Each sequence was composed of nucleotides A, C, G, and T. The dataset included a class label indicating the gene family to which each sequence belonged. There were a total

---

[2] https://www.gisaid.org/.

of seven unique gene family labels, namely G Protein Coupled, Tyrosine Kinase, Tyrosine Phosphatase, Synthetase, Synthase, Ion Channel, and Transcription Factor. The objective of the study was to classify the gene family of each DNA sequence. The dataset exhibited variations in sequence lengths. The maximum, minimum, and average sequence lengths in the dataset were found to be 18,921, 5, and 1,263.59, respectively. These statistics provide insights into the range and distribution of sequence lengths within the dataset. The classes along with their counts in this dataset are the following: G Protein Coupled (531), Tyrosine Kinase (534), Tyrosine Phosphatase (349), Synthetase (672), Synthase (711), Ion Channel (240), Transcription Factor (1343).

5   Results and Discussion

In this section, we report the representation capacity results for different embedding methods generated for different datasets.

The results for the Spike7k dataset are reported in Table 1. In terms of representation capacity, we can observe that AutoEncoder-based embedding achieves the highest performance. If we break down the performance for different metrics, the Spike2Vec embedding shows the best classification accuracy, AutoEncoder shows the best clustering performance as well as the best trustworthiness value. Moreover, PWM2Vec shows the highest performance in the case of neighborhood agreements. From the "Optimal Weights (Performance Values)", we can observe that Classification, Clustering, and Trustworthiness got almost equal weight based on the Bayesian optimization. However, neighborhood agreement god very small weight values. Because of this reason, despite PWM2Vec showing the best performance for neighborhood agreement, its representation capacity score is the lowest among all embedding methods (because of the 0.0003 weight for the neighborhood agreement). The overall behavior shows that the neighborhood agreement may provide additional insights about local structures but might not carry as much discriminative power in the overall analysis.

Table 1. Representation Capacity results for Spike7k dataset. The best values are shown in bold.

Embedding	Representation Capacity	Optimal Weights (Performance Values)			
		Classification	Clustering	Neighborhood Agreement	Trustworthiness
Spike2Vec	0.7638	0.3329 (**0.8533**)	0.3326 (0.5447)	0.0074 (0.8623)	0.3270 (0.9325)
Spaced k-mers	0.7728	0.3332 (0.8471)	0.3330 (0.5589)	0.0004 (0.8425)	0.3332 (0.9141)
PWM2Vec	0.7629	0.3333 (0.8171)	0.3272 (0.5732)	0.0003 (**0.8933**)	0.3390 (0.8942)
AutoEncoder	**0.8190**	0.3303 (0.7576)	0.3301 (**0.7870**)	0.0094 (0.8336)	0.3300 (**0.9597**)

The results for the Protein Subcellular dataset are reported in Table 2. In terms of representation capacity, we can observe that Spaced $k$mers-based embedding achieves the highest performance. If we break down the performance for different metrics, the Spaced k-mers embedding shows the best classification accuracy (with an optimal weight of 0.3472) and Clustering performance (with an optimal weight of 0.3136). AutoEncoder shows the best Neighborhood Agreement performance while PWM2Vec shows the highest performance in the case of trustworthiness. Again, from the "Optimal Weights (Performance Values)", we can observe that Classification, Clustering, and Trustworthiness got almost equal weight based on the Bayesian optimization. However, neighborhood agreement god very small weight values, which shows that although neighborhood agreement may provide additional insights about local structures, however, it might not carry as much discriminative power in the overall analysis.

Table 2. Representation Capacity results for Protein Subcellular dataset. The best values are shown in bold.

Embedding	Representation Capacity	Optimal Weights (Performance Values)			
		Classification	Clustering	Neighborhood Agreement	Trustworthiness
Spike2Vec	0.4010	0.3335 (0.5687)	0.3314 (0.0351)	0.0020 (0.7570)	0.3329 (0.6045)
Spaced k-mers	**0.4603**	0.3472 (**0.6677**)	0.3136 (**0.1548**)	0.0001 (0.6183)	0.3389 (0.5309)
PWM2Vec	0.4094	0.3292 (0.5151)	0.3303 (0.0634)	0.0053 (0.6992)	0.3350 (**0.6644**)
AutoEncoder	0.3639	0.3425 (0.4485)	0.3145 (0.0017)	0.00007 (**0.7634**)	0.3427 (0.6122)

The results for the Protein Subcellular dataset are reported in Table 3. In terms of representation capacity, we can observe that Spaced $k$mers-based embedding achieves the highest performance despite achieving the best individual performance for only classification metric. If we breakdown the performance for different metrics, the Spike2Vec embedding shows the best Neighborhood agreement value (with optimal weight of 0.0000006 and neighborhood agreement value of 0.9646) and Trustworthiness value (with optimal weight of 0.3305 and neighborhood agreement value of 0.9732). The PWM2Vec shows the best Clustering performance. Here we can observe the same pattern as with the previous two datasets where classification, clustering, and Trustworthiness got almost equal weights while neighborhood agreement contains almost 0 weight.

Table 3. Representation Capacity results for Human DNA dataset. The best values are shown in bold.

Embedding	Representation Capacity	Optimal Weights (Performance Values)			
		Classification	Clustering	Neighborhood Agreement	Trustworthiness
Spike2Vec	0.6515	0.3320 (0.5859)	0.3373 (0.4009)	0.0000006 (**0.9646**)	0.3305 (**0.9732**)
Spaced k-mers	**0.6667**	0.3329 (**0.7313**)	0.3275 (0.3184)	0.0002 (0.9637)	0.3392 (0.9408)
PWM2Vec	0.5985	0.3317 (0.3036)	0.3319 (**0.9337**)	0.0103 (0.7935)	0.3258 (0.6017)
AutoEncoder	0.5485	0.3459 (0.6605)	0.3079 (0.0497)	0.0001 (0.9168)	0.3459 (0.8810)

6   Conclusion

In this paper, we have presented a comprehensive evaluation framework to measure the representation capacity of embeddings, addressing the need for robust and quantitative assessment methods. By combining classification, clustering, t-SNE-based neighborhood analysis, and trustworthiness, our framework provides a holistic understanding of the effectiveness of embeddings in capturing structural and contextual information. To ensure an objective evaluation, we have employed Bayesian optimization for weight optimization, allowing for the automatic selection of optimal weights for different evaluation metrics. This data-driven approach maximizes the representation capacity score and provides a balanced assessment of embeddings. Applying our evaluation framework to real-world biological sequence datasets, including proteins and nucleotides, we have analyzed the representation capacity of four embedding methods. Future work in this area could focus on incorporating additional evaluation metrics or tasks that could provide a more comprehensive assessment of representation capacity. Exploring other intrinsic and extrinsic evaluation measures specific to different domains or applications could further enhance the evaluation process.

References

1. Najafabadi, M.M., Villanustre, F., Khoshgoftaar, T.M., Seliya, N., Wald, R., Muharemagic, E.: Deep learning applications and challenges in big data analytics. J. Big Data **2**(1), 1–21 (2015)
2. Runck, B.C., Manson, S., Shook, E., Gini, M., Jordan, N.: Using word embeddings to generate data-driven human agent decision-making from natural language. GeoInformatica **23**, 221–242 (2019)
3. Banerjee, I., Madhavan, S., Goldman, R.E., Rubin, D.L.: Intelligent word embeddings of free-text radiology reports. In: AMIA Annual Symposium Proceedings, vol. 2017. American Medical Informatics Association, p. 411 (2017)
4. Glielmo, A., Husic, B.E., Rodriguez, A., Clementi, C., Noé, F., Laio, A.: Unsupervised learning methods for molecular simulation data. Chem. Rev. **121**(16), 9722–9758 (2021)
5. Bian, J., Gao, B., Liu, T.-Y.: Knowledge-powered deep learning for word embedding. In: Calders, T., Esposito, F., Hüllermeier, E., Meo, R. (eds.) ECML PKDD 2014. LNCS (LNAI), vol. 8724, pp. 132–148. Springer, Heidelberg (2014). https://doi.org/10.1007/978-3-662-44848-9_9
6. Chourasia, P., Ali, S., Patterson, M.: Informative initialization and kernel selection improves t-sne for biological sequence. In: IEEE International Conference on Big Data (IEEE Big Data) 2022)
7. Pandey, S., Vaze, R.: Trustworthiness of t-distributed stochastic neighbour embedding. In: Proceedings of the 3rd IKDD Conference on Data Science, 2016, pp. 1–2 (2016)
8. Ali, S., Sahoo, B., Ullah, N., Zelikovskiy, A., Patterson, M., Khan, I.: A k-mer based approach for SARS-CoV-2 variant identification. In: International Symposium on Bioinformatics Research and Applications, pp. 153–164 (2021)

9. Ali, S., Patterson, M.: Spike2vec: an efficient and scalable embedding approach for covid-19 spike sequences. In: IEEE International Conference on Big Data (Big Data), pp. 1533–1540 (2021)
10. Farhan, M., Tariq, J., Zaman, A., Shabbir, M., Khan, I.: Efficient approximation algorithms for strings kernel based sequence classification. In: Advances in Neural Information Processing Systems (NeurIPS), pp. 6935–6945 (2017)
11. Leslie, C., Eskin, E., Weston, J., Noble, W.S.: Mismatch string kernels for svm protein classification. In: Advances in neural information processing systems, pp. 1441–1448 (2003)
12. Hoffmann, H.: Kernel PCA for novelty detection. Pattern Recogn. **40**(3), 863–874 (2007)
13. Zhang, D., Yin, J., Zhu, X., Zhang, C.: MetaGraph2Vec: complex semantic path augmented heterogeneous network embedding. In: Phung, D., Tseng, V.S., Webb, G.I., Ho, B., Ganji, M., Rashidi, L. (eds.) PAKDD 2018. LNCS (LNAI), vol. 10938, pp. 196–208. Springer, Cham (2018). https://doi.org/10.1007/978-3-319-93037-4_16
14. Wang, B., Wang, A., Chen, F., Wang, Y., Kuo, C.-C.J.: Evaluating word embedding models: methods and experimental results. APSIPA Trans. Signal Inf. Process. **8**, e19 (2019)
15. Schnabel, T., Labutov, I., Mimno, D., Joachims, T.: Evaluation methods for unsupervised word embeddings. In: Proceedings of the 2015 Conference on Empirical Methods in Natural Language Processing, pp. 298–307 (2015)
16. Antoniak, M., Mimno, D.: Evaluating the stability of embedding-based word similarities. Trans. Assoc. Comput. Linguist. **6**, 107–119 (2018)
17. Hartmann, N., Fonseca, E., Shulby, C., Treviso, M., Rodrigues, J., Aluisio, S.: Portuguese word embeddings: Evaluating on word analogies and natural language tasks. arXiv preprint arXiv:1708.06025 (2017)
18. Wang, Y., et al.: A comparison of word embeddings for the biomedical natural language processing. J. Biomed. Inform. **87**, 12–20 (2018)
19. Shor, J., et al.: Towards learning a universal non-semantic representation of speech. arXiv preprint arXiv:2002.12764 (2020)
20. Yu, L.-C., Wang, J., Lai, K.R., Zhang, X.: Refining word embeddings for sentiment analysis. In: Conference on Empirical Methods in Natural Language Processing, pp. 534–539 (2017)
21. Akbik, A., Bergmann, T., Vollgraf, R.: Pooled contextualized embeddings for named entity recognition. In: Conference of the North American Chapter of the Association for Computational Linguistics: Human Language Technologies, Volume 1 (Long and Short Papers), pp. 724–728 (2019)
22. Zou, W.Y., Socher, R., Cer, D., Manning, C.D.: Bilingual word embeddings for phrase-based machine translation. In: Conference on Empirical Methods in Natural Language Processing, pp. 1393–1398 (2013)
23. Wang, X., Bo, D., Shi, C., Fan, S., Ye, Y., Philip, S.Y.: A survey on heterogeneous graph embedding: methods, techniques, applications and sources. IEEE Trans. Big Data (2022)
24. Bhatia, K., Jain, H., Kar, P., Varma, M., Jain, P.: Sparse local embeddings for extreme multi-label classification. In: Advances in Neural Information Processing Systems, vol. 28 (2015)
25. Rudkowsky, E., Haselmayer, M., Wastian, M., Jenny, M., Emrich, Š, Sedlmair, M.: More than bags of words: sentiment analysis with word embeddings. Commun. Methods Meas. **12**(2–3), 140–157 (2018)

26. Ben-David, S., Eiron, N., Simon, H.U.: Limitations of learning via embeddings in euclidean half spaces. J. Mach. Learn. Res. **3**, 441–461 (2002)
27. Plank, B., Moschitti, A.: Embedding semantic similarity in tree kernels for domain adaptation of relation extraction. In: Proceedings of the 51st Annual Meeting of the Association for Computational Linguistics (Volume 1: Long Papers), pp. 1498–1507 (2013)
28. Wang, B.: On position embeddings in bert. In: International Conference on Learning Representations (2021)
29. Nayak, N., Angeli, G., Manning, C.D.: Evaluating word embeddings using a representative suite of practical tasks. In: Proceedings of the 1st Workshop on Evaluating Vector-Space Representations for nlp, pp. 19–23 (2016)
30. Beckman, S.L., Barry, M.: Innovation as a learning process: embedding design thinking. Calif. Manage. Rev. **50**(1), 25–56 (2007)
31. Yu, L., Hermann, K.M., Blunsom, P., Pulman, S.: Deep learning for answer sentence selection. arXiv preprint arXiv:1412.1632 (2014)
32. Ali, S., Bello, B., Chourasia, P., Punathil, R.T., Zhou, Y., Patterson, M.: PWM2Vec: an efficient embedding approach for viral host specification from coronavirus spike sequences. Biology **11**(3), 418 (2022)
33. Kuzmin, K., Adeniyi, A.E., DaSouza, A.K., Jr., Lim, D., Nguyen, H., Molina, N.R., Xiong, L., Weber, I.T., Harrison, R.W.: Machine learning methods accurately predict host specificity of coronaviruses based on spike sequences alone. Biochem. Biophys. Res. Commun. **533**(3), 553–558 (2020)
34. Ali, S., Murad, T., Chourasia, P., Patterson, M.:Spike2signal: classifying coronavirus spike sequences with deep learning. In: 2022 IEEE Eighth International Conference on Big Data Computing Service and Applications (BigDataService), pp. 81–88. IEEE (2022)
35. Tayebi, Z., Ali, S., Patterson, M.: Robust representation and efficient feature selection allows for effective clustering of SARS-CoV-2 variants. Algorithms **14**(12), 348 (2021)
36. Wang, Z., Yan, W., Oates, T.: Time series classification from scratch with deep neural networks: a strong baseline. In: IJCNN, pp. 1578–1585 (2017)
37. Shwartz-Ziv, R., Armon, A.: Tabular data: deep learning is not all you need. Inf. Fusion **81**, 84–90 (2022)
38. Löchel, H., Heider, D.: Chaos game representation and its applications in bioinformatics. Comput. Struct. Biotechnol. J. **19**, 6263–6271 (2021)
39. Löchel, H., Eger, D., Sperlea, T., Heider, D.: Deep learning on chaos game representation for proteins. Bioinformatics **36**(1), 272–279 (2020)
40. Devijver, P., Kittler, J.: Pattern Recognition: A Statistical Approach, pp. 1–448. Prentice-Hall, London (1982)
41. Singh, R., Sekhon, A., et al.: Gakco: a fast gapped k-mer string kernel using counting. In: Joint ECML and Knowledge Discovery in Databases, pp. 356–373 (2017)
42. Xie, J., Girshick, R., Farhadi, A.: Unsupervised deep embedding for clustering analysis. In: International Conference on Machine Learning, pp. 478–487 (2016)
43. Van der Maaten, L., Hinton, G.: Visualizing data using t-SNE. J. Mach. Learn. Res. (JMLR) **9**(11) (2008)
44. Protein Subcellular Localization (2023). https://www.kaggle.com/datasets/lzyacht/proteinsubcellularlocalization. Accessed 10 Jan 2023
45. Human DNA. https://www.kaggle.com/code/nageshsingh/demystify-dna-sequencing-with-machine-learning/data. Accessed 10 Oct 2022

Multivariable-Unistep Prediction of Travel Times in Public Transport Buses Using LSTM and Convolutional LSTM

Elizon F. Carcausto-Mamani[1]([⊠]) [iD], Etson R. Rojas-Cahuana[1] [iD],
Edwin Alvarez-Mamani[2] [iD], and Harley Vera-Olivera[1] [iD]

[1] Universidad Nacional San Antonio Abad del Cusco, Cusco, Peru
{170427,124821,harley.vera}@unsaac.edu.pe
[2] Pontificia Universidad Católica del Perú, San Miguel, Lima, Peru
edwin.alvarez@pucp.edu.pe

Abstract. Public transportation plays a vital role in the daily mobility of a city, especially in tourist destinations like Cusco, Peru. Although intelligent transportation systems exist to control and monitor public transportation, improving efficiency and service management, tools for predicting travel time between stops are still lacking. To enhance the utility of these systems, various techniques and deep learning models have been employed. Our proposal is based on experimenting with LSTM (Long Short-Term Memory) and Convolutional LSTM architectures, used as an Encoder-Decoder with a multivariate-unistep approach. We utilized a dataset of 1.6 million records of public transportation routes, including GPS points from buses and their stops. Experimental results show that the selected model is capable of predicting travel time, considering the spatiotemporal context, with an MAE of 19.55 s. Code: https://github.com/eFrank-cm/travel-time-prediction.

Keywords: LSTM · ConvLSTM · deep learning · prediction · travel time · multivariable · unistep · public transport

1 Introduction

One of the most important cities in Peru is the city of Cusco, also known as one of the world's highly-rated tourist destinations. Cities like Cusco have the particularity of attracting a significant number of people, including residents and both national and international tourists [12]. Consequently, it also hosts social and economic activities that have a great impact on the country. Therefore, one of the key elements to facilitate these activities is the mobility of people and goods. Addressing this situation, the most crucial resource is the public transportation service, as it provides an economical, fast, and accessible option [9].

J. A. Lossio-Ventura et al. (Eds.): SIMBig 2023, CCIS 2142, pp. 46–61, 2024.
https://doi.org/10.1007/978-3-031-63616-5_4

In this context, public transportation services currently fulfill the basic needs of users. However, one of their main concerns is travel time from one stop to another. Therefore, knowing the travel time allows users to determine when a bus will arrive at a stop, enabling them to better organize their waiting time. In Cusco, public transportation services are managed by private companies, and for our study, we focus on the case of Patrón San Jerónimo company. Although some of these companies have Intelligent Transportation Systems (ITS), they lack a tool that enables them to predict travel time between stops.

The problem of travel time prediction has been the subject of study in previous research. Proposed solutions suggest various alternatives, such as estimation based on historical data and statistical techniques [8], support vector regression [16], or simple regression models [17]. In rural areas, where there are fewer factors influencing travel time, traditional methods can be used [1]. However, calculating travel time in urban areas becomes more complex due to the existence of a greater number of factors, such as traffic congestion, traffic flow, and passenger demand at certain hours. Considering these circumstances, methods using Artificial Intelligence (AI) techniques, such as expert systems and neural networks, have been implemented. In particular, models based on recurrent neural networks like Long Short-Term Memory (LSTM) have shown promising results in predicting travel times for public transportation buses.

This study aims to experiment with Simple LSTM, LSTM Encoder-Decoder, Simple Convolutional LSTM, and Convolutional LSTM Encoder-Decoder models, leveraging the capacity in LSTM networks to capture long-term dependencies [5]. A dataset of 1.6 million GPS points on the routes of each bus from the company was utilized. This dataset was preprocessed and transformed for training the described models. It is important to mention that travel times are the resource used for training, which is handled on a scale of seconds, and this data can be extracted from the GPS points.

This work is structured as follows: Sect. 2 describes the related works that served as references for this study. Section 3.1 outlines the strategy used to address the travel time prediction problem. Section 3 provides details about the materials and methods employed. Section 5 presents the experiments conducted and the results obtained, and Sect. 6 includes the conclusions of the study.

2   Related Works

According to [13], the deployment of a ConvLSTM network significantly improves arrival time accuracy. In this study, a multi-output ConvLSTM model is implemented in an Encoder-Decoder architecture. The model achieves an RMSE of 3.11 min when predicting three or more instances ahead. One of the peculiarities in the context of the study is the existence of more distant route links. For this reason, the unit of time is in minutes. Additionally, this method is computationally costly. On the other hand, in [4], a simple LSTM model with 66 units is trained, which can also make unistep and multistep predictions of four instances or more ahead. The reported error is 7% on the test dataset with a lower computational cost.

In work [10], the problem is addressed using a simple LSTM neural network architecture, referred to as LSTM-A. This architecture combines a simple LSTM network with a dense Artificial Neural Network (ANN). The relevance of this work lies in the approach used to consider traffic variations at different hours of the day. Time feature vectors were implemented, allowing the model to take into account peak demand hours. A similar approach is presented in [6], where LSTM models are used to calculate real-time traffic, bus dwell time at stops, and travel time between stops. All these calculations are weighted with real-time traffic, resulting in a sum of the weighted times to obtain the bus arrival time. Additionally, a GPS calibration algorithm is applied to improve the accuracy of coordinates, considering historical data from 30 buses over a year. Their evaluation involves comparing four prediction methods, with Weighted LSTM standing out, achieving an MAE metric of 1.62 min and an RMSE of 4.0 min in multiple-stop tests.

In [14], an attention mechanism is implemented to address the limitations of LSTM networks and enable multi-step predictions. Upon reviewing various works, it is found that the majority experiment with LSTM models or their variations. In [15], although they use travel time prediction to solve the next location problem, they also implement LSTM models with self-attention mechanisms and compare them with a Sequential LSTM model. Subsequently, in [11], the focus is on experimenting with 16 hyperparameter configurations to train different LSTM models, where LSTM-DD (Long Short-Term Memory Deep Neural Network) achieves the most prominent results. On the other hand, other research emphasizes the relevance of travel time information, as it can lead to cost reduction for both the service providers and users, thereby increasing service reliability and quality, as indicated by the authors of [9].

3   Materials and Method

3.1   Travel Time Prediction

The present work aims to experiment with four architectures: a simple LSTM network, an Encoder-Decoder LSTM, a simple ConvLSTM, and an Encoder-Decoder ConvLSTM. The target is to enhance the accuracy of travel time prediction by generating travel time series for model training. These series include the time it takes for the bus to travel each link (space between stops) of the route and space-time context information through feature vectors. Travel times are calculated in seconds, as the stops are close to each other. Figure 1 shows the route in blue (covering 21 km) and its 84 stops in yellow.

A series is composed of travel times for the 83 links. Figure 2a displays travel time series, revealing sets of peaks in specific areas, indicating the existence of patterns. Leveraging the advantages of LSTM networks in processing time series

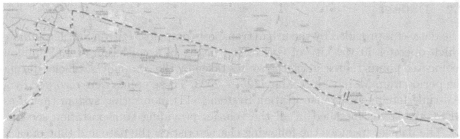

Fig. 1. Route of Patrón San Jerónimo company.

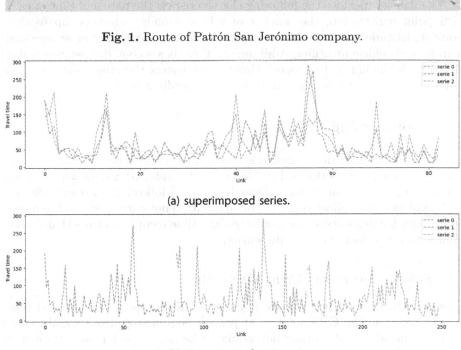

(a) superimposed series.

(b) Concatenated series.

Fig. 2. Travel time series.

data [7], we concatenate the travel time series to present the peaks at frequencies that the model can grasp, as if it were dealing with a time series, as shown in Fig. 2b. During certain hours of the day and in specific locations within the city, travel times may increase or decrease due to traffic. For this reason, we include feature vectors representing the time and location where the travel time is obtained.

3.2   Dataset

The dataset is provided by the urban transport company "Patrón San Jerónimo", which operates in the city of Cusco. It consists of a collection of 1.68 million geolocated points representing the routes taken by the company's vehicles during the period from March 1st to March 25th, 2023. These points were recorded by a real-time Intelligent Transportation System (STI) monitoring system that uses GPS subsystems installed in all the vehicles providing transportation services [2]. The dataset includes the following characteristics: the date and time of each GPS point registration, the number of vehicle rounds completed up to that moment, latitude and longitude coordinates, vehicle navigation in sexagesimal degrees, and vehicle identifier. Additionally, there is a second dataset containing the stops belonging to the route. This dataset covers the stop identifier, stop name, navigation, and latitude and longitude coordinates.

4   Preprocessing

To generate the travel time series, it is crucial to work with reliable data. Therefore, data cleaning is performed to identify and handle GPS data with reading errors. Upon closer examination of the dataset, the following cases were discovered: existence of duplicated points, points that do not correspond to the route, coordinates located outside the roadways, and time recording errors that do not align with the sequence of a route journey.

4.1   Selection of Points Using Geofencing

Subsequently, travel time for each link was calculated using the date and time information from the GPS points that pass through a stop. However, the company's monitoring system does not validate whether a point passed through a stop, necessitating the use of geofencing techniques. Geofencing employs virtual boundaries to define the perimeter of an object, and when another object crosses this perimeter, a notification is triggered. To implement this technique, we calculated the radius (R) for each stop since this information was not available in the dataset. The radius for each stop was computed taking into account the precision error of GPS systems, the size of the vehicles, and the vehicular traffic density in specific areas of the city. There are cases where more than one point falls within the perimeter of a stop. To address this, we verify if the navigation of the point aligns with the stop's navigation or falls within a 45° arc concerning the stop's navigation. If multiple points coincide, the closest one is selected. On the other hand, there are also instances where no points are registered within the perimeter of certain stops. In such cases, it was determined that to form a series, a maximum of 24 stops without GPS points is allowed. This approach allows us to apply Algorithm 1 to handle missing data. After filtering the points, we calculate the travel time between stops, forming a total of 3 361 travel time series.

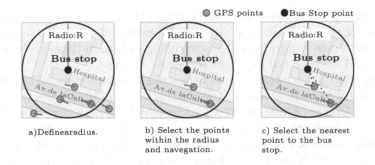

a) Define a radius.

b) Select the points within the radius and navegation.

c) Select the nearest point to the bus stop.

Fig. 3. Application of geofencing to the GPS points.

4.2 Outliers

Upon visualizing the scatter plot in Fig. 4a, the x-axis represents the quantity of data, and the y-axis represents the travel times for the entire dataset, we observe that a significant portion of the travel times falls within the interval [10, 500]. However, there are three points that are distant from this interval, representing GPS reading errors. Additionally, there are points that are distant but still within a short distance, with values less than 2 500. Considering that travel times can be influenced by various factors and that the times are in seconds, it is not appropriate to remove all outliers, as some of them may represent valid data.

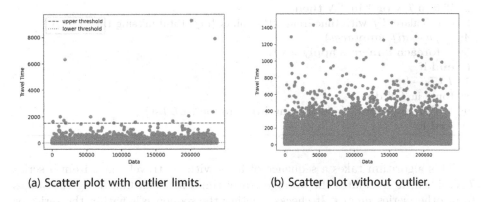

(a) Scatter plot with outlier limits.

(b) Scatter plot without outlier.

Fig. 4. Scatter plots with and without outliers.

Conducting a case study, we found that some of the travel times falling within the range of [500, 2500] are indeed GPS reading errors, while a significant portion represents valid and real data. The reason is that travel times are subject to traffic conditions, as well as waiting queues at the busiest stops, and instances where drivers stop for a few minutes during certain stretches of the route, particularly at specific times of the day, to pick up additional passengers. As a consequence, it is not appropriate to remove all outliers from the dataset since a considerable proportion of them constitute accurate and meaningful data points. These outliers provide valuable insights into the variability of travel times under different scenarios and are essential for a comprehensive analysis.

Taking into consideration the events described above, a threshold of [10, 1500] was chosen due to atypical cases in travel times less than 10 s between stops and a maximum tolerance of 1500 s for bus departures only from the first stop. This will eliminate excessive travel times as well as others that we consider not relevant for training purposes. Filtering the data points resulted in a loss of only 14 time travel series, which is acceptable. Figure 4b displays the travel times filtered by the threshold.

4.3   Handling Missing Data

Since there are bus stops that did not record any GPS points within their perimeter, there are links without travel times, resulting in an incomplete time travel series. For the training process, all links must have their corresponding travel times to form continuous sequences. We designed Algorithm 1 for imputing average travel times to complete the missing times in each link.

Algorithm 1. Imputation of averages

Require: TN: Travel time-free link sequences.
Ensure: TTL: List of travel times for the links.
1: $avgs \leftarrow [mean(t_n)$ **for** n **in** $TN]$ $\{t_n$: travel time for the link $n\}$
2: **if** 0 **in** TN **or** 1 **in** TN **then**
3:     calculate dif with time from GPS points $\{dif$: total missing time in $TN\}$
4:     $fp \leftarrow dif/\textbf{sum}(avgs)$
5:     **foreach** u **in** $avgs$ **apply** $u * fp$
6: **end if**
7: $TTL \leftarrow [\,]$
8: **for** n **in** TN **do**
9:     TLL **append** t_n $\{$add the travel time to the TLL list$\}$
10: **end for**

This algorithm takes a sequence of links without travel times from a series TN. Then, it calculates the average travel times for each link using the values from other series *means*. It checks whether the sequence is within the series or if it is at either end. If it is within the sequence, it calculates the total missing time dif that forms a sequence TN, and then maps the averages *means* by multiplying with a proportion factor fp. The factor fp allows us to adjust the average value in relation to the proportion that a section without travel time represents in relation to the total remaining time dif. Otherwise, if it is at either extreme, the averages are imputed directly. Finally, to avoid potential biases after applying this algorithm to all the series, the average travel time, maximum, and minimum values should remain unchanged. For this reason, the series is filtered again using the previously defined thresholds.

4.4 Spatiotemporal Feature Vector

Travel times are dependent variables on both the schedule and the stops. For instance, at a stop with a higher concentration of people at 08:00 hr, travel times tend to be higher due to the massive movement of people. To ensure that the model also considers this factor, we associate a vector of features representing the stop and a time interval. The stop is represented by a link identifier, resulting in 83 identifiers. To represent the time interval, 15 min intervals were considered, and the GPS point time was rounded to the nearest quarter-hour. Subsequently, the time is divided into two categorical variables: one indicating the hour and the other one indicating the minutes. This process yields the feature vector associated with the travel times of a vehicle across all links of the route, as shown in Table 1.

Table 1. Travel time serie.

Link	Hour	Minute	Travel time
100:101	7	15	191.0
101:102	7	15	106.0
102:103	7	30	90.0

4.5 Dataset Preparation for Training

For the experiments, the dataset was divided into training, validation, and testing sets, with proportions of 80%, 10%, and 10%, respectively. The models follow a supervised learning approach, requiring the generation of a dataset that transforms our travel time series into inputs and outputs. Following the approach described in Sect. 3.1, all travel time series are concatenated linearly to form a single series containing all of them, as shown in Fig. 2a. With this single series, the sliding window method is used to create inputs and outputs. This method allows capturing local patterns and relationships in sequential data to facilitate learning, rather than analyzing the entire sequence at once, series of 83 are analyzed. It is also utilized to train models that predict future values based on past observations.

Figure 5 illustrates the application of the sliding window method. To form the first input, a sequence of length 83 is taken to predict element 84. Then, we shift one link to form the second input and output, and so on, until the entire series is covered. Upon completion, we have a set of inputs (X) and another set of outputs (Y) for training purposes.

Figure 6 displays the dimension of the input data, represented by N, W, and Z, where N denotes the total number of samples (batches), W indicates the number of evaluated sequences (input length), and Z is the number of variables

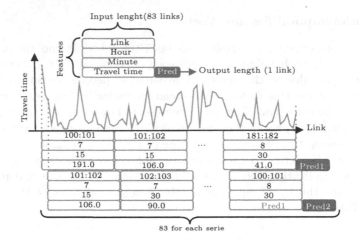

Fig. 5. Sliding window.

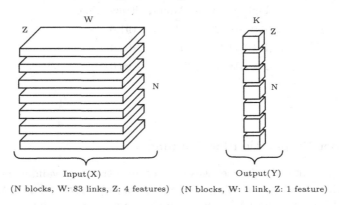

Input(X)   Output(Y)

(N blocks, W: 83 links, Z: 4 features)   (N blocks, W: 1 link, Z: 1 feature)

Fig. 6. Tensor-3D, input y output.

being assessed (features). It is structured as a 3D tensor of size N with dimensionality $N \times W \times Z$. On the other hand, for the output Y, a 3D tensor of size N with dimensionality $N \times k \times Z$ is used. Since we construct datasets for supervised learning models, only the variable to be predicted is considered, thus Z is equal to 1, and k indicates how many time steps into the future we need to predict. Being this a unistep model, k is equal to 1.

Once the supervised dataset is structured, normalization is performed using three scalers: Robust scaler, Standard scaler, and Min-max scaler. As shown in Fig. 4a, the dataset contains outliers; therefore, the performance of the models is evaluated using these scalers.

4.6   Multivariable-Unistep Models

The study focuses on the evaluation of four models: Base LSTM, Encoder-Decoder LSTM, Base ConvLSTM, and Encoder-Decoder ConvLSTM. Figures 7a, 7b and 7c illustrate the detailed structure of each model, including the layers used and their connections. The models were implemented using the Tensorflow and Keras frameworks [3].

With these configurations, we obtain a total number of trainable parameters of 68 233, 661 123, 463 753 and 3 284 867 for the models described in Figs. 7a.1, 7a.2, 7b, and 7c respectively. It can be observed that the models incorporating ConvLSTM layers have a higher total number of trainable parameters.

5   Experiments

For conducting the experiments, default values were established for the hyperparameters: batch size, memory units, optimizer, and activation and loss functions, set to 256, 128, Adam, linear function, and RMSE, respectively. Additionally, in order to achieve optimal performance in the model predictions, experiments were conducted, considering various aspects. Firstly, the impact of the number of covariates was investigated, starting with two main features: travel time and link. These features provided a solid foundation for later incorporating the variables hour and minute. Different training epochs were also evaluated, taking into account the computational cost of models with ConvLSTM2D layers. Epoch values of 50, 75, 100, 150, 200, and 500 were explored. To accelerate the training time in the experiments, TPUs (Tensor Processing Units) from Google Colaboratory were used. Finally, experiments were performed with different scalers (Min-max scaler, Standard scaler, and Robust scaler) on the supervised dataset.

5.1   Predictions and Selection of Test Data

The model approach is unistep, meaning it makes predictions for $t + 1$, where t indicates the current time step. However, it is also possible to perform multiple sequential predictions for $t + 2$, $t + 3, \ldots, t + i$, where i represents the number of future time steps. To achieve this, the model considers the predictions made for each i and concatenates them sequentially to form predictions for the i future time steps. Additionally, a previous initial sequence before t is required, corresponding to the time references (hours and minutes) and stops (links).

To evaluate the models performance when making multiple sequential predictions, test data was collected using two methods: The first method involved a dataset of GPS points from July 6th, provided by the same transportation company. This dataset was processed as described in Sect. 4 up to Subsect. 4.2, a maximum of 55 prediction data points were obtained between 09:00 and 18:00 h, divided into 1, 5, 10, 15, and 20 time steps to ensure equitable comparison at different times of the day. Subsequently, the points were filtered based on the historical average of each link and a standard deviation to tolerate the maximum

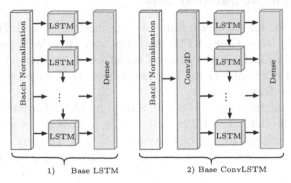

(a) Base LSTM and ConvLSTM models.

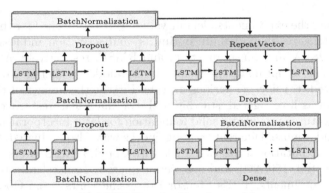

(b) LSTM Encoder-Decoder model.

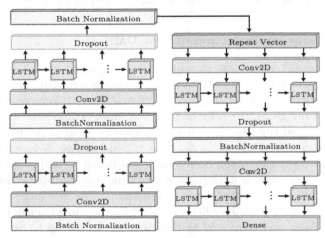

(c) ConvLSTM Encoder-Decoder model.

Fig. 7. Multivariable-unistep models.

and minimum acceptable values. This was done to obtain reliable data for model evaluation. The second method consisted of calculating travel times tradition-ally, i.e., by boarding the bus and timing the travel time between stops on July 17th and 18th. For greater data collection accuracy, a mobile application called "Save Location GPS" was used. However, this method is used in a referential manner due to a minimal number of samples.

5.2 Results Evaluation

The models were evaluated using the root mean squared error (RMSE), mean absolute error (MAE), and mean absolute percentage error (MAPE) metrics. The comparison of these metrics was carried out for each model since calculating them on the scaled datasets resulted in non-interpretable values. Nonetheless, it aided in verifying the model convergence in each epoch and detecting anomalies such as overfitting or underfitting. To assess performance and compare results across different models, the values generated by the models are inversely scaled to seconds. This ensures that the results are on a consistent scale regardless of the scaler used previously.

Table 2 shows the performance of the models on the test set described in Sect. 4.5, along with their corresponding scaler. Achieving an MAE of around 17 s.

Table 2. Training RMSE and MAE values.

Model	RMSE	MAE	Scaler
Base LSTM	28.57	17.62	Robust
Base ConvLSTM	28.92	17.85	Robust
Encoder-Decoder LSTM	29.78	16.99	Standard
Encoder-Decoder ConvLSTM	28.50	17.50	Robust

Table 3 presents the evaluation metrics for multiple sequential predictions of the best-performing models on the test set from July 6th, within the time range from 09:00 hr to 18:00 hr. The evaluation metrics MAE and MAPE indicate that the Encoder-Decoder ConvLSTM architecture outperforms the other models.

Table 4 displays the overall performance with all the cases of multiple pre-dictions at various time instances on the test set applied in Table 3, highlighting the Encoder-Decoder ConvLSTM model for achieving lower error in both MAE and MAPE when using the standard scaler compared to the 3 models. Figure 8 displays the training and validation history of the top models. Throughout the training process, both the training and validation datasets exhibited consistency.

Figures 9a, 9b and 9c depict the predictions of the top four models for a sequence from the test set, encompassing all stops and peak demand hours.

Table 3. Comparison of performance in multiple time steps predictions.

Model	Number of steps				
	1	5	10	15	20
	MAE	MAE	MAE	MAE	MAE
Base LSTM	22.64	62.18	44.27	96.91	90.55
Base ConvLSTM	24.00	57.91	43.91	81.82	82.09
Encoder- Decoder LSTM	24.36	64.36	**34.18**	87.64	**81.91**
Encoder-Decoder ConvLSTM	**19.55**	**56.55**	37.54	**76.64**	83.73

Table 4. Comparison of general performance.

General performance					
Model	MAE	RMSE	MAPE (%)	SCALER	Training time (Min)
Base LSTM	64.35	89.62	14.27	Robust	71.58
Base ConvLSTM	58.56	77.99	14.36	Standard	116.09
Encoder- Decoder LSTM	59.75	82.90	13.98	Robust	98.43
Encoder-Decoder ConvLSTM	**58.33**	82.17	**13.77**	Standard	211.26

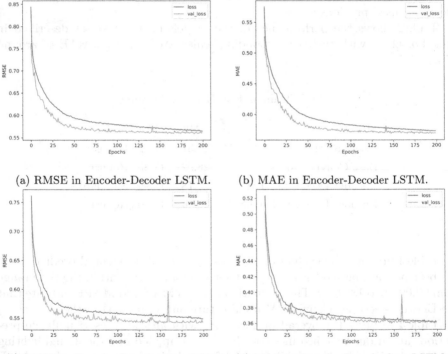

(a) RMSE in Encoder-Decoder LSTM.   (b) MAE in Encoder-Decoder LSTM.

(c) RMSE in Encoder-Decoder ConvLSTM. (d) MAE in Encoder-DecoderConvLSTM.

Fig. 8. Training history of top models.

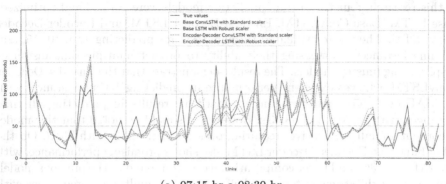

(a) 07:15 hr a 08:30 hr.

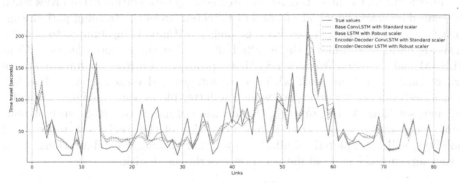

(b) 15:00 hr a 16:15 hr.

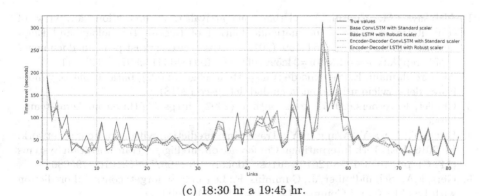

(c) 18:30 hr a 19:45 hr.

Fig. 9. Prediction of the four models at different hours.

6   Conclusions

In this research, four travel time prediction models were trained and optimized: Base LSTM, Base ConvLSTM, Encoder-Decoder LSTM, and Encoder-Decoder ConvLSTM. They were evaluated through tests for predicting 1, 5, 10, 15, and 20 time instances, showcasing their ability to predict multiple time instances despite being unistep models. The results demonstrate that the Encoder-Decoder ConvLSTM achieves excellent performance in predicting 1 time instance, with an MAE of 19.55 s, and even more remarkable results in predicting all time instances, with an MAE of 58.33 s. However, it should be noted that this model is computationally expensive, requiring over 3 h of training with TPU. On the other hand, the Encoder-Decoder LSTM also shows promising performance, with an MAE of 24.36 s and lower computational cost compared to the previous model. Moreover, it exhibits consistency and effectiveness in multi-step predictions with an MAE equal to 59.75 s.

Furthermore, the models demonstrated good generalization capabilities when evaluated on travel time data from dates different from the training period, suggesting their usefulness across various months without being limited to specific training data. In summary, the results indicate that the Encoder-Decoder ConvLSTM and Encoder-Decoder LSTM are promising options for multi-instance travel time prediction, each with its advantages and disadvantages. The former stands out for its precision, while the latter offers a more computationally efficient solution. As future work, the inclusion of more covariates, such as real-time bus location, traffic conditions, speed, day of the week, new routes, and holidays, will be explored. Similarly, new hyperparameter configurations and a larger amount of historical data will be experimented with.

References

1. Altinkaya, M., Zontul, M.: Urban bus arrival time prediction: a review of computational models. International Journal of Recent Technology and Engineering (IJRTE) **2**(4), 164–169 (2013). https://citeseerx.ist.psu.edu/document? repid=rep1&type=pdf&doi=34e59070faa4472fb94e3d3413c897f5ad409b11
2. Alvarez Mamani, E.: Sistema de transporte inteligente (sti), para el control y monitoreo del servicio urbano en la ciudad del cusco (2018)
3. Chollet, F.: others.(2015). keras. github (2007). https://github.com/keras-team/keras
4. Duan, Y., L.V., Y., Wang, F.Y.: Travel time prediction with lstm neural network. In: 2016 IEEE 19th International Conference on Intelligent Transportation Systems (ITSC), pp. 1053–1058 (2016). https://doi.org/10.1109/ITSC.2016.7795686
5. Gers, F.A., Schmidhuber, J., Cummins, F.: Learning to forget: continual prediction with LSTM. Neural Comput. **12**(10), 2451–2471 (2000)
6. Han, Q., Liu, K., Zeng, L., He, G., Ye, L., Li, F.: A bus arrival time prediction method based on position calibration and LSTM. IEEE Access **8**, 42372–42383 (2020). https://doi.org/10.1109/ACCESS.2020.2976574, https://ieeexplore.ieee.org/abstract/document/9015964

7. Hochreiter, S., Schmidhuber, J.: Long short-term memory. Neural Comput. **9**(8), 1735–1780 (1997)
8. Khosravi, A., Mazloumi, E., Nahavandi, S., Creighton, D., van Lint, J.W.C.: Prediction intervals to account for uncertainties in travel time prediction. IEEE Trans. Intell. Transp. Syst. **12**(2), 537–547 (2011). https://doi.org/10.1109/TITS.2011.2106209
9. Lin, H.E., Zito, R., Taylor, M., et al.: A review of travel-time prediction in transport and logistics. In: Proceedings of the Eastern Asia Society for transportation studies. vol. 5, pp. 1433–1448. Bangkok, Thailand (2005)
10. Liu, H., Xu, H., Yan, Y., Cai, Z., Sun, T., Li, W.: Bus arrival time prediction based on lstm and spatial-temporal feature vector. IEEE Access **8**, 11917–11929 (2020). https://doi.org/10.1109/ACCESS.2020.2965094, https://ieeexplore.ieee.org/abstract/document/8954709
11. Liu, Y., Wang, Y., Yang, X., Zhang, L.: Short-term travel time prediction by deep learning: a comparison of different lstm-dnn models. In: 2017 IEEE 20th International Conference on Intelligent Transportation Systems (ITSC), pp. 1–8 (2017https://doi.org/10.1109/ITSC.2017.8317886, https://ieeexplore.ieee.org/abstract/document/8317886
12. Marsano Delgado, J.M.: Cusco: turismo cultural e inclusión económica. Turismo y patrimonio (12), 131–156 (Sep 2018).https://doi.org/10.24265/turpatrim.2018.n12.08, http://revistaturismoypatrimonio.com/index.php/typ/article/view/172
13. Petersen, N.C., Rodrigues, F., Pereira, F.C.: Multi-output bus travel time prediction with convolutional LSTM neural network. Expert Syst. Appl. **120**, 426–435 (2019). https://doi.org/10.1016/j.eswa.2018.11.028. https://www.sciencedirect.com/science/article/pii/S0957417418307486
14. Ran, X., Shan, Z., Fang, Y., Lin, C.: An LSTM-based method with attention mechanism for travel time prediction. Sensors **19**(4) (2019).https://doi.org/10.3390/s19040861, https://www.mdpi.com/1424-8220/19/4/861
15. Sun, J., Kim, J.: Joint prediction of next location and travel time from urban vehicle trajectories using long short-term memory neural networks. Transp. Res. Part C: Emerg. Technol. **128**, 103114 (2021). https://doi.org/10.1016/j.trc.2021.103114. https://www.sciencedirect.com/science/article/pii/S0968090X21001339
16. Wu, C.H., Ho, J.M., Lee, D.: Travel-time prediction with support vector regression. IEEE Trans. Intell. Transp. Syst. **5**(4), 276–281 (2004). https://doi.org/10.1109/TITS.2004.837813
17. Zhang, X., Rice, J.A.: Short-term travel time prediction. Transp. Res. Part C: Emerg. Technol. **11**(3), 187–210 (2003). https://doi.org/10.1016/S0968-090X(03)00026-3, https://www.sciencedirect.com/science/article/pii/S0968090X03000263, traffic Detection and Estimation

Reinforcement Learning and Biologically Inspired Artificial Neural Networks

Fiuri Ariel M.[1(✉)], Dominguez Martin A.[1], and Francisco Tamarit[1,2]

[1] Facultad de Matemática, Astronomía, Física y Computación, Universidad Nacional de Córdoba, Córdoba, Argentina
{ariel.fiuri,martin.dominguez,francisco.tamarit}@unc.edu.ar
[2] Instituto de Física Enrique Gaviola (UNC y CONICET), Córdoba, Argentina

Abstract. Over the last few years, machine learning methods have used Deep Neural Network architectures to tackle complex problems. In this paper, we applied biologically inspired neural machine learning to solve two classical and well-known challenging problems, the Mountain Car Continuous and the Cart Pole. We use a neural network extracted from the connectome of C-Elegans to learn a policy able to yield a good solution. We used Reinforcement Learning (RL) and optimization techniques to train the models, in addition to proposing a novel neural dynamics model. We use different metrics to make a detailed comparison of the results obtained, combining different neuronal dynamics and optimization methods. We obtained very competitive results compared with the solution provided in the literature, particularly with the novel dynamic neuronal model.

Keywords: Artificial Neural Network · Reinforcement Learning · Optimization · Neural Dynamics · Biologically Inspired

Throughout the history of theoretical and computational neuroscience, the study of how animal nervous systems function has sparked the use of models across a wide range of fields of knowledge, encompassing the dynamics of a single neuron to the macroscopic behavior of vast neural networks. The connectionist approach, based on the storage and processing of information within the intricate architecture of neuronal synapses, has shown remarkable predictive power in recent decades. This capability now allows for the construction of artificial neural networks capable of replicating the most sophisticated human mental abilities, a feat that was once unimaginable. A very interesting example that clearly illustrates the close relationship between biology and computation is the study of a small and ubiquitous animal called C-Elegans [9,10], of which we have extensive knowledge of its neural functions. A promising approach in this area is to incorporate machine learning techniques into these models, particularly reinforcement learning (RL) [8], which exhibits a more direct association with the natural mechanisms of learning from experience.

Our study focused on three key aspects: the architecture of the neural network, the modeling of neural dynamics, and the learning mechanism. Our main

J. A. Lossio-Ventura et al. (Eds.): SIMBig 2023, CCIS 2142, pp. 62–79, 2024.
https://doi.org/10.1007/978-3-031-63616-5_5

objective was to address the problem of understanding the relative importance of biological inspiration as far as using it to efficiently solve specific problems. Throughout this process, we successfully tackled two learning problems based on accumulated experience using a small network. Our main contributions are as follows: (1) providing a novel model of neural dynamics that yields excellent results in solving classic state-of-the-art problems, (2) identifying metrics to measure the models and determine which ones excel in the 'intelligence to solve problems' aspect, as well as considering computational costs, and (3) ultimately, shedding light on the relative importance of the biological approach to neural architecture and its underlying dynamics, where we obtained better results in configurations that diverged further from biological reality.

1   Background

Reinforcement learning (RL) is a machine learning technique in which an agent learns to perform a task through a succession of trial and error interactions with a changing environment, usually modeled with Markov decision processes. To train the agent to solve a problem, the environment provides us with a reward and a detailed description of the state of the problem. Each time we execute an action on the environment, we obtain a reward and a state descriptor again. A desired solution is one that maximizes the rewards obtained in a given number of interactions [8]. An episode refers to the sequence of interactions with the environment starting from its initial state. In each episode, the rewards from each interaction accumulate to obtain an overall reward for the episode.

Table 1. Pseudo codes.

```
Require: agent, env, optSteps
   step ← 0
   while step < optSteps do
      setParams(agent, policy)
      return ← episode(agent, env)
      if (is the best reward) then
         saveAgent(agent)
      end if
      step ← step + 1
   end while
   return the best agent
```

```
Require: agent, env
   totReward ← 0
   reset(agent)
   reset(env)
   obs ← getState(env)
   while ¬done do
      action ← getAction(agent, obs)
      obs, rew, done ← step(env, action)
      totReward ← totReward + rew
   end while
   return totReward
```

Code 1. The optimization procedure which explores the different internal parameters and returns the best configuration.

Code 2. The episode procedure which represents the interaction between the agent and the environment.

In the right side of Table 1, we present the pseudocode of an episode. This code shows the interaction between the **agent** and the environment (represented by **env**) through the variables **obs**. The agent uses **obs** and **rew** to define the actions to be executed on the environment, querying the artificial neural network (**model**) through the function **getAction**. Next, the function **step** modifies the environment and returns the new values of **obs** and **rew**.

In the left side of Table 1, we present the optimization procedure that iterates a defined number of steps (`optSteps`) assigning values to the internal parameters of the network (`setParams`) and calculating in each step the reward obtained in an episode. The assignment of the values is represented by the `policy` which is associated to optimizer.

From now on, we will use the word model to refer to the neural network that we are using as an agent.

1.1 Two Classical RL Tasks

In this section, we will present two problems commonly addressed with **RL** techniques that we will use throughout the work to carry out the experiments.

The **Mountain Car Problem** (**MCP**) is a typical **RL** challenge, described by Sutton & Barto in [8]. In this problem, a low-powered car tries to reach the highest point of one of its two surrounding hills starting from a random position in the valley between them. The engine power cannot go up in one attempt, so it has to learn to manage the impulses up and down the hill. To solve this problem, the solver has access to two system state variables, the speed and the position of the vehicle, and it can take action based on the information provided by these variables. In addition to the two state variables, the value of a reward is also available, which somehow describes how effective was the chosen action. The initial state is random and the problem is solved when the mobile reaches the flag at the top of the hill in less than 1000 interactions. In Table 2 there is a simple scheme of this problem.

Table 2. Solved Problems.

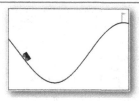

Mountain Car Problem, the mobile must reach the flag with the proper sequence of impulses.	**Cart Pole Problem**, the mobile must keep the pole between the limits, applying impulses to the left and right.

The **Cart Pole Problem** (**CPP**) is another classic problem in **RL**, also described by Sutton and Barto in [8]. It involves a cart holding a pole with an ideal (frictionless) joint. The goal is to learn to balance the pole and keep it as vertical as possible while the cart moves on a frictionless flat surface. The initial state is random; four variables describe the state of the mobile (position and velocity of the mobile along with angle and angular velocity of the pole). The agent receives a reward value for taking an action that either moves left or right.

If the pole is kept upright for an average of 195 actions in 100 separate attempts, the problem is considered solved. The Table 2 provides a visual representation of this scenario.

2 Related Works

Many approaches have been used to solve these classical **RL** problems. For example, the **MCP** was solved using SARSA with a semi-gradient approximation [8]. Other authors have also employed tabular methods, as seen in Nguyen's work [13]. Some studies combine techniques like tabular approximation with RBF [12], while others attempt to incorporate domain knowledge, such as potential functions, as done by Xiao [11].

Regarding the **CPP**, a similar pattern emerges. Initially, it was solved using a tabular method. However, in Berez's work [14], domain knowledge was incorporated through constraints. Towers in [16] employed a single DQN, while Kurban in [17] utilized both DQN and Double DQN, like Simmons in [18]. Furthermore, Lanillos in [15] tackled the problem by utilizing images generated by the environment.

The previously mentioned citations are related to this work solely because of the problems they aim to solve. However, particularly interesting work for us is that of Lechner M. in [1], where the authors propose to solve the **MCP** using **RL**, employing an architecture called **Tap Withdrawal Circuit (TWC)** and the **Integrate and Fire (IandF)** neural dynamics model, using **Random Seek (RS)** as the search method in the solution space. This work reports the successful resolution using libraries Open AI for **MCP** and rllabbs for **CPP**. It is important to note that the authors did not compare their results and performance with other state-of-the-art techniques.

In the present work, we propose to extend this idea by adding other models of neural dynamics, other optimization methods, and other architectures. To evaluate the performance of the different models, we established metrics that allowed us to differentiate the best solutions and compare them with other recent works in the area.

3 Our Approach

3.1 Exploring the Solution Space

As discussed in the previous section, traversing the space of potential solutions is crucial when training a **RL** model. In this paper, we employ three well-known methods for exploring the parameter search space: **Random Seek (RS)**, **Genetic Algorithm (GA)** [5], and **Bayesian Optimization (BO)** [6, 7]. In all cases, we conducted a grid search for hyperparameters optimization, and the chosen options remained fixed throughout the experiments.

3.2   Neural Architecture

Due to is associated to an animal's oscillatory response, in the first stage, we worked with the well-studied **Tap Withdrawal Circuit** (**TWC**) architecture that models a small portion of the *C-elegance* connectome [9,10]. This small network consists of eleven neurons, with four sensory, two motor, and five internal neurons. To model the synaptic connections, we took into account whether neurons are excitatory, inhibitory, or electrical connections.

Table 3. Architecture examples.

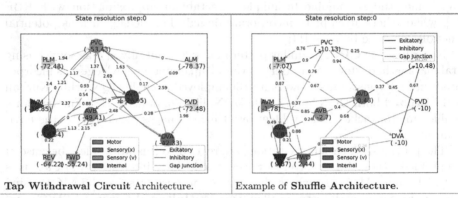

| Tap Withdrawal Circuit Architecture. | Example of Shuffle Architecture. |

In the second stage, we also included the search for an optimal architecture to compare with the biological connectome by creating what we have called **shuffle architecture** (**SA**). A **SA** is derived by randomly mixing the set of synaptic connections, ensuring that no neuron remains disconnected. In Figs. 3 and 4 (Table 3), we compare the **TWC** of C-Elegance with a **SA**.

Each model contains internal parameters that need to be learned to solve different problems. It is important to mention that they have an internal representation that in none of the cases coincides with the state variables of the environment or the actions that can be executed on the problem. Furthermore, it is important to note that it is necessary to define an interface to communicate the motor and sensory neurons with the environment. In this sense, the interface with the motor neurons will translate what action will be applied in the environment. With the sensory ones, information from the environment will be given.

3.3   Neuronal Dynamics Models

So far, we have discussed the training methodology (i.e. **RL**), the neural network architecture, and how we will explore the solution space. However, a fundamental piece still needs to be included: the model of neural dynamics. We work with two well-studied in the literature and also our proposal. Next, we will detail the three neural models.

The **Integrate and Fire (IandF)** model [1] is a continuous model that describes the temporal evolution of the voltage across of the neuronal membrane (which may be stimulated in the dendritic connections) through a single ordinary differential equation. It has been widely used in the literature, although it is not suitable for modeling neuronal spikes.

The **Izhikevich (IZH)** model [2] is a simplification of the famous Hodgkin-Huxley model and models the neuronal evolution through a system of two coupled ordinary differential equations. Unlike the **IandF** model, this model not only allows reproducing the firing and bursting behavior of different types of biological neurons but also provides a more detailed description of neuronal dynamics.

Finally, in this work, we introduce a new neuron model originally proposed by Fiuri and then named **FIU** model (**FIU**). It attempts to represent a simplified neuronal state and, consequently, the resulting dynamics without losing sight of biological inspiration. A neuron n will then have in this model two well-differentiated variables, one internal one (E_n) and an output one (O_n). Both of them depend on the dendritic stimulus, and in Table 4, we explain the updating rules of each one. Each neuron is characterized by its threshold Th_n and a parameter d_n which represents the decaying of E_n in absence of stimulus. Unlike **IandF** and **IZH** models, in this case we have a discrete model in time, making it much more efficient from a computational point of view.

Table 4 shows the equations that define each dynamic. We can see that each **IandF** neuron has three parameters to be learned, and each connection 2. Therefore, for the **TWC**, there are 33+52=85 parameters to learn. For the case of **IZH**, we have four parameters per neuron and 1 per connection, so to train **TWC**, we have 44+26=70 learning parameters. Finally, for **FIU**, we have two parameters per neuron and 1 per connection, totaling 22+26=48 parameters to learn. The difference in the number of parameters and a faster computation in dynamics (since differential equations do not have to be solved at each simulation step) put the **FIU** model in the spotlight for its computational speed. This advantage can explain the time advantage of being almost five times faster than the others in training and testing.

3.4   Experimental Setup

In this section, we present the experiments carried out to evaluate the performance of various combinations of dynamics, optimizers, and architectures that we have applied to the two classical **RL** problems under consideration.

To achieve this, we conducted the same experiment for each configuration. In other words, given an architecture A, a model M, and an optimizer O, the network was trained with the problem under different scenarios (while keeping A, M and O fixed), depending on the number of optimization steps.

Furthermore, we introduced two parameters called `batch` and `worst` to mitigate the stochastic effect on the training performance of the networks. For example, a network trained with `batch=5` and a `worst=2` means that during training, five episodes are executed, and we keep the two worst solutions. In other words,

Table 4. Neural Dynamics.

$$C_{mn}\frac{dv_n}{dt} = G_{Leack_n}(V_{Leack_n} - v_n(t)) + \sum_{j=1}^{m} I_{in}^j \tag{1}$$

$$I_{in}^j = \omega_j(v_n(t) - v_j(t)) \tag{2}$$

$$I_{in}^j = \frac{\omega_j(E - v_j)}{1 + e^{\sigma_j(v_n + \mu)}} \tag{3}$$

In *Integrate & Fire*, $C_m, G_{Leack}, V_{Leack}$ are neuronal parameters (capacitance, proportionality, and threshold). I_{in}^j are input currents actuating on the synaptic connections (j's) of the neuron n. Such currents are defined by the expression 2 for electrical connections. For chemical connections, expression 3 defines the currents. E is the reverse potential and currently implements the connection excitatory or inhibitory. The differential equations system is solved using a hybrid iterative method merging explicit and implicit Euler all in one.

$$\frac{dv_n}{dt} = 0.04v_n^2 + 5v_n + 140 - u_n + \sum_{j=1}^{m} I_{in}^j \tag{4}$$

$$\frac{du_n}{dt} = a_n(b_n v_n - u_n) \tag{5}$$

$$if\ v_n \geq 30mV\ then\ v_n := c_n,\ u_n := u_n + d_n \tag{6}$$

$$I_{in}^j = \omega_j(E_{type} - v_j) \tag{7}$$

$$I_{in}^j = \omega_j(v_j - v_n) \tag{8}$$

In *Izhikevich* v y u are dimensional variables representing neural membrane voltage and the recovery factor after a fire respectively. The other variables are dimensionless, a describe the recovery temporal scale u, b its sensitivity, and c describe the membrane reset value after a neuron fire (with the reset condition due by expression 6), and d is the reset value for u. By last I_{in}^j is the input current actuating on the synaptic connection coming from neuron j to neuron n, and ω_j is the connection capacitance. We propose the expression 7) for chemical connections where the reverse potential E implements excitatory and inhibitory connections and 8) for electrical connections, which is based on the Ohm law. We also propose to solve the differential equations using a hybrid iterative method, merging explicit and implicit Euler all in one.

$$S_n = E_n + \sum_{j=1}^{m} I_{in}^j \tag{9}$$

$$O_n = \begin{cases} S_n - T_n & if\ S_n > T_n \\ 0 & other\ case \end{cases} \tag{10}$$

$$E_n = \begin{cases} S_n - T_n & if\ S_n > T_n \\ E_n - d_n & if\ S_n \leq T_n\ and\ S_n = E_n \\ S_n & other\ case \end{cases} \tag{11}$$

$$I_{in}^j = \begin{cases} \omega_j * O_j & if\ O_j \geq E_n\ y\ gap\ junct. \\ -\omega_j * O_j & if\ O_j < E_n\ y\ gap\ junct. \\ \omega_j * O_j & chemical\ excitatory \\ -\omega_j * O_j & chemical\ inhibitory \end{cases} \tag{12}$$

In *Fiuri*, E_n and O_n represent the input and output states of the neuron n, respectively. If S_n represents the stimulus coming through the dendritic connections (j's) due to the currents I_{in}^j (9), then the expressions 10) and 11) define the dynamic of n. T_n y d_n are neuronal parameters that have to be learned and represent the firing threshold and the decay factor (due to not enough stimulus). The currents I_{in}^i are defined by 12) for each connection type. ω_j is the connection capacitance.

the selection is based on the average performance of the two worst models. Note that in the pseudocode of Table 1, we present the case of `batch=1` and `worst=1`.

For each network, we run five training sessions for each scenario. Once the number of optimizer steps (`Steps`) is chosen, the `batch` and `worst` parameters are used to run five instances (called `a,b,c,d,e`) of the same configuration. This differentiation helps in organizing and comparing the results.

In summary, for example, in the case of the **MCP** considering a network `R` characterized by an architecture `A` $\in \{TWC, SA\}$, model `M` $\in \{IandF, IZH, FIU\}$, optimizer `O` $\in \{RS, GA, BO\}$ and number of steps `Steps` $\in \{S_1, S_2, S_3\}$ (where each S_i depends on the optimizer), five instances of `R` were trained in five different scenarios with (`batch,worst`) $\in \{(1,1), (5,2), (5,5), (10,5), (10,10)\}$. For each scenario, five training sessions were run (`a,b,c,d,e`) . Therefore, we can say that 1350 trainings were executed for **MCP** in both architectures. A similar situation occurs with the **CPP**. The only difference is that it was decided to switch to four different `Steps` $\in \{S_1, S_2, S_3, S_4\}$ for each optimizer and only three combinations (`batch,worst`) $\in \{(1,1), (5,2), (5,5)\}$. So the total number of trainings for **CPP** in both architectures was 1080. This change was sufficient for our purposes.

We will identify a network by constructing its name following the pattern `M+O+Steps+batch+worst+version`, where `M` $\in \{IandF, IZH, FIU\}$ represents the model type, `O` $\in \{RS, GA, BO\}$ indicates the optimizer used, `Steps` refers to the number of optimization steps, and `batch` and `worst` have been explained previously. Additionally, `version` $\in \{a,b,c,d,e\}$ is included to differentiate between different instances of the same configuration. For instance, a network named `FIUBO150052e` means that it is built upon the **FIU** model, uses the **BO** optimizer with 1500 optimization steps, and has `batch` and `worst` values of 5 and 2, respectively. It is also the instance `e` of that specific configuration.

Typically, in the area of reinforcement learning, training results are reported, commonly using rewards as performance indicators. However, evaluations in most other learning areas (such as supervised and unsupervised learning) are conducted in a separate way. By adopting this approach, we can more effectively assess whether one model outperforms another in solving a given task. To achieve this, we carry out experiments to solve the problem, but instead of being in the training mode, we execute the experiments **1000** times in the evaluation mode, collecting different metrics for comparison. In the next section, we will establish specific performance metrics for each problem, allowing us to conduct a thorough comparison of the trained models.

3.5 Metrics

It is well known in the state of the art that, to evaluate **RL** models, the rewards obtained in training (*T. Rew.* in our tables) and evaluation are the metrics to report. However, given the problem's stochastic nature, some solutions performed very well in the training phase but, in the evaluation stage, did not maintain this behavior. For this reason, we decided to collect two metrics, in addition to the obtained reward, to discriminate the quality of the learned models, thus, setting a fairer criterion.

In the case of the **MCP**, we collect the average number of steps (*Me Stp* in the tables) for the mobile to reach its destination in the 1000 test executions. In addition, we keep the minimum value of steps (*Mi Stp* in the tables) in which we get to solve the problem. In the case of the **CPP**, we define something similar, collecting the average (in the 1000 tests) of steps in which the post managed to stay within limits (also *Me Stp*). In addition, we record the value of the most significant number of steps that the pole remained upright in the 1000 attempts (*Ma Stp*). The execution times were also recorded on the same machine in training and evaluation to compare the performance of computational costs between different models.

4   Results

In this section, we report the results obtained for all the combinations described in Sect. 3.4 and that we evaluated with the metrics that we introduced in the previous section.

MCP: For this problem, the authors in [1,11] reported reward values between 90 and 96, based on a sample size of 100 experiments. In our experiments, we achieved a higher reward of 98.9 ± 0.9, averaging over 1000 experiments. Additionally, for a more detailed analysis of our results, the average number of steps taken by our best network was 121.17 ± 5.58, and the minimum number of steps for solving the problem with our best model was 85. We could not find any previous reports of these last metrics for comparison. The results presented in the top section of Table 5 display the nine best rewards obtained for different neural dynamics and each optimizer, considering both **TWC** and **SA**. The resulting models achieved excellent results, particularly for **IandF** and **FIU** in both architectures, when compared with the previously mentioned results. The bottom part of Table 5 showcases the best results for each dynamic model and optimizer, taking into account the mean number of steps required to solve the **MCP** problem. Notably, the proposed model (**FIU**) achieved outstanding results, ranking among the top positions.

Table 6 displays the results for the **TWC** and **SA**. The graph on the left shows the **TWC** architecture, while the one on the right shows a **SA**. Different colors are used in each graph to identify the neural dynamic and to show the variance of the mean steps taken to solve the **MCP** problem for the top 15 models. In this case, the ordering criteria is the mean number of steps taken by the model to solve the problem, and the sample is the result of 1000 tests. The **FIU** model performs best for both architectures, obtaining a model with fewer steps to solve **MCP** and with more stability. The **IandF** and **IZH** models also obtain good results but with more standard deviation.

CP: Regarding the issue at hand, the problem is deemed resolved in the literature if a sample of 100 tests produces an average of 195 ticks within the defined boundaries of the pole. The most noteworthy results have been reported to be close to 500 ticks (referenced in sources [14–19]). We are pleased to report excellent results as we have discovered numerous models with a favorable step mean.

Table 5. MCP: Experimental results, T. Rew. stands for training reward, Me Rew. is the mean of rewards for 1000 sized test and σ corresponds to its standard deviation, Me Stp and its respective σ are similar as for rewards and Mi Stp is the min amount of steps a tests returned.

Tap Withdrawal Circuit				Shuffle Architecture			
Network	T. Rew	Me Rew	σ	Network	T. Rew	Me Rew	σ
Ordered by mean reward.							
$IandFRS2K55d$	98.95	98.90	0.08	$IandFRS2K105c$	99.08	99.09	0.08
$IandFGA8055d$	98.54	98.49	0.10	$IandFBO50052a$	99.06	99.14	0.08
$FIURS5K1010a$	98.42	98.43	0.15	$FIUBO1K1010c$	98.62	98.56	0.15
$FIUGA501010a$	97.09	97.13	0.48	$FIUGA5055b$	98.64	98.55	0.09
$IandFBO50052a$	97.34	97.40	0.84	$IandFGA20105a$	97.73	97.70	0.26
$FIUBO1K1010b$	98.37	98.38	0.09	$FIURS5K52b$	98.56	97.69	8.93
$IZHRS5K105a$	96.03	96.29	0.46	$IZHBO1K105b$	96.95	97.12	0.31
$IZHBO150011c$	97.46	96.11	0.56	$IZHRS5K52a$	96.10	96.77	0.52
$IZHGA8055b$	96.77	96.11	0.68	$IZHGA8055e$	96.49	95.87	0.61
Network	Mi Stp	Me Stp	σ	Network	Mi Stp	Me Stp	σ
Ordered by mean steps							
$FIURS5K105e$	116.0	122.92	5.77	$FIUBO50055a$	111.0	121.17	5.58
$FIUGA50105a$	124.0	134.72	2.26	$IZHRS5K11b$	105.0	172.89	30.33
$IandFGA2055a$	150.0	166.85	32.35	$FIURS5K52c$	130.0	187.65	47.13
$FIUBO1K11b$	124.0	186.53	37.6	$IandFGA2052a$	184.0	195.016	7.85
$IandFRS5K11b$	160.0	220.54	28.13	$FIUGA5052a$	191.0	206.58	37.93
$IZHRS2K105b$	166.0	226.37	39.34	$IZHGA8055b$	164.0	248.74	36.58
$IZHBO1500105b$	160.0	226.3	33.31	$IandFRS5K55c$	144.0	280.11	110.80
$IZHGA8052a$	211.0	283.18	37.58	$IandFBO500105b$	251.0	300.40	31.38
$IandFBO5001010a$	157.0	313.61	79.83	$IZHBO1K55d$	129.0	449.52	227.40

The top of Table 7 shows the best models for different neuronal dynamic and optimizers, considering the reward obtained in 1000 experiments, we can see very good results for **IandF** and **FIU** model in both architectures. Notice that in **CPP** the reward is same as the amount of steps the pole is considered in good position. The bottom of Table 7 shows the best models for different neuronal dynamic and optimizers, considering the average of steps that sticks is up, using 1000 evaluation attempts. It is important to mention that many

Table 6. Models comparison.

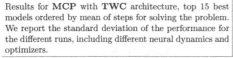

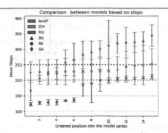
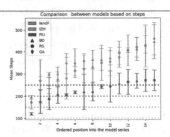

Results for **MCP** with **TWC** architecture, top 15 best models ordered by mean of steps for solving the problem. We report the standard deviation of the performance for the different runs, including different neural dynamics and optimizers.	Results for **MCP** with **shuffle architecture**, top 15 best models ordered by mean of steps for solving the problem. We report the standard deviation of the performance for the different runs, including different neural dynamics and optimizers.

models earned 500 on average and almost all the maximum amount of steps is 500. Table 8 displays the results for the **TWC** and **SA**, solving **CPP** problem. The graph on the left shows the **TWC** architecture, while the one on the right shows the **SA** one. We report graphs showing the variance of the performance achieved for models, using the mean of steps that the model hods the stick (over the 1000 test attempts). Note that **FIU** and **IandF** performs very well, and, it is difficult to differentiate between model qualities due to the most models reach a value of 500.

Extending CPP Limit: The Table 9 shows the detail of the number of networks that obtain an average of 500 steps (again, we notice a tendency in which the **IandF** and **FIU** models obtain a more significant number of good models). As we can see, many models obtained a maximum of 500 steps required. Therefore, to distinguish if one model is better than others, we carried out new experiments extending the cutoff limit of the standard problem. We extended the limit from 500 to 5000 and reran the 1000-attempt test, but this time only included models that resulted in an average of 500 steps for the standard environment version. Table 10 shows the evaluation graphs with the extended limit for the top 15 models for both architectures. Surprisingly, we obtained that these networks trained with a limit of 500 steps for the end of the episode mean much higher than those reported in the literature, some even reaching 5000 steps.

The Table 11 contains details of the best results for different dynamics and optimizers on both architectures. For most retested networks, we get maximums of 5000 steps for an episode. In this case, we noted a tendency for the **IandF** dynamic to find better networks than the rest.

Time Results: Until now, the variable that was not analyzed was the time it took to train models and the time it takes a model to get a response. In order to analyze the time performance to obtain results from a model, we use the **TWC**, measure the time spent finding the sensorial neurons, and read the output from

Table 7. CPP: Experimental results, T. Rew. stands for training reward, Me Rew. is the mean of rewards for 1000 sized test and σ corresponds to its standard deviation, Me Stp and its respective σ are similar as for rewards and Ma Stp is the max amount of steps a tests returned.

Tap Withdrawal Circuit				Shuffle Architecture			
Network	T. Rew	Me Rew	σ	Network	T. Rew	Me Rew	σ
Ordered by mean reward.							
$FIUBO5K52e$	500.10	500.0	0.0	$IandFRS1M55e$	500.07	500.0	0.0
$FIURS250K11c$	500.08	500.0	0.0	$IandFBO850055d$	500.07	500.0	0.0
$IandFBO10K55a$	500.07	500.0	0.0	$IandFGA5K52b$	500.06	500.0	0.0
$IandFRS1M55b$	500.04	500.0	0.0	$FIUGA1K55e$	500.02	499.99	0.30
$IandFGA5K52b$	500.03	499.93	1.34	$IZHBO5K55e$	500.07	456.45	51.97
$FIUGA1K52e$	500.02	499.91	2.97	$IZHRS500K11c$	500.10	428.50	122.50
$IZHGA5K55d$	425.8	233.03	140.61	$FIUBO15K55e$	500.0	373.90	166.37
$IZHRS500K55e$	123.0	157.50	89.01	$FIURS500K11e$	419.0	360.98	153.38
$IZHBO10K52e$	126.5	122.37	58.96	$IZHGA10K11e$	500.09	159.92	71.99
Network	Ma Stp	Me Stp	σ	Network	Ma Stp	Me Stp	σ
Ordered by mean steps and σ							
$FIUBO500052e$	500.0	500.0	0.0	$IandFRS1M55e$	500.0	500.0	0.0
$FIURS25000011c$	500.0	500.0	0.0	$IandFGA500052b$	500.0	500.0	0.0
$IandFRS1M55b$	500.0	500.0	0.0	$IandFBO850055d$	500.0	500.0	0.0
$IandFBO1000055a$	500.0	500.0	0.0	$FIUGA100055c$	500.0	499.99	0.29
$IandFGA500052b$	500.0	499.93	1.34	$IZHBO500055e$	500.0	456.45	51.97
$FIUGA100052e$	500.0	499.91	2.97	$IZHRS50000011c$	500.0	428.50	122.50
$IZHGA500055d$	500.0	233.03	140.61	$FIUBO1500055e$	500.0	373.90	166.37
$IZHRS50000055e$	500.0	157.50	89.01	$FIURS50000011e$	500.0	360.98	153.38
$IZHBO1000052e$	328.0	122.37	58.96	$IZHGA1000011e$	500.0	159.92	71.99

Table 8. Models Comparison.

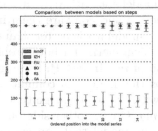
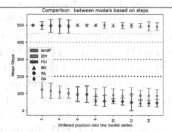

CPP with **TWC** results corresponding to the 15 better ANN differenced by neural dynamics and optimizer, ordered by mean steps. We report the standard deviation of the performance for the different runs. | **CPP** with **SA** results corresponding to the 15 better ANN differenced by neural dynamics and optimizer, ordered by mean steps. We report the standard deviation of the performance for the different runs.

Table 9. CPP: Amount of models with mean of steps of 500.

	Tap Withdrawal Circuit			Shuffle Architecture		
	IandF	IZH	FIU		IandF	IZH	FIU
RS	18	0	57	*RS*	9	4	0
GA	54	5	58	*GA*	53	6	58
BO	33	0	38	*BO*	9	10	1
Tot.	105	5	153	*Tot.*	71	20	59

Table 10. Models Comparisons.

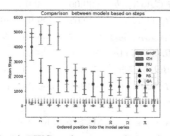 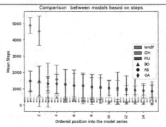

ECPP with TWC results corresponding to the 15 better ANN differenced by neural dynamics and optimizer, ordered by mean steps.	ECPP with SA results corresponding to the 15 better ANN differenced by neural dynamics and optimizer, ordered by mean steps.

the motor neurons. We repeated this experiment 1000000 times. We performed this experiment for different configurations and recorded the time it took on each neural dynamic model. The resulting time cumin are the followings: for the **FIU** model:7 m 34.156 s; for the **IandF** model, 38 m 59.682 s; and finally, for **IZH** model, 34 m 5.389 s. Clearly, we can see that **FIU** is almost five times quicker than **IZH** and more than five times quicker than **IandF**. To analyze the time spent in the training phase, in the next section, we report the training times for the different optimization method.

Finding the Best Models: We select one model for each dynamic model - optimizer combination to identify the best models and compare them in the Table 12. We established criteria to decide when a model m_1 is better than other m_2 based on the mean of steps of solving the problem metric for both problems. Let us suppose $s_i \pm \sigma_i$ is the mean steps metric of m_i. In **MCP**, if we intend that $s_i + \sigma_i$ is the upper mean number of steps the model can commit in the problem solution, we want to select the model with the minor magnitude. So if $s_1 + \sigma_1 < s_2 + \sigma_2$ we consider m_1 better than m_2. On the other side but with similar reasoning for **CPP**, we want to select the model that can assure the maximum amount of mean steps that the car can, as a minimum, maintain the pole between the limits so if $s_1 - \sigma_1 < s_2 - \sigma_2$ we will take m_2 to be better than m_1.

Table 11. ECPP: Step based experimental results.

Tap Withdrawal Circuit				Shuffle Architecture			
Network	Ma Stp	Me Stp	σ	Network	Ma Stp	Me Stp	σ
			Ordered by	mean steps			
$IandFBO15K52c$	5000.0	4940.95	290.67	$IandFGA10K52d$	5000.0	4887.00	482.30
$IandFRS1M11b$	5000.0	4830.34	683.87	$IandFBO850055a$	5000.0	4569.27	899.78
$IandFGA250052b$	5000.0	4802.17	654.12	$IandFRS1M55a$	5000.0	4260.44	1131.03
$FIUBO5K52a$	5000.0	4113.76	1300.66	$FIUGA5K55c$	5000.0	3477.72	1602.62
$FIURS250K11c$	5000.0	4000.83	909.43	$IZHRS500K11a$	4146.0	850.72	634.45
$FIUGA1K52d$	5000.0	2711.80	1208.94	$FIUBO15K55a$	4633.0	709.29	716.37
$IZHGA10K11a$	685.0	155.76	72.53	$IZHBO15K55a$	4953.0	631.82	726.19
$IZHRS$	–	–	–	$IZHGA10K11c$	517.0	154.88	70.18
$IZHBO$	–	–	–	$FIURS$	–	–	–

Table 12. Best models. In gray the best values of each box architecture - problem and in light gray the second best values for each model. In case of MCP a ttest analysis was done between the gray and the light gray in the same problem and also between the best of MCP with TWC and MCP with SA. Here the results: TWC/FIURS vs TWC/IandFGA = $2.9e - 226$, TWC/FIURS vs TWC/IZHBO = 0.0, SA/FIUBO vs SA/IandFGA=0.0, SA/FIUBO vs SA/IZHRS=$5.9e-304$, TWC/FIURS vs SA/FIUBO = $7.15e - 12$.

Problem	Op	Tap Withdrawal Circuit			Shuffle Architecture		
		IandF	IZH	FIU	IandF	IZH	FIU
MCP	RS	248.68	263.38	128.69	543.29	203.22	211.46
	GA	199.20	320.77	136.98	202.85	285.32	223.34
	BO	499.77	259.61	210.04	331.78	555.81	126.75
CPP	RS	500.0	None	500.0	500.0	321.63	207.59
	GA	498.59	92.42	496.94	500.0	None	499.67
	BO	500.0	None	500.0	500.0	404.48	207.53
ECPP	RS	4146.47	None	3091.39	3129.41	216.28	None
	GA	4148.05	None	1529.32	4404.67	None	1927.39
	BO	4650.28	None	1748.70	3669.49	391.00	None

Grouping Results: For **MCP**, clearly, **FIU** obtains best results in both architectures. In order to show this statistically significant of the improvements between the different models we performs the **ttest** comparing the results in the 1000 runs. The results are shown in the comment of Table 12. The values reflect the solution's independence.

For **CPP**, we have the exceptional situation that many models reach very good results (i.e., 500). The results corresponding to the **ECPP** show that

Table 13. MCP grouping results.

Tap Withdrawal Circuit					
Metric	Op	IandF	IZH	FIU	Row Stats
Training Time (hr)	RS	14.99 ± 70.07%	12.50 ± 87.23%	2.17 ± 71.56%	9.89 ± 72.29%
	GA	1.79 ± 66.11%	2.15 ± 45.52%	0.33 ± 43.57%	1.42 ± 51.73%
	BO	2.85 ± 55.28%	1.92 ± 45.50%	0.37 ± 52.46%	1.70 ± 51.08%
Col Stats		6.54 ± 63.82%	5.52 ± 59.42%	0.96 ± 55.86%	
Mean Steps	RS	478.27 ± 91.89	337.84 ± 65.32	473.61 ± 89.84	429.91 ± 82.35
	GA	396.02 ± 64.21	412.27 ± 95.55	283.02 ± 50.78	363.77 ± 70.18
	BO	527.69 ± 136.61	358.39 ± 62.54	374.37 ± 55.51	429.15 ± 84.87
Col Stats		467.33 ± 97.57	369.50 ± 74.47	377 ± 65.38	
Shuffle Architecture					
Metric	Op	IandF	IZH	FIU	Row Stats
Training Time (hr)	RS	18.93 ± 83.17%	8.94 ± 73.39%	1.53 ± 84.20%	9.8 ± 80.25%
	GA	0.74 ± 60.31%	1.65 ± 47.86%	0.23 ± 42.74%	0.87 ± 50.30%
	BO	2.21 ± 66.42%	1.48 ± 44.22%	0.26 ± 54.50%	1.32 ± 50.05%
Col Stats		7.29 ± 69.97%	4.02 ± 56.88%	0.67 ± 60.48%	
Mean Steps	RS	589.67 ± 102.44	494.5 ± 76.79	375.38 ± 73.42	486.52 ± 84.22
	GA	421.23 ± 73.38	411.97 ± 90.22	371.1 ± 67.34	401.43 ± 76.98
	BO	503.47 ± 93.3	552.66 ± 90.79	400.72 ± 81.24	485.62 ± 88.44
Col Stats		504.79 ± 89.71	486.38 ± 85.93	382.4 ± 74	

IandF models reach better performances than others followed by **FIU** which also gets outstanding results.

In this section, we try to analyze the behavior of the optimization methods to reach the solution space of the hyperparameters. To do so, we try to do a global analysis calculating only one magnitude for all models considered to be a good solution, in order to characterize the method as a whole. So we try to infer some kind of preference, if exists, between the different dynamic models or even between the different optimizers. The first step was to select the models with certain quality as base defining in this way some kind of sample, then calculate the means for training time and mean of steps over each sample. For **MCP**, a model is included in the sample if the obtained reward (training and test) is more than 91.5. For **CPP**, a model is added to the sample if the obtained reward (training and test) is more than 190. The following tables show training time and mean of steps metrics for all combinations of the dynamic model - optimizer - architecture. For the training time metric we report as an error the standard deviation of the sample. For the mean of steps metric, we report as an error the mean of the individual standard deviations.

Now we will analyze the time the optimizers considered took for the hyper-parameter search of our models. In the Table 13, in the rows labeled "Training

Table 14. CPP grouping results.

		Tap Withdrawal Circuit			
Metric	Op	IandF	IZH	FIU	Row Stats
Training Time (hr)	RS	11.13 ± 68.19%	0.0 ± 0.0%	1.70 ± 93.23%	6.42 ± 80.71%
	GA	43.84 ± 100.01%	11.48 ± 0.0%	11.37 ± 95.35%	22.23 ± 65.12%
	BO	7.57 ± 88.05%	0.0 ± 0.0%	2.91 ± 6.83%	9.03 ± 47.44%
Col Stats		20.85 ± 85.42%	11.48 ± 0.0%	5.33 ± 65.13%	
Mean Steps	RS	412.34 ± 61.10	0.0 ± 0.0	430.32 ± 88.71	421.33 ± 74.91
	GA	411.02 ± 85.32	233.03 ± 140.6	401.05 ± 115.16	348.37 ± 113.69
	BO	440.82 ± 58.04	0.0 ± 0.0	428.81 ± 89.86	434.82 ± 73.95
Col Stats		421.39 ± 68.15	233.03 ± 140.6	420.06 ± 97.91	
		Shuffle Architecture			
Metric	Op	IandF	IZH	FIU	Row Stats
Training Time (hr)	RS	13.54 ± 113.19%	11.08 ± 111.40%	0.65 ± 1.66%	8.42 ± 75.42%
	GA	52.72 ± 102.31%	0.0 ± 0.0%	11.68 ± 96.16%	32.20 ± 99.24%
	BO	9.29 ± 71.86%	11.10 ± 65.23%	5.97 ± 0.0%	8.79 ± 48.63%
Col Stats		25.18 ± 95.79%	11.09 ± 88.32%	6.10 ± 32.61%	
Mean Steps	RS	412.74 ± 83.39	310.19 ± 143.24	284.63 ± 101.86	335.85 ± 109.50
	GA	399.04 ± 83.31	0.0 ± 0.0	408.71 ± 113.23	373.87 ± 98.27
	BO	400.45 ± 70.59	315.42 ± 105.53	373.9 ± 166.37	363.26 ± 114.16
Col Stats		404.08 ± 70.09	359.45 ± 124.39	355.75 ± 127.15	

Time," we can see at the top the amount of time consumed by each of the optimizers in the different neural and architectural models. We can see that the times consumed by **GA** and **BO** are much lower than those consumed by **RS**. Note that the performance of the solutions obtained, in Table 13 for the rows labeled "Mean Steps," on average, the best solutions were inserted by the GA, both in mean and variance. Regarding the **CPP**, we can do a similar analysis; however, when looking at the Table 14, in the rows labeled as "Training Time," we see that the time consumed by **GA** is higher than that consumed by **BO** and **RS**. However, this is because the best solutions in the **CPP** are the ones that take more steps to have the stick hold. Therefore, in Table 9, we can see that the **GA** obtains many more models that have an average of 500 steps, and this may explain the more extended amount of time since many of the genes analyzed take longer to compute as they are better models on average.

5   Conclusion and Future Work

In this work, our main focus was on addressing several questions. First, we investigated the feasibility of employing biologically-inspired models in architecture and neural dynamics for applications in solving standard problems within the area of **Reinforcement Learning**. Specifically, we examined whether this approach could serve as a viable alternative to conventional methods such as tabular, Deep RL, and others. We explored the different configurations and compared their performance with the metrics obtained through the **Mountain Car Problem** and the **Cart Pole Problem** using two typical dynamics, **Integrate and Fire**, **Izhikevich**, and our proposal **Fiuri**.

The second question is related to how to explore the solution space of neuronal dynamic hyperparameters. We investigated different optimizer methods, and all of them obtained competitive networks. However, concerning the time and computation used to obtain the solutions, the **Genetic Algorithm** and the **Bayesian Optimizer** significantly outperformed **Random Seek**.

In third place and most importantly, we introduced a new neural dynamics model, intending to be competitive in results and efficient in computation. The **Fiuri** model easily met both wishes, although comparing computing times and resources with traditional methods remains pending.

Fourthly, we questioned the importance of biologically-inspired architecture to obtain a good performance. To answer this question, we explored **Shuffle Architectures** that achieved excellent results, often even better than biological architecture.

Finally, a particularly remarkable finding is our capability to solve a problem with a network comprising only eleven neurons, which is substantially fewer than what is typically utilized in Deep RL techniques.[1]

In the development of this work, we pursued two main lines of research. On one side, we aimed to solve the same problems using pure **Reinforcement Learning** techniques, such as tabular RL, Deep RL, among others. We collected specific metrics to conduct a comprehensive comparison of these methods.

Another line of research we intend to address is exploring the resolution of quantum physics problems applying **Reinforcement Learning**. For example, in [21] authors use Deep RL to solve the quantum state transfer in a one-dimensional spin chain. We plan to use our neural model to solve the problem of transmission of chains in quantum computing, looking for the most suitable architecture using the methods we have already explored in the present work.

Finally, we want to to test the setup of **Deep Reinforcement Learning** but using the **Fiuri** neural model instead of the commonly used one.

References

1. Lechner, M., Hasani, R., Grosu R.: Neuronal circuit policies. https://arxiv.org/abs/1803.08554 (2018)
2. Izhikevich Eugene, M.: Simple model of spiking neurons. IEEE Trans. Neural Netw. **14**(6) (2003). https://arxiv.org/pdf/2106.06158.pdf
3. Haimovici, A., Tagliazucchi, E., Balenzuela, P., Chialvo, D.: Brain organization into resting state networks emerges at criticality on a model of the human connectome (2013). https://arxiv.org/abs/1209.5353
4. Open AI.: Toolkit for standar RL problems (2021). https://gym.openai.com/

---

[1] Code available at https://github.com/afiuriG/BiMPuRLE_CMP/tree/MCP.

5. Ahmed, F.: PyGAD: An Intuitive Genetic Algorithm Python Library (2021). https://arxiv.org/pdf/2106.06158.pdf
6. Brochu, E., Cora, V., De Freitas, N.: A Tutorial on Bayesian Optimization of Expensive Cost Functions, with Application to Active User Modeling and Hierarchical Reinforcement Learning (2010). https://doi.org/10.48550/arXiv.1012.2599
7. Bergstra, J., Yamins, D., Cox, D.D.: Making a science of model search: hyperparameter optimization in hundreds of dimensions for vision architectures. In: 30th International Conference on Machine Learning. http://hyperopt.github.io/hyperopt/. (ICML 2013)
8. Sutton, R.S., Barto, A.G.: Reinforcement Learning: An Introduction., MIT Press., Cambridge., (1998)
9. White, J.G., Southgate, E., Thomson, J.N., Brenner, S.: The structure of the nervous system of the nematode Caenorhabditis elegans. Philos. Trans. Royal Society of London B. Biol. Sci. **314** (1165), 1–34 (1986)
10. Chen, B.L., Hall, D.H., Chklovskii, D.B.: Wiring optimization can relate neuronal structure and function. Proc. Natl. Acad. Sci. U.S.A. **103**(12), 4723–4728 (2006)
11. Xiao, B., Ramasubramanian, B., Poovendran, R.: Shaping Advice in Deep Reinforcement Learning (2022). https://arxiv.org/pdf/2202.09489.pdf
12. Unzueta, D.: Reinforcement Learning Applied to the Mountain Car Problem. Towards Data Science (2022). https://towardsdatascience.com/reinforcement-learning-applied-to-the-mountain-car-problem-1c4fb16729ba
13. Nguyen, H.: Playing Mountain Car with Q-learning and SARSA. Medium (2021). https://ha-nguyen-39691.medium.com/playing-mountain-car-with-q-learning-and-sarsa-4e7327f9e35c
14. Barez, F., Hasanbieg, H., Abbate, A.: System III: Learning with Domain Knowledge for Safety Constraints (2023). https://doi.org/10.48550/arXiv.2304.11593
15. van der Himst, O., Lanillos, P.: Deep active inference for partially observable MDPs. In: IWAI 2020. CCIS, vol. 1326, pp. 61–71. Springer, Cham (2020). https://doi.org/10.1007/978-3-030-64919-7_8
16. Paszke, A., Towers, M.: https://pytorch.org/tutorials/intermediate/reinforcement_q_learning.html (2023)
17. Kurban, R.: Deep Q Learning for the CartPole. Towards Data Science (2019). https://towardsdatascience.com/deep-q-learning-for-the-cartpole-44d761085c2f
18. Simmons, L.: Double DQN Implementation to Solve OpenAI Gym's CartPole. Medium (2019). https://medium.com/@leosimmons/double-dqn-implementation-to-solve-openai-gyms-cartpole-v-0-df554cd0614d
19. Surma, G.: Cartpole - Introduction to Reinforcement Learning (DQN - Deep Q-Learning). Medium https://gsurma.medium.com/cartpole-introductionto-reinforcement-learning-ed0eb5b58288
20. Dayan, P., Abbott, L.: Theoretical Neuroscience. Computational and Mathematical Modeling of Neural Systems. The MIT Press Cambridge, Massachusetts, London, England (2005)
21. Zhang, X.M., Cui, Z.W., Wang, X., Yung, M.H: Automatic spin-chain learning to explore the quantum speed limit. Am. Phys. Society. Phys. Rev. A **97**(5), 052333 (2018)

Efficient Classification of SARS-CoV-2 Spike Sequences Using Federated Learning

Prakash Chourasia[1], Taslim Murad[1], Zahra Tayebi[1], Sarwan Ali[1(✉)], Imdad Ullah Khan[2], and Murray Patterson[1]

[1] Georgia State University, Atlanta, GA 30303, USA
{pchourasia1,tmurad2,ztayebi1,sali85}@student.gsu.edu,
mpatterson30@gsu.edu
[2] Lahore University of Management Sciences, Lahore Punjab 54792, Pakistan
imdad.khan@lums.edu.pk

Abstract. This paper presents a federated learning (FL) approach to train an AI model for SARS-Cov-2 variant classification. We analyze the SARS-CoV-2 spike sequences in a distributed way, without data sharing, to detect different variants of this rapidly mutating coronavirus. Our method maintains the confidentiality of local data (that could be stored in different locations) yet allows us to reliably detect and identify different known and unknown variants of the novel coronavirus SARS-CoV-2. Using the proposed approach, we achieve an overall accuracy of 93% on the coronavirus variant identification task. We also provide details regarding how the proposed model follows the main laws of federated learning, such as Laws of data ownership, data privacy, model aggregation, and model heterogeneity. Since the proposed model is distributed, it could scale on "Big Data" easily. We plan to use this proof-of-concept to implement a privacy-preserving pandemic response strategy.

Keywords: Federated Learning · Bio-sequence Analysis · SARS-CoV-2 · Spike Sequence

1 Introduction

The COVID-19 pandemic, caused by the SARS-CoV-2 coronavirus, has impacted the entire globe [31]. It is responsible for almost 6 million in deaths and 561 million infected people as of July 2022 as reported by the World Health Organization (WHO) [46]. This influence has drawn the attention of the research community to actively contribute their tools and techniques toward pandemic response strategies, such as the design and assessment of containment measures [14,23], image processing for diagnosis [36,42], optimal vaccine distribution [1,2,27,40], computational tomography for genome sequencing [42], etc.

Moreover, to comprehend the diversity and dynamics of the virus, its genome sequences are analyzed by using phylogenetic methods [20,33]. These methods

© The Author(s), under exclusive license to Springer Nature Switzerland AG 2024
J. A. Lossio-Ventura et al. (Eds.): SIMBig 2023, CCIS 2142, pp. 80–96, 2024.
https://doi.org/10.1007/978-3-031-63616-5_6

can help in variant identification, however, they are not scalable [20,33]. Due to the presence of large amounts of publicly available biological sequence data on databases such as GISAID [19], it is desirable to design a scalable analytical model to get a deeper understanding of the virus.

Furthermore, the detailed SARS-CoV-2 genome structure is illustrated in Fig. 1. It consists of many sub-parts including the spike region, which is essential because the virus attaches to the host cell through this region. It also contains many of the mutations of the SARS-CoV-2 virus, which can result in creating different variants of this virus. Therefore, rather than using the full genome sequence of the virus, the spike sequence alone provides sufficient information to reliably analyze this virus. Recently, classification and clustering approaches are proposed to analyze the SARS-CoV-2 virus using only spike sequences, like host classification [5,26], variant classification [6,8,41], etc. These methods first generate numerical embeddings of the sequences and then employ either vector-space or kernel-based classifiers.

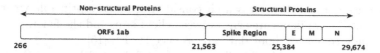

Fig. 1. The SARS-CoV-2 genome is roughly 30kb in length, encoding structural and non-structural proteins. The spike region is composed of 3821 base pairs.

Traditionally, the training of a machine learning (ML) model happens in a centralized way with all of the data stored on or is available to be sampled from a single server [24]. However, privacy and data security concerns discourage disparate entities (e.g., healthcare governing bodies in different countries) from sharing the data. The under-reporting of COVID-19 statistics and other related data has already been observed in various regions [25,47], due to political or other reasons. Even in cases where there are no ethical, regulatory, or legal issues in data sharing, healthcare bodies are known to prefer models validated on their data [11]. Moreover, the local context is already lost in a model trained on global data. On the other hand, models trained on "limited local" data tend to overfit and do not generalize.

Federated learning (FL), an AI paradigm, offers a more pragmatic and proven approach to dealing with many facets of data-sharing challenge. FL [32] enables collaborative model learning over data from several (decentralized) places without any data relocation. In FL, as shown in Fig. 2, first, (many) local models are trained using the private data at each location. A *global model* is then trained using *federated learning*. The global model is kept on a central server called a *federated server*. Model parameters from the local models are pushed onto the federated server, aggregating them using an *aggregation function*. FL preserves data privacy, overcomes data ownership barriers, and yields generalized models.

The concept of federated learning has been used in many different areas [3, 12,37], including mobile apps, internet-of-things (IoT), transportation, bioinfor-

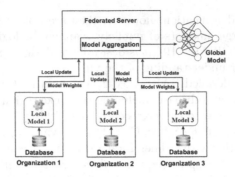

Fig. 2. The federated learning approach for a learning task using private data from three separate organizations.

matics and defense. Due to its applicability and the numerous trials that have previously been done, it is quite dependable. Recently, FL has been suggested for inter-institutional healthcare research considering its core principle where only model weights or gradients are sent between client sites and the federated server, easing privacy concerns about data governance for FL [15].

In this paper, we build a small prototype of federated learning (FL) model using a set of spike sequences for coronavirus variant classification. We compare the performance of our proposed FL-based approach on spike sequence data versus expensive baseline methods. In addition, we compare our proposed solution with other traditional state-of-the-art (SOTA) approaches, which involve a centralized model training approach using different embedding methods to address the classification problem.

We envision the use of an FL-based solution as a solution for authorities and governments to facilitate different privacy and simultaneously extract the knowledge from these large public (global) datasets (repositories such as GISAID) along with private (local) datasets from other countries (private dataset) for a customized model catered to solving public health issues and designing policies in a specific context (e.g., state, country, geographical region). Here, we propose a federated learning-based approach to efficiently utilize a publicly available data set (i.e. GISAID), and a mechanism to extract helpful information from the private data of others while facilitating the differential privacy of contributors to the problem of classifying variants of the SARS-CoV-2 virus. For this purpose, we extracted 9000 spike protein sequences from GISAID along with their lineage information to perform multi-class classification. Our dataset comprised 9 unique lineages. Our scalable model provides a framework for solving similar problems in other domains. Moreover, we show that using the spike protein instead of the whole genomic sequence can give the same or better accuracy, thus reducing computational complexity significantly.

Our contributions are as follows:

1. For coronavirus spike sequence classification, we provide federated learning (FL) based models, which are scalable and can be applied in a distributed fashion with less computational overhead.
2. Using the proposed FL model in a distributed manner allows us to maintain data privacy by only sending outputs (differential privacy) from the local small models to the global model (secure multi-party computation).
3. We compare FL-based models with different state-of-the-art (SOTA) embedding techniques and show that the proposed model outperforms SOTA methods in terms of predictive accuracy.
4. We demonstrate that the underlying machine learning classifiers can achieve high predictive performance with a fraction of the information (spike sequences rather than full-length genome sequences).

The rest of the paper is organized as follows: Sect. 2 contains the related work. Our proposed federated learning model is explained in detail in Sect. 3. Section 4 provides the details on the dataset and experimental setup. Results are given in Sect. 5, and we conclude the paper in Sect. 6.

2   Related Work

There are several approaches to convert biological sequences into machine learning-compatible inputs for classification and clustering, like k-mers-based methods [4,8,39,45]. Similarly, a position weight matrix (PWM) based classification approach is proposed in [5], which generates a fixed-length representation of spike sequences based on weights of k-mers computed using PWM.

Although the methods discussed above show higher predictive performance, they do not consider the privacy of data. To ensure the privacy of the information, a novel technique called federated learning (FL) has caught the attention of researchers. In [34], authors use the data gathered by individual user entities/equipment utilizing ambient sensors and wearable devices to propose a lightweight FL model that may be used to privately and collectively learn medical symptoms (like COVID-19). Moreover, Many FL-based methods for image classification are put forward, like the authors in [28] proposed MOON framework to deal with the heterogeneity of data distribution among local parties in FL. In another work [22], early breast cancer prediction is made by a memory-aware curriculum federated learning-based model using mammography images. The system given in [29] is performing neuroimage analysis by following an FL-based strategy. In [49] authors used FL for COVID detection using x-ray images. Using data from 20 institutions throughout the world, the authors in [15] proposed a model called EXAM (electronic medical record (EMR) chest X-ray AI model). However, the model uses inputs of vital signs, laboratory data, and chest X-rays to forecast the future oxygen requirements of symptomatic COVID-19 patients. It is heterogeneous but is clinical and image data. Unlike these image-based approaches, our proposed method directly works on the sequence data. Although there are studies related to medical federated learning, specifically for Oncology and Cancer Research [13] along with biases in the genomic data collection to perform federated learning [9], these studies do not present an end-to-end federated learning-based pipeline to perform privacy aware spike sequence classification.

3 Proposed Approach

In this section, we describe the proposed FL-based approach for the classification of coronavirus variants from spike protein sequences. We explain in detail the overall architecture of the proposed model.

3.1 Architecture

The architecture consists of two types of components: 1) client models (local) and 2) Federated Learning models (global). The approach is based on a decentralized data approach that involves dividing the dataset into different smaller parts and processing each part separately. The client model is composed of three parts of the dataset to train the models locally. These trained local models are pushed to a central (global) neural network (NN) based model. Only the weights, biases, and other parameters are provided to the global NN. To further reduce the size of the global model, it may undergo pruning (removing the less important parameters). The NN model gets all the locally trained models and averages them out, effectively creating a new global model (Federated Learning model). The Federated Learning model coordinates the federated learning process and uses a fourth part of the dataset to train the global model. Each step is explained in more detail below:

Step 1: Feature Vector Generation

A fixed-length numerical feature vector called One Hot Encoding (OHE) is proposed in [8,26]. It generates a binary $(0-1)$ vector based on the character's position in the sequence given alphabet Σ, where Σ is "$ACDEFGHIKLMN$-$PQRSTVWXY$", the unique characters in each sequence. The $0-1$ vectors for all characters are concatenated to make a single vector for a given sequence. For a given sequence i of length l, the dimension of OHE based vector i.e., ϕ_i can be denoted by $\phi_i = |\Sigma| \times l$.

Step 2: Federated Learning Approach

After generating the numerical vectors ϕ for SARS-CoV-2 spike sequences, we use these feature vectors as input for our federated learning-based model. We divide the dataset into training (ϕ_{tr}) and testing (ϕ_{ts}). The training dataset ϕ_{tr} is further divided into four equal parts $(\phi_{tr1}, \phi_{tr2}, \phi_{tr3}, \phi_{tr4})$. Our final Federated Learning-based model is comprised of a local and a global model, which work together to classify the spike sequences.

In the current architecture, we divide the data randomly into different models with equal proportions. In a real-world scenario, the data distribution among local models could be very different as some models can be trained on more data compared to other models. However, since we are using simple machine-learning classifiers in the local models, and since they are not as data-hungry as typical neural networks, they could generalize easily to different distributions of data in different local models.

Local Models. We initialize 3 individual classification (local) models (using classifiers such as XGB, Logistic Regression (LR), and Random Forest (RF)) and train them using three parts of the data $(\phi_{tr1}, \phi_{tr2}, \phi_{tr3})$. After training the "local model", these models are used to create a new aggregated model (global).

Global Model. Our global model consists of a neural network architecture, which takes λ_1, λ_2, and λ_3 as input where λ_1, λ_2, and λ_3 are the outputs from local trained models for the dataset ϕ_{tr4}, thus training the neural network using ϕ_{tr4}. It is important to point out that only the weights, biases, and other parameters are transferred to a new global model (from the local models). In the global model, none of the data from the three parts of the dataset $(\phi_{tr1}, \phi_{tr2}, \phi_{tr3})$ is used, which is the core concept of federated learning. Using the fourth part of the training data (ϕ_{tr4}) we get output λ_1, λ_2, and λ_3 from respective trained classification models (local) for each data sample. This output of dimension $9 \times 3 = 27$ (probability for 9 class labels from 3 models) is supplied to the neural network as input to train the Neural Network in the (global) model. We get our final trained ensemble model after this step. Figure 3 shows the precise architecture of the deep learning (DL) model, which is employed as the global model. The number of neurons in the input layer is 27 (weights from 3 local model for 9 class labels). The output layer, which has 9 neurons, represents the nine classes we predict. The neural network has two hidden layers with 25 and 15 neurons, respectively. Each hidden layer has a ReLu activation function, while the final classification layer uses a Softmax function to handle our multi-class classification problem. Furthermore, we use the ADAM optimizer with 16 batch size and 100 training epochs as hyperparameters. The number of parameters is listed in Table 1, the number of trainable parameters for hidden layer 1 is 700, hidden layer 2 is 390, and the output layer is 144. In total, the global model uses 1254 trainable parameters.

Testing the Ensemble Model. Finally, using the ensemble-trained global model, we predict for the test dataset ϕ_{ts} for the final predictions and evaluate our proposed model using different evaluation metrics.

Workflow for Proposed Approach

Figure 4 shows the complete workflow for our proposed approach. The left box shows the feature vector (ϕ) generation process where we used One Hot Encod-

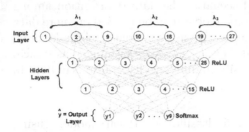

Fig. 3. Federated learning - Neural network.

Table 1. Detail regarding the parameters in different layers of the Neural Network.

Layer (type)	Input/Output Shape	Trainable Parameters
Input Layer	Input : (None, 27) Output : (None, 27)	–
Hidden Layer 1	Input : (None, 27) Output : (None, 25)	700
Hidden Layer 2	Input : (None, 25) Output : (None, 15)	390
Output Layer	Input : (None, 15) Output : (None, 9)	144
Total	–	1254

ing to generate the numerical representation (feature vectors) from the spike sequences. Each amino acid in the spike sequence, as shown in Fig. 4 (a), is encoded into numerical representation by placing 1 at the position of a character. For example, for amino acid "A" we place 1 at the first position in the respective numerical representation as shown in (b). Afterward, we divide the feature vector dataset into training ϕ_{tr} and testing ϕ_{ts}. Box 2 on the right side of Fig. 4 shows our federated learning-based approach. We divide the training dataset into 4 equal parts ($\phi_{tr1}, \phi_{tr2}, \phi_{tr3}$ and ϕ_{tr4}) and use 3 of these for training the "local models" (e.g. random forest) as shown in Fig. 4 (f-h). After training, these models are aggregated and assembled to create a new global model Fig. 4 (j). The weights uploaded by each node (local model) for the training dataset ϕ_{tr4} are received on the server side as input. They are used to train the global neural network model. In the end, we use the testing dataset (ϕ_{ts}) to predict and evaluate the model.

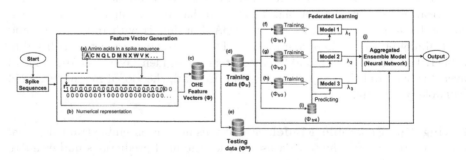

Fig. 4. Flowchart of Federated Learning approach.

The pseudo-code of our proposed approach is shown in Algorithm 1. The given spike sequence-based data is converted to numerical vectors by employing a one-hot encoding technique. The resultant vectors are aligned following the trailing zero padding method. Then we split the aligned vectors into training and test sets. The training set is further divided into four exclusive training sets, among which the three sets are used individually to train three local models respectively. We feed the fourth training set to the local models to obtain their respective weights. Furthermore, we combine all the extracted weights and pass them to the global model as input. After the training, we employ the test dataset to get the predictions from the global model. These predictions can provide insight into the global model's performance.

Algorithm 1. Ensemble Model Workflow.

1: **Input:** Sequence data S
2: **Output:** Sequences Variant Predictions V
3: ϕ = OHE (S)   ▷ get one-hot encodings of S
4: ϕ_{tr}, ϕ_{ts} = SplitDataTrainTest (ϕ)   ▷ 70-30% split
5: ϕ_{tr1}, ϕ_{tr2}, ϕ_{tr3}, ϕ_{tr4} = SplitTrainingData (ϕ_{tr})
      ▷ split training data into 4 sets
6: $model_1$ = Train (ϕ_{tr1})
      ▷ train local $model_1$ with ϕ_{tr1} training set
7: $\lambda_1 = model_1(\phi_{tr4})$
8: $model_2$= Train (ϕ_{tr2})
      ▷ train local $model_2$ with ϕ_{tr2} training set
9: $\lambda_2 = model_2(\phi_{tr4})$
10: $model_3$ = Train (ϕ_{tr3})
      ▷ train local $model_3$ with ϕ_{tr3} training set
11: $\lambda_3 = model_3(\phi_{tr4})$
12: $model_g$ = Train ($\lambda_1 + \lambda_2 + \lambda_3$)
      ▷ pass $\lambda_1 + \lambda_2 + \lambda_3$ as input to global $model_g$
13: $V = model_g(\phi_{ts})$ ▷ $model_g$ output V for ϕ_{ts}
14: return(V)

---

4   Experimental Setup

In this section, we detail the spike sequence dataset used for experimentation. Followed by the details of the baseline models. In the end, we talk about the evaluation metrics used to test the performance of the models. All experiments are conducted using an Intel(R) Core i5 system @ 2.10 GHz having Windows 10 64 bit OS with 32 GB memory. For the classification algorithms, we use 70% of the data for training and 30% for testing. The data is split randomly and experiments are repeated 5 times to report average results. For hyperparameter tuning, we used 10% data from the training set as a validation set.

4.1   Dataset Statistics

We extract the spike sequence data from GISAID[1]. It is a popular database in the bioinformatics domain that provides free open access to a large amount of

---

[1] https://www.gisaid.org/.

sequence data related to the SARS-CoV-2 virus and Influenza virus. Moreover, GISAID facilitates genomic epidemiology and real-time surveillance to monitor the emergence of new COVID-19 viral strains across the planet. The extracted data contains 9 coronavirus variants within 9000 total sequences (1000 sequences for each variant) that are selected randomly. Detailed statistics of the dataset can be seen in Table 2. The variant information is used as class labels for classification. Every sequence is associated with a lineage or variant. The variant is generated by certain mutations in the spike protein region. For example, the epsilon variant is created when the mutations S13I, W152C, and L452R happen in the spike region, where S13I means the amino acid S at position 13 is replaced by amino acid I. We use these sequence-based datasets to predict the corresponding variant names.

Remark 1. Note that the spike sequences in our data are not of the same length. The average, minimum, and maximum length of sequences (in the whole data) is 1263.16, 9, and 1277, respectively. We use data padding in one-hot encoding to get a fixed-length representation. The sequence length statistics for individual variants are given in Table 2.

4.2   Baseline Model

We use the following models from the literature as baselines for the comparison of results with the proposed federated learning model.

Spike2Vec [6] Spike2Vec is a method to convert bio-sequences into numerical form for enabling ML-based classification of the sequences. A sequence of length N will have $N - k + 1$ k-mers. For our experiments, we used $k = 3$.

WDGRL: A neural network (NN) based method that takes the one-hot representation of biological sequence as input and designs an NN-based embedding method by minimizing loss [38].

PWM2Vec [5]: Using the idea of the position-weight matrix (PWM), this technique is intended to generate fixed-length numerical embeddings. It starts by creating a $|\Sigma| \times k$ dimensional PWM matrix from a protein sequence, which comprises the count of each amino acid inside k-mers of the sequence. Each k-mer is given a numerical weight based on the counts. The final representation is generated by concatenating all of the weights.

String Kernel: Kernel Matrix-based method which designs $n \times n$ kernel matrix that can be used with kernel classifiers or with kernel PCA [21] to get feature vector based on principal components [7,16,17].

ProteinBert: It is a pre-trained Transformer, a protein sequence model to classify the given biological sequence using Transformer/Bert [10].

  A summary of the comparison of different baseline models and the proposed federated learning-based approach is also shown in Table 3.

Table 2. Statistics for 9 lineages from the SARS-CoV-2 dataset.

Lineage	Region of First Time Detection	Variant Name	No. Mut. S/Gen.	No. of sequences	Sequence Length Min.	Max.	Avg.
B.1.351	South Africa [18]	Beta	9/21	1000	9	1274	1260.46
B.1.427	California [50]	Epsilon	3/5	1000	100	1274	1272.18
B.1.429	California [44]	Epsilon	3/5	1000	100	1277	1271.93
B.1.525	UK and Nigeria [44]	Eta	8/16	1000	32	1273	1257.19
B.1.526	New York [48]	Iota	6/16	1000	9	1273	1266.62
B.1.617.2	India [46]	Delta	8/17	1000	99	1273	1265.12
B.1.621	Colombia [44]	Mu	9/21	1000	9	1275	1255.93
C.37	Peru [44]	Lambda	8/21	1000	86	1273	1248.55
P.1	Brazil [35]	Gamma	10/21	1000	99	1274	1270.45
Total	-	-	-	9000	-	-	-

Table 3. Baseline and Proposed Methods advantages and disadvantages.

Embedding	Alignment Free	Privacy	Low Communication Cost	Space Efficient	Runtime Efficient
Spike2Vec	✓	✗	✗	✓	✗
WDGRL	✗	✗	✗	✓	✗
PWM2Vec	✗	✗	✗	✓	✓
String Kernel	✓	✗	✗	✗	✗
ProteinBert	✓	✗	✗	✗	✗
Federated Learning (ours)	✓	✓	✓	✓	✓

4.3 Machine Learning Classifiers

For the classification task on state-of-the-art methods, we use Support Vector Machine (SVM), Naive Bayes (NB), Multi-Layer Perceptron (MLP), K Nearest Neighbors (KNN) $K = 5$, Random Forest (RF), Logistic Regression (LR), and Decision Tree (DT).

For the FL, we use eXtreme Gradient Boosting (XGB), LR, and RF classifiers to train the local models. XGB is a boosting algorithm based on the gradient-boosted decision trees approach. It applies a better regularization technique to reduce over-fitting. We select important features from the training dataset using a meta-transformer approach. This approach involves selecting features based on importance weights and is used for feature selection (dimensionality reduction). The goal of dimensionality reduction is to either improve the accuracy scores of the estimators or to boost the model's performance on high-dimensional datasets, hence avoiding the curse of dimensionality.

4.4 Evaluation Metrics

We use average accuracy, precision, recall, weighted F_1, macro F_1, and ROC-AUC (one-vs-rest) metrics to evaluate the performance of classification algorithms. We also report the training runtime for the classifiers. Note that for the federated learning-based model, the reported runtime is for the whole end-to-end model.

4.5 Data Visualization

The t-distributed stochastic neighbor embedding (t-SNE) [30] is utilized to identify any hidden patterns in the data. This method works by mapping the high dimensional input data into $2D$ space but preserves the pairwise distance between data points. This visualization aims to highlight if different embedding methods introduce any changes to the overall distribution of the data. For various (baseline) embedding methods, Fig. 5 illustrates the t-SNE-based visualization (with SARS CoV-2 variants as labels shown in the legends). In the case of WDGRL, we can observe that the variants are not clearly grouped together. For Spike2Vec, PWM2Vec, and String Kernel, the majority of the variants, such as P.1 (Gamma), B.1.526 (Iota), and C.37 (Lambda), make a single group.

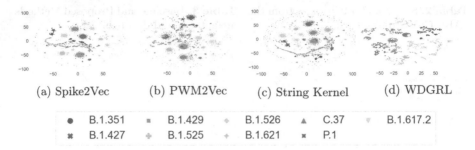

(a) Spike2Vec   (b) PWM2Vec   (c) String Kernel   (d) WDGRL

● B.1.351	■ B.1.429	◆ B.1.526	▲ C.37	▽ B.1.617.2
✳ B.1.427	✦ B.1.525	✚ B.1.621	✖ P.1	

Fig. 5. t-SNE plots for different embedding. The figure is best seen in color.

5 Results and Discussion

This section reports the classification results of the various methods using different evaluation metrics. We report the average and standard deviation scores of 5 runs to minimize the effects of any randomness.

Table 4 summarizes the results for our proposed system and the state-of-the-art (SOTA) models for different ML classifiers. We can observe that our proposed method with the LR classifier setting outperforms the baselines for all the evaluation metrics except for the training run time. While our method involves training multiple models which incurs high run times, it is able to preserve the privacy of data while maintaining the highest predictive performance, which is the prime goal of this paper. The federated learning-based model illustrates better performance than the feature-engineering-based baselines (Spike2Vec, PWM2Vec), achieving 3.3% and 0.4% more accuracy than the PWM2Vec and Spike2Vec methods, respectively, for the LR classifier. Similarly, it outperforms String Kernel with 0.4% accuracy using the LR classifier. Moreover, the proposed model outperforms WDGRL by 2.2% and pre-trained Protein Bert by 2.9% in terms of predictive accuracy using LR.

The confusion matrix for the FL-based model using RF is shown in Table 5. Similarly, the confusion matrix for the FL-based model using LR is shown in Table 6. We can observe that in most cases, the model is able to classify the variants correctly. An interesting observation here is in the results of variants B.1.427 and B.1.429. Since both of these variants are classified as Epsilon originating in California (see Table 2), the proposed model cannot distinguish between them because of their high similarity. Note that both of these variants share the same mutations in the spike region but have different mutations in other SARS-CoV-2 genes. Since we are dealing with spike regions in this study, differentiating between them becomes very difficult, that's why the model is getting confused between these two variants of Epsilon.

5.1 Local Model Analysis

We present the training and validation accuracy for individual ML models in Fig. 6 to assess the performance of individual models throughout the training

Table 4. Variants classification results (average ± standard deviation of 5 runs) for spike sequences data. The best average values are shown in bold.

Method	Algo	Acc. ↑	Prec. ↑	Recall ↑	F1 (Weig.) ↑	F1 (Macro) ↑	ROC AUC ↑	Train Time (Sec.) ↓
Spike2Vec [6]	SVM	0.925 ± 0.001	0.926 ± 0.001	0.925 ± 0.001	0.924 ± 0.001	0.924 ± 0.002	0.958 ± 0.001	242.499 ± 4.623
	NB	0.919 ± 0.001	0.925 ± 0.003	0.919 ± 0.001	0.918 ± 0.001	0.918 ± 0.002	0.955 ± 0.001	6.452 ± 0.334
	MLP	0.890 ± 0.015	0.894 ± 0.012	0.890 ± 0.015	0.889 ± 0.014	0.889 ± 0.013	0.938 ± 0.008	156.453 ± 14.703
	KNN	0.866 ± 0.002	0.871 ± 0.002	0.866 ± 0.002	0.867 ± 0.002	0.866 ± 0.004	0.925 ± 0.002	16.039 ± 1.079
	RF	0.926 ± 0.003	0.927 ± 0.004	0.926 ± 0.003	0.925 ± 0.003	0.925 ± 0.003	0.958 ± 0.002	11.032 ± 0.175
	LR	0.927 ± 0.001	0.929 ± 0.002	0.927 ± 0.001	0.927 ± 0.001	0.927 ± 0.002	0.959 ± 0.001	23.966 ± 0.866
	DT	0.922 ± 0.004	0.924 ± 0.004	0.922 ± 0.004	0.922 ± 0.003	0.922 ± 0.002	0.956 ± 0.001	4.414 ± 0.172
PWM2Vec [5]	SVM	0.888 ± 0.001	0.891 ± 0.001	0.888 ± 0.001	0.887 ± 0.002	0.885 ± 0.002	0.936 ± 0.001	13.718 ± 1.894
	NB	0.423 ± 0.014	0.449 ± 0.026	0.423 ± 0.014	0.352 ± 0.019	0.351 ± 0.017	0.675 ± 0.007	0.496 ± 0.047
	MLP	0.866 ± 0.006	0.869 ± 0.008	0.866 ± 0.006	0.864 ± 0.006	0.862 ± 0.006	0.923 ± 0.003	12.656 ± 3.516
	KNN	0.841 ± 0.010	0.843 ± 0.009	0.841 ± 0.010	0.841 ± 0.010	0.839 ± 0.009	0.910 ± 0.005	1.442 ± 0.181
	RF	0.899 ± 0.003	0.900 ± 0.003	0.899 ± 0.003	0.899 ± 0.003	0.897 ± 0.003	0.942 ± 0.002	6.608 ± 0.056
	LR	0.898 ± 0.004	0.898 ± 0.004	0.898 ± 0.004	0.896 ± 0.004	0.894 ± 0.004	0.941 ± 0.002	152.62 ± 7.102
	DT	0.882 ± 0.005	0.883 ± 0.005	0.882 ± 0.005	0.882 ± 0.005	0.880 ± 0.005	0.933 ± 0.003	3.406 ± 0.110
String Kernel [17]	SVM	0.926 ± 0.005	0.931 ± 0.005	0.926 ± 0.005	0.924 ± 0.005	0.924 ± 0.003	0.959 ± 0.002	12.46 ± 2.543
	NB	0.600 ± 0.008	0.705 ± 0.010	0.600 ± 0.008	0.611 ± 0.008	0.611 ± 0.008	0.775 ± 0.004	0.218 ± 0.013
	MLP	0.853 ± 0.013	0.855 ± 0.014	0.853 ± 0.013	0.852 ± 0.013	0.853 ± 0.013	0.917 ± 0.007	6.948 ± 0.622
	KNN	0.866 ± 0.007	0.872 ± 0.008	0.866 ± 0.007	0.868 ± 0.008	0.868 ± 0.005	0.925 ± 0.003	0.827 ± 0.068
	RF	0.918 ± 0.004	0.919 ± 0.003	0.918 ± 0.004	0.917 ± 0.004	0.917 ± 0.002	0.954 ± 0.001	5.120 ± 0.191
	LR	0.927 ± 0.004	0.930 ± 0.003	0.927 ± 0.004	0.926 ± 0.004	0.926 ± 0.002	0.959 ± 0.001	9.258 ± 0.702
	DT	0.897 ± 0.006	0.899 ± 0.005	0.897 ± 0.006	0.897 ± 0.006	0.897 ± 0.004	0.942 ± 0.002	1.426 ± 0.065
WDGRL [38]	SVM	0.902 ± 0.003	0.905 ± 0.004	0.902 ± 0.003	0.901 ± 0.004	0.902 ± 0.003	0.946 ± 0.002	0.403 ± 0.038
	NB	0.825 ± 0.004	0.789 ± 0.007	0.825 ± 0.004	0.792 ± 0.004	0.795 ± 0.004	0.904 ± 0.002	**0.016 ± 0.003**
	MLP	0.908 ± 0.004	0.910 ± 0.004	0.908 ± 0.004	0.907 ± 0.005	0.908 ± 0.004	0.949 ± 0.002	4.691 ± 0.736
	KNN	0.910 ± 0.012	0.913 ± 0.011	0.910 ± 0.012	0.909 ± 0.012	0.910 ± 0.011	0.950 ± 0.006	0.116 ± 0.014
	RF	0.909 ± 0.002	0.911 ± 0.001	0.909 ± 0.002	0.907 ± 0.002	0.909 ± 0.002	0.949 ± 0.001	0.446 ± 0.057
	LR	0.877 ± 0.012	0.880 ± 0.005	0.877 ± 0.012	0.877 ± 0.015	0.878 ± 0.014	0.931 ± 0.006	0.168 ± 0.016
	DT	0.898 ± 0.005	0.900 ± 0.006	0.898 ± 0.005	0.897 ± 0.005	0.899 ± 0.004	0.943 ± 0.002	0.020 ± 0.005
Protein Bert [10]	-	0.902 ± 0.004	0.903 ± 0.003	0.902 ± 0.004	0.904 ± 0.005	0.903 ± 0.009	0.945 ± 0.007	16127.76 ± 0.019
Federated Learning (ours)	XGB	0.930 ± 0.004	0.932 ± 0.003	0.930 ± 0.004	0.930 ± 0.005	0.928 ± 0.004	0.960 ± 0.003	1578.27 ± 0.045
	LR	**0.931 ± 0.011**	**0.933 ± 0.010**	**0.931 ± 0.012**	**0.931 ± 0.011**	**0.929 ± 0.011**	**0.961 ± 0.010**	396.296 ± 0.024
	RF	0.929 ± 0.005	0.932 ± 0.004	0.928 ± 0.006	0.927 ± 0.005	0.925 ± 0.006	0.959 ± 0.004	125.322 ± 0.079

Table 5. Random Forest

	B.1.351	B.1.427	B.1.429	B.1.525	B.1.526	B.1.617.2	B.1.621	C.37	P.1
B.1.351	283	0	0	1	4	3	0	0	0
B.1.427	0	173	140	0	4	0	0	0	0
B.1.429	1	48	267	0	1	0	0	1	1
B.1.525	1	1	0	287	1	0	0	0	0
B.1.526	0	0	0	1	297	0	0	0	0
B.1.617.2	0	0	0	0	0	283	0	0	0
B.1.621	0	0	0	0	2	0	296	0	0
C.37	1	0	1	0	1	0	0	297	0
P.1	0	0	0	0	0	0	0	0	304

phase. We can observe that these charts demonstrate accuracy improvements as the training set size increases, showing the improvement of the model.

Table 6. Logistic Regression

	B.1.351	B.1.427	B.1.429	B.1.525	B.1.526	B.1.617.2	B.1.621	C.37	P.1
B.1.351	302	0	0	0	0	0	0	0	0
B.1.427	0	166	138	0	1	0	0	0	0
B.1.429	1	57	262	1	0	0	0	0	0
B.1.525	0	0	1	285	0	3	0	0	0
B.1.526	0	1	0	0	309	0	0	0	0
B.1.617.2	0	0	0	0	0	293	0	0	0
B.1.621	0	0	0	0	1	0	297	0	0
C.37	0	0	0	0	0	0	0	306	0
P.1	1	0	2	0	0	0	0	0	273

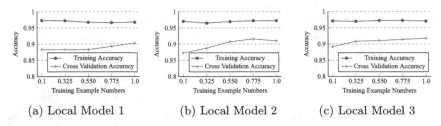

(a) Local Model 1   (b) Local Model 2   (c) Local Model 3

Fig. 6. Training and Cross-Validation accuracy of different local models with increasing (fraction of) training set size (x-axis). The figure is best seen in color.

5.2 Global Model Analysis

The accuracy and loss curves for the global model are shown in Fig. 7. We can observe in Fig. 7a that the loss is stable after 20 epochs, and accuracy ranges around 94–96% as shown in Fig. 7b.

5.3 Laws of Federated Learning

In this section, we discuss the different laws of federated learning that the proposed model holds.

Law of Data Ownership. This law is upheld in the proposed model since the data is kept locally on each local model's device, and only the model outputs are shared among the devices.

Law of Data Privacy. This law is upheld in the proposed algorithm since the data is not shared between the devices, only the model parameters are shared.

Law of Model Aggregation. This law is upheld in our model since the model parameters from each participant are combined at a central server to create a global model.

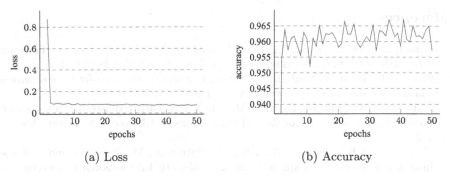

(a) Loss   (b) Accuracy

Fig. 7. Loss and Accuracy of final ensemble (Global) model (NN).

Law of Model Heterogeneity. This law is upheld in our algorithm since each participant may use a different local training algorithm and hyperparameters to train their model.

6 Conclusion

We propose federated learning-based models for SARS-CoV-2 variant classification. We show that by using spike sequences only, we can achieve good predictive performance. We compare the results using different evaluation metrics with several SOTA models and show that the federated learning-based approach outperforms those existing models from the literature. An important property of the proposed model is that since it only transfers the output from local models to the global model, it preserves the privacy of users, which could be a major problem in many big organizations. Especially in healthcare addressing the issue of privacy is of major concern and the proposed model addresses the issue while not compromising the performance. One possible extension of this approach is to apply deep learning-based local models to classify the sequences. Another interesting direction would be to propose an approximate approach to compute feature embeddings for the biological sequences to further improve computational overhead. Using different ML classifiers in combination within a single FL architecture could also be an interesting future extension for SARS-CoV-2 variant classification. We will also explore incorporating other attributes (e.g., regions, time) and variants along with the spike sequences to generate a vertical federated learning model. Investigating the generalization of the proposed model to other protein region sequences is also an exciting future direction.

References

1. Ahmad, M., Ali, S., Tariq, J., Khan, I., Shabbir, M., Zaman, A.: Combinatorial trace method for network immunization. Inf. Sci. **519**, 215–228 (2020)
2. Ahmad, M., Tariq, J., Shabbir, M., Khan, I.: Spectral methods for immunization of large networks. arXiv preprint arXiv:1711.00791 (2017)
3. Aledhari, M., Razzak, R., Parizi, R.M., Saeed, F.: Federated learning: a survey on enabling technologies, protocols, and applications. IEEE Access **8**, 140699–140725 (2020)
4. Ali, S., Ali, T.E., Khan, M.A., Khan, I., Patterson, M.: Effective and scalable clustering of sars-cov-2 sequences. In: 2021 the 5th International Conference on Big Data Research (ICBDR), pp. 42–49 (2021)
5. Ali, S., Bello, B., Chourasia, P., Punathil, R.T., Zhou, Y., Patterson, M.: Pwm2vec: an efficient embedding approach for viral host specification from coronavirus spike sequences. MDPI Biology (2022)
6. Ali, S., Patterson, M.: Spike2vec: an efficient and scalable embedding approach for covid-19 spike sequences. In: IEEE International Conference on Big Data (Big Data), pp. 1533–1540 (2021)
7. Ali, S., Sahoo, B., Khan, M.A., Zelikovsky, A., Khan, I.U., Patterson, M.: Efficient approximate kernel based spike sequence classification. IEEE/ACM Transactions on Computational Biology and Bioinformatics (2022)
8. Ali, S., Sahoo, B., Ullah, N., Zelikovskiy, A., Patterson, M., Khan, I.: A k-mer based approach for sars-cov-2 variant identification. In: International Symposium on Bioinformatics Research and Applications, pp. 153–164 (2021)
9. Boscarino, N., Cartwright, R.A., Fox, K., Tsosie, K.S.: Federated learning and indigenous genomic data sovereignty. Nature Mach. Intell. **4**(11), 909–911 (2022)
10. Brandes, N., Ofer, D., Peleg, Y., Rappoport, N., Linial, M.: ProteinBERT: a universal deep-learning model of protein sequence and function. Bioinformatics **38**(8), 2102–2110 (02 2022)
11. Buch, V., et al.: Development and validation of a deep learning model for prediction of severe outcomes in suspected Covid-19 infection. arXiv preprint arXiv:2103.11269 (2021)
12. Chourasia, P., Tayebi, Z., Ali, S., Patterson, M.: Empowering pandemic response with federated learning for protein sequence data analysis. In: 2023 International Joint Conference on Neural Networks (IJCNN), pp. 01–08. IEEE (2023)
13. Chowdhury, A., Kassem, H., Padoy, N., Umeton, R., Karargyris, A.: A review of medical federated learning: applications in oncology and cancer research. In: Crimi, A., Bakas, S. (eds.) Brainlesion: Glioma, Multiple Sclerosis, Stroke and Traumatic Brain Injuries: 7th International Workshop, BrainLes 2021, Held in Conjunction with MICCAI 2021, Virtual Event, September 27, 2021, Revised Selected Papers, Part I, pp. 3–24. Springer International Publishing, Cham (2022). https://doi.org/10.1007/978-3-031-08999-2_1
14. Coccia, M.: The impact of lockdown on public health during the first wave of Covid-19 pandemic: lessons learned for designing effective containment measures to cope with second wave. medRxiv (2020)
15. Dayan, I., et al.: Federated learning for predicting clinical outcomes in patients with Covid-19. Nat. Med. **27**(10), 1735–1743 (2021)
16. Devijver, P., Kittler, J.: Pattern recognition: A statistical approach. In: London, GB: Prentice-Hall, pp. 1–448 (1982)

17. Farhan, M., Tariq, J., Zaman, A., Shabbir, M., Khan, I.U.: Efficient approximation algorithms for strings kernel based sequence classification. In: Advances in Neural Information Processing Systems vol. 30 (2017)
18. Galloway, S.,et al.: Emergence of sars-cov-2 b. 1.1. 7 lineage-united states, december 29, 2020–january 12, 2021. Morbidity Mortality Weekly Report **70**(3), 95 (2021)
19. GISAID Website: https://www.gisaid.org/ (2021). Accessed 29 Dec 2021
20. Hadfield, J., et al.: Nextstrain: real-time tracking of pathogen evolution. Bioinformatics **34**(23), 4121–4123 (2018)
21. Hoffmann, H.: Kernel PCA for novelty detection. Pattern Recogn. **40**(3), 863–874 (2007)
22. Jiménez-Sánchez, A., Tardy, M., Ballester, M.A.G., Mateus, D., Piella, G.: Memory-aware curriculum federated learning for breast cancer classification. arXiv preprint arXiv:2107.02504 (2021)
23. Kaimann, D., Tanneberg, I.: What containment strategy leads us through the pandemic crisis? An empirical analysis of the measures against the covid-19 pandemic. PLoS ONE **16**(6), e0253237 (2021)
24. Kairouz, P., et al.: Advances and open problems in federated learning. Found. Trends® in Mach. Learn. **14**(1–2), 1–210 (2021)
25. Kisa, S., Kisa, A.: Under-reporting of Covid-19 cases in Turkey. Int. J. Health Plann. Manage. **35**(5), 1009–1013 (2020)
26. Kuzmin, K., et al.: Machine learning methods accurately predict host specificity of coronaviruses based on spike sequences alone. Biochem. Biophys. Res. Commun. **533**(3), 553–558 (2020)
27. Lee, R., Herigon, J., Benedetti, A., Pollock, N., Denkinger, C.: Performance of saliva, oropharyngeal swabs, and nasal swabs for SARS-COV-2 molecular detection: a systematic review and meta-analysis. J. Clin. Microbiol. **59**(5), 20-e02881 (2021)
28. Li, Q., He, B., Song, D.: Model-contrastive federated learning. In: Proceedings of the IEEE/CVF Conference on Computer Vision and Pattern Recognition, pp. 10713–10722 (2021)
29. Li, X., Gu, Y., Dvornek, N., Staib, L.H., Ventola, P., Duncan, J.S.: Multi-site fMRI analysis using privacy-preserving federated learning and domain adaptation: abide results. Med. Image Anal. **65**, 101765 (2020)
30. Van der Maaten, L., Hinton, G.: Visualizing data using t-sne. J. Mach. Learn. Res. **9**(11) (2008)
31. Majumder, J., Minko, T.: Recent developments on therapeutic and diagnostic approaches for Covid-19. AAPS J **23**(1), 1–22 (2021)
32. McMahan, B., Moore, E., Ramage, D., Hampson, S., y Arcas, B.A.: Communication-efficient learning of deep networks from decentralized data. In: Artificial Intelligence and Statistics, pp. 1273–1282. PMLR (2017)
33. Minh, B.Q., et al.: Iq-tree 2: new models and efficient methods for phylogenetic inference in the genomic era. Mol. Biol. Evol. **37**(5), 1530–1534 (2020)
34. Nasser, N., Fadlullah, Z.M., et al.: A lightweight federated learning based privacy preserving b5g pandemic response network using unmanned aerial vehicles: A proof-of-concept. Comput. Netw. **205**, 108672 (2022)
35. Naveca, F., et al.: Phylogenetic relationship of Sars-Cov-2 sequences from Amazonas with emerging Brazilian variants harboring mutations e484k and n501y in the spike protein. Virological. org **1**, 1–8 (2021)
36. Panwar, H., Gupta, P., Siddiqui, M.K., Morales-Menendez, R., Singh, V.: Application of deep learning for fast detection of Covid-19 in x-rays using ncovnet. Chaos, Solitons Fractals **138**, 109944 (2020)

37. Shaheen, M., Farooq, M.S., Umer, T., Kim, B.S.: Applications of federated learning; taxonomy, challenges, and research trends. Electronics **11**(4), 670 (2022)
38. Shen, J., Qu, Y., Zhang, W., Yu, Y.: Wasserstein distance guided representation learning for domain adaptation. In: AAAI (2018)
39. Solis-Reyes, S., Avino, M., Poon, A., Kari, L.: An open-source k-mer based machine learning tool for fast and accurate subtyping of hiv-1 genomes. Plos One (2018)
40. Tariq, J., Ahmad, M., Khan, I., Shabbir, M.: Scalable approximation algorithm for network immunization. In: Pacific Asia Conference on Information Systems (PACIS), p. 200 (2017)
41. Tayebi, Z., Ali, S., Patterson, M.: Robust representation and efficient feature selection allows for effective clustering of Sars-Cov-2 variants. Algorithms **14**(12), 348 (2021)
42. Udugama, B., et al.: Diagnosing Covid-19: the disease and tools for detection. ACS Nano **14**(4), 3822–3835 (2020)
43. West Jr, A., et al.: Detection and characterization of the Sars-Cov-2 lineage b. 1.526 in new york. Nature Commun. **12**(1), 4886 (2021)
44. WHO   Website: https://www.who.int/en/activities/tracking-SARS-CoV-2-variants/
45. Wood, D., Salzberg, S.: Kraken: ultrafast metagenomic sequence classification using exact alignments. Genome Biol. **15**(3), 1–12 (2014)
46. World Health Organization: Who coronavirus (covid-19) dashboard. https://covid19.who.int/. Accessed 20-July-2022
47. Xu, W., Wu, J., Cao, L.: Covid-19 pandemic in china: context, experience and lessons. Health Policy Technol. **9**(4), 639–648 (2020)
48. Yadav, P., et al.: Neutralization potential of Covishield vaccinated individuals sera against b. 1.617. 1. bioRxiv **1** (2021)
49. Zhang, W., et al.: Dynamic-fusion-based federated learning for Covid-19 detection. IEEE Internet Things J. **8**(21), 15884–15891 (2021)
50. Zhang, W., Davis, B.D., et al.: Emergence of a novel Sars-Cov-2 variant in southern California. JAMA **325**(13), 1324–1326 (2021)

Comparing Incremental Learning Approaches for a Growing Sign Language Dictionary

Joe Huamani-Malca[1]([✉]) [iD] and Gissella Bejarano[2] [iD]

[1] Pontificia Universidad Católica del Perú, San Miguel, Peru
huamani.jn@pucp.edu.pe
[2] Marist College, Poughkeepsie, USA
gissella.bejarano@marist.edu.pe

Abstract. Machine Learning-based Sign Language Dictionaries recognize a sign performed in front of a camera and return the most probable written language word. Due to the scarce number and variety of datasets for sign languages, these dictionaries need an incremental approach to include new signs each time a new dataset is available. Current sign language recognition models used in these dictionaries are trained for a fixed number of classes. For this reason, our work systematically compares three incremental learning approaches in a skeleton and transformer-based sign language recognition model to train up to 60 classes or Peruvian Sign Language (LSP) signs. In addition, we also evaluate two distinct incremental groups: only taking new classes and, taking new instance of old and new classes. This last incremental group is considerably less explored compared to the incremental approach involving only new classes at each step. We found that a method inspired by distillation loss outperforms others in most scenarios.

Keywords: incremental learning · class incremental learning · sign language dictionary

1 Introduction

Sign Language - Oral Language Dictionaries consist of receiving a sign performed by a user in front of a camera and returning an oral language word related to the most probable or similar sign recognized. This video-based search is usually performed through machine learning models trained to solve the isolated sign language recognition (ISLR) task.

Due to the scarce number and variety of datasets for sign language, new signs or classes are available at different times. To build a dataset, researchers record, annotate, and preprocess videos. When these recordings belong to sentences, new samples of previous signs can also be included. However, ISLR models are usually trained for a finite number of classes. Integrating new classes into the dataset necessitates retraining the model from scratch, which can be time-consuming

J. A. Lossio-Ventura et al. (Eds.): SIMBig 2023, CCIS 2142, pp. 97–106, 2024.
https://doi.org/10.1007/978-3-031-63616-5_7

and resource-intensive. Moreover, in some cases, we might want to integrate new classes immediately like when a user provides or correct several examples online and want the knowledge to be reflected in the platform. Another significant challenge arises in the growth of a dataset where data may be lost or not stored correctly, making it inaccessible for future use. In some scenarios, access might be limited to only the final model rather than the entire historical dataset. This limitation underscores the importance of addressing the issue of continuous data management in the context of incremental learning for sign language dictionaries.

For this reason, building a Sign Language Dictionary highly benefits from incremental learning approaches that adapt to the challenge of having new classes available at different moments and that have to be included in the model. In this work, we compare three class-incremental learning approaches on a skeleton and transformer-based ISLR model to train up to 60 classes or Peruvian Sign Language signs. Moreover, we explore three incremental groups of only taking new classes and taking new instance of old and new classes. The details of these groups will be discussed in Sect. 3.1.

Online Sign language dictionaries continue to expand in diverse countries as a tool for bridging the gap between sign languages and oral languages. Our work shade light on a real-world application of incremental learning, usually tested in toy dataset examples. Besides, our comparison and analysis of the incremental learning techniques can help other researchers focus on the continuous growth of the vocabulary in these kinds of dictionaries [10,12].

2   Related Work

Traditional SLR methods that rely on training a model once for the entire set of classes have been widely studied [6,7] and have shown promising results. However, when these kinds of models are used in final user applications, they need to learn new instances as new datasets are produced.

To address this specific challenge, the adoption of incremental learning, more specifically of class-incremental learning, emerges as a solution supported by evidence of its application across diverse domains. For instance, incremental image recognition has explored various approaches tested in toy datasets such as MNIST and CIFAR usually. Some of these works propose the addition of similar classifiers for each incremental group of classes or also considered feature extractors to a common last layer to output a final class [2]. Others suggest partially freezing model weights [4], maintaining a consistent feature extraction size while modifying the last layer [17], or employing distillation techniques to preserve previous knowledge [5]. Furthermore, researchers have also employed techniques such as an out-of-distribution detector for memory management that works with the classification model for gesture recognition [14]. In the context of Sign Language Recognition (SLR), a partially frozen weight model has also been employed [13].

Another important aspect involves including new examples from previously learned classes. This is something often seen in Task-Incremental Learning [15,

16, 18, 19]. However, it is important to mention that some studies have examined this particular element in the context of Class-Incremental Learning, as shown by studies like [5] for image recognition and [13] for SLR.

3   Methodology

For testing the incremental learning techniques, we split our dataset in groups. Each new group is fine-tuned by loading the weights of the model trained for the classes of all the previous groups in a cumulative form. This new group, a subset of the original dataset, is composed mainly of new instances of new classes but can also include new instances of previous classes. The process to create more sign language datasets fit with this setting given that the sentences annotated in new datasets probably include several instances of previously learned signs. In this section we explain the skeleton and transform-based ISLR model, how we created the incremental subsets and details on the incremental techniques we compare. We provide code of our scripts in our GitHub repository[1]

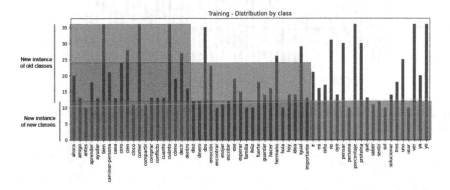

Fig. 1. Training dataset that shows the new instance of new classes (used in NC) and also the instances of previous classes (used in NINOC) for each training increment. Green area is taken for the first 20 classes; purple area for the increment of "20 to 40" classes, the section above green represents the new instances of previous classes, and the red area for "40 to 60" classes, which also includes new instances of the original group and the 40-class group (Color figure online)

3.1   Incremental Groups

The incremental techniques are tested by providing groups or subsets of the original dataset. These incremental groups include NC a NINOC as explained in the following subsections. Figures 1 and 2 show an example of how we split the classes included in each incremental step at the training and validation stages. Different colors represent the incremental groups consisting of the instances of the new classes and the instances or previous classes.

---

[1] https://github.com/JoeNatan30/sign_recognition_incremental.

New Classes - NC. In this incremental group, we exclusively consider new instances of new classes during each incremental step. The purpose of using this group is to evaluate how the technique performs when faced with an incremental step of solely new classes.

New Instances of New and Old Classes - NINOC. Within this group, we include new instances from both new and old classes to observe how the performance of the model changes when incorporating instances from previous classes along with new ones.

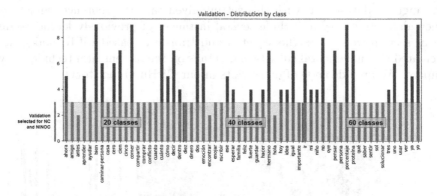

Fig. 2. Validation dataset distribution used for NC and NINOC in each training increment.

3.2   Model Architecture

The architecture of ISLR is a skeleton and transformer-based model. In other words, our model works with the landmarks of the pose estimation predicted for the body of the person in each of the frames of the video. The input is a sequence of keypoint landmarks which are processed by the transformer-based model, known as SPOTER, proposed in [8] to output the class or sign recognized through the final linear layer. The 54 keypoint landmarks utilized in the model represent the pose, face, and both hands, which were obtained using the Mediapipe "Holistic" model for keypoint estimation [9]. The architecture includes a customized transformer decoder layer that omits the repeated self-attentional operation found in standard implementation. Although we utilized SPOTER as the foundation, we made certain parameter reductions to avoid overfitting. These modifications resulted in the model having approximately 3,7 million parameters.

3.3   Class-Incremental Learning Techniques

Formally, class-incremental learning is categorized as one of the variants of continual learning, wherein the model progressively acquires the ability to distinguish newly introduced classes over time [1]. We test three techniques: Fixed last layer, Expanded last layer and Weighted last layer.

Technique 1: Fixed Last Layer. To enable the model to accommodate varying numbers of classes, we set the last layer to match the maximum possible number of classes even when the initial training on the first group does not include all the classes. At each incremental learning step, the architecture of the model is not modified at all, and the weights of the previously trained model are loaded. It uses approximately 3.7 million trainable parameters.

Technique 2: Expanded Last Layer. To integrate new classes into the model, we employ an approach that expands the dimensions of the final linear layer to correspond to the new total class count. An advantage of this technique lies in the preservation and transfer of weights from the model of the previous training. By leveraging its existing knowledge, the model can seamlessly adapt to the inclusion of new classes, accelerating learning. This strategy enables the model to build upon its prior experience while accommodating the evolution of the dataset [2]. It uses approximately 3.7 million trainable parameters.

Technique 3: Weighted Last Layer. This technique is inspired by the distillation loss framework used in [20] and part of the parameter configuration in distillation section in [5]. With the difference that our approach is not performing traditional distillation where the student model is a less-complex model which train from scratch. The weights of the first or the previous trained model are loaded into a second model with a similar architecture. The first one keeps the last layer size for the number of classes in the first group. The second model expanded its last layer to include the new classes. Two loss functions are calculated from the last layers of the two models. The first loss (TL) is calculated based on the first model's output layer and the section that corresponds to the previous classes from the second model's output layer as shown in Eq. 2. The second loss (SL) is calculated based on the second model's complete output layer and the ground truth. Then, both cross-entropy losses are sum in a weighted function based on the α parameter as shown in Eq. 3. The value of α is obtained by dividing the number of previous classes by the total number of classes, as shown in Eq. 1. The back-propagation affects only the weights of the second model. It utilizes approximately 3.7 million trainable parameters but demands more GPU memory due to the inclusion of the teacher model.

$$\alpha = \frac{M}{M + N} \tag{1}$$

where: M represents the previous number of classes, and N represents the new number of classes being added.

$$TL = -\frac{1}{M} \sum_{i=1}^{M} \left(P(O_i^t/T) \cdot \log(P(O_i^s/T)) \right) \tag{2}$$

where: O_i^t represents the output of the teacher model, O_i^s represents the output of the student model and T the Temperature set whose value is 2 for our experiments.

$$FinalLoss = \alpha \cdot TL + (1 - \alpha) \cdot SL \tag{3}$$

4   Experiments

This section details the two datasets used for the training (Sect. 4.1) and explains how we configure the experiment using the dataset (Sect. 4.2).

4.1   Dataset Description

We utilized a combination of the two previously mentioned datasets for our experiments. From this combined dataset, we selected the first 60 most frequently occurring classes from this mix, ensuring a minimum of 12 instances for each class. On average, there are 16.7 instances per class, with a median of 20 instances. Although some classes have more than 20 instances, we set a criterion of having a minimum of 12 instances per class in the dataset, which allows to work up to 60 classes.

PUCP-PSL-DGI 305 Dataset. The PUCP-DGI305 dataset comprises videos featuring deaf signers from Peru generating sentences in 1920×1080 resolution at 29.9 fps. The videos are standardized, featuring a consistent white background, and were all recorded from an equal camera distance and signer body position. The dataset was annotated by a native LSP speaker and reviewed by a deaf individual and a linguistic master student proficient in LSP. Additionally, The labels of the dataset were standardized by a linguistic expert. As of the current date of this paper's publication, the dataset is still in the process of development.

AEC Dataset. The dataset comprises content extracted from two 30-min videos of the Peruvian TV show titled 'Aprendo en casa' (Learning at home). The videos feature two distinct interpreters. The frames from these videos were captured at 29.9 fps and cropped to 220×220 pixels of the small corner square where the interpreter appears. The signs in the dataset were segmented based on the spoken words in the program and reviewed by a linguistic Master student familiar with LSP [11].

4.2   Experiment Configuration

In this work, we are exploring the definition of certain benchmarks that can better adjust to different case studies or applications. For our work in a sign language dictionary, at each stage we could have as many classes as the previous group. For that reason, we experiment with two sizes of increments. In the first size, we began with 40 classes and increased by 10 classes at each step, simulating a smaller dataset growth. In the second size, we started with 20 classes and increased by 20 classes at each step, representing a larger increment in the number of classes. In both cases, we imposed a maximum limit of 60 classes.

We maintain a consistent learning rate of 0.00005 and utilize the SGD optimizer throughout all the experiments. These parameter selections have been subject to comprehensive validation in our previous research demonstrating promising results. We evaluate the performance of our model using accuracy Top 1 and Top 5 as metrics. During the training process, we also implemented an early stop strategy with a patience value set to 200 to prevent overfitting.

5   Results and Analysis

We report the mean and standard deviation based on three training samplings for each technique within each increment group. We prepared three lists of randomly ordered words, with each list corresponding to one of these training samplings.

Even when training from scratch for 20, 40, and 60 classes will always overcome incremental approaches, we present these results in Table 1 to provide context for the values achieved by our incremental techniques. The model trained from scratch with 20 classes will serve as the base model for the 20-40 class increment, while the model trained with 40 classes will serve as the base model for the 40-50 class increment.

Table 1. Summary of the results after training from scratch for 20, 40 and 60 classes

Incremental technique	Accuracy (%)
Base 20	74.93 ± 0.99
Base 40	64.14 ± 3.45
Base 60	60.62 ± 6.20

In Table 2, we present the results for each technique in the 20-40 and 40-60 class increments. Taking a general view, it becomes evident that NINOC tends to show better accuracy compared to NC. This behavior can be expected, considering that NINOC uses new instances of old classes. In a closer examination, we notice that the Weighted technique consistently achieves the highest accuracy in most of these cases. Even in NINOC for the increment step of "40-60," where it did not reach the highest accuracy, its value is close to the highest achieved.

Table 2. Summary of the results obtained through training in two incremental steps "20-40" and "40-60" for NC and NINOC incremental groups

Incremental technique	Increment step	NC-Acc (%)	NINOC-Acc (%)
Fixed	20 - 40	33.91 ± 2.83	42.09 ± 1.30
Expanded	20 - 40	35.31 ± 0.28	44.36 ± 3.77
Weighted	20 - 40	**39.83 ± 1.19**	**44.93 ± 3.43**
Fixed	40 - 60	24.62 ± 3.13	28.41 ± 3.94
Expanded	40 - 60	23.67 ± 1.99	**28.59 ± 1.74**
Weighted	40 - 60	**26.32 ± 0.33**	28.22 ± 1.18

We observe consistent results for the behavior of the Weighted technique in Table 3, which presents the results for each technique in the 40-50 and 50-60 increments. It is also interesting to mention that the Weighted technique performs better than the other techniques in smaller incremental step sizes. Specifically, for 40-50 increment, where the alpha value in Eq. 1 and 3 of this technique is set to 80%-20%, and for 50-60 increment, with an alpha value of 83%-17%, it consistently performs better. In larger incremental steps, such as 20-40 and 40-60 increments, which corresponds to 50%-50% and 66%-33%, it performs better in the NC setting. We believe that these setting of the alpha value favors more the class of previous steps or the base classes. By examining the accuracy of both old and new classes in each sampling, we observe that the accuracy in older classes is generally better than in new ones. Additionally, when the number of classes to add is fewer than the existing classes, Weighted technique converges to its peak performance in a shorter time.

Table 3. Summary of the results obtained through training in two incremental steps "40-50" and "50-60" for NC, NINOC incremental groups

Incremental technique	Incremental step	NC-Acc (%)	NINOC-Acc (%)
Fixed	40–50	30.54 ± 4.88	49.09 ± 1.93
Expanded	40–50	37.10 ± 5.11	47.97 ± 1.55
Weighted	40–50	**55.42 ± 2.35**	**52.93 ± 5.25**
Fixed	50–60	19.32 ± 3.73	32.01 ± 2.81
Expanded	50–60	26.51 ± 3.65	33.14 ± 3.99
Weighted	50–60	**45.07 ± 1.18**	**42.99 ± 3.70**

We performed an extra test by freezing the entire model except for the last layer for all the techniques, and observed improved results. However, no technique consistently outperformed the others in our datasets. We believe that a more robust conclusion could be drawn through testing on more datasets.

In general, we could state that the Weighted Last Layer technique has the potential to be more robust across various incremental settings. While it exhibits superior performance in smaller increments, supported by the flexibility provided by adjusting the alpha value, fine-tuning the alpha value may present an opportunity for a more balanced learning approach between old and new classes.

6   Conclusions

We compared three class-incremental techniques for the case of a growing sign language dictionary that receives new classes and new instances of previous classes at each incremental step. Our results indicate that the Weighted Last Layer technique outperforms the other two techniques for new classes (NC) and new instances of new and old classes (NINOC). Our findings shed light on the future and more extensive work that should be performed to design and improve class-incremental learning in this and other related applications.

Acknowledgements. Results presented in this paper were obtained using the Chameleon testbed supported by the National Science Foundation [3]

References

1. Van de Ven, G.M., Tuytelaars, T., Tolias, A.S.: Three types of incremental learning. Nature Mach. Intell. 4(12), 1185–1197 Nature Publishing Group UK London (2022)
2. Yan, S., Xie, J., He, X.: DER: dynamically expandable representation for class incremental learning. In: Proceedings of the IEEE Conference on Computer Vision and Pattern Recognition (CVPR) (2021)
3. Keahey, K., et al.: Lessons learned from the chameleon testbed. In: Proceedings of the 2020 USENIX Annual Technical Conference (USENIX ATC 2020). USENIX Association (2020)
4. Liu, Y., Schiele, B., Sun, Q.: Adaptive aggregation networks for class-incremental learning. In: IEEE/CVF Conference on Computer Vision and Pattern Recognition (CVPR), pp. 2544–2553 (2020)
5. He, J., Mao, R., Shao, Z., Zhu, F.: Incremental learning in online scenario. In: 2020 IEEE/CVF Conference on Computer Vision and Pattern Recognition (CVPR), pp. 13923-13932 (2020). https://doi.org/10.1109/CVPR42600.2020.01394
6. Amaliya, S., Handayani, A., Akbar, M., Wahyu, H., Fukuda, O., Kurniawan, W.: Study on Hand Keypoint Framework for Sign Language Recognition, pp. 446-451 (2021). https://doi.org/10.1109/ICEEIE52663.2021.9616851
7. De Coster, M., Van Herreweghe, M., Dambre, J.: Sign language recognition with transformer networks. In: Proceedings of the Twelfth Language Resources and Evaluation Conference, pp. 6018–6024. European Language Resources Association, Marseille (2020)
8. Boháček, M., Hrúz, M.: Sign pose-based transformer for word-level sign language recognition. In: Proceedings of the IEEE/CVF Winter Conference on Applications of Computer Vision (WACV) Workshops, pp. 182–191 (2022)

9. Camillo, L., et al.: MediaPipe: A Framework for Building Perception Pipelines. ArXiv (2019)
10. McKee, R., Mckee, D.: The Online Dictionary of New Zealand Sign Language: A case study of contemporary sign language lexicography, pp. 495–520 (2017)
11. Bejarano, G., Huamani-Malca, J., Cerna-Herrera, F., Alva-Manchego, F., Rivas, P.: PeruSIL: a framework to build a continuous peruvian sign language interpretation dataset. In: Proceedings of the LREC2022 10th Workshop on the Representation and Processing of Sign Languages: Multilingual Sign Language Resources, pp. 1–8. European Language Resources Association, Marseille, France (2022)
12. Bragg, D., Rector, K., Ladner, R.E.: A user-powered American sign language dictionary. In: Proceedings of the 18th ACM Conference on Computer Supported Cooperative Work and Social Computing, pp. 1837–1848. Association for Computing Machinery, New York (2015)
13. Gupta, R.: Expanding Indian sign language recognition system using class incremental learning. In: 2022 International Conference on Advances in Computing, Communication and Materials (ICACCM), pp. 1–5 (2022). https://doi.org/10.1109/ICACCM56405.2022.10009218
14. Li, M., Cong, Y., Liu, Y., Sun, G.: Class-incremental gesture recognition learning with out-of-distribution detection. In: 2022 IEEE/RSJ International Conference on Intelligent Robots and Systems (IROS), pp. 1503–1508 (2022). https://doi.org/10.1109/IROS47612.2022.9981167
15. Maltoni, D., Lomonaco, V.: Continuous learning in single-incremental-task scenarios. Neural Networks **116**, 56–73 (2019). https://doi.org/10.1016/j.neunet.2019.03.010
16. Huang, B., Chen, Z., Zhou, P., Chen, J., Wu, Z.: Resolving task confusion in dynamic expansion architectures for class incremental learning. In: Proceedings of the AAAI Conference on Artificial Intelligence 37, pp. 908–916 (2023). https://doi.org/10.1609/aaai.v37i1.25170
17. Zhou, D.-W., Wang, Q.-W., Ye, H.-J., Zhan, D.-C.: A model or 603 exemplars: towards memory-efficient class-incremental learning. In: The International Conference on Learning Representations (2023)
18. Kumar Sah, R., Mirzadeh, S.I., Ghasemzadeh, H.: Continual learning for activity recognition. In: Annual International Conference of the IEEE Engineering in Medicine and Biology Society, pp. 2416–2420 (2022). https://doi.org/10.1109/EMBC48229.2022.9871690
19. Graffieti, G., Borghi, G., Maltoni, D.: Continual learning in real-life applications. IEEE Robot. Automation Lett. **7**(3), 6195–6202 (2022). https://doi.org/10.1109/LRA.2022.3167736
20. Wu, Y., et al.: Large scale incremental learning. In: 2019 IEEE/CVF Conference on Computer Vision and Pattern Recognition (CVPR), pp. 374–382 IEEE Computer Society, Los Alamitos, CA, USA (2019). https://doi.org/10.1109/CVPR.2019.00046

User-Agnostic Model for Retweets Prediction Based on Graph-Embedding Representation of Social Neighborhood Information

Pablo Gabriel Celayes[✉], Martín Ariel Domínguez, and Damián Barsotti

FaMAF, Universidad Nacional de Córdoba, Córdoba, Argentina
{celayes,mdoming,damian}@famaf.unc.edu.ar

Abstract. Predicting the content-sharing behavior of users is fundamental for improving our understanding of the processes of opinion shaping and information spread on social media. Twitter, in particular, is among the most interesting platforms to study, given its central role in social debate and the accessibility and richness of its data.

This paper continues to investigate the problem of developing a user-independent model for predicting retweets based on the retweeting behavior within the second-degree social neighborhood of the targeted user. Our proposed method uses node-level graph embeddings to create a compact feature representation of the targeted user and the retweeting activity within their neighborhood. This allows for effective learning through an XGBoost model. The model builds embeddings based on followership connections, eliminating the need for computing auxiliary network centrality or activity metrics as in previous work.

Despite its simplicity, this representation yields comparable performance to the previous approach based on aggregating neighborhood activity by centrality and activity metrics, attaining an F_1 score of 83.8% over a large test dataset containing tweets from sampled users. Furthermore, similar classification performance is also observed when analyzing individual users, regardless of their activity and centrality levels or whether they were observed during training.

Keywords: Retweet Prediction · Machine Learning · Graph Embeddings · XGBoost · Social Network Analysis

1 Introduction

In recent years, the public opinion has been shaped by social networking services, transforming the way individuals express themselves, stay informed, and influence each other. Within these services, Twitter stands as the most important online platform for real-time microblogging, offering users the capability to compose, read, and distribute short messages, wich are called tweets. At the heart of this social networking service is the "retweet" feature, which allows users to

ⓒ The Author(s), under exclusive license to Springer Nature Switzerland AG 2024
J. A. Lossio-Ventura et al. (Eds.): SIMBig 2023, CCIS 2142, pp. 107–120, 2024.
https://doi.org/10.1007/978-3-031-63616-5_8

choose and share tweets generated by users they follow. One of the distinguishing features of Twitter is that the generated content is public by default, offering structured data about user interactions easily accessible through the official API. This is why most of the research work in the area is about the Twitter platform.

Our paper develops and analyzes a general machine-learning model to predict user retweets. The task uses only the retweet dynamics within their immediate social environment. We employ graph-embedding techniques to represent users and their social interactions within equal-length vector representations to accomplish this. We build this model extending the results of our previous work [4], where we show that a single user-agnostic model, trained with data about different central users, can predict interactions for new users for which no retweet preference information was available during the training phase. To address this problem, we define a schema to aggregate neighborhood information into a fixed number of clusters and distinguished users. The present work applies a more streamlined technique to the problem of generating a model of the social environment activity. In this approach, we replace aggregated features with representations based on node-embeddings of the users in the graph of followership relation. This method still provides the advantages of being extensible to other users and offers a compact representation. However, it requires less feature engineering effort and eliminates the need for auxiliary computations related to network centrality and activity metrics.

The main contributions of this work are:

- The implementation of a graph-embedding-based model that achieves a comparable prediction performance to previous work that uses individual models. Furthermore, our results match those of previous heuristic-based models but with added generalization power, reduced training time, and simplified feature extraction.
- A detailed analysis of the prediction performance for both known and unknown users and comparisons with our previous approach based on neighborhood aggregation of retweet features.

The rest of this paper is structured as follows: Sect. 2 overviews related works. Section 3 describes how we build the datasets from Twitter for our experiments. Section 4 describes the model's technical details: the learning of graph embeddings for users and how they are combined for social feature extraction, the tuning and training process of the proposed model, and different evaluation methods. In Sect. 5, the obtained results are summarized and compared to the performance of single-user models. Finally, in Sect. 6. We finish presenting the conclusions and also include possible lines of future research.

2   Related Work

Along with social media's increased popularity and impact, the research interest has grown in modeling users' preferences and the distribution of popular content.

One exciting line of research on this problem focuses on the interactions and connections between users, regardless of the nature of the shared content.

In [4], we implemented a general model that uses centrality and activity metrics to distinguish a top-K of the most important neighbors and groups the rest in equal-sized buckets. This improved previous works since it established a shared framework to learn about multiple central users instead of training separate models for each central user. This approach was proved to attain prediction performance comparable to individual models, with much shorter training times. The present work seeks to maintain these models' generalization power and training advantages without using complex feature computation or auxiliary network and social activity metrics.

Previously [5], we had studied the prediction of retweets for a given user, using the behavior of users in their second-degree social neighborhood (followed, and followed by followed) to build a classifier that determines whether or not they will *retweet* a given post. Based purely on social information, these models achieved high predictive performance, with an average F_1 score of 87.6%. In that work, we also explored extending the models with content features for the cases where the purely social models were not performing well. Using a topic modeling algorithm adapted to tweets (TwitterLDA) obtains an average performance uplift of 1.7%.

In [14], we extended the previous work to the problem of predicting popularity within a community of users instead of just individual preferences. The target here was to build classifiers that could identify if a given tweet would become popular or not, based only on the activity that a selected set of *influencers* (i.e., highly central and active users) had on it. This work also leveraged features based on embeddings, not for the users themselves as in the present work, but to represent the text content of tweets. This second work utilizes a metric of user importance that combines user activity and network centrality. We adapt it to our problem to define a ranking of environment users that will enable us to extract general features. This work also proposes a unified model, but in contrast to the present paper, it is only applied to the prediction of collective preferences and cannot predict retweets of individual users.

In [11], we study the problem of individual retweet prediction and trend prediction based on the evolution in the amount of information available since the creation of the original tweet. The results establish an interesting trade-off between elapsed time and prediction performance, concluding that it is possible to reasonably predict the preference of a user retweet or how massive a publication will be, using only the information available during the first 30–60 minutes since creating a tweet. However, the models in this work are still either user-specific or general models that predict general preferences.

The 2020 and 2021 editions of the RecSys challenge [2] focused on a real-world task of tweet engagement prediction in a dynamic environment. The goal was to predict the probability for different types of engagement (Like, Reply, Retweet, and Retweet with Comment) of a target user for a set of tweets based on heterogeneous input data. It is worth noting that the winning approaches for both editions [13] [7] (and other competitors like [17]) make use of the XGBoost algorithm (combined with Deep Learning approaches in the 2021 edition). However, the problem is very different from ours: the predicted target is more generic, and even though user and tweet input data are richer than in our problem, there is no explicit information about the graph of followed connections being leveraged. Instead, the predictions are based solely on features about the content of the tweet being predicted, its author, and the user for which the engagement prediction is produced.

AnalytiCup [1] is another data analysis competition within the ACM International Conference on Information and Knowledge Management (CIKM). In the year 2020, one of the challenges was predicting the number of retweets during the COVID-19 pandemic. The solution that won first prize [12] used techniques similar to ours. The predictive algorithm presented was an ensemble of boosting models (LightGBM, Catboost) with a Deep Learning approach. Also, feature engineering was performed by extracting embeddings from graphs representing tweet-user, hashtag-users, and URL-user relationships using the PyTorch-biography library. Unlike our work, the solution employs inherent information from tweets (sentiment analysis of the text, hashtags, URLs, etc.).

3   Dataset

We now describe the datasets used in this work. We explain how we built the social graph of users and how we collected a dataset of tweets shared by them.

3.1   Social Graph

The experiments in this paper reutilize the dataset from our previous works [4] [5], which consists of Twitter users and the who-follows-whom relation between them. The motivation behind its construction was to create a representative subgraph of Twitter where all users would have a similar amount of social information about their neighborhood of connected users. The decision was to build a homogeneous network where each user would have the same number of followed users. To this end, we performed a two-step process: first, building a large enough *universe graph* and filtering it to get a homogeneous subgraph.

The *universe graph* was built starting with a singleton graph containing just one Twitter user account $\mathcal{U}_0 = \{u_0\}$ and performing 3 iterations of the following procedure: (1) Fetch all users followed by users in $\mathcal{U}_i$; (2) keep only those having at least 40 followers and following at least 40 accounts; (3) add filtered users and their edges to get an extended $\mathcal{U}_{i+1}$ graph. This process generated a *universe graph* $\mathcal{U} := \mathcal{U}_3$ with $2,926,181$ vertices and $10,144,158$ edges.

For the second step, a subgraph was extracted following the procedure below to get a homogeneous network.

- We started with a small sample of seed users S, consisting of users in $\mathcal{U}$ having out-degree 50, this is, users following exactly 50 other users.
- For each of those, we added their 50 most socially affine followed users. The affinity between two users was measured as the ratio between the number of users followed by both and the number of users followed by at least one of them.

– We repeated the last step for each newly added user until there were no more new users to add.

This filtering produced a graph $\mathcal{G}$ with $5,180$ vertices and $229,553$ edges called the homogeneous K-degree closure ($K = 50$ in this case) of S in the universe graph $\mathcal{U}$.

3.2   Content

For each user in the graph $\mathcal{G}$ we fetched their *timelines* (all tweets written or retweeted) for one month, from Aug 25th until Sep 24th, 2015. Finally, we only kept the tweets written in the Spanish language –according to their language tag in the Twitter API results–, resulting in a set $\mathcal{T}$ of $1,636,480$ tweets.

Visible Tweets. Using the Twitter API, we do not have explicit information about whether or not a user saw a given tweet. However, we can at least take a universe of *potentially viewed* tweets; then, we can use it as examples for training and testing our model. This set is the set of all the tweets written or shared by the users, followed by u. We exclude from this set those tweets *written* by u herself since our focus is on recognizing interesting external content and not on studying content generation from a particular user. Formally this set is defined as: $T(u) := \left(\bigcup_{x \in \{u\} \cup \mathtt{followed}(u)} \mathtt{timeline}(x) \right) - \{t \in \mathcal{T} | \mathtt{author}(t) = u\}$, where $\mathtt{followed}(u) := \{x \in \mathcal{G} | (u, x) \in \mathtt{follow}\}$, and $\mathtt{timeline}(x)$ is the set of all tweets written or retweeted by x for tweets fetched in $\mathcal{T}$.

Target Retweeted Label. The retweet prediction task is modeled as a binary classification problem where the target for a user u and a tweet $t \in T(u)$ is whether or not t was retweeted in the timeline of u: $y_{u,t} := \mathtt{tweet\_in\_tl}(t, u)$. Putting together all values of the target variable for user u and tweets in $T(u) = \{t_1, \ldots, t_m\}$, we obtain the target vector $y_u := [y_{t_i,u}]_{1 \leq i \leq m}$.

Down-Sampling of Negative Examples. For some users, the set $T(u)$ was too large, making experimenting and model training too computationally intensive. We decided to prune each $T(u)$ to a maximum of $5,000$ tweets, keeping all positive examples (the minority class) and randomly removing the necessary number of negative examples (non-retweets from u). This dataset still results in a highly imbalanced prediction problem, with only 2.58% of positive examples.

3.3   User Selection

Given their inherent unpredictability, we exclude *passive* users from our experiments, considering as such any users having less than 10 retweets in our dataset. Removing them leaves us with a set A of $3,240$ active users in $\mathcal{G}$. We also remove from $\mathcal{T}$ any tweets shared only by passive users.

3.4   Dataset Partitions

User Level Partition. In our previous work [5], the computational limitations of training one retweet prediction model per user led us to work with a small set U of 194 users, selected as the intersection of the top 1000 most active users (in terms of retweets in their timelines) and the top 1000 most central users (in terms of Katz centrality [8] in $\mathcal{G}$). In the interest of comparing the results of our general model to a good number of those users, we decided to reserve 50% of them for testing, resulting in a random partition of U into sets U_{train} and U_{test}, of 97 users each. For the remaining users in the set $V := A - U$, we randomly select 70% of them for training (V_{train}) and reserve 30% for test (V_{test}).

Tweet Level Partition For each user $u \in A$ we split her set $T(u)$ of visible tweets as follows:

– $T_{tr}(u) :=$ first 70% of tweets from $T(u)$, ordered by creation date.
– $T_{te}(u) :=$ last 30% remaining tweets.

We extend this notation to denote the combined training or test tweets of any set S of users. For instance $T_{tr}(S) := \bigcup_{u \in S} T_{tr}(u)$.

This split divides the data into 8 pieces, as seen in Fig. 1. Only the two partitions of training users and their training tweets will be used to train the model. The remaining data will be reserved for different types of evaluation (general performance, new tweets by known users, and unknown users).

			Tweets	
			70% train	30% test
A = active users from closed graph G with timelines (3240)	U = most active and central (194)	50% U_{tr} (97)	$T_{tr}(U_{tr})$	$T_{te}(U_{tr})$
		50% U_{te} (97)	$T_{tr}(U_{te})$	$T_{te}(U_{te})$
	V = A - U (3046)	70% V_{tr} (2111)	$T_{tr}(V_{tr})$	$T_{te}(V_{tr})$
		30% V_{te} (935)	$T_{tr}(V_{te})$	$T_{te}(V_{te})$

Fig. 1. Dataset partitions at user and tweet level. Only highlighted partitions will be used for training. The remaining ones are used for different types of evaluation.

4   Experimental Setup

In this section, we formulate the general user retweet prediction problem and describe the graph-embedding features and model that will be used to solve it, as well as the process of tuning hyperparameters, training, and evaluating against previous models.

4.1 Social Environment

Even though any user u can only see tweets shared by those users he follows, the information about the activity on her extended network can provide more indicators of the degree of interest of a tweet t. This is the reason why we decided to take as a user's environment not only the users she follows but also to continue one more step in the $\mathtt{follow}$ relation and include the users followed by them. Therefore, we take all users (other than u herself) to 1 or 2 steps forward from u in the directed graph $\mathcal{G}$, formally: $E_u = \left(\bigcup_{x \in \{u\} \cup \mathtt{followed}(u)} \mathtt{followed}(x) \right) - \{u\}$.

4.2 Raw Environment Features

For any user u and visible tweet $t \in T(u)$, the raw neighborhood features of t relative to u are defined as the boolean features describing which users from the social environment retweeted t. Formally, if we enumerate the neighbors in E_u as $\{u_1, u_2, \ldots, u_n\}$, we can define:

$$v_{u,t} := [\mathtt{tweet\_in\_tl}(t, u_i)]_{i=1,\ldots,n},$$

where $\mathtt{tweet\_in\_tl}(t, u) := \begin{cases} 1 & t \in \mathtt{timeline}(u) \\ 0 & \text{otherwise} \end{cases}$

The raw dataset assigned to a user u (denoted M_u) is the matrix that contains one row $v_{u,t}$ per tweet $t \in T(u)$ and has one column per user in E_u. Note that each M_u has a dimensionality $|E_u|$, which varies from one user to another.

4.3 Node-Embedding Environment Features

We aim to implement a general model that can learn from multiple users and be applied to any user. To do that, we need to transform these neighborhood-dependent features M_u into a fixed-length representation that doesn't depend on the given user.

The proposed transformation will be based on aggregations of node embeddings of the central user (u), its neighborhood (E_u), and the subset of its neighborhood retweeting the target tweet t:

$$E_{u,t} := \{v \in E_u | t \in \mathtt{timeline}(v)\}$$

Given a fixed embedding dimensionality d, a table of node-embeddings is learned over the graph $\mathcal{G}$ using the PyTorch-BigGraph library [9] to train a ComplEx [15] model, which produces a d-dimensional vector e_u for each $u \in \mathcal{G}$. This is achieved by running 7 epochs of minibatch stochastic gradient descent to minimize a softmax loss capturing the similarity between connected nodes.

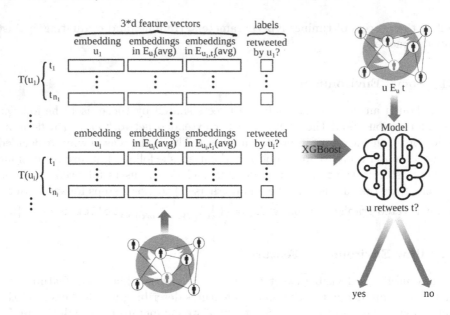

Fig. 2. Schematic of the experimental setup.

Using these embeddings, we represent the activity of t relative to u, as the concatenation between the embeddings of central users and the averages of embeddings of all neighbors and retweeting neighbors. Formally:

$$w_{u,t} = e_u \,||\, \overline{\{e_v | v \in E_u\}} \,||\, \overline{\{e_v | v \in E_{u,t}\}}$$

, where $\overline{S}$ represents the coordinate-wise mean of the set of embedding vectors S.

Note that this representation gives us a common length of $3 * d$ for the feature vector of any u, t pair, independent of the size of E_u, depending only on the chosen dimensionality d of the node embeddings. This will be treated as one additional hyperparameter and tuned jointly with the hyperparameters of the chosen classifier model.

In Fig. 2, we show a schematic of the whole experimental setup. On the left-hand side of the figure, we synthesized the featurization of the training phase, and on the right-hand side, we show how the resulting model is applied.

4.4   Classifier Model

For this work, we chose to use the XGBoost [6] gradient boosted trees classification algorithm, which gave us good results in our last paper [4] and makes better use of parallelism and is generally faster to train than the Support Vector Machines we used in previous works [5,11,14]. The classification performance of our algorithms will be measured using the F_1 score metric on the positive class, which is suitable for unbalanced problems like this one. It is important to remark that, for this work, we decided not to include content features of the tweets (NLP features like word embeddings). The results of previous works [4,5] show that the content of tweets has a marginal contribution to the classification.

4.5 Hyperparameter Tuning

Since hyperparameter tuning is a computationally expensive process, we chose to perform it on a smaller sample of training tweets, namely the set $T_{tr}(W)$ of training tweets corresponding to a set W of 200 randomly selected training users from $U_{train} \cup V_{train}$. $T_{tr}(W)$ consists of around $700,000$ examples.

We employed the hyperopt [3] Python package to perform an efficient bayesian search over the parameter space described by the intervals in Table 1. The process consisted of 20 iterations of 4-fold cross-validation over $T_{tr}(W)$, and the explored parameter space included both hyperparameters for the XGBoost classification algorithm and d_node_embeddings for the vector size of the embedding representation of users. The best CV F_1 score was 0.892, and it was obtained for the hyperparameter configuration detailed in the right column of Table 1 below:

Table 1. Intervals of hyperparameter values explored with hyperopt Bayesian search. This includes both hyperparameters for the XGBoost classifier and d for the neighborhood representations.

hyperparameter	search interval	best configuration
colsample_bytree	[0.5, 1]	0.7
eta	[0.025, 0.5]	0.075
gamma	[0.5, 1]	0.7
max_depth	[1, 13]	10
min_child_weight	[1, 6]	2.0
n_estimators	[50, 1000)	571
subsample	[0.5, 1]	0.95
d_node_embeddings	[10, 20, 50, 100]	100

4.6 Model Training

The model was trained using the training tweets from all training users, that is, the set $T_{tr}(U_{tr} \cup V_{tr})$, which consists of $7,535,386$ labeled (user, tweet) pairs. We will denote this trained general model with M_{emb}. We will denote with M_{gen} the general model based on features of aggregated and distinguished neighbors that we implemented in our previous work [4]. In the next section, we will perform a variety of evaluations of M_{emb} that reflect its performance under specific scenarios (known users, unknown users, comparison to individual models).

5   Results

We describe following the performance metrics obtained by our general retweet prediction model M_{emb}. We will perform the following evaluations:

- General F_1 score metrics over all test data.
- Comparison to the performance of single-user models.
- Evaluation over known vs. unknown users and how the performance is affected by users' activity level.

5.1   General Evaluation

To get a general metric of the classification performance of M_{emb}, we evaluate it over all the data not seen during training, that is $D_{test} := T_{te}(U_{tr}) \cup T_{tr}(U_{te}) \cup T_{te}(U_{te}) \cup T_{te}(V_{tr}) \cup T_{tr}(V_{te}) \cup T_{te}(V_{te})$. This dataset consists of $8,170,959$ samples, with $217,624$ positive labels (2.66%). The metrics obtained are:

   precision = 99.9%, recall = 72.2% and F_1 score = 83.8%.

These are very similar to the ones obtained for M_{gen}:

   precision = 99.5%, recall = 72.5% and F_1 score = 83.9%.

5.2   Comparison to Single User Models

We now proceed to compare the model to the performance of single-user models [5]. To this end, we consider all users in the selected set of active and central users U for which we built individual SVC classifier models in our previous works. The metrics obtained by M_{emb} over the combined set $T_{te}(U)$ of test tweets on all these users are: precision = 99.9%, recall = 77.4% and F_1 score = 87.3%.

For any user $u \in A$, we will denote with $F_1^{emb}(u)$ and $F_1^{gen}(u)$ the F_1 scores over $T_{te}(u)$ of the M_{emb} and M_{gen} models respectively. If $u \in U$, we denote with $F_1^{ind}(u)$ the F_1 score over $T_{te}(u)$ of the individual SVC model of u. The distributions of scores over U can be seen here:

	F_1^{emb}	F_1^{gen}	F_1^{ind}
mean	86.2%	85.5%	87.7%
std	0.128	0.155	0.109
Q1	80.9%	79.7%	82.4%
median	88.9%	89.2%	88.5%
Q3	96.0%	95.9%	95.9%

Fig. 3. Distribution of F_1 scores of general vs. individual models over selected 194 active and centrals users in U.

We observe that the mean F_1 score per user is 1.5% less for the general embedding model M_{emb}. For more difficult-to-learn users with lower scores (see lower quartile $Q1$), single-user models still perform better (1.5% higher at $Q1$). It is worth noting that here, the performance of the embeddings model is closer to individual models than that of the previous M_{gen} model. If we look at the median and upper quartile $Q3$, M_{emb} has similar scores to those of single-user models and the M_{gen} model.

It is also interesting to mention that M_{emb} achieved better scores than single-user models for 49 of the test users and 32 of the train users, which accounts for 42% of all the users in U.

5.3 Performance on General Users

We now turn away from the limitation to users in U imposed by individual models and analyze the performance of the M_{emb} model on more general users in V. We start by computing performance metrics over the combined set of samples of users from V not used during training; this is $D_{test}^V := T_{te}(V_{tr}) \cup T_{tr}(V_{te}) \cup T_{te}(V_{te})$ The metrics obtained by M_{emb} over D_{test}^V are:
precision $= 99.9\%$, recall $= 70.3\%$ and F_1 score $= 82.6\%$.
These are very similar to what was obtained for the M_{gen} model:
precision $= 99.4\%$, recall $= 70.7\%$ and F_1 score $= 82.6\%$.

5.4 Performance on Known Vs. Unknown Users

To understand the generalization power of the M_{emb} model, we compare its performance for users known during training versus previously unseen ones. In Fig. 5, we compare the distributions of F_1^{emb} scores for known and unknown users in the set of selected users U. In Fig. 4, we can see a similar analysis for the set of regular users V. Table 2 summarizes these distributions, extending the comparison to individual model performance for users in U.

We generally do not observe better performance for users known during training, which indicates that M_{emb} generalizes well to previously unseen users, the same as previously observed for the M_{gen} model. However, we observe that M_{emb} performs better for users in U, more active and central than those in V. In the case of known users, the mean F_1^{emb} score per user is 10.1% higher for users in U_{tr} than for users in V_{tr}. For unknown users, the corresponding difference (mean F_1^{emb} over U_{te} vs. V_{te}) is 10.4%.

Table 2. Distribution of F_1 scores on $T_{te}(u)$ over selected (U) and regular users (V), grouped by users known and unknown during training of M_{emb}.

	General embeddings model (M_{emb})				General heuristic model (M_{gen})				Individual models			
	Q1	mean	median	Q3	Q1	mean	median	Q3	Q1	mean	median	Q3
U_{tr}	79.2%	85.6%	89.1%	96.1%	79.5%	84.8%	89.2%	95.7%	83.1%	88.6%	91.8%	96.4%
U_{te}	80.1%	86.2%	88.9%	96.0%	80.0%	86.2%	89.4%	95.9%	82.1%	86.7%	87.3%	95.7%
V_{tr}	66.7%	75.5%	83.3%	94.1%	66.7%	75.4%	82.4%	93.7%				
V_{te}	66.7%	75.8%	84.2%	94.7%	66.7%	75.9%	83.6%	94.7%				

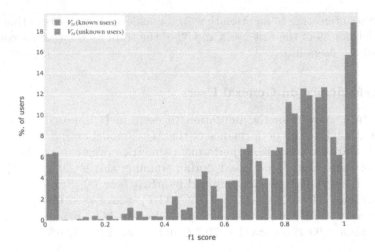

Fig. 4. Distribution of F_1 scores of M_{emb} over known vs. unknown regular users (V).

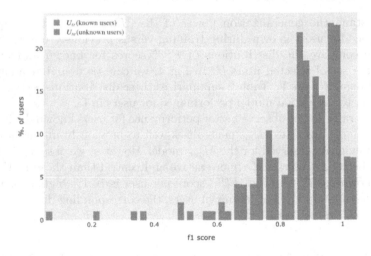

Fig. 5. Distribution of F_1 scores of M_{emb} over known vs. unknown selected users (U).

6   Conclusions and Future Work

In conclusion, it is possible to achieve good predictive performance for the individual retweet prediction problem by means of modeling the social neighborhood activity with graph embedding techniques. The results are on par with those previously obtained using aggregated features that required additional feature engineering work and computation of auxiliary activity and network centrality metrics. On the contrary, the graph-embeddings approach requires only information about user followership connections.

This research opens many doors to evolve the model. We describe next the most relevant to us.

Leveraging graph embeddings is a first step towards more sophisticated modeling techniques involving Graph Neural Networks [18], which can potentially capture the complexities of retweets happening in different positions of the network of neighborhood users and improve the performance of the predictions even further. Also, even though the presented model can handle users for whom we do not see any tweets during training, we still observe that the prediction quality is much higher for known users. Hence, it would be interesting to explore better ways of dealing with cold start users and better understand the relation between the amount of past activity and the prediction quality for each user. This is another aspect where GNN approaches can present an improvement since they enable the propagation of learned preferences across connected users. Additionally, the GNN architectures could be combined with others that capture the temporal sequence of retweet events, such as a Long Short-Term Memory (LSTM) neural network [10] or a Transformer architecture [16].

Another extension would be to incorporate content-related features into the general model. The challenge here is modeling content in a user-independent way. The difficulty of this direction lies in the fact that more information is needed to model the content of the target tweet, and, in addition, we need to encode somehow the content preferences of the user we are predicting for.

Finally, an interesting line of research is trying to replicate the experiments for other social networks such as Facebook, Instagram, or Sina Weibo, and see to what extent our conclusions apply to those. The purely social nature of the proposed model makes it suitable to be extended to any network of users sharing content, even in image-based networks such as Instagram. However, we are limited by the availability of data to build datasets.

References

1. CIKM 2020 AnalytiCup. https://cikm2020.org/analyticup/
2. Recsys challenge. https://recsys.acm.org/challenges/
3. Bergstra, J., Komer, B., Eliasmith, C., Yamins, D., Cox, D.D.: Hyperopt: a Python library for model selection and hyperparameter optimization. Comput. Sci. Disc. 8(1), 014008 (2015). http://stacks.iop.org/1749-4699/8/i=1/a=014008
4. Celayes, P.G., Domínguez, M.A., Barsotti, D.: User-agnostic model for prediction of retweets based on social neighborhood information. In: Lossio-Ventura, J.A., Valverde-Rebaza, J., Díaz, E., Alatrista-Salas, H. (eds.) Information Management and Big Data: 9th Annual International Conference, SIMBig 2022, Lima, Peru, November 16–18, 2022, Proceedings, pp. 18–31. Springer Nature Switzerland, Cham (2023). https://doi.org/10.1007/978-3-031-35445-8_2
5. Celayes, P.G., Domínguez, M.A.: Prediction of user retweets based on social neighborhood information and topic modelling. In: Castro, F., Miranda-Jiménez, S., González-Mendoza, M. (eds.) Advances in Computational Intelligence: 16th Mexican International Conference on Artificial Intelligence, MICAI 2017, Enseneda, Mexico, October 23-28, 2017, Proceedings, Part II, pp. 146–157. Springer International Publishing, Cham (2018). https://doi.org/10.1007/978-3-030-02840-4_12

6. Chen, T., Guestrin, C.: XGBoost: A scalable tree boosting system. In: Proceedings of the 22nd ACM SIGKDD International Conference on Knowledge Discovery and Data Mining, pp. 785–794. KDD '16, ACM, New York, NY, USA (2016). https://doi.org/10.1145/2939672.2939785
7. Deotte, C., Liu, B., Schifferer, B., Titericz, G.: Gpu accelerated boosted trees and deep neural networks for better recommender systems. In: RecSysChallenge '21: Proceedings of the Recommender Systems Challenge 2021. p. 7–14. RecSysChallenge 2021, Association for Computing Machinery, New York, NY, USA (2021). https://doi.org/10.1145/3487572.3487605
8. Katz, L.: A new status index derived from sociometric analysis. Psychometrika **18**(1), 39–43 (1953)
9. Lerer, A., et al.: PyTorch-BigGraph: A large-scale graph embedding system (2019). https://arxiv.org/abs/1903.12287
10. Lu, Z., Lv, W., Cao, Y., Xie, Z., Peng, H., Du, B.: Lstm variants meet graph neural networks for road speed prediction. Neurocomputing **400**, 34–45 (2020). https://doi.org/10.1016/j.neucom.2020.03.031, https://www.sciencedirect.com/science/article/pii/S0925231220303775
11. Meriles, E., Domínguez, M.A., Celayes, P.G.: Twitter early prediction of preferences and tendencies based in neighborhood behavior. In: Lossio-Ventura, J.A., Valverde-Rebaza, J.C., Díaz, E., Alatrista-Salas, H. (eds.) Information Management and Big Data: 7th Annual International Conference, SIMBig 2020, Lima, Peru, October 1–3, 2020, Proceedings, pp. 29–44. Springer International Publishing, Cham (2021). https://doi.org/10.1007/978-3-030-76228-5_3
12. Nguyen, T.T., et al.: Word and graph embeddings for covid-19 retweet prediction. In: 2020 International Conference on Information and Knowledge Management AnalytiCup, CIKM AnalytiCup 2020 **2881** (2020). https://api.semanticscholar.org/CorpusID:235484491
13. Schifferer, B., et al.: Gpu accelerated feature engineering and training for recommender systems. In: Proceedings of the Recommender Systems Challenge 2020, pp. 16–23. RecSysChallenge '20, Association for Computing Machinery, New York, NY, USA (2020). https://doi.org/10.1145/3415959.3415996
14. Silva, M., Domínguez, M., Celayes, P.: Analyzing the retweeting behavior of influencers to predict popular tweets with and without considering their content. In: Communications in Computer and Information Science, Springer, 5th International Conference on Information Management and Big Data (SimBig 2018). Springer, ISBN 978-3-030-02840-4 (2018)
15. Trouillon, T., Welbl, J., Riedel, S., Gaussier, É., Bouchard, G.: Complex embeddings for simple link prediction. CoRR **abs/1606.06357** (2016). http://arxiv.org/abs/1606.06357
16. Vaswani, A., et al.: Attention is all you need. In: Guyon, I., Luxburg, U.V., Bengio, S., Wallach, H., Fergus, R., Vishwanathan, S., Garnett, R. (eds.) Advances in Neural Information Processing Systems. vol. 30. Curran Associates, Inc. (2017). https://proceedings.neurips.cc/paper_files/paper/2017/file/3f5ee243547dee91fbd053c1c4a845aa-Paper.pdf
17. Volkovs, M., et al.: User engagement modeling with deep learning and language models. In: Proceedings of the Recommender Systems Challenge 2021, pp. 22–27. RecSysChallenge '21, Association for Computing Machinery, New York, NY, USA (2021). https://doi.org/10.1145/3487572.3487604
18. Zhou, J., Cui, G., Zhang, Z., Yang, C., Liu, Z., Sun, M.: Graph neural networks: a review of methods and applications (2018). http://arxiv.org/abs/1812.08434, arxiv:1812.08434

CollabVR: A Social VR Architecture for Social Interaction Between College Students

Diego Johnson⑩, Brayan Mamani⑩, and Cesar Salas⁽✉⁾⑩

Universidad Peruana de Ciencias Aplicadas, Lima, Peru
`cesar.salas@upc.edu.pe`

Abstract. This paper explores the challenges and solutions to the decrease in social interaction in the university environment due to the adoption of online classes. The proposal frames the use of Virtual Reality (VR) for the creation of CollabVR, a social interaction platform. CollabVR is based on a technological architecture oriented towards managing extracurricular activities in VR environments, with the aim of enhancing social interaction among university students. This architecture follows a microservices approach and includes a web application and a VR application. To assess the technological feasibility of CollabVR, a focus group of software architecture experts was organized. The results showed that 66% of them agreed that the proposed architectural diagrams provide a clear and complete representation of the interaction between users, devices, applications, and servers. In addition, 100% of the experts deemed the proposed solution as highly viable. They highlighted that the suggested services and components would contribute to significantly improve students' social interaction. In summary, the conceptual model of CollabVR provides a space for socialization, paving the way to enhance the remote educational experience and contributing to the social well-being of the students.

Keywords: Social interaction · Remote learning · Virtual Reality · Social Virtual Reality · Educational experience

1 Introduction

As a result of the pandemic, the implementation and adoption of asynchronous or remote learning have been promoted. Although technologies such as Learning Management Systems have provided the possibility to continue with online education, their use has generated some challenges related to the decline of social interaction (DSI).

DSI is an issue that affects the quality of learning and student performance. According to [1], it was identified that 71% of students experienced negative effects on their learning due to a lack of interaction between teachers and peers. Likewise, as indicated by [2], DSI results in a sense of isolation and lack of motivation in student learning, which negatively affects their commitment to the educational process.

UNESCO has recognized the importance of social interaction as a key component in the process of learning and human development [3]. On the other hand, there has been

J. A. Lossio-Ventura et al. (Eds.): SIMBig 2023, CCIS 2142, pp. 121–130, 2024.
https://doi.org/10.1007/978-3-031-63616-5_9

a growing interest in extracurricular activities (ECAs) in higher education, especially in developing countries. These activities, which go beyond the traditional academic curriculum, have shown to have a significant impact on the academic and professional development of students, as well as on their psychological well-being and their attitude towards community participation [4]. The social interactions that occur in ECAs are particularly valuable, as they enhance motivation, foster the construction of shared knowledge, and develop personal and social skills. Moreover, ECAs promote positive attitudes towards oneself and others, contributing to the development of a more sustainable society. This growing interest in ECAs in higher education is an important aspect to consider in the design of remote learning platforms that seek to improve social interaction among students.

Although there are education-focused solutions that use extended reality (XR) technologies, [5] identified that the role of XR technologies, particularly the capabilities of social virtual reality (SVR) in distance learning contexts, remains largely unexplored.

In this context, this paper proposes an architecture for CollabVR, a social platform in virtual reality aimed at promoting socialization among students. Unlike other VR platforms, a distinctive feature of CollabVR is its ability to allow universities to manage VR environments geared towards socialization. These environments are designed to promote interaction through ECAs such as clubs, presentations, cultural events, and workshops. The proposal addresses the emerging problem in higher education: the decrease in social interaction among students due to the adoption of remote classes. Furthermore, it relies on the growing interest in ECAs as an opportunity to promote social interaction and counteract the negative effects of remote learning.

To achieve this proposal, CollabVR integrates a web application with a VR application to offer a unified user experience. The platform employs microservices to ensure efficient modularization and management of its various functionalities. In designing CollabVR's architecture, we adopted both Attribute Driven Design and Domain Driven Design methodologies.

2   Related Works

DSI in classes has been a common problem in distance education. In this section, we will review some work related to social interaction in virtual environments.

Recent studies have shown the effectiveness of virtual reality platforms in enhancing social interaction in educational contexts. Xu [6] designed a VR platform to enable a virtual graduation ceremony amid the pandemic, resulting in an improvement in social interaction and participant satisfaction. The post-implementation survey indicated that the use of the platform was well received, with participants feeling little mental pressure or cognitive load during activities. Similarly, Mushtaha et al. [1] conducted a qualitative survey, where 75% of respondents approved a hybrid teaching scenario that combines online and in-person learning.

The potential of VR platforms to improve psychological health has also been explored, Barreda-Ángeles and Hartmann [7] provided a model of the associations between spatial and social presence and the psychological benefits of using VR platforms, with a qualitative analysis identifying the main activities and objectives of users in the use of VR environments, which were related to perceived psychological benefits, the study found that greater spatial and social presence is associated with more intense feelings of socialization. Siani and Marley [8] found that recreational use of VR can have a positive impact on physical and mental well-being during periods of social isolation. Their quantitative analysis indicated that almost 70% of participants reported spending 1 to 4 h in VR for recreational purposes, while a similar percentage reported using VR for physical conditioning purposes.

In addition to psychological benefits, the potential of VR to enhance communication and interpersonal skills has also been examined. In the study conducted by Baccon et al. [9], they compared self-disclosure in face-to-face, virtual reality, and text-based communication, suggesting that virtual reality could be as effective as face-to-face communication in facilitating self-disclosure and interpersonal communication. Yan and Lv [10] also found that communication through VR is more efficient and natural than text-based communication, with users reporting a communication experience more similar to face-to-face communication. The study used a Likert scale to evaluate the VR communication model and found that users reported a significantly more positive experience with VR communication than with text-based communication.

Finally, in a study conducted Young et al. [5], they indicate that Social VR can potentially address the shortcomings of existing virtual learning environments. Therefore, there is a need for further in-depth reflection on how pedagogical approaches and methods are implemented to effectively use virtual reality technology, to investigate the impact of these technologies and how they can contribute to the design of instruction systems for remote classroom experiences.

These studies demonstrate the potential of virtual environments using VR to improve social interaction, psychological well-being, and communication skills in university education.

3 Main Contribution

In this section, the main concepts and the principal contribution of this study will be presented.

3.1 Preliminary Concepts

Here, the main concepts used in our proposal are presented.

VR and SVR, part of the XR technology that also includes Augmented Reality, is an artificial experience that immerses the user in a 3D space visually isolated from the physical world [11]. This technology extends to SVR, an interactive 3D space where users communicate through real-time tracked full-body avatars. This interaction, similar to face-to-face communication, includes voice, gestures, proxemics, gaze, and facial expression [12], and can enhance communication among geographically dispersed groups [13]. CollabVR, our proposal, aspires to be a SVR environment as described, fostering interaction and collaboration in a virtual space.

Microservices. This is a design approach where an application is built as a collection of small services, each running in its own process and communicating with lightweight mechanisms [14, 15]. In the context of CollabVR, we are employing microservices to handle the business logic that a platform like ours requires, ensuring scalability and flexibility.

Attribute-Driven Design (ADD). This is a method that uses quality attributes as a basis to guide the design process of a system's architecture [16]. In the context of CollabVR, ADD is applied to shape the system's architecture, allowing informed decisions that reinforce identified quality attributes: scalability and performance [17], availability and security [18].

Domain-Driven Design (DDD). This is an approach to software design that focuses on understanding the business domain and seeks to reflect this structure in the application design, leading to a more organized application [19]. Moreover, DDD is a popular approach to identifying microservices by modeling subdomains and context maps [20]. In our project, we are use DDD for the software architecture design process, ensuring that our application faithfully reflects the business domain and is structured efficiently.

3.2 Method

This article seeks to propose the architecture for CollabVR, an SVR platform designed for universities. CollabVR facilitates ECAs such as clubs, presentations, cultural events, and workshops, aiming to support and enhance the social interactions of remote students.

This architectural proposal has been meticulously crafted to address the inherent challenges of virtual collaboration in SVR environments. To this end, we employed the ADD approach with the aim of creating a general structure of the system based on identified quality attributes.

Solution Architecture. We can see the general flow of the application, with the types of users, the devices they use to interact with CollabVR, and the main technologies used for the web application, the VR application, and the server (See Fig. 1).

As shown, CollabVR is composed of two applications:

VR Platform: Developed in Unity, it offers a cross-platform solution, allowing students and moderators to connect and participate in ECAs in a collaborative environment. The application will be accessible from personal computers, mobile devices, or using VR headsets, such as Oculus Quest.

Web Application: Built in Angular, it is designed for administrators to manage the activities that will take place within the VR platform. Here is where they can create different types of activities using the default available assets or customized assets that seek to represent the university identity. Moreover, it is where metrics about the activities that are performed can be visualized.

The main features of CollabVR are presented. Furthermore, based on the concepts of DDD, we identify the subdomains belonging to our solution that can be observed in the services column (See Fig. 2).

With these considerations, the proposed architecture for CollabVR was developed following the microservices approach, which goes hand in hand with DDD (See Fig. 3).

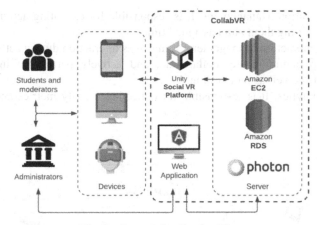

Fig. 1. General Application Flow

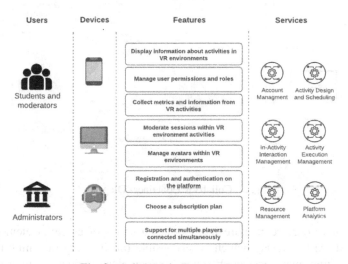

Fig. 2. Collab Main Features Proposal

This container diagram illustrates the server, where each microservice encapsulates a subdomain of our solution providing a structure with less coupling between software components. In this way, system maintainability and scalability are ensured. The responsibilities of each microservice are explained below:

- Account Management: It oversees account management, roles, and user authentication.
- Activity Design and Scheduling: It is responsible for the design and scheduling of activities, allowing administrators to create and schedule events such as clubs, workshops, and conferences.
- Assets Management: It handles assets management, such as activity templates and virtual rooms, ensuring their availability and efficient use in the environments.

- Activity Execution Management: It is responsible for executing activities, such as starting and ending them at an assigned time.
- In-Activity Interaction Management: It manages interaction during activities, allowing users to communicate, collaborate, and actively participate in the virtual environment, as well as moderation.
- Platform Analytics: It is responsible for collecting activity metrics and generating reports.

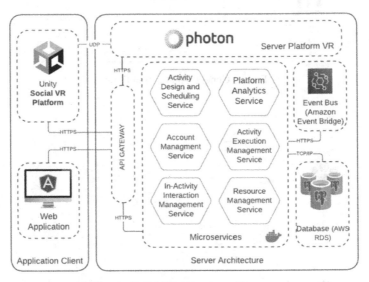

Fig. 3. CollabVR Containers Diagram.

To conclude, our architecture incorporates a series of essential elements for its operation. An API Gateway, which is responsible for directing incoming requests to the corresponding microservices. Likewise, communication between microservices is orchestrated through an Event Bus, which uses a publish-subscribe event system. Additionally, real-time interactions within the VR platform are managed through Photon Unity Networking (PUN), ensuring a seamless experience. By integrating these components, CollabVR would become a scalable and resilient SVR platform designed to foster socialization.

Hypothesis: The CollabVR platform, based on the proposed VR architecture, has the potential to offer easy management, scalability, and efficient performance for social interaction among college students.

4 Experimentation

4.1 Experimental Protocol

In this section, the Virtual Focus Group aimed at software architecture experts is described. The goal was to evaluate the perception and usefulness of the proposed architecture diagram to support CollabVR's functionalities, with the objective of improving social interaction. To recruit participants, an email was sent to four professors from the Universidad Peruana de Ciencias Aplicadas who teach software architecture courses, as well as a graduate from the Software Engineering program at the same university. The experts who agreed to participate were sent a questionnaire with 4 open-ended questions and Likert scale responses regarding the extent to which the proposed architecture contributes to social interaction and suggestions for possible improvements. As a result, in-depth opinions from three experts who completed the survey between June 7th and June 12th, 2023, in Lima, Peru, were recorded.

Participants. Among the 3 participants, all 3 are males, two are Computer Engineers working as Software Architects in MTC and Seguros Rimac, and the third participant is a Software Engineer who worked as a Quality Engineer at Snapchat and currently works at Blizzard. The participants' experience ranges from 5 years to over 10 years working with Software Architectures in real-world solutions.

4.2 Results

After analyzing the results of the Focus Group, Microsoft Excel was used to process the questionnaire data, which allowed obtaining quantifiable results such as:

- 66% of the experts agreed that the proposed architecture diagrams provide a clear and comprehensive representation of the interaction between users, devices, applications, and servers in virtual reality environments. They suggested that it would be beneficial to include a use case diagram and recommended segmenting and establishing relationships at the microservices level. On the other hand, 33% had a neutral opinion, suggesting that a deployment diagram of the proposed solution could be included.
- 100% of the experts agreed that the proposed architecture for CollabVR would contribute to the improvement of social interaction among students. They considered that the microservices-based architecture would be essential when it comes to scaling the system with a larger number of users, which would benefit the application's performance and ensure smooth interaction between users. Additionally, they mentioned that the proposed components would contribute to social interaction and could be utilized by academic staff. They believed that such services are ideal for complementary classes that aim to achieve student engagement.
- 100% of the experts considered the proposed solution to be highly viable, arguing that the field of virtual reality applications in the university context is still in an early stage and lacks an established leading solution. They highlighted that the necessary technological elements are becoming increasingly accessible, which boosts the potential for the proposal's success. Furthermore, they pointed out that virtual reality technology is reaching significant levels of maturity, allowing for the development of an optimal solution tailored to the specific needs of the sector.

Regarding the qualitative questions, the following was obtained:

- The experts stated that usability is the most important quality attribute of CollabVR, as it is essential to ensure that the application is easy to use and understand, enabling users to engage in socialization activities efficiently and effortlessly. They also mentioned that usability should include voice communication functionality, and the solution should support it, as it would enhance interaction and facilitate user participation. Additionally, the importance of the security attribute was highlighted. The experts mentioned that strengthening authentication mechanisms is crucial to ensure data protection and user privacy, which is vital in an academic environment.

Based on the feedback received, it is inferred that CollabVR has the potential to significantly improve the "social interaction" variable, suggesting that the platform's architecture is suitable for addressing the current challenges of distance education.

4.3 Discussion

Based on the results obtained, it is established that the proposed architecture for managing virtual reality environments for ECAs in universities contributes favorably to social interaction among asynchronous or remote university students.

Consequently, the DSI due to the adoption of asynchronous teaching and online education would improve with the implementation of CollabVR, providing asynchronous students with the possibility to interact in immersive and remote ECAs.

5 Conclusions and Perspectives

The current study addresses an emerging issue in higher education: the decline in social interaction among students due to the adoption of remote classes. In response to this challenge, we have conducted a literature analysis, based on which we have proposed the architectural design of CollabVR, a virtual reality platform aiming to offer students in remote learning scenarios a means to actively engage in and benefit from ECAs, which are crucial for a comprehensive educational experience.

The validation of our proposal by experts has been generally positive, highlighting the clarity and comprehensiveness of the architectural diagrams. However, although the experts see potential in the proposed architecture to enhance social interaction and believe the solution is feasible in the current context of higher education, it's important to note that this validation is based on the architecture and not on actual user testing.

These findings lead us to conclude that the proposed architecture for CollabVR has the technical potential to be a valuable tool in improving social interaction among students in a remote educational environment. It not only provides a space for socialization but also offers opportunities for engagement in ECAs. Nonetheless, it is essential to conduct further research evaluating usability, acceptability, and user appropriation to determine its real effectiveness in enhancing social interaction among college students.

Looking towards the future, we see a horizon full of possibilities for the expansion and improvement of CollabVR and other similar initiatives. In this regard, we propose three possible directions for future projects:

- Develop VR architecture and application using the proposed architecture: A future direction would be to create a robust and scalable SVR platform that allows students to participate in ECAs and socialize in an immersive virtual environment, utilizing the proposed architecture as a foundation.
- Evaluate the impact of CollabVR on social interaction: Another important area for future projects would be to conduct a comprehensive analysis of how students interact in CollabVR and how they are affected by its functionalities. This study would provide empirical data on the frequency and quality of students' social interaction, which would help optimize the design and functionality of CollabVR in future versions.
- Sentiment analysis to overcome barriers of shyness and social isolation: Using artificial intelligence, CollabVR could identify signs of shyness or social isolation in students' interactions and respond by adapting the platform and suggesting activities to foster less intimidating social interaction, thereby creating a more inclusive and welcoming environment.

References

1. Mushtaha, E., Abu Dabous, S., Alsyouf, I., Ahmed, A., Abdraboh, N.R.: The challenges and opportunities of online learning and teaching at engineering and theoretical colleges during the pandemic. Ain Shams Eng. J. **13**(6), 2090–4479 (2022). https://doi.org/10.1016/j.asej.2022.101770
2. Canela-Ruano, A., Arboleda, R., Pessina, M.: Efectos y perspectivas de la educación en pandemia y la interacción social en las relaciones de enseñanza y aprendizaje. Caso de la Universidad UTE. Tsafiqui Revista Científica En Ciencias Sociales **12**(18), 64–75 (2022). https://doi.org/10.29019/tsafiqui.v12i18.1037
3. Unesco. https://learningportal.iiep.unesco.org/es/fichas-praticas/mejorar-el-aprendizaje/el-entorno-psicosocial-de-la-escuela. Accessed 20 June 2023
4. Díaz-Iso, A., Eizaguirre, A., García-Olalla, A.: Understanding the role of social interactions in the development of an extracurricular university volunteer activity in a developing country. Int. J. Environ. Res. Public Health **17**(12), 4422 (2020). https://doi.org/10.3390/ijerph17124422
5. Young, G.W., O'Dwyer, N.C., Smolic, A.: A case study on student experiences of social VR in a remote STEM classroom. In: Extended Abstracts of the 2023 CHI Conference on Human Factors in Computing Systems (CHI EA 2023), no. 374, pp. 1–8. Association for Computing Machinery, New York (2023). https://doi.org/10.1145/3544549.3573852
6. Xu, X.: To social with social distance: a case study on a VR-enabled graduation celebration amidst the pandemic. Virtual Real. (2022). https://doi.org/10.1007/s10055-022-00646-2
7. Barreda-Ángeles, M., Hartmann, T.: Psychological benefits of using social virtual reality platforms during the Covid-19 pandemic: the role of social and spatial presence. Comput. Hum. Behav. **127** (2022). https://doi.org/10.1016/j.chb.2021.107047
8. Siani, A., Marley, S.A.: Impact of the recreational use of virtual reality on physical and mental wellbeing during the Covid-19 lockdown. Health Technol. **11**, 425–435 (2021). https://doi.org/10.1007/s12553-021-00528-8
9. Baccon, L.A., Chiarovano, E., MacDougall, H.G.: Virtual reality for teletherapy: avatars may combine the benefits of face-to-face communication with the anonymity of online text-based communication. Cyberpsychol. Behav. Soc. Netw. **22**(2), 158–165 (2019). https://doi.org/10.1089/cyber.2018.0247

10. Yan, Z., Lv, Z.: The influence of immersive virtual reality systems on online social application. Appl. Sci. **10**(15), 5058 (2020). https://doi.org/10.3390/app10155058
11. Rauschnabel, P.A., Felix, R., Hinsch, C., Shahab, H., Alt, F.: What is XR? Towards a framework for augmented and virtual reality. Comput. Hum. Behav. **133** (2022). https://doi.org/10.1016/j.chb.2022.107289
12. Freeman, G., Maloney, D.: Body, avatar, and me: the presentation and perception of self in social virtual reality. Assoc. Comput. Mach. **4**, CSCW3 (2021). https://doi.org/10.1145/3432938
13. Burova, A., et al.: Distributed asymmetric virtual reality in industrial context: enhancing the collaboration of geographically dispersed teams in the pipeline of maintenance method development and technical documentation creation. Appl. Sci. **12**(8), 3728 (2022). https://doi.org/10.3390/app12083728
14. Merson, P., Yoder, J.: Modeling microservices with DDD. In: 2020 IEEE International Conference on Software Architecture Companion (ICSA-C), Salvador, Brazil, pp. 7–8 (2020). https://doi.org/10.1109/ICSA-C50368.2020.00010
15. Dave, C.V., Patel, A., Keshri, U.: Microservices software architecture: a review. Int. J. Res. Appl. Sci. Eng. Technol. **9**(11), 1494–1496 (2021). https://doi.org/10.22214/ijraset.2021.39036
16. Suaza, C.A.A., Plaza, J.E.G., Gamboa, A.X.R.: Impacto del método attribute-driven design ADD 3.0 en la definición de arquitecturas de software. In: Ingeniería y Desarrollo en la Nueva Era. Instituto Antioqueño de Investigación (IAI), pp. 768–778 (2022)
17. Latoschik, M.E., Kern, F., Stauffert, J.-P., Bartl, A., Botsch, M., Lugrin, J.-L.: Not alone here?! Scalability and user experience of embodied ambient crowds in distributed social virtual reality. IEEE Trans. Vis. Comput. Graph. **25**(5), 2134–2144 (2019). https://doi.org/10.1109/TVCG.2019.2899250
18. Valluripally, S., Gulhane, A., Mitra, R., Hoque, K.A., Calyam, P.: Attack trees for security and privacy in social virtual reality learning environments. In: 2020 IEEE 17th Annual Consumer Communications & Networking Conference (CCNC), Las Vegas, NV, USA, pp. 1–9 (2020). https://doi.org/10.1109/CCNC46108.2020.9045724
19. Hippchen, B., Schneider, M., Landerer, I., Giessler, P., Abeck, S., Lavazza, L.: Methodology for splitting business capabilities into a microservice architecture: design and maintenance using a domain-driven approach. In: The Fifth International Conference on Advances and Trends in Software, Valencia, Spain (2019). https://www.researchgate.net/publication/332833041
20. Kapferer, S., Zimmermann, O.: Domain-driven service design. In: Dustdar, S. (ed.) SummerSOC 2020. CCIS, vol. 1310, pp. 189–208. Springer, Cham (2020). https://doi.org/10.1007/978-3-030-64846-6_11

Analysis of Mexican Women's Decision-Making Power Using Machine Learning Strategies

Paulina Aldape Bretado�ⓘ, Mariano de Jesús Gómez Espinozaⓘ,
Juanita Hernández López(✉)ⓘ, Azucena Yoloxóchitl Ríos Mercadoⓘ,
and Alvaro Eduardo Cordero Francoⓘ

Universidad Autónoma de Nuevo León, Pedro de Alba s/n San Nicolás de los Garza,
Nuevo León C.P. 66451, Mexico
{paulina.aldapebrtd,mariano.gomezes,juanita.hernandezl,
azucena.riosmr,alvaro.corderofr}@uanl.edu.mx

Abstract. In Mexico, as in the rest of the world, there are different problems to solve regarding social analysis. One of them is gender violence, which primarily affects women. Thanks to the development of technology and algorithms based on artificial intelligence, it is possible to use techniques capable of determining situations of violence. This article uses two of these algorithms to classify Mexican women's decision-making power in the home. The methodology employed included the ENDIREH 2016 database, with 29,708 records. Experiments were conducted employing Random Forest and k-Nearest Neighbors algorithms. The results suggest no statistical difference between the methods with a $p=0.741$ Student's t-test value. Both algorithms obtained 99% in terms of accuracy, sensitivity, and specificity and a false-positive ratio of 0.31% and 0.33%, respectively.

Keywords: Social analysis · Women's decision-making power · Machine learning

1 Introduction

Computational methods based on artificial intelligence (AI) allow us to identify patterns automatically and detect groups of interest for further analysis and interpretation. Currently, AI is gaining relevance in different areas of knowledge, being used in sentiment analysis, in the social analysis of behavior patterns (among which is gender violence), and the analysis of the social behavior patterns of women [10,11]. In Mexico, as in other countries, gender violence is one of the leading public problems that mainly affects women [4,5]. Data from the National Institute of Women in Mexico reveal that in 2020 there was a daily average of 11 female victims of intentional homicide and femicide[1]. Also, this

---

[1] https://mexico.unwomen.org.

© The Author(s), under exclusive license to Springer Nature Switzerland AG 2024
J. A. Lossio-Ventura et al. (Eds.): SIMBig 2023, CCIS 2142, pp. 131–141, 2024.
https://doi.org/10.1007/978-3-031-63616-5_10

same source revealed in 2021 that during the SARS-CoV2 health emergency, violence in conditions of confinement disproportionately affected women and girls[2].

Some of the first approaches for the automatic analysis of gender violence in Mexico are the decision-making power index and the violentometer. The decision-making power index establishes women's decision-making power based on their performance in three distinct areas of decision-making in couple relationships: control over the woman's life and children, control of fertility, and household decisions [2,9][3], while the violentometer is a tool that divides the different types of violence into three conglomerate segments: "be careful!", "react!", and "need professional help!"[4].

In the literature, we find some works in which machine learning has been used to analyze violence. Rodríguez et al. [11] propose a computational method for forecasting spousal violence in Spanish women; this method is based on time series analysis. The work of Muraleedharan et al. [10] is based on audio analysis and a deep-learning strategy for detecting domestic violence. On the other hand, Lu et al. [7] have proposed a machine learning method for the prediction of aggregation in the Chinese population. Another paper, by Yallico et al. [13], analyzed multimedia information to detect violence against women. In addition, Miranda et al. [8] propose analyzing tweets to identify gender violence in Mexico. These are some of the recent works related to the detection and identification of violent patterns toward women. As can be seen, most of these works aim to identify some violence against women. However, no article is related to classifying women's decision-making power using machine learning algorithms.

The main contribution to state of the art is a method for automatically classifying Mexican women's decision-making power. The sections of the article are divided into (1) Introduction, (2) Materials and methods, (3) Results, and (4) Conclusions and future work.

2   Materials and Methods

2.1   Methodology

Figure 1 describes the development methodology used. The following subsections detail the procedure performed further.

2.2   Database

The database was obtained from the National Survey on the Dynamics of Household Relationships 2016 (ENDIREH 2016) conducted by the National Institute of Statistics and Geography (INEGI) in Mexico. This database provides

---

[2] http://cedoc.inmujeres.gob.mx.

[3] http://cedoc.inmujeres.gob.mx/documentos_download/100925.pdf.

[4] https://www.ipn.mx/genero/materiales/violentometro.html.

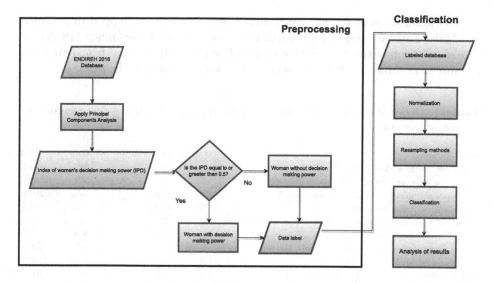

Fig. 1. Flow chart of the development methodology used.

information regarding women's experiences of violence (family, intimate partner, school, work, and community). It collects information on the aggressor(s)
and the place where the physical, economic, sexual, emotional, or patrimonial
aggression occurred. The age range of the women surveyed is 15 years and older.
The database has a total of 29,708 records. This compilation of records was
obtained using information from Section 14 in the national survey and focused
on the responses of women interviewed who were married or in a free union,
either with a resident partner or with a partner who was temporarily absent at
the time of the survey.

Section 14 of the national survey is called "Decisions and Personal Freedom."
It addresses questions about the dynamics of the decisions made in the household
and includes 15 scenarios or questions, of which only 11 were considered in this
paper as a reference to the methodology proposed by Castro and Casique [2].
Table 1 shows the distribution of the 11 questions related to women's decision-
making in Mexican households.

The possible answers that could be given by the interviewees to the 11 scenarios posed are the following: "Only you (the interviewee)", "Only your husband or
partner", "Between the two of you, but he a little more", "Between the two of you,
but you a little more", "Between the two of you equally", "Other people" or "Does
not apply". "Other people" or "Does not apply" were excluded from the analysis
to analyze women's decision-making power within a couple's relationship. Thus,
the codes assigned to the response categories are (1) only the husband or partner,
(2) between the two (both), and (3) only the woman (respondent). We merged
the answers "Between the two of you, but he a little more", "Between the two of
you, but you a little more", and "Between the two of you equally" into category
2, because all these responses describe the input of both parties.

To obtain the dataset, the categorical feature space was mapped to a numerical feature space using the principal component analysis technique (PCA) [3]. The application of this technique consists of mapping the dataset from categories to numerical values so that the range of data was bounded in the range of $[-1,1]$.

Table 1. Distribution of the information in the database for the 29,708 records considered in this study.

Who decides...	Only he	Between the two	Only her	Total
1. Are you able to work or study?	6%	39%	55%	100%
2. Can you leave your home?	5%	27%	68%	100%
3. Are you able to use the money you have earned?	4%	41%	56%	100%
4. Can you buy things for yourself?	3%	24%	74%	100%
5. Can you participate in your community's social or political life?	4%	31%	65%	100%
6. Who spends or saves money?	5%	57%	38%	100%
7. Can you give permission to your children?	4%	78%	17%	100%
8. Can you move out of the house or city?	7%	82%	11%	100%
9. Who decides when to have sexual relations?	3%	88%	8%	100%
10. Are you using a contraceptive method?	3%	79%	18%	100%
11. Who should use contraceptive methods?	4%	75%	21%	100%

2.3   Principal Component Analysis for Labeling Data

For constructing the decision-making power index, factor analysis was applied using the Principal Component Analysis technique (PCA) [3]. This analysis is the starting point to integrate the 11 variables of the survey and to obtain through their addition an index of decision-making power as suggested by Castro and Casique [2].

PCA is based on two important mathematical concepts known as eigenvectors and eigenvalues. Each principal component is obtained by a linear combination of the original variables so that each can capture the whole's variance. For example, the first principal component of a group of variables $(X_1, X_2, \ldots, X_p)$ is the normalized linear combination of these variables that has the highest variance. The following equation represents this:

$$Z_1 = \phi_{11}X_1 + \phi_{21}X_2 + \ldots + \phi_{p1}X_p \tag{1}$$

Weights (ϕ) can be interpreted as the importance of each variable in each component. Therefore, they help us determine what type of information is collected by each component.

It is essential to mention that, before applying the PCA, Bartlett's Sphericity test was applied to the data to find a correlation between the variables. The test resulted in a p-value of 0, which indicates that the null hypothesis can be rejected with a 95% confidence level, further indicating that the correlation between each pair of variables is zero. The results obtained through the PCA are presented in Table 2.

Table 2. Factors identified in the PCA and explained variance.

Factor	Autovalues	% Variance	Accumulated Variance
1	4.4	39.63%	39.63%
2	1.7	15.67%	55.30%
3	1.0	8.93%	64.24%
4	0.7	6.74%	70.97%
5	0.6	5.23%	76.20%
6	0.5	4.97%	81.17%
7	0.5	4.66%	85.83%
8	0.5	4.12%	89.95%
9	0.4	3.96%	93.91%
10	0.4	3.60%	97.51%
11	0.3	2.49%	100%

Based on this analysis, it was determined that the number of factors to be considered is three, which explains 64% of the variance, similar to the findings of Castro and Casique [2], where they considered three factors for their analysis with 61% percent of variance explained.

In addition, the principal components matrix allows us to identify, through the correlation values, the variables that make up each of the three factors considered. The values of each of the components are represented in Table 3. The three factors identified are integrated as follows:

- **Factor 1** comprises decisions related to the woman, whether she can work or study, whether she can leave the house, what to do with the money she earns, whether she can buy things for herself, whether she can actively participate in her community, and how money is spent or saved in the home. We identify this factor as the sub-index of women's control and it represents 40% of the variance.
- **Factor 2** comprises decisions about when to have sex and whether to use contraceptives. We identify this factor as the fertility control sub-index and it represents 16% of the variance.
- **Factor 3** comprises household decisions regarding permissions for children, moving out of the house or city, and who should use contraceptive methods. We identify this factor as the sub-index of household control and it represents 9% of the variance.

The sub-indices generated from each of the factors are summed and divided by their maximum value to obtain a range of values between [0,1] and thus we are able to generate the index of women's decision-making power (IPD), as shown in the equation below:

$$IPD = (Factor\ 1 * 0.3963) + (Factor\ 2 * 0.1517) + (Factor\ 3 * 0.0893) \qquad (2)$$

Table 3. Principal components matrix. In the last column, the factor associated with each question.

Questions	PC1	PC2	PC3	Factor
1. Are you able to work or study?	−0,2978	0,2418	−0,0128	Factor 1
2. Can you leave your home?	−0,3199	0,2968	−0,1066	Factor 1
3. Are you able to use the money you have earned?	−0,3323	0,2630	−0,0564	Factor 1
4. Can you buy things for yourself?	−0,3193	0,3029	−0,1524	Factor 1
5. Can you participate in your community's social or political life?	−0,3247	0,2657	−0,0780	Factor 1
6. Who spends or saves money?	−0,3162	0,1072	0,1758	Factor 1
7. Can you give permission to your children?	−0,2863	−0,2199	0,4605	Factor 3
8. Can you move out of the house or city?	−0,2835	−0,2559	0,5109	Factor 3
9. Who decides when to have sexual relations?	−0,2846	−0,3663	0,1657	Factor 2
10. Are you using a contraceptive method?	−0,2823	−0,4324	−0,4222	Factor 2
11. Who should use contraceptive methods?	−0,2611	−0,4188	−0,4962	Factor 3

The percentage of variance explained will be the weighting of each factor generated. The index of women's decision-making power is integrated according to their performance in three different areas of decision-making: control over the woman (Factor 1), fertility control (Factor 2), and control in the home (Factor 3). This index has a range of values from 0 to 1, where values close to 0 represent the cases of those women without any decision-making power when all or almost all decisions are made by their male partners. At the same time, values close to 1 are equivalent to the other extreme: those women who make each decision autonomously without involving their male partners.

A threshold was used to obtain a class label based on decision power α of 0.5 to decide which women have decision-making power in the home ($\alpha \geq 0.5$) and those that do not have it or it is limited ($\alpha < 0.5$). It is worth mentioning that this last class includes cases with little or no decision-making power. Thus, the distribution of the total number of records in the database is shown in Fig. 2, where 58% of women have decision-making power and the remaining 42% have limited decision-making power.

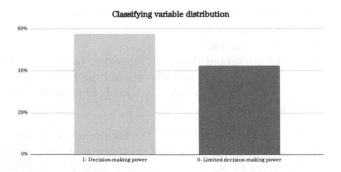

Fig. 2. Distribution of the classification variable for the identification of two groups of empowered and non-empowered women.

2.4 Techniques and Methods of Classification

Two classification algorithms were used to classify women's decision-making power: the k-Nearest Neighbors (kNN) algorithm and the Random Forest (RF) algorithm. Each of these algorithms is described in detail below:

- K-Nearest Neighbors (kNN) [6] is a widely used classification technique because of its straightforward interpretation and low computational time. This algorithm depends on a parameter k, associated with the number of neighbors to be considered when assigning a class label. Among the general steps employed by this technique are: (1) calculate the distance between the data point to be classified and the rest of the data points in the training set. (2) select the k closest elements (with a smaller distance), and (3) choose a classification based on the predominant class among the k closest elements. In this study, different values of k were experimented with and it was determined that the value $k = 3$ was the most optimal. Additionally, the kNN method employed the Minkowski distance.
- Random Forest (RF) [1] is a classification technique based on an ensemble of classifiers. Being an ensemble of homogeneous classifiers, the RF uses binary decision trees as the base classifier. The main advantage of classifier ensembles is that they obtain better results than a single base classifier because the decision trees are different within the RF, thus achieving better generalization. The random subspace method is used to diversify the classifiers in the RF by restricting the decision space at each node to a random subset of size m, smaller than the size of the complete feature set n. The random subset is chosen for each node in the tree. In this study, the value of $m = \frac{n}{2}$.
  Among the general steps employed by this technique are: (1) randomly select samples using bootstrap resampling, (2) partition each node of the tree by the best cutoff point found over a random selection of a subset of m predictor variables (instead of all n predictor variables that make up the complete feature set) using a measure of purity such as the Gini index, and let each RF tree grow without pruning. (4) The RF scheme combines the responses of B decision trees to produce a majority vote toward the winning class. In this study, different values of B decision trees were explored by optimization and the most satisfactory B value was the value of $B = 6$.

2.5 Evaluation and Statistical Comparison

The Hold-out resampling technique was used to evaluate the models using 70% of the data for training and 30% for testing on a base of 29,708 records. This evaluation was performed at least 31 times in order to be able to analyze the results statistically.

The following performance indices were used to measure the performance of the classification [12]:

The Accuracy Ratio (ACC) is defined as the total number of correct predictions divided by the total number of predictions. It refers to how close the result of a measurement is to the true value. The following equation represents it:

$$\frac{TP + VN}{TP + VN + FP + FN} \tag{3}$$

where TP represents True Positive values, VN represents True Negative values, FP represents False Positive values and FN represents False Negative values.

The Sensitivity index or True Positive Ratio (TPR) is the proportion of positive cases that were correctly identified by the algorithm. The following equation represents this index:

$$\frac{TP}{TP + FN} \tag{4}$$

The specificity index (also called Recall) is also known as the true negative rate. This measure indicates the proportion of negative cases that are correctly detected. The mathematical definition is as follows:

$$\frac{VN}{VN + FP} \tag{5}$$

Additionally, the false positive rate (FPR). This measure indicates the proportion of positive cases that are erroneously detected. The mathematical definition is as follows:

$$\frac{FP}{FP + VN} \tag{6}$$

Finally, the Precision (Eq. 7), and F1 score (Eq. 8) index were calculated.

$$\frac{TP}{TP + FP} \tag{7}$$

$$\frac{2 \times Precision \times Recall}{Precision + Recall} \tag{8}$$

3   Results

Table 4 shows the corresponding confusion matrix obtained from the results generated by the k-Nearest Neighbors (kNN) and the Random Forest (RF).

Table 5 shows the results of the kNN and RF methods in terms of Accuracy, Sensitivity, Specificity, and False Positive Ratio (FPR).

The results suggest that both methods adequately predict women's decision power at 99%. The total errors for the kNN and RF classifiers were 21 and 18, respectively, which is reflected in the performance of the Sensitivity and Specificity indices. Regarding the FPR index, RF and kNN obtained a ratio of 0.31% and 0.33%, respectively.

Table 4. Confusion matrix: a) kNN, y b) RF.

a)

True label	Predicted label	
	0	1
0	**3,765**	8
1	13	**5,127**

b)

True label	Predicted label	
	0	1
0	**3,771**	6
1	12	**5,124**

Table 5. Summary performance of 30 runs of the Nearest Neighbors (kNN) and Random Forest (RF) algorithms. Mean (Standard Deviation).

Classification Index	Method	
	kNN	**RF**
Accuracy	0.9975 (0.0004)	**0.9977 (0.0005)**
Sensitivity	**0.9973 (0.0007)**	0.9971 (0.0008)
Specificity	0.9980 (0.0004)	**0.9986 (0.0004)**
FPR	0.0033 (0.0009)	**0.0031 (0.0007)**
Precision	**0.9980 (0.0005)**	0.9980 (0.0005)
F1 Score	0.9970 (0.0004)	**0.9980 (0.0004)**

To validate the statistical significance, the Shapiro-Wilk test was applied to validate the normality of the sample, obtaining a value of $p=0.6$, suggesting that the data follow a normal distribution. Also, the Student's t-test was applied; the test statistic was -0.333 with a $p = 0.741$ value for an $\alpha = 95\%$ confidence. Therefore, it is concluded that there is no significant difference between the methods.

4 Conclusions and Future Work

This article addressed the classification of the decision-making power that Mexican women have in the household. For this purpose, INEGI's ENDIREH 2016 database and the Castro and Casique method were used [2] for obtaining the labeled data. The feature set included a data transformation from the original feature space to numerical features employing Principal Component Analysis (PCA). Two machine learning methods were tested to perform decision power classification of Mexican women, the k-Nearest Neighbors (kNN) and Random Forest (RF) algorithms. Test results had both methods obtaining 99% in terms of Accuracy, Sensitivity, and Specificity. The Student's t-test showed no statistical difference between the methods and that either of them can be employed to resolve this problem adequately. In terms of error reduction, Random Forest improves over kNN by obtaining a lower False Positive Rate (FPR) equal to 0.31%; this could be because the boundaries generated by RF are more complex. In the case of kNN, because the decision is made concerning the number of nearest neighbors, the prediction could be biased toward the majority class.

We considered that the outstanding performance of these algorithms depended on the decision power index, which was an essential part of the discrimination between two data groups to classify.

In future work, we wish to analyze different patterns associated with women's violence and the relationship between the decision-making power factor and the violentometer, for which collaboration with health professionals, such as clinical psychologists, will be required.

Conflict of Interest. The authors declare that they have no conflict of interest.

References

1. Breiman, L.: Random forests. Mach. Learn. **45**(1), 5–32 (2001). https://doi.org/10.1023/A:1010933404324
2. Castro, R., Casique, I.: Violencia de género en las parejas mexicanas: análisis de resultados de la encuesta nacional sobre la dinámica de las relaciones en los hogares, 2006. Instituto Nacional de las Mujeres (2008)
3. Pearson, K.: LIII. on lines and planes of closest fit to systems of points in space. The London, Edinburgh, and Dublin Philos. Mag. J. Sci. **2**(11), 559–572 (1901). https://doi.org/10.1080/14786440109462720
4. López Rosales, F., de la Rubia, J.M.: Violencia en la pareja. un análisis desde una perspectiva ecológica. CIENCIA ergo-sum **20**(1), 6–16 (2017). https://cienciaergosum.uaemex.mx/article/view/7757
5. Gutiérrez-Esparza, G.O., Vallejo-Allende, M., Hernández-Torruco, J.: Classification of cyber-aggression cases applying machine learning. Appl. Sci. **9**(9), 1828 (2019). https://doi.org/10.3390/app9091828, https://www.mdpi.com/2076-3417/9/9/1828
6. Kramer, O.: K-Nearest Neighbors, pp. 13–23. Springer, Heidelberg (2013). https://doi.org/10.1007/978-3-642-38652-7_2
7. Lu, Z., Xie, C., Liu, N., Xie, Y., Lu, H.: 'can we predict aggression?'-determining the predictors of aggression among individuals with substance use disorder in china undergoing enforced detoxification through machine learning. J. Affect. Disorders. **320**, 628–637 (2023). https://doi.org/10.1016/j.jad.2022.10.005, https://www.sciencedirect.com/science/article/pii/S0165032722011880
8. Miranda, G., Alejo, R., Castorena, C., Rendón, E., Illescas, J., García, V.: Deep neural network to detect gender violence on Mexican Tweets. In: Hernández Heredia, Y., Milián Núñez, V., Ruiz Shulcloper, J. (eds.) IWAIPR 2021. LNCS, vol. 13055, pp. 24–32. Springer, Cham (2021). https://doi.org/10.1007/978-3-030-89691-1_3
9. Munguía, J.A.T., Martínez-Zarzoso, I.: Determinants of emotional intimate partner violence against women and girls with children in Mexican households: an ecological framework. J. Interpers. Violence **37**(23-24), NP22704–NP22731 (2022). https://doi.org/10.1177/08862605211072179
10. Muraleedharan, A., Garcia-Constantino, M.: Domestic violence detection using smart microphones. In: Bravo, J., Ochoa, S., Favela, J. (eds.) Proceedings of the International Conference on Ubiquitous Computing & Ambient Intelligence (UCAmI 2022), pp. 357–368. Springer International Publishing, Cham (2023). https://doi.org/10.1007/978-3-031-21333-5_36

11. Rodríguez-Rodríguez, I., Rodríguez, J.V., Pardo-Quiles, D.J., Heras-González, P., Chatzigiannakis, I.: Modeling and forecasting gender-based violence through machine learning techniques. Appl. Sci. **10**(22), 8244 (2020). https://doi.org/10.3390/app10228244, https://www.mdpi.com/2076-3417/10/22/8244
12. Sokolova, M., Lapalme, G.: A systematic analysis of performance measures for classification tasks. Inf. Process. Manag. **45**(4), 427–437 (2009). https://doi.org/10.1016/j.ipm.2009.03.002
13. Yallico Arias, T., Fabian, J.: Automatic detection of levels of intimate partner violence against women with natural language processing using machine learning and deep learning techniques. In: Lossio-Ventura, J.A., Valverde-Rebaza, J., Díaz, E., Muñante, D., Gavidia-Calderon, C., Valejo, A.D.B., Alatrista-Salas, H. (eds.) Information Management and Big Data, pp. 189–205. Springer International Publishing, Cham (2022). https://doi.org/10.1007/978-3-031-04447-2_13

Design Optimization for High-Performance Computing Using FPGA

Murat Isik[1]([✉]), Kayode Inadagbo[2], and Hakan Aktas[3]

[1] Electrical and Computer Engineering Department, Drexel University, Philadelphia, USA
mci38@drexel.edu
[2] Electrical and Computer Engineering Department, A&M University, Prairie View, USA
[3] Computer Engineering Department, Omer Halisdemir University, Nigde, Turkey
haktas@ohu.edu.tr

Abstract. Reconfigurable architectures like Field Programmable Gate Arrays (FPGAs) have been used for accelerating computations in several domains because of their unique combination of flexibility, performance, and power efficiency. However, FPGAs have not been widely used for high-performance computing, primarily because of their programming complexity and difficulties in optimizing performance. We optimize Tensil AI's open-source inference accelerator for maximum performance using ResNet20 trained on CIFAR in this paper in order to gain insight into the use of FPGAs for high-performance computing. In this paper, we show how improving hardware design, using Xilinx Ultra RAM, and using advanced compiler strategies can lead to improved inference performance. We also demonstrate that running the CIFAR test data set shows very little accuracy drop when rounding down from the original 32-bit floating point. The heterogeneous computing model in our platform allows us to achieve a frame rate of 293.58 frames per second (FPS) and a %90 accuracy on a ResNet20 trained using CIFAR. The experimental results show that the proposed accelerator achieves a throughput of 21.12 Giga-Operations Per Second (GOP/s) with a 5.21 W on-chip power consumption at 100 MHz. The comparison results with off-the-shelf devices and recent state-of-the-art implementations illustrate that the proposed accelerator has obvious advantages in terms of energy efficiency.

Keywords: High-performance computing · Tensil AI · Design optimization · FPGA · Open-source inference accelerator

1 Introduction

Real-time vision-based motion tracking is necessary for many applications. Real-time video streaming for surveillance applications requires advanced encoding

J. A. Lossio-Ventura et al. (Eds.): SIMBig 2023, CCIS 2142, pp. 142–156, 2024.
https://doi.org/10.1007/978-3-031-63616-5_11

and decoding techniques as well as compute-intensive image processing designs. The ability to operate in real-time is especially important for applications in which speed is paramount, such as production areas, traffic speed control systems, or when the camera activity needs to be synchronized with other system components. The developers of machine vision frameworks and respectability may be engrossed in determining which of these steps to implement while developing the rest of the framework. The organize option is commonly selected when prototyping the system for the first time. The number of sections or outlines the application must prepare each instant depends on how many sections the prototyped application must handle at any given moment. Researchers are developing methods to design embedded systems that require less power, which is critical for most applications in modern embedded systems [1–3]. High-resolution image preparation applications demand faster, configurable, high-throughput frameworks with superior productivity for preparing enormous data sets [4–6]. FPGAs (Field-Programmable Gate Arrays) can play an important role since they provide configurability, adaptability, and parallelism to coordinate the necessary throughput rates of the application under consideration [7]. An FPGA device provides an execution method that allows it to be used in real-life applications. FPGAs have significantly increased the flexibility of hardware in general. A wider community of builders can now make use of these devices thanks to advancements in the toolchains for developing applications on them. Applications that require concurrency, high transfer speeds, and re-programmability typically use FPGAs. Modern digital life is increasingly reliant on image-processing applications. They are used in a variety of applications, including medical imaging, security, autonomous vehicles, and entertainment. In order to meet the increasing demand for more accurate and faster image processing, high-performance computing systems are needed. Image processing systems can be improved through FPGA-based design optimization. There are several factors that require pushing for higher performance in image processing. The following factors are discussed in more detail.

- Resolution and Image Size: Image processing performance is tied to image resolution and size. High-resolution medical images, like CT scans and MRI, can be several gigabytes. Such images necessitate high-performance computing systems for swift and accurate handling.
- Real-Time Processing: Applications like video streaming, security systems, and autonomous vehicles demand real-time image processing. For instance, autonomous vehicles need real-time processing to detect obstacles. High-performance systems are vital to manage vast data volumes promptly.
- Complex Algorithms: The intricacy of image processing algorithms, especially in tasks like object recognition, demands high processing power and memory. High-performance systems ensure faster execution of these intricate algorithms.
- Parallel Processing: Parallel processing enhances image processing as it allows simultaneous computations. FPGAs enable this high parallelism, making multi-pixel image processing faster, especially vital in video processing.

The increasing demand for faster and more accurate image processing requires image processing applications to push for higher performance. High-performance computing systems are needed because of factors such as high resolution and image size, real-time processing, complex algorithms, and parallel processing. Optimising FPGA-based designs for image processing applications is a very effective way to increase performance, and it is likely to become more relevant as the demand for faster and more accurate image processing increases. FPGAs are integrated circuits that can be programmed and reprogrammed to perform specific tasks. The unique features that make them well-suited to high-performance computing make them increasingly popular. High-performance computing can benefit from FPGAs as outlined below:

- High Parallelism: FPGAs excel in parallelism, executing multiple tasks simultaneously using configurable logic blocks. This feature is crucial for high-performance computing applications.
- Customizable Architecture: FPGAs boast a flexible architecture that can be tailored to specific performance needs, offering an advantage over general-purpose processors.
- Low Latency: FPGAs process inputs rapidly, in nanoseconds, making them ideal for real-time applications like video and audio processing.
- High Bandwidth: With the capacity to transfer vast data amounts swiftly through high-speed transceivers, FPGAs can achieve bandwidths of several gigabits per second.
- Energy Efficiency: FPGAs are energy-efficient with lower power consumption compared to general-purpose processors, making them suitable for high-performance applications.

FPGAs are an attractive option for applications requiring a significant amount of processing power, such as image processing, machine learning, and real-time processing. FPGAs are likely to become even more important in high-performance computing as the demand grows. Tensil AI creates hardware and software solutions for machine learning applications. They offer high-performance machine learning inference on FPGA platforms through an open-source inference accelerator. As an open-source machine learning library developed by Google, TensorFlow Lite Inference Engine underpins Tensil AI's inference accelerator. The Tensil AI accelerator can therefore be easily integrated with existing machine learning applications. The Tensil AI inference accelerator performs quantization as one of its key features. A quantification process reduces the precision of machine learning models, making them easier to store and deploy. A Tensil AI accelerator performs quantization on the fly, which reduces the memory and power requirements of the inference engine. Its ability to support dynamic shapes is another key feature of the Tensil AI inference accelerator. Machine learning applications that require real-time processing of sensor or camera data can benefit from variable input data sizes and shapes. The Tensil AI accelerator is able to change the size of the inference engine on the fly based on the size of the input data, so it can handle a wide range of input sizes and shapes. Tensil AI inference accelerators are highly configurable, allowing developers to optimize their performance according to their needs. The low latency, high bandwidth, and high throughput processing it provides make it an ideal solution for high-performance computing applications. The Tensil AI inference accelerator is not only highly scalable but also highly efficient. The technology can be employed in edge devices such as smartphones, smart cameras, and IoT devices, as well as in cloud-based applications that require high-performance machine learning inferences. Tensil AI accelerators can be deployed on a wide range of FPGA platforms, including Xilinx's Alveo accelerator cards, making them ideal for high-performance computing applications. The Tensil AI open-source inference accelerator is a powerful tool for accelerating machine learning inference on FPGA platforms. A wide range of input sizes and shapes can be supported, making it a highly scalable and versatile solution. High-performance computing will likely become even more reliant on solutions like the Tensil AI inference accelerator as machine learning becomes more important [8,9].

The rest of the paper is organized as follows: Sect. 2 presents the motivation and related works. Section 3 introduces open-source ml inference accelerators. The proposed method and its experimental results and analysis are reported in Sects. 4 and 5. Section 6 concludes the contents of this paper and gives future aspects of this paper.

2 Background

FPGAs have been around for several decades, and they are used in many different applications. High-performance computing has been limited by a number of challenges and difficulties. FPGAs have not been widely used in high-performance computing due to their high development cost and complexity. The tools and technologies required for FPGA development are often expensive and complex, which makes it difficult to develop systems based on FPGAs. FPGA-based solutions have proven challenging to adopt for many organizations, especially for smaller organizations or those with limited resources. The limited availability of high-level software tools is another challenge with FPGAs in high-performance computing. Developing software for FPGAs requires a deep understanding of the underlying hardware architecture, which is more difficult than for traditional processors. However, high-level synthesis tools are not as mature as those used for traditional processors, making development more challenging [10–12]. Some high-performance computing applications can also be limited by the limited amount of on-chip memory on FPGAs. There is a significant amount of data transfer between the FPGA and external memory, which slows performance and increases latency. For many high-performance computing applications, floating-point operations are also not supported by FPGAs. FPGAs used in high-performance computing also have a limited number of prebuilt IP blocks. The development of FPGA-based solutions often requires the use of pre-built intellectual property (IP) blocks, such as memory controllers and data interfaces. The availability of these IP blocks for FPGAs is often limited, which makes developing FPGA-based systems more difficult and time-consuming. High-performance computing applications benefit from the advantages of FPGAs, despite these challenges. FPGAs can be highly optimized for specific tasks and often perform better than traditional processors in specific applications. A hardware-level parallelism capability also enhances performance for certain tasks. Recent developments have made FPGAs more accessible for high-performance computing, thus addressing these challenges. The availability of high-level synthesis tools for FPGAs makes software development easier, for example. A number of pre-built IP blocks are also being developed and made available for FPGAs. A number of FPGA-based solutions are now available that require less specialized hardware design knowledge and are easier to use. Despite the challenges and difficulties involved in developing and implementing FPGAs, they have not been widely used for high-performance computing, but efforts are being made to resolve these issues and make FPGA-based solutions more accessible and usable for high-performance computing. The adoption of FPGAs in high-performance computing will increase as development tools, IP blocks, and FPGA-based solutions improve [13]. High-performance computing applications have attracted significant interest in FPGAs in recent years. FPGA-based systems can be highly optimized for specific tasks, and they can often perform better than traditional processors in specific applications. The image and video processing industry has extensively used FPGAs for high-performance computing. The processing of high-resolution images and video can be carried out in real-time using FPGAs. A high-level synthesis tool called Vivado HLS has been used by researchers at UCLA to develop an FPGA-based system for real-time image processing [14]. A throughput of 52 frames per second was achieved when filtering images, and 20 frames per second when segmenting images. High-performance computing has also been done using FPGAs in the financial industry. Complex mathematical operations are often involved in financial calculations, which are well suited for FPGAs. A high-frequency trading system developed by the Tokyo Stock Exchange (TSE) can process trades in less than one microsecond using FPGAs [15,16]. The system leverages FPGAs for various high-performance computing tasks. In the financial sector, FPGAs are employed to compute instruments such as options and futures. Beyond finance, the application of FPGAs in the domains of artificial intelligence and machine learning is noteworthy. They are particularly adept at being optimized for neural network computations, which facilitates faster and more efficient data processing. However, it's crucial to note that while FPGAs can process data efficiently, they are constrained by a limited amount of local memory. This limitation can pose challenges when working with extensive datasets. Additionally, FPGAs have been beneficial in scientific calculations, offering optimized performance that enhances data processing speeds. Furthermore, a number of existing works focus on optimizing FPGA-based systems for high-performance computing in general. Researchers have developed a tool called FireSim to simulate large-scale FPGA-based systems using cloud resources [17]. The tool can be used to optimize system performance and evaluate different design options. There are many existing works that focus on using FPGAs for high-performance computing. Several applications, including image and video processing, finance, machine learning, artificial intelligence, and scientific research, have been demonstrated using FPGAs in these studies. With the continued development of FPGA-based tools and technologies, we can expect to see even increased adoption of FPGAs for high-performance computing in the future.

3   Open-Source ML Inference Accelerators

Many high-performance computing applications rely on machine learning inference. Models are used to analyze input data and generate output results. High-performance computing systems can help speed up ML inference, which is often computationally intensive. High-performance computing applications may benefit from open-source ML inference accelerators. An ML inference accelerator is a specialized hardware device designed specifically for efficient ML inference tasks. While general-purpose processors are commonly used for these tasks, graphics processing units (GPUs) have also been widely recognized in the HPC community as highly efficient solutions for ML inference. Contrary to the claim on page 16, GPUs are indeed optimized and extensively used for ML inference in many high-performance computing scenarios. An ML inference accelerator provides efficient and optimized execution of ML inference tasks. Open-source ML inference accelerators offer the advantage of being free and customizable to fit specific use cases. An open-source ML inference accelerator offers a transparent and open development process, which encourages community participation and feedback. Open-source accelerators can also reduce the cost and time associated with developing ML inference accelerators. Recently, the Versatile Tensor Accelerator (VTA) has gained significant attention as an open-source ML inference accelerator. Inference tasks using VTA are performed with the help of a highly optimized hardware accelerator. TensorFlow, PyTorch, and ONNX are among the popular ML frameworks supported by VTA. There are a variety of hardware platforms that can be used with VTA, including FPGAs and ASICs [18] (Fig. 1).

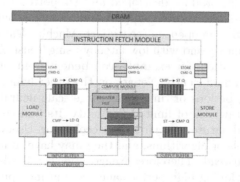

Fig. 1. VTA Framework [18]

By providing open-source tools and platforms, developers can collaborate to create new and more efficient ML inference solutions. Collaboration can lead to faster development and adoption of new ML techniques and applications. Other open-source ML inference accelerators, such as Intel's OpenVINO and Xilinx's Deep Learning Processor, are available alongside VTA [19,20]. These accelerators provide developers with a variety of options for building and optimizing machine learning systems. High-performance computing applications can take advantage of open-source ML inference accelerators because they provide a flexible and powerful tool. Development of ML inference systems can be customized and optimized, resulting in lower development costs and time, collaboration and innovation, and wide adoption of new ML techniques and applications. As the field of ML continues to grow and evolve, we can expect to see even more powerful and efficient open-source ML inference accelerators become available. High-performance computing applications using FPGAs can be built with Nengo and Tensil AI frameworks. A variety of hardware platforms, including FPGAs, can be used to build large-scale neural models with Nengo software. In addition, Nengo is designed to be flexible and extensible, allowing users to create customized models and algorithms. Nengo is well-suited for applications such as robotics and cognitive modeling because it can build complex models with many neurons and synapses. The Tensil AI hardware accelerator, on the other hand, performs machine learning inference tasks. The Tensil AI is designed to provide high performance at low power consumption, making it ideal for applications such as image recognition and natural language processing. Tensil AI is designed to be easily integrated with existing hardware architectures and supports a wide range of machine learning frameworks, including TensorFlow and PyTorch. Their focus is one of the key differences between Nengo and Tensil AI. Tensil AI focuses on accelerating machine learning inference tasks, whereas Nengo is primarily focused on building large-scale neural networks [21–23]. Nengo is more versatile and can be used for a wider variety of tasks, whereas Tensil AI is more focused on particular tasks. Their development processes are also key differences between Nengo and Tensil AI. The Open-source project Nengo is actively developed and maintained by a large developer community. The Tensil AI product, on the other hand, is a commercial product developed and supported by Tensil AI. Due to this, users have access to dedicated support and resources, but not as much community support as with an open-source project. Machine learning inference tasks can be performed quickly and with low latency using Tensil AI. Self-driving cars and industrial automation, for example, can benefit from their ability to make inferences quickly and efficiently. Nengo, on the other hand, simulates complex behaviors over long periods of time using large-scale neural models. Tensil AI has the potential drawback of limited flexibility. Its limited versatility may be due to its specialized nature as a hardware accelerator. Users may not be able to create custom models or algorithms, and they may have to use pre-built models and architectures instead. Therefore, Nengo and Tensil AI are both powerful frameworks for developing high-performance computing applications. A variety of applications can be carried out with Nengo, whereas Tensil AI is more suited for specific tasks, such as machine learning inference. Developers should carefully evaluate the strengths and weaknesses of each framework before selecting one, and ultimately their choice will depend on the specific needs of the application [8,9].

4 Method

We propose methods like Vivado hardware design, Xilinx Ultra RAM utilization, and advanced compiler strategies to boost inference performance. In Tensil AI's ResNet20-ZCU104 tutorial, various techniques optimize the ResNet20 neural network for the Xilinx ZCU104 board using their open-source accelerator. ResNet-20, trained on the CIFAR-10 dataset with 60,000 32×32 RGB images, achieves about 91% accuracy using PyTorch. Post-training, several optimizations prepare it for device deployment. Pruning, a standard technique in many frameworks, reduces computations by removing unnecessary network connections. The tutorial also introduces quantization, which, using the TensorRT framework, minimizes weights and activations to 8-bit precision, saving memory and computational resources. However, the methodology mainly taps into TensorRT's existing features, lacking deeper insights into Tensil AI's unique contributions. Tensil AI's accelerator, designed for sparse neural networks on FPGAs, deploys the optimized network on the ZCU104. This achieves high performance and energy efficiency through FPGA reconfigurability and parallelism. In summary, Tensil AI's tutorial demonstrates key optimization techniques, including pruning and quantization, for FPGA-based neural network designs.

4.1 Baseline Design

Specifying 32 by 32 systolic array size contributed to the high utilization of multiply-accumulate units (DSP). Note how we pushed Block RAM (BRAM) utilization almost to its limit by specifying 16 KV local memory and 4 KV accumulators (KV = 1024 vectors = 1024 * 32 * 16 bits). The ZCU104 board supports an SD card interface. This allows us to use Tensil embedded driver file system functionality to read the ResNet model and a set of images to test it with. The set we will be using is the test set for the original CIFAR-10. The ResNet model is trained with separate training and validation sets from the CIFAR-10. The test set is what the model hasn't seen in training and therefore gives an objective estimate of its accuracy. The CIFAR-10 provides a test set of 10,000 images in several formats. We will use the binary format that is more suitable for the embedded application. With the SD card inserted and containing the CIFAR-10 test data set and the ResNet model compiled for Tensil, you should see the inference printing every 100's images and the corresponding prediction along with measured inferences (frames) per second. After running the inference on the entire test data set the program will print the final average frames per second and the accuracy of the inference. For the baseline solution, we are getting an average of 133.54 frames per second with %90 accuracies. Note that the accuracy we are seeing when testing the same ResNet model with TensorFlow is %92. The %2 drop is due to changing the data type from a 32-bit floating point in TensorFlow to a 16-bit fixed point in Tensil.

4.2 Dual Clock Solution

The first optimization is based on the following observation. The Tensil RTL block is clocked at 100MHz. The Tensil block DRAM0 and DRAM1 ports are connected to AXI interfaces on the ZYNQ block. The instruction port is indirectly connected to the AXI on the ZYNQ block via AXI DMA. ZYNQ Ultra-Scal+ AXI ports support up to 333MHz and a maximum width of 128 bits. This gives us the opportunity to introduce a second clock domain for 333MHz while at the same time making the Tensil AXI ports wider. Figure 2 shows how this may work in a simpler 100MHz to 400MHz, 512- to 128-bit conversion. Each clock in the Tensil clock domain would pump one 512-bit word in or out. This would match 4 clocks in the ZYNQ clock domain with 512-bit words split to or composed from 4 128-bit words.

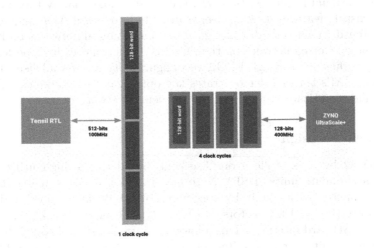

Fig. 2. Tensil RTL clock domain.

For the dual clock solution, we are getting an average of 152.04 frames per second-a meaningful improvement over the baseline. This improvement is roughly proportional to the ratio of time spent in moving data to and from the FPGA to the time spent in internal data movement and computation. An accelerator is designed in two parts - a data path and a control path. Data paths process input data through neural networks, while control paths manage data flow and control the overall operation of the accelerator. Data and control paths are clocked separately at different frequencies, with the data path clocked at a higher frequency to maximize the accelerator's throughput. Data synchronization and timing violations between the two paths can also impact the accelerator's performance and reliability with this approach. Tensil AI's dual clock solution includes a number of design techniques such as pipelining, synchronization signals, and careful timing analysis to ensure proper data synchronization and avoid timing violations. A high level of throughput is still maintained while these techniques improve the accelerator's performance and reliability.

4.3 Ultra RAM Solution

Ultra RAM refers to a design approach that optimizes memory access and utilization in FPGA-based inference accelerators. An Ultra RAM is a high-density memory block that is available in Xilinx FPGAs and offers high bandwidth and low latency access to memory. The Ultra RAM solution is used in the ResNet20-ZCU104 project to store the weights of the neural network model, which is a critical part of inference. Ultra RAMs are used to store weights so they can be accessed quickly and efficiently during the inference process. As part of the Ultra RAM configuration, the accelerator also supports concurrent reads and writes, further improving performance. Tensil AI's design approach makes optimal use of Ultra RAMs by using techniques such as weight compression and quantization, which reduce the memory footprint of weights without compromising accuracy. Using these techniques increases the capacity and efficiency of Ultra RAMs, improving the accelerator's performance overall. Inference accelerators based on FPGAs benefit greatly from the Ultra RAM solution for optimizing memory access and utilization. A ResNet20-ZCU104 neural network model has been successfully inferred with high performance and efficiency using the ResNet20-ZCU104. The second optimization is based on the higher-end ZYNQ UltraScale+ device's support for another type of on-chip memory called Ultra RAM. By default, Vivado maps dual-port memory to Block RAM. In order for it to map to the Ultra RAM it needs hints in the Verilog code. To enable these hints we will use the Xilinx ultra ram option of the Tensil RTL tool. The amount of Ultra RAM available on ZCU104 allows us to add around 48 KV memory in addition to 20 KV available through Block RAM. We start by creating a new Tensil architecture for ZCU104 in which we allocate all of the Block RAM (20 KV) to accumulators and all of the Ultra RAM (48 KV) to local memory. For the Ultra RAM solution, we are getting an average of 170.16 frames per second, another meaningful improvement. This improvement is based purely on having larger on-chip memory. With a small on-chip memory the Tensil compiler is forced to partition ResNet convolution layers into multiple load-compute-save blocks. This, in turn, requires that the same input activations are loaded multiple times, assuming weights are loaded only once. This is called weight-stationary dataflow. In the future, we will add an option for input-stationary dataflow. With it, when partitioned, the input activations are loaded once and the same weights are loaded multiple times.FPGA utilization for Ultra RAM design is shown in Table 1.

Table 1. Resource Usage.

Utilization	XCZU7EV
LUT	181440
DSP	1054
BRAM	293
URAM	96

Figure 3 shows such a 3-partitioned compilation. Layer N has 2 stages. In each stage, a unique subset of weights is loaded. Then, each stage is further split into 2 partitions. Partition is defined by the largest amount of weights, input and output activations, and intermediate results that fit local memory and accumulators.

Having larger on-chip memory reduces this partitioning and, by extension, the need to load the same data multiple times. Figure 4 shows how layer N now has 1 stage and 1 partition that fits larger local memory and accumulators, which allows weights and activations to be loaded only once.

4.4 Compiler Strategy with Large Local Memory

This strategy involves optimizing the speed and latency of local memory resources in FPGAs, such as block RAMs and Ultra RAMs, which are faster than external memory resources such as DRAM. Inference is carried out using the data and weights stored in the local memory, which are used for data storage and weight storage. Several techniques are used by ResNet20-ZCU104 to implement the compiler strategy with large local memory, such as weight compression and quantization, which reduce the memory footprint of weights without compromising their accuracy. The reduced memory footprint allows for larger portions of the neural network model and data to be stored in the local memory resources. The final optimization is based on the same hardware design and Tensil architecture we created to support the Ultra RAM. We will only change the Tensil compiler strategy. Tensil compilers, by default, assume that the model is much larger than the FPGA's local memory in terms of its weights and activations. This is true for large models and for low-end FPGA devices. For small and medium-sized models running on large FPGA devices, there is a possibility that local memory is large enough to contain the weights plus input and output activations for each layer. Our Proposed compiler strategy is shown in Fig. 5.

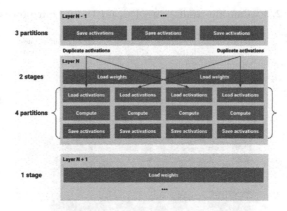

Fig. 3. 3-Partitioned Compilation

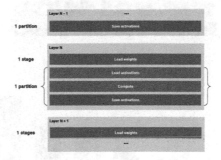

Fig. 4. 1-Partitioned Compilation.

5 Results

Our results demonstrate the effectiveness of Tensil AI's open-source inference accelerator for optimizing neural networks and implementing them on FPGAs for high-performance computing applications. It has been done using CPUs, GPUs, and FPGAs. CPU/GPU-based NNs consume a lot of power and have a limited throughput due to limited memory bandwidth which is shown in Table 2. In Table 3 Many researchers have developed FPGA-based designs for accelerating network inference workloads in order to achieve better energy efficiency.FPGAs function as programmable devices that can construct unique logic, alleviating constraints on neural network implementation. We demonstrated how improving the Vivado hardware design, leveraging Xilinx Ultra RAM, and using advanced compiler strategies can improve the performance of inference. As a result, one of the current research hotspots involves the development of hardware systems supporting NN inference based on FPGA to achieve high throughput and power efficiency. Figure 6 summarizes presented solutions and their frames per second performance.

Table 2. Evaluation results on CPU, GPU, and our processor.

	Technology [nm]	Frequency [MHz]	Latency [ms]	Throughput [GOP/s]	Power [Watt]	Energy Efficiency [GOP/s/W]
Intel Xeon E5-2697 (CPU)	14	2300	1137.62	27.20	145	0.19
NVIDIA GTX 1080 TI (GPU)	14	1481	6.15	235.77	250	0.94
Xilinx ZCU104 (FPGA)	16	100	2.91	21.12	5.21	4.05

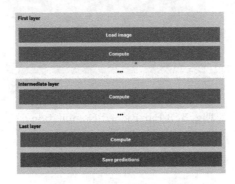

Fig. 5. Compiler Strategy.

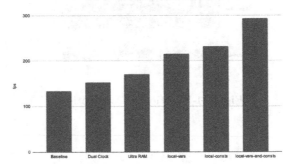

Fig. 6. Performance Chart.

Table 3. Comparisons with previous implementations.

Work	Device	Frequency	Quant	Power	FPS	Throughput	Energy Efficiency
Ma et al. [24]	Arria-10 GX	$150MHz$	8-16 bit fixed	$21.2W$	–	$645.25(GOP/s)$	$30.44(GOP/s/W)$
Mei et al. [25]	Virtex-7	$200MHz$	16-bit float	$10.81W$	6.58	$202.42(GOP/s)$	$1.64(GOP/s/W)$
Zhang et al. [26]	Zynq ZU7EV	$300MHz$	8-bit fixed	$17.67W$	–	$290.40(GOP/s)$	$0.80(GOP/s/W)$
Blott et al. [27]	Zynq ZU3EG	$220MHz$	8-bit fixed	$10.2W$	200	$400(GOP/s)$	$39.21(GOP/s/W)$
Zhang et al. [28]	Virtex-7	$200MHz$	8-bit fixed	$6.32W$	6.77	$209.60(GOP/s)$	$33.16(GOP/s/W)$
Li et al. [29]	Zynq 7010	$200MHz$	16-bit fixed	19.52	–	$452.8(GOP/s)$	$23.20(GOP/s/W)$
Suda et al. [30]	Stratix-V	$120MHz$	8-16 bit fixed	$25.8W$	–	$117.8(GOP/s)$	$4.56(GOP/s/W)$
Ours	Zynq ZU7EV	$100MHz$	32-bit floating	$5.21W$	290.58	$21.12(GOP/s)$	$4.05(GOP/s/W)$

6 Conclusions

The ResNet20-ZCU104 project demonstrates the potential of using FPGA-based acceleration for machine learning tasks. By leveraging the unique capabilities of FPGAs, such as low latency and efficient memory usage, the project achieved impressive results in terms of both performance and accuracy. The model is implemented for hardware acceleration with various heterogeneous devices and resulting in an energy-efficient, reconfigurable system on the latter. In the further phase of our work, we will propose to use Dynamic Partial Reconfiguration which is state-of-art technology of reconfigurable hardware into an achieved high-performance framework. Within this feature, we will solve reshaping and offloading the initial and post-data processing for high-performance computing with Tensil AI. The Tensil AI already can take a different model by compiling something new, but the data going in and out could require manipulation which works between the input process and output process of the Tensil AI.

References

1. Wang, H., et al.: Convolutional neural network accelerator on FPGA. In: 2019 IEEE International Conference on Integrated Circuits, Technologies and Applications (ICTA), pp. 61–62. IEEE (2019)
2. Vanderbauwhede, W., Benkrid, K.: High-performance Computing Using FPGAs vol. 3. Springer, New York (2013). https://doi.org/10.1007/978-1-4419-9320-6
3. Isik, M., Paul, A., Varshika, M.L., Das, A.: A design methodology for fault-tolerant computing using astrocyte neural networks. In: Proceedings of the 19th ACM International Conference on Computing Frontiers, pp. 169–172 (2022)
4. Blaiech, A.G., Khalifa, K.B., Valderrama, C., Fernandes, M.A., Bedoui, M.H.: A survey and taxonomy of FPGA-based deep learning accelerators. J. Syst. Architect. **98**, 331–345 (2019)
5. Zou, D., Dou, Y., Guo, S., Ni, S.: High performance sparse matrix-vector multiplication on FPGA. IEICE Electron. Express **10**(17), 20130529–20130529 (2013)
6. Isik, M., Oldland, M., Zhou, L.: An energy-efficient reconfigurable autoencoder implementation on fpga. arXiv preprint arXiv:2301.07050 (2023)
7. Woods, R., McAllister, J., Lightbody, G., Yi, Y.: FPGA-based Implementation of Signal Processing Systems. John Wiley & Sons, London (2008)
8. Tensil AI Website. https://www.tensil.ai/. Accessed 17 Dec 2022
9. Tensil AI Github. https://github.com/tensil-ai. Accessed 17 Dec 2022
10. Sundararajan, P.: High performance computing using FPGAs. Technical report, Citeseer (2010)
11. Sklyarov, V., Skliarova, I., Utepbergenov, I., Akhmediyarova, A., et al.: Hardware accelerators for information processing in high-performance computing systems. Int. J. Innov. Comput. Inf. Control **15**(1), 321–335 (2019)
12. Inadagbo, K., Arig, B., Alici, N., Isik, M.: Exploiting FPGA capabilities for accelerated biomedical computing. arXiv preprint arXiv:2307.07914 (2023)
13. Huang, S., Pearson, C., Nagi, R., Xiong, J., Chen, D., Hwu, W.: Accelerating sparse deep neural networks on FPGAs. In: 2019 IEEE High Performance Extreme Computing Conference (HPEC), pp. 1–7. IEEE (2019)

14. Chen, Z., Zhou, J., Blair, G.J., Blair, H.T., Cong, J.: FPGA-based in-vivo calcium image decoding for closed-loop feedback applications. arXiv preprint arXiv:2212.04736 (2022)
15. Kohda, S., Yoshida, K.: Characteristics of high-frequency trading and its forecasts. In: 2021 IEEE 45th Annual Computers, Software, and Applications Conference (COMPSAC), pp. 1496–1501. IEEE (2021)
16. Kohda, S., Yoshida, K.: Characteristics and forecast of high-frequency trading. Trans. Jpn. Soc. Artif. Intell. **37**(5), 1–44 (2022)
17. Karandikar, S., et al.: Using Firesim to enable agile end-to-end RISC-V computer architecture research (2019)
18. Moreau, T., et al.: A hardware-software blueprint for flexible deep learning specialization. IEEE Micro **39**(5), 8–16 (2019)
19. Zunin, V.: Intel openvino toolkit for computer vision: object detection and semantic segmentation. In: 2021 International Russian Automation Conference (RusAutoCon), pp. 847–851. IEEE (2021)
20. Xilinx's DPU Website. https://docs.xilinx.com/r/en-US/ug1414-vitis-ai/Deep-Learning-Processor-Unit. Accessed 17 Dec 2022
21. Morcos, B.: NengoFPGA: an FPGA backend for the nengo neural simulator. Master's thesis, University of Waterloo (2019)
22. DeWolf, T., Jaworski, P., Eliasmith, C.: Nengo and low-power AI hardware for robust, embedded neurorobotics. Front. Neurorobot. **14**, 568359 (2020)
23. Gosmann, J., Eliasmith, C.: Automatic optimization of the computation graph in the nengo neural network simulator. Front. Neuroinform. **11**, 33 (2017)
24. Ma, Y., Cao, Y., Vrudhula, S., Seo, J.: Optimizing loop operation and dataflow in FPGA acceleration of deep convolutional neural networks. In: Proceedings of the 2017 ACM/SIGDA International Symposium on Field-Programmable Gate Arrays, pp. 45–54 (2017)
25. Mei, C., Liu, Z., Niu, Y., Ji, X., Zhou, W., Wang, D.: A 200mhz 202.4 gflops@ 10.8 w VGG16 accelerator in Xilinx vx690t. In: 2017 IEEE Global Conference on Signal and Information Processing (GlobalSIP), pp. 784–788. IEEE (2017)
26. Zhang, M., Li, L., Wang, H., Liu, Y., Qin, H., Zhao, W.: Optimized compression for implementing convolutional neural networks on FPGA. Electronics **8**(3), 295 (2019)
27. Blott, M., et al.: Finn-r: An end-to-end deep-learning framework for fast exploration of quantized neural networks. ACM Trans. Reconfig. Technol. Syst. (TRETS) **11**(3), 1–23 (2018)
28. Zhang, X., Wei, X., Sang, Q., Chen, H., Xie, Y.: An efficient FPGA-based implementation for quantized remote sensing image scene classification network. Electronics **9**(9), 1344 (2020)
29. Li, L., Zhang, S., Wu, J.: Efficient object detection framework and hardware architecture for remote sensing images. Remote Sens. **11**(20), 2376 (2019)
30. Suda, N., et al.: Throughput-optimized OpenCL-based FPGA accelerator for large-scale convolutional neural networks. In: Proceedings of the 2016 ACM/SIGDA International Symposium on Field-Programmable Gate Arrays, pp. 16–25 (2016)

CLPSafe: Mobile Application for Avoid Cloned of License Plates Using Deep Learning

Diego Sánchez⑩, John Silva⑩, and Cesar Salas⁽✉⁾ ⑩

Universidad de Ciencias Aplicadas del Perú, Lima, Peru
cesar.salas@upc.edu.pe

Abstract. The problem of cloning vehicle license plates in Peru is detailed, by criminals to sell vehicles at a lower price or commit crimes with the stolen vehicle. A mobile application is proposed that uses convolutional neural networks and deeplearning algorithms: TensorFlow, EasyOCR and OpenCV to identify the license plate and its alphanumeric code, obtain detailed information about the vehicle and its owner, and issue reports to the authorities in case of cloned plate or stolen. The objective of the project is to speed up identification, consultation, and issuance of reports regarding vehicular identity theft, thus contributing to improving citizen security missing results. The analyzed results indicate that 75% of the experts expressed favorable opinions regarding the validation of the proposed architecture diagram for CLPSafe. The positive evaluations received endorse the feasibility and effectiveness of the proposed architecture, affirming its potential to effectively tackle the problem of license plate cloning in Peru.

Keywords: Mobile Application · vehicle license plate fraud · Deep Learning · Optical Character Recognition (OCR) · vehicle license plate cloning

1 Introduction

At present, the cloning of license plates still persists in Peru in such a way that they are committed by groups of criminals or mafias with the purpose of selling a vehicle with the same characteristics at a lower price or to commit criminal acts with it, already that when using a vehicle with a license plate that belongs to another [1], with the consequence that the original owner of the license plate is guilty of the crimes committed by the cloners, also on the side of the authorities, they cannot efficiently identify vehicle data.

Citizen insecurity, given the wave of theft of vehicles and parts, has been increasing over the years despite the efforts made by the authorities to reduce this increase. These crimes commonly carried out by vehicle drivers are driving under the influence of illegal substances, vehicle in poor condition, driving without a license or an expired license, not having the SOAT. However, among the crimes that are carried out against the owners of a vehicle, the most alarming due to the number of complaints that there is identity theft seconded by vehicle theft [2]. The perpetrators steal vehicles to supplant the license plate and use it to carry out criminal acts [3].

J. A. Lossio-Ventura et al. (Eds.): SIMBig 2023, CCIS 2142, pp. 157–166, 2024.
https://doi.org/10.1007/978-3-031-63616-5_12

That is why many countries, including Peru, have opted for new preventive measures against this type of modality, which is to make a query using a web platform for vehicle consultation, to find out if it is presenting an active cloning complaint [4]. In other countries, they opted for the vehicle license plate recognition method, which has been successful not only in the issue of license plate identification but also in the recognition and monitoring of vehicle entrances, as well as identifying them when they enter places such as hotels, shopping centers, etc. [5]. One of the main problems that the Peruvian national police currently have, especially the traffic police, when carrying out a police intervention on a vehicle that has a cloned license plate is the process of making the consultation and reporting the intervention. Since they have a communication channel, to which they consult about the data of the intervened vehicle. This consultation process is delayed, because the area in charge of carrying out the consultation attends to several requests at the same time using a government system with opportunities for improvement [6]. The proposed solution is the design of a mobile application, which allows the police force to consult the government system directly using the camera of their mobile device to identify the characters of the vehicle license plate.

CLPSafe is a mobile application, which through a data entry of photos that can be taken directly from the application or uploaded from the device's photo gallery, will allow the identification of the license plate and its alphanumeric code and additionally obtain detailed information about the vehicle and its owner to verify if the license plate is cloned or not, in addition to allowing a report to be issued and sent to the corresponding entity in case it is a cloned or stolen license plate.

The objective that will be considered in this article is to speed up identification, consultation, and issuance of reports regarding cases of vehicular identity theft. In addition, our motivation for the development of this research is to provide the necessary tools to contribute to the identification or detection of vehicular identity theft.

2 Related Works

To provide an effective and precise solution, it is necessary to train neural networks, which is why a wide variety and data set of license plates of Peruvian nationality are needed, since entering international license plates can decrease the accuracy of the detection of these. That is why Weihong and Jiaoyang, in [7] detail how a solution with the Deep Learning algorithm was implemented to improve the license plate recognition process. This is how they comment that they carried out an experimental test to verify the precision and processing time in different Deep Learning algorithms. At the end of the testing process, the YOLO model was selected as the most suitable to implement it in the solution with an accuracy of 96.8% and a processing time of 13.92 ms.

One of the most interesting solutions was the one proposed by [8] in which they developed an automatic system for the recognition of multinational vehicle license plates. Through the YOLOv3 architecture, said system could be developed, through some tests carried out by the authors, it was possible to detect and recognize characters from vehicle license plates from 17 different countries, having a processing time of 42 ms. Likewise, this solution consists of three stages in which the first is the detection of the vehicle license plate in which its location is detected, as a second stage is the unified character recognition where each character of the vehicle plate is segmented for its due recognition of each one and finally there is the detection of multinational license plate design, an algorithm is proposed to extract the correct order of the number of vehicle plates that is generalized to multinational vehicle plates. This results in an accuracy of 98.85% and a recovery of 99.76% by the system proposed by the authors.

Regarding the article [9], YOLOv4 uses an algorithm based on other neural network models that allows object detection, what makes this algorithm better is that the model is co-trained, so it is faster than others object detection algorithms, in addition to the fact that detection is carried out in real time. Their proposed system starts with image processing to clean up every noise or other obstacle that prevents license plate detection, then YOLOv4-Tiny is used for license plate frame detection, then a virtual judgment line is used to determine if a vehicle license plate framework has passed, so as to apply M-YOLOv4 for character recognition within the license plate, finally, a logical auxiliary judgment system is applied to improve the license plate recognition accuracy. As a result of the proposed solution, a license plate character recognition rate was obtained with 97% and 95% accuracy during the day and night respectively. With the proposed system based on an edge AI, it will allow the transmission and recognition of vehicle license plate characters in real time with low computational cost, through a real-life test environment of selected vehicle license plates in Taiwan.

Likewise, with a much more recent approach, Sestrem and his team [10] with the proposed next-generation storage architecture guarantee privacy in license plate recognition systems. Such architecture uses a private blockchain along with smart contracts. In addition to presenting a detailed description and evaluation of the performance and security of a blockchain-based storage architecture to protect the privacy of users of vehicle license plate recognition systems. According to the main result of the proposed solution, a maximum of 0.46 s was obtained as execution time to obtain a blockchain contract, this referring to 100 blocks and a minimum of 0.43 s referring to one block.

3   Main Contribution

For the development of the design of the logical architecture of the mobile application, a diagram has been chosen in which the process of each functionality that the application contains is detailed, as well as the relationships that each component of the solution has between them and with each other the end users [11].

A. Mobile App Users

Two users have been defined, the police officer is the user who uses the application to consult information about a vehicle and make a report of a case that vehicle identity theft has been identified; the citizen uses the application to consult information about a vehicle and file a complaint about vehicle identity theft. Both consult the information of the vehicles through the recognition of license plates and the reports and complaints are issued to be sent by email on cases of vehicle identity theft. For these two users to enter the application, they must create an account within it, in which they will be assigned the user role from which they will identify themselves within the mobile application,

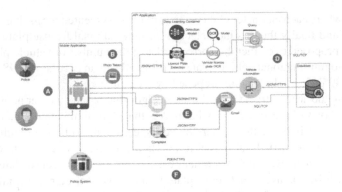

Fig. 1. Solution architecture

such as police or citizen. An extra functionality is the login using token authentication to verify your identity.

B. Vehicle Image

For users to be able to query vehicle information, they must first access the vehicle registration detection and recognition functionality, in which a photograph of the vehicle to be consulted will be needed. The user can take a photograph of the vehicle or upload it from the multimedia gallery of your mobile device from the application, where your board is as visible as possible, the application can accept image files in JPG, JPEG, PNG and SVG format, the image will be sent by JSON format to the Application API of the application for the detection and recognition of the license plate of the image.

C. Vehicle License Plate Detection and Recognition

When the Backend receives the image sent through the JSON format using HTTPS, it will go through two Deep Learning models that have been previously trained to be able to detect and recognize license plates and extract the alphanumeric code of said license plate to be able to perform the query, these models will be developed using Python using TensorFlow and EasyOCR for detection and recognition respectively. The image will first go through the vehicle license plate detection model, this model will allow the vehicle license plate to be located and focused, in which only the vehicle license plate will be framed, to transfer it to the second Deep Learning model which is based on optical recognition of characters, this allows segmenting each character found on the vehicle license plate in order to extract the alphanumeric code and digitize it to perform the query. Once the vehicle registration code is extracted and digitized, it will be saved using a variable to be able to query the database where the vehicle information is located.

D. Vehicle Information Query

A query is made directly about the vehicle information to a simulated database through the alphanumeric code of the image of the vehicle license plate to be consulted, the connectivity with the database that will be developed with MySQL, is done through a DJango framework. Which is a framework to develop Backend in Python, to then show on the application screen all the necessary information that the user needs to identify if a crime of vehicular identity theft is being committed, this information will be saved in JSON format through the HTTPS protocol to be displayed on the screen of the user's mobile device.

E. Issuance and Review of Reports and Complaints

In the process of issuing reports, only the police can do it, since they oversee identifying this type of crime, which is why they are responsible for issuing a case report. Once the report is created, it is sent to them through a notification system mail the report to the relevant authority in this case the same police in which the report will be in PDF format, this same case happens with citizen users, they can only issue complaints but not reports of the case, but like the process of Reports are sent to the police through a mail system. The issuance and complaint creation functionality allows you to create these two documents through a form in which you must fill it out to send it. Once the form is completed, the document will go to PDF format and then to JSON format for sending to the e-mail system of the application by HTTP, once said document is sent, the sender will see said document attached in PDF format in his inbox.

The use of layers: presentation, application, deep learning, database are present in Fig. 1, detailed below:

Presentation Layer (Mobile): Provides functionality to query vehicle information and send reports or complaints through mobile devices. Developed with Flutter (mobile framework) using the Dart programming language, coded in Android Studio.

Deep Learning Layer: Consisting of two models previously trained to perform the detection and recognition of vehicle license plates, receiving as input data photos or images of vehicles for which you want to consult information, after the detection and recognition process the alphanumeric code is sent of the license plate extracted from the image to the API of the application in computer format. These models will be developed with Python for training.

Application Layer (API): Provides functions for querying vehicle information, sending reports and denouncing cases of vehicle identity theft through a JSON/HTTPS API. This Backend is developed with the Django Python framework for Backend development and as a Python programming language.

Data Layer: Stores user registration information, hash authentication credentials, access logs, etc., in addition to the reports and complaints made within the mobile application, MySQL will be the chosen tool.

The architecture is aimed at increasing the efficiency of the detection and identification of vehicle identity theft (D&ISV), with the objective of implementing a mobile application, which allows recognizing and detecting license plates that are suspected of vehicle identity theft (D&ISV), to speed up the query and report, using Deep Learning. Having to analyze the technologies of object detection and optical character recognition, also to design the architecture of the software to be developed. The use of Deep Learning would allow rapid and accurate detection and recognition to identify cases of vehicle identity theft.

The DL-based solution presents three layers: Input layer, for license plate detection, receives images of predefined size and prepares them to be processed by the subsequent layers of the network, where features will be extracted, and license plate detection will be performed.

Hidden layers are responsible for extracting relevant features and learning more abstract representations of the input images. This allows the network to identify specific patterns related to the plates and perform the necessary classification.

Output layer provides the final classification of the image regions and, in some cases, also provides information about the location of license plates using bounding boxes.

The Pooling process (located within the training phase) is based on making convolution and reduction layers to better resize the output image. When this process ends, the final model will have a clear idea to be able to create the output data and/or make a prediction. As can be seen in the example shown, depending on the image, a label will also be generated, based on the detection, and its percentage of precision [12]. This is detailed in Fig. 2, where it takes as a case images of license plates.

POOLING

Fig. 2. Contribution graph: Pooling

In [13], optical character recognition (OCR) is defined as a technology that uses image processing algorithms to identify and convert printed or handwritten text into digitalized images or documents in editable text format. We utilize this technology to extract each character found on the license plate and digitize it, to query the vehicle information.

In object detection technologies, computer vision techniques are employed, utilizing deep learning algorithms to identify and classify objects in images or videos, as defined in [14]. We utilize this technology to locate the license plate within the input image.

Each object detection technology has its strengths and weaknesses in terms of accuracy and speed. TensorFlow and Detectron2, these two technologies are ideal choices for those looking for high accuracy and speed, although implementing these technologies may require advanced programming and deep learning skills [15].

Based on the comparison criteria, it can be concluded that TensorFlow is an excellent option for projects that require high-precision object detection and scalability. Although it may require a higher level of knowledge in programming and deep learning compared to other options, TensorFlow offers a wide variety of tools and resources that can facilitate the implementation and training of object detection models, its flexibility and versatility applies to learning automatic [16].

EasyOCR stands out as a solid option for optical character recognition. It offers good detection accuracy, fast processing speed, and an easy-to-implement interface [17]. Furthermore, its flexibility in terms of supported languages and supported image formats make it a versatile solution. Overall, EasyOCR provides a balanced combination of key features, making it an excellent choice for projects looking for easy implementation, high accuracy, and multi-language recognition.

It is important to note that the accuracy and speed of detection may vary depending on the type of document and the quality of the scan, so it is advisable to carry out tests with the technologies considered before making a final decision. In addition, ease of implementation, scalability, and flexibility must also be considered when choosing the right OCR technology for a specific project [18, 19].

Design of CPLSafe Architecture improves the identification of vehicle license plates in Metropolitan Lima.

4 Experiments

4.1 Experimental Protocol

The objective is to validate the design of the CLPSafe architecture, which will allow the identification of vehicles with fake license plates. To validate the hypothesis, a Focus Group is proposed, led by three experts in software architecture from the Faculty of Engineering at the Universidad Peruana de Ciencias Aplicadas. They will be responsible for evaluating the CLPSafe architecture.

The virtual Focus Group will take place in Lima, Peru, and will involve a comprehensive evaluation of the architecture. To gather data and opinions from the participants, a structured questionnaire consisting of four questions will be used. These questions are designed to enable the experts to provide feedback on each component of the software architecture.

The identified variable in this case is the low efficiency in detecting and reporting vehicles with forged license plates.

4.2 Results

The responses from the software architecture experts were obtained, which were analyzed and scored based on a scale of 1 to 5.

The results of the analysis conducted on the expert's responses yielded the following outcomes:

- 75% of the experts expressed a favorable opinion regarding the diagram design of the proposed architecture for CLPSafe.
- 50% of the experts had a positive view regarding the use of artificial intelligence technologies such as Deep Learning-based pooling, considering it a substantial contribution to the research project's objectives.
- 75% of the experts expressed a favorable opinion concerning the guarantee of scalability and performance of the deployed CLPSafe application.
- 75% of the experts had a positive opinion regarding the components utilized in the diagram of the proposed architecture for CLPSafe.

4.3 Discussion

We analyzed the results obtained in relation to the posed questions, providing an unbiased discussion and offering recommendations to improve CLPSafe. Additionally, relevant aspects of the presented architecture are highlighted, and areas for improvement in terms of scalability and performance are identified.

Firstly, we agree with the responses given by the experts and the overall result of the first question, which showed a favorable perception in 75% of the responses. Regarding the need to consider security mechanisms for vehicle plates using machine learning, our results support the importance of implementing an approach that combines the ability to recognize key features such as holograms, three-dimensional braids, and watermarks, with the visual and tactile inspection carried out by the police. This combination of approaches enhances the accuracy and reliability of the plate authenticity verification system.

The results of the second question, with an acceptance percentage of 50%, reflect the different perspectives regarding the relevance of the detailed contribution in Fig. 2. While some experts consider it valuable and that it contextualizes the explored mechanisms, others may view it as a general framework or suggest consulting specialized sources for more accurate information.

Regarding the third question, with a 75% acceptance rate among experts, we agree with them regarding scalability, emphasizing the need to address this aspect in the proposed architecture diagram. It is recommended to consider the use of "Deep Learning Containers" in conjunction with technologies like Kubernetes or serverless services in cloud computing, which allow the system to scale automatically based on workload. In the current version of the diagram, a lack of clear indications of scalability and performance is observed, making it necessary to address this aspect to ensure an efficient and adaptable system.

5   Conclusions and Perspectives

5.1   Conclusions

License plate cloning remains a persistent problem in Peru, leading to criminal activities and falsely implicating the original owners of the license plates in crimes. According to the analyzed results, which have an overall average of 75% of expert responses expressing favorable views towards the validation of the proposed architecture diagram for CLPSafe. The proposed diagram has received positive evaluations from the experts, validating its feasibility and effectiveness. These results support the robustness of the proposed architecture in addressing the presented problem and providing an effective solution to license plate cloning in Peru.

5.2   Perspectives

Regarding the development and validation of the proposed solution in the future, a promising performance is envisioned for CLPSafe, which will enable the detection of vehicle license plate identity theft using Deep Learning techniques. It is expected that the continuous advancement of technology and the availability of larger and more diverse datasets will further enhance the accuracy and efficiency of the system. Additionally, exploring new technologies like blockchain is being considered, as it could provide an additional layer of security and reliability to the solution by offering an immutable and transparent record of transactions related to license plate identification. These perspectives suggest a promising outlook for CLPSafe, where the combination of cutting-edge techniques and emerging technologies could drive significant advancements in the detection and prevention of identity theft in the realm of vehicle license plates in Metropolitan Lima.

References

1. Caretas Nacional: Sunarp emitió más de 13 mil Tarjetas de Identificación Vehicular Electrónica. Ilustración Peruana Caretas (2020). https://caretas.pe/nacional/sunarp-emitio-mas-de-13-mil-tarjetas-de-identificacion-vehicular-electronica/
2. Caretas Nacional: Policía Desarticula Banda Dedicada a Robo de Autos de Lujo Que Estaría Liderada Por Fritz Moreno. Ilustración Peruana Caretas (2022). https://caretas.pe/nacional/sunarp-emitio-mas-de-13-mil-tarjetas-de-identificacion-vehicular-electronica/
3. Caretas Nacional: Fiscalía Detiene a Conductores de Motos En Operativo Preventivo de Falsificación de Documentos, Robo de Vehículos y Posesión Ilegal de Armas. Ilustración Peruana Caretas (2022). https://caretas.pe/nacional/fiscalia-detiene-a-conductores-de-motos-en-operativo-preventivo-de-falsificacion-de-documentos-robo-de-vehiculos-y-posesion-ilegal-de-armas/
4. Leon Zaa, R., Rojas Rocca, P.C.: Implementación de un sistema informático, orientado a optimizar la eficiencia en la gestión de emisión del certificado de identificación vehicular de la DIPROVE, Lima Metropolitana (2022). https://renati.sunedu.gob.pe/handle/sunedu/3280945
5. Abdellatif, M.M., Elshabasy, N.H., Elashmawy, A.E., AbdelRaheem, M.: A low cost IoT-based Arabic license plate recognition model for smart parking systems. Ain Shams Eng. J. **14** (2023). https://doi.org/10.1016/J.ASEJ.2023.102178
6. Sanchez Chamachi, W.R.: El delito de falsedad genérica en la modalidad de suplantación de identidad vehicular - "clonación"y su afectación al derecho a la propiedad y seguridad jurídica, Lima 2019–2020 (2021)
7. Weihong, W., Jiaoyang, T.: Research on license plate recognition algorithms based on deep learning in complex environment. IEEE Access **8**, 91661–91675 (2020). https://doi.org/10.1109/ACCESS.2020.2994287
8. Henry, C., Ahn, S.Y., Lee, S.W.: Multinational license plate recognition using generalized character sequence detection. IEEE Access **8**, 35185–35199 (2020). https://doi.org/10.1109/ACCESS.2020.2974973
9. Lin, C.J., Chuang, C.C., Lin, H.Y.: Edge-AI-based real-time automated license plate recognition system. Appl. Sci. **12** (2022). https://doi.org/10.3390/APP12031445
10. Zou, Y., et al.: A robust license plate recognition model based on Bi-LSTM. IEEE Access **8**, 211630–211641 (2020). https://doi.org/10.1109/ACCESS.2020.3040238
11. Tesoriero, R., Rueda, A., Gallud, J.A., Lozano, M.D., Fernando, A.: Transformation architecture for multi-layered WebApp source code generation. IEEE Access **10**, 5223–5237 (2022). https://doi.org/10.1109/ACCESS.2022.3141702
12. He, M.X., Hao, P.: Robust automatic recognition of Chinese license plates in natural scenes. IEEE Access **8**, 173804–173814 (2020). https://doi.org/10.1109/ACCESS.2020.3026181
13. Onim, M.S.H., et al.: BLPnet: a new DNN model and Bengali OCR engine for automatic licence plate recognition. Array **15** (2022). https://doi.org/10.1016/J.ARRAY.2022.100244
14. Huang, Q., Cai, Z., Lan, T.: A single neural network for mixed style license plate detection and recognition. IEEE Access **9**, 21777–21785 (2021). https://doi.org/10.1109/ACCESS.2021.3055243

15. Lim, J.J., et al.: Application of convolutional neural network (CNN) to recognize ship structures. Sensors **22** (2022). https://doi.org/10.3390/S22103824
16. Filus, K., Domańska, J.: Software vulnerabilities in TensorFlow-based deep learning applications. Comput. Secur. **124** (2023). https://doi.org/10.1016/J.COSE.2022.102948
17. Laptev, P., Litovkin, S., Davydenko, S., Konev, A., Kostyuchenko, E., Shelupanov, A.: Neural network-based price tag data analysis. Future Internet **14** (2022). https://doi.org/10.3390/FI1 4030088
18. Salma, Saeed, M., Ur Rahim, R., Gufran Khan, M., Zulfiqar, A., Bhatti, M.T.: Development of ANPR framework for Pakistani vehicle number plates using object detection and OCR. Complexity **2021** (2021). https://doi.org/10.1155/2021/5597337
19. Zhang, C., Wang, Q., Li, X.: V-LPDR: towards a unified framework for license plate detection, tracking, and recognition in real-world traffic videos. Neurocomputing **449**, 189–206 (2021). https://doi.org/10.1016/J.NEUCOM.2021.03.103

Analyzing Sentiments and Topics
on Twitter Towards Rising Cost of Living

Yanyi Li[✉], Nian Ran, Yifu Chen, Renhua Zhou, and Riza Batista Navarro

University of Manchester, Manchester, England
`yanyi.li@student.manchester.ac.uk`

Abstract. In September 2022, the United Kingdom experienced an unprecedented 40-year high in its inflation rate, resulting in a cost of living crisis that has significantly impacted British citizens. To assess public opinion on this issue, we developed a social media analytics pipeline to collect and analyze microblogs posted on Twitter. Our primary objective was to conduct sentiment analysis on the collected tweets to determine the dominant sentiment towards the topic of the cost of living. Additionally, we performed named entity recognition to identify the entities most frequently mentioned and used topic modeling to uncover the most discussed topics. Our approach employed a hybrid sentiment analysis method that utilized three lexicons for preliminary tweet labeling and fine-tuned a RoBERTa model. Our results demonstrate the superior effectiveness of our methods, which provided an in-depth analysis of the cost-of-living situation in the UK.

Keywords: Text Mining · Sentiment Analysis · Topic Modelling

1 Introduction

Social media analytics is a prevalent method for understanding and analyzing public opinions on products or services, as well as perceptions of social events and discussions about political or economic news [18,19,25]. The primary objective of this project is to apply a social media analytics pipeline to assess British people's perceptions of the cost of living in the United Kingdom using tweets retrieved from Twitter [26,27]. The Consumer Prices Index including owner occupiers' housing costs (CPIH) is a measure of inflation. According to the Office for National Statistics, the CPIH index rose from 0.9% in January 2021 to 8.8% in March 2023 [3], indicating that the cost of living crisis is a serious problem. To gain insight into British people's perspectives on this issue, we conducted sentiment analysis, topic modeling and named entity recognition tasks on tweets and analyzed the results obtained.

2 Related Work

2.1 Sentiment Analysis

Twitter sentiment analysis represents a novel and challenging domain within the field of sentiment analysis. The length limitations and informal nature of tweets

J. A. Lossio-Ventura et al. (Eds.): SIMBig 2023, CCIS 2142, pp. 167–183, 2024.
https://doi.org/10.1007/978-3-031-63616-5_13

make them particularly difficult to analyze [4, 7, 9, 24, 26, 28]. There are four predominant methods for conducting sentiment analysis on Twitter: lexicon-based, graph-based, machine learning-based, and hybrid methods that combine lexicon-based and machine learning-based approaches [4]. Deep learning techniques have been applied to Twitter sentiment analysis tasks with great success, demonstrating high levels of precision and effectiveness [10]. Hybrid methods that utilize learning-based approaches to help the model learn new rules and lexicons have proven to be a practical approach for labeling and analyzing sentiment [13]. In our study, we combine lexicon-based approaches and machine learning and achieve better accuracy and more meaningful and authentic results.

2.2   Topic Modeling

Topic modeling is a fundamental technique to uncover latent topics from a given document, it can also be used for fast recommendation by hashtags on Twitter [29]. The two primary types of approaches used for topic modeling are statistical-based and machine-learning-based methods. Among them, Latent Dirichlet Allocation (LDA) [5] has emerged as the most successful statistical one, assuming that a document can be represented as a distribution of topics, while a topic can be represented as a distribution of words. To better capture the complexities of modern social media such as Twitter, Author Topic Model (ATM) [6] and conversation-based LDA [8] were proposed to aggregate documents by authors and conversations, respectively. Recent advancements in pretraining word vectors have led to more granular topic modeling approaches such as Top2Vec [11] and BERTopic [12] using word vector pretraining and deep learning techniques. A comparison between these methods and LDA has been conducted in [14]. In this study, we employ LDA as our topic model due to its prominent performance and applications on Twitter data [15, 16], as well as social prevalent topics such as energy companies [18] and COVID-19 [19].

2.3   Aspect-Based Sentiment Analysis

Sentiment analysis can be categorized into three levels: document-level, sentence-level and aspect-level. Aspect-based sentiment analysis (ABSA) associates sentiments with specific aspects or entities within a sentence [20]. Named entity recognition can be used to extract entities from sentences and then combined with a sentiment analyzer model to conduct sentiment analysis at the aspect level [21].

3   Data Collection and Preprocessing

3.1   Data Collection

Twitter API for academic research was used to search for tweets from 2021 to 2023 that contain keywords or hashtags such as cost of living, food prices, energy bills, etc. We retrieved over 30,000 tweets posted in the United Kingdom by specifying geological coordinates. The raw data contained a wealth of information; replies and retweets were also collected as they contain important expressions of sentiment and perceptions. Additionally, we took into account the like count of each tweet when conducting sentiment analysis.

3.2   Pre-processing

All tasks require certain common pre-processing procedures, such as the removal of usernames, URLs and punctuation. However, different tasks have specific requirements for input data. For instance, while emojis and emoticons can contribute to polarity scores in sentiment analysis, they are irrelevant to topic modeling and named entity recognition (NER) tasks. Additionally, topic modeling is case-sensitive whereas sentiment analysis is not. As a result, different pre-processing steps were conducted for each task. The *clean-text*[1] package was used to filter out emojis, usernames, hashtags and web links from tweets for fundamental data cleaning. These elements have certain patterns; hence we used regular expressions to match the corresponding formats and remove them.

4   Methodology

4.1   Sentiment Analysis

Due to the fact that tweets are naturally unlabeled and the volume of data is vast, manually labeling all tweets is impractical. As such, supervised learning is unlikely to be feasible for this task. However, a hybrid method represents a suitable approach. In this project, we initially used *Valence Aware* Dictionary and Sentiment Reasoner (*VADER*), a lexicon and rule-based sentiment analysis tool that is particularly accurate and effective for analyzing sentiment expressed in social media. However, *VADER* has certain limitations; it calculates valence scores for each word in a sentence and then adjusts the score according to predefined rules. This means that it cannot fully comprehend the context and semantics of sentences [17]. As a result, sarcasm and irony may be misinterpreted and corresponding tweets may be labeled with the opposite sentiment.

Traditional hybrid methods as a solution to above issue use only one sentiment lexicon to annotate data before employing machine learning techniques to increase precision. In contrast, we employed an ensemble of three different sentiment lexicons — *VADER*[2], *TextBlob*[3] and *SentiWordNet*[4] — to improve annotation accuracy and provide a solid training dataset for our machine learning model.

---

[1] https://github.com/prasanthg3/cleantext.
[2] https://github.com/cjhutto/vaderSentiment.
[3] https://github.com/sloria/TextBlob.
[4] https://github.com/aesuli/SentiWordNet.

Tweets that received consensus from a minimum of two lexicons were assigned a corresponding sentiment label and utilized as training data. On the other hand, tweets that failed to achieve consensus across the lexicons were employed as test data without any sentiment annotations. This approach effectively capitalizes on the individual strengths of each lexicon to establish a robust consensus regarding the sentiment expressed within each tweet.

However, setting appropriate thresholds for the sentiment score of each lexicon is a crucial step in improving accuracy. The commonly used threshold for VADER in classifying a sentence is ¿ 0.05 as 'positive' and ¡ -0.05 as 'negatives' [1]. However, this threshold was not accurate or suitable for our data and resulted in numerous misclassification and counterintuitive sentiments. Similarly, the commonly used threshold for TextBlob and SentiWordNet to separate 'positive' and 'negative' sentiments was not used by our dataset due to low F1-score they cause.

To address this particular concern, we randomly selected a subset of 500 data samples from the entire dataset. Each individual data sample was then annotated by two members of our team. In order to enhance the sentiment interpretation of each data sample, we introduced an additional "Neutral" tag, acknowledging that certain tweets may convey factual information or serve as mere reports. Consequently, for each lexicon, there are two thresholds that need to be determined and set. To ensure the reliability of our annotated data, we utilized the Cohen's kappa coefficient [30], treating the annotations provided by the first annotator as the "Ground truth" and those provided by the second annotator as the "Reference". This allowed us to calculate metrics such as "True positives", "True negatives", "False negatives", and "False positives", ultimately yielding the Cohen's kappa coefficient. Our objective was to maximize the Cohen's kappa coefficient, aiming for a value close to 1 since a value of 1 indicates perfect agreement between the annotators. Additionally, we implemented a validation process within our team, involving an independent auditor who scrutinized our labeled tags whenever the Cohen's kappa coefficient fell below a predetermined threshold.

After obtaining the 500 data samples as our gold standard, we proceeded to adjust the threshold values for each lexicon until the predicted labels achieved a relatively high F1-score when compared to the gold standard. To determine these optimal thresholds, we conducted a random search [31] within a range of -1 to 1. Specifically, we initialized 5000 samples within this range for each lexicon and iteratively evaluated our objective function, the F1-score, to identify the highest achievable value. Subsequent to the random search process, we obtained the best thresholds and their corresponding F1-scores for each lexicon, which are presented in Table 1.

Subsequently, we proceeded to apply the thresholds associated with the highest F1-scores for each lexicon to the complete dataset, thereby generating preliminary predictions using the three lexicons. Data points that achieved consensus among two or more lexicons were selected to form the training set.

Table 1. Thresholds to reach highest F1-scores and highest F1-scores

Lexicons	Threshold1	Threshold2	F1-score
VADER	0.809	-0.102	0.588
TextBlob	0.262	-0.126	0.408
SentiWordNet	0.122	-0.121	0.338

As a result, our training set exhibited a sentiment distribution comprising 14,833 instances analyzed as neutral, 9,622 instances analyzed as negative, and 2,129 instances analyzed as positive.

Finally, we used **RoBERTa**[5] [2], a more robust version of **BERT** that is pre-trained on a larger corpus of English data, as our machine learning model. We fine-tuned the pre-trained **RoBERTa** model on our training dataset to learn latent patterns in the tweets and make predictions about the sentiment of tweets in our test dataset.

The methodology employed for conducting sentiment analysis is delineated in Fig. 1.

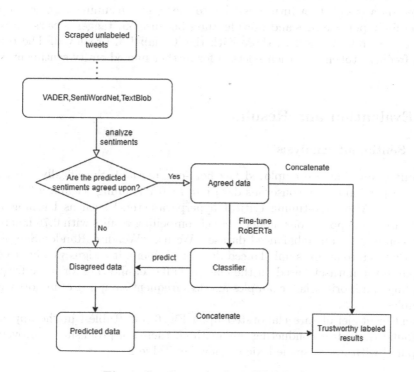

Fig. 1. Sentiment Analysis Workflow

---

[5] https://huggingface.co/RoBERTa-base.

4.2   Topic Modeling

Effective data preprocessing is critical for accurate topic modeling. In addition to the preprocessing steps mentioned in 3.2 Pre-processing, we follow the suggested order in [22] and make some empirical modifications. After data cleaning, we first apply lemmatization, followed by the removal of stopwords. This approach is necessary because some words can become stopwords after lemmatization. For example, 'where's' becomes 'where' and 's.' After preprocessing, bi-grams are constructed to provide more context for topic analysis.

To obtain the best performance from the LDA model, a Bayesian Optimization technique is employed to search for optimal hyperparameters, including the number of topics, training passes, and the parameters of two distributions in LDA. The search is guided by the topic model coherence score, which uses both normalized pointwise mutual information (NPMI) [23] and cosine similarity.

4.3   Aspect-Based Sentiment Analysis

This study employs the Stanford NER Tagger, a 7-class model, to extract named entities including location, person, organization, money, percent, date, and time. Tagged data is saved for future use due to the time-consuming tagging process. We retain uppercase tags and word features because our tagger is case-sensitive. To remove irrelevant words, those with the 'O' label are removed. The top 20 most frequent tokens are then selected for further named entity sentiment analysis.

5   Evaluation and Results

5.1   Sentiment Analysis

For our evaluation, we employed the hold-out method. Specifically, we partitioned a portion of the consensus data into a 70% training set and a 30% evaluation set. After fine-tuning critical hyperparameters[6] such as learning rate, batch size, and epochs, our model yielded compelling results with 0.75 macro F1 score confronting an unbalanced dataset. We use "WeightedRandomSampler"[7] from PyTorch to address unbalanced dataset problem, it assigns weights to each sample in the dataset based on the class unbalance, allowing for more frequent sampling of minority class examples and less frequent sampling of majority class examples.

Sentiment details are elaborated upon Fig. 6 and Table 4 in the appendix. We found that after conducting our method, there's a promising improvement compared with initial single lexicon shown in Table 2.

---

[6] Learning rate:5e-5, batch size:64, epochs:10.
[7] https://pytorch.org/docs/stable/data.html.

Table 2. Improvement rate for each lexicon

Lexicons	Threshold1	Threshold2	F1-score	Improved_F1	Improvement rate (%)
VADER	0.809	-0.102	0.588	0.650	10.544
TextBlob	0.262	-0.126	0.408	0.650	54.762
SentiWordNet	-0.122	-0.121	0.338	0.650	95.783

We later employed the fine-tuned model to predict the sentiment of the discordant data. Finally, we concatenated the predicted data with the original consensus data to generate our conclusive results. To discern the dominant sentiments, we took into consideration the count of likes, as they convey the support and endorsement of the original tweets and consequently express the same sentiment. Therefore, the frequency of a sentiment is the sum of all likes associated with that sentiment. (We omitted retweets and replies as they may express disparate sentiments from those of the original tweets.) In Figs. 2 and 3, we present the sentiment frequency and monthly sentiment frequency, respectively, as well as statistics without counting likes in Figs. 7 and 8 in the appendix. We also provide WordClouds for both positive and negative sentiments in Figs. 9, 10 in the appendix for a more clear view of these sentiments

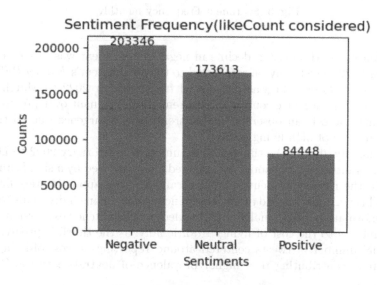

Fig. 2. Sentiment Frequency

The figures presented in the analysis reveal a clear predominance of negative sentiment towards the rising cost of living, exceeding positive sentiment by over twofold, combined with the number of likes. Notably, this negative sentiment exhibits a consistent upward trend from January 2021 to August 2022, with a surge observed between June and August 2022, coinciding with the surge

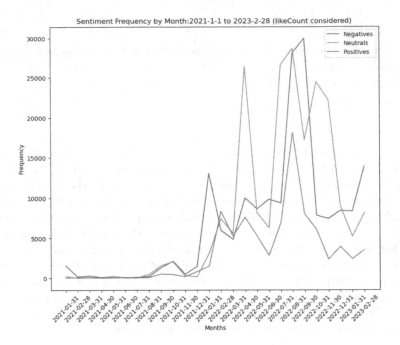

Fig. 3. Sentiment Frequency monthly

in inflation rates. However, a decline in negative sentiment was observed until November 2022, which may be attributed to the government's *Energy Bills Support Scheme(EBSS)*[8] that was introduced from October 2022 to March 2023. Nevertheless, the negative sentiment still remained dominant over positive sentiment, and there is an observed recent trend of a resurgence due to the yet unresolved issue of high living costs.

Additionally, during the timeframe spanning from February 2022 to December 2022, an intriguing phenomenon emerged, characterized by a significant fluctuation in the number of neutral tweets, ranging from approximately 6,000 to 27,500. This period witnessed an increased inclination among individuals to share factual information, occasionally accompanied by a heightened expression of sentiments related to the cost of living. Additionally, as the timeline progressed, a substantial number of tweets centered around reporting on cost-of-living policies, thereby contributing to a higher prevalence of neutral sentiments within the dataset.

5.2   Topic Modeling

We extracted the top 7 topics with the highest occurrence in our dataset, as shown in Fig. 4. The remaining topics have infrequent occurrences, so it's trivial

---

[8] https://www.gov.uk/get-help-energy-bills.

to list them. Each topic is represented by a set of the most significant keywords. Topics 6, 23, 7, 20, and 3 indicate public concern about the rising cost of living, including the prices of energy, heat, and food. People are struggling to pay their bills, and they expect relevant policies from the government and energy companies to address this energy crisis. To provide a more granular visualization, we created WordClouds for each topic, some of which are displayed in Fig. 5, while the full image is available in Fig. 12 in the Appendix. The WordClouds further reveal that people are seeking support from the government and energy companies to alleviate their problems. The WordCloud in Fig. 12 also indicates that people are concerned about the cold, inflation, food demand, and resources for kids.

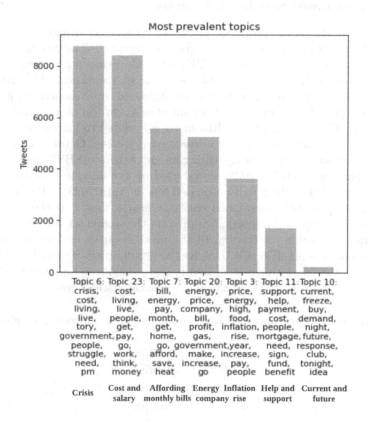

Fig. 4. Most prevalent topics from LDA, the top 7 topics are extracted, each of them is represented by a word that best summarizes the topic, which is in black bold.

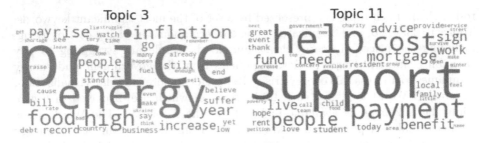

Fig. 5. WordCloud of the topics most talked about(partial)

5.3   Aspect-Based Sentiment Analysis

To conduct a thorough sentiment analysis of the most-discussed entities, we extracted the 20 entities with the highest occurrence. The results show that organizations and locations such as UK, NHS, Government, Scotland, London, Johnson, Britain, Labour, and Rishi are the most mentioned. This suggests a correspondence between our sentiment analysis and topic modeling with regard to government policies and related organizations. On the other hand, Ukraine, EU, Europe, Energy, winter, and Russia are all related to international politics, which is a significant factor in the current energy crisis. October and April are mentioned because of the Energy Bills Support Scheme (EBSS) and the rise of bills starting from October 2022, as reported by the London government[9], and the energy price cap which will be carried out in April 2023[10]. The appearance of BBC as a frequently mentioned entity indicates that it is the main source of news for our topics. Moreover, we provide the dominant sentiment towards these entities in Table 3 according to the most frequent entities in Table 5. It presents an interesting discovery: despite the proliferation of negative sentiments prompted by the escalating cost of living, there remains a noteworthy degree of positive sentiment directed towards governmental institutions.

Table 3. The dominant sentiment towards mostly mentioned entities

Entity	Sentiment
NHS	Positive
Ukraine	Positive
UK	Positive
EU	Positive
April	Positive
Government	Positive
Russia	Positive

---

[9] https://www.london.gov.uk/city-hall-blog/rising-energy-prices-latest-advice.
[10] https://www.ofgem.gov.uk/news-and-views/blog/what-april-2023-price-cap-means-consumers.

6   Future Work

Although our model has demonstrated advancements compared to lexicon-based methods, there are several pertinent concerns that necessitate attention. Firstly, the limited sample size of 500 data points may engender potential bias towards specific sentiments, thereby warranting an expansion in sample size to yield more compelling outcomes. Secondly, the utilization of only 500 data points often results in underfitting when training using RoBERTa, which restricts our ability to make substantial progress despite our endeavors to compare our methods with state-of-the-art models. Consequently, it is imperative to augment the sample size beyond 500 in order to effectively address these concerns and achieve more dependable results. Furthermore, it is crucial to acknowledge that relying solely on Twitter data may not sufficiently capture the diversity of individuals' thoughts. To address this limitation, we recognize the need to collect data from other social media platforms. Although we have amassed 30,000 data points, we acknowledge that this quantity is still insufficient to establish robust conviction. Therefore, in future endeavors, we intend to gather additional data from diverse platforms to enhance the comprehensiveness and persuasiveness of our findings.

7   Conclusion

In this paper, we propose a novel approach for sentiment classification on Tweets. Due to the inherent complexity of the language used in tweets, we employ three lexicon-based approaches for preliminary sentiment labeling, which are then refined using the state-of-the-art RoBERTa language model. Our model achieves a macro 0.94 F1 score, indicating high accuracy in sentiment classification. Through our analysis, we have uncovered significant insights into the sentiments expressed on Twitter and its trend and causes, as well as a range of topics, including energy bills, and government policies and support. Specifically, we found that users frequently express negative sentiments towards rising living costs, citing underlying causes such as Russia and Ukraine. We also observed that people seek support from the government, energy companies, and related organizations, and that government policies aimed at alleviating energy bills have had a positive impact. In addition, our topic modeling and named entity recognition have enabled us to draw further connections between different aspects of the data (Fig. 11).

A   Appendix

Table 4. Classification Report for Fine-tuning RoBERTa the Consensus data (0-negative,1-neutral,2-positive)

	precision	recall	F1-score	support
0	0.74	0.86	0.79	2348
1	0.85	0.74	0.79	4457
2	0.67	0.78	0.72	1370
accuracy			0.78	8175
macro avg	0.75	0.79	0.77	8175
weighted avg	0.79	0.78	0.78	8175

Table 5. Top 20 most frequent words in cost of living topic

	token	label	count
0	NHS	ORGANIZATION	760
1	Ukraine	LOCATION	607
2	UK	ORGANIZATION	424
3	EU	ORGANIZATION	409
4	Government	ORGANIZATION	402
5	Europe	LOCATION	374
6	April	DATE	349
7	Energy	ORGANIZATION	346
8	BBC	ORGANIZATION	346
9	winter	DATE	341
10	Scotland	LOCATION	321
11	October	DATE	321
12	of	ORGANIZATION	316
13	London	LOCATION	292
14	Johnson	PERSON	288
15	Britain	LOCATION	247
16	Labour	ORGANIZATION	221
17	Russia	LOCATION	220
18	Rishi	PERSON	210
19	today	DATE	209

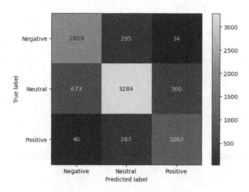

Fig. 6. Confusion Matrix after Fine-tuning RoBERTa on Consensus data

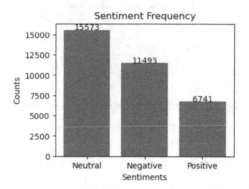

Fig. 7. Sentiment Frequency without Counting Likes

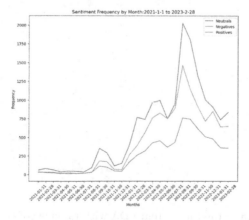

Fig. 8. Sentiment Frequency Monthly without Counting Likes

Fig. 9. WordCloud for positive sentiment

Fig. 10. WordCloud for negative sentiment

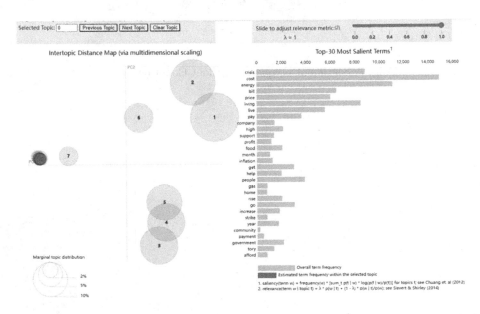

Fig. 11. Visualization of the topics from LDA with rankings of the words most talked about

Fig. 12. WordCloud of the topics most talked about

References

1. Collomb, A.A., Brunie, L., Costea, C.: A Study and Comparison of Sentiment Analysis Methods for Reputation Evaluation (2013)
2. Liu, Y., et al.: Roberta: a robustly optimized Bert pretraining approach. arXiv preprint arXiv:1907.11692 (2019)
3. Office for National Statics.: CPIH ANNUAL RATE. https://www.ons.gov.uk/economy/inflationandpriceindices/timeseries/l55o/mm23. Accessed 2 Mar 2023

4. Giachanou, A., Crestani, F.: Like it or not: a survey of twitter sentiment analysis methods. In: Association for Computing Machinery. New York, USA. vol. 49, num. 2 (2017). https://doi.org/10.1145/2938640

5. Blei, D.M., Ng, A.Y., Jordan, M.I.: Latent Dirichlet Allocation. In: JMLR.org, vol. 3. (2003)

6. Steyvers, M., Smyth, P., Rosen-Zvi, M., Griffiths, T.: Probabilistic author-topic models for information discovery. In: Proceedings of the Tenth ACM SIGKDD International Conference on Knowledge Discovery and Data Mining, Seattle, USA, pp. 306–315 (2004). https://doi.org/10.1145/1014052.1014087

7. Zimbra, D., Abbasi, A., Zeng, D., Chen, H.: The state-of-the-art in twitter sentiment analysis: a review and benchmark evaluation. ACM Trans. Manage. Inf. Syst. 9(2), 1–29 (2018). https://doi.org/10.1145/3185045

8. Alvarez-Melis, D., Saveski, M.: Topic modeling in twitter: aggregating tweets by conversations. In: Proceedings of the International AAAI Conference on Web and Social Media, vol. 10. num. 1 (2021). https://ojs.aaai.org/index.php/ICWSM/article/view/14817

9. Kouloumpis, E., Wilson, T., Moore, J.: Twitter sentiment analysis: the good the bad and the OMG! In: Proceedings of the International AAAI Conference on Web and Social Media, vol. 5 (2021). https://ojs.aaai.org/index.php/ICWSM/article/view/14185, https://doi.org/10.1609/icwsm.v5i1.14185

10. Severyn, A., Moschitti, A.: Twitter sentiment analysis with deep convolutional neural networks. In: Proceedings of the 38th International ACM SIGIR Conference on Research and Development in Information Retrieval, pp. 959–962 (2015). https://doi.org/10.1145/2766462.2767830

11. Angelov, D.: Top2Vec: Distributed Representations of Topics (2020). https://arxiv.org/abs/2008.09470

12. Grootendorst, M.: BERTopic: Neural topic modeling with a class-based TF-IDF procedure (2022). https://arxiv.org/abs/2203.05794

13. Zhang, L., Ghosh, R., Dekhil, M., Hsu, M., Liu, B.: Combining Lexicon-based and Learning-based Methods for Twitter Sentiment Analysis (2011)

14. Egger, R., Yu, J.: A Topic Modeling Comparison Between LDA, NMF, Top2Vec, and BERTopic to Demystify Twitter Posts. In: Frontiers in Sociology, vol. 7 (2022). https://www.frontiersin.org/articles/10.3389/fsoc.2022.886498

15. Zhao, W.X., Jiang, J., Weng, J., He, J., Lim, E.-P., Yan, H., Li, X.: Comparing twitter and traditional media using topic models. In: Clough, P., Foley, C., Gurrin, C., Jones, G.J.F., Kraaij, W., Lee, H., Mudoch, V. (eds.) ECIR 2011. LNCS, vol. 6611, pp. 338–349. Springer, Heidelberg (2011). https://doi.org/10.1007/978-3-642-20161-5_34

16. Alash, H.M., Al-Sultany, G.A.: Improve topic modeling algorithms based on Twitter hashtags. J. Phys. Conf. Ser. 1660(1), 012100 (2020). https://dx.doi.org/10.1088/1742-6596/1660/1/012100

17. Hutto, C., Gilbert, E.: VADER: a parsimonious rule-based model for sentiment analysis of social media text. In: Proceedings of the International AAAI Conference on Web and Social Media, vol.8, num. 1, pp. 216–225 (2014). https://ojs.aaai.org/index.php/ICWSM/article/view/14550

18. Ikoro, V., Sharmina, M., Malik, K., Batista-Navarro, R.: analyzing sentiments expressed on twitter by UK energy company consumers. In: 2018 Fifth International Conference on Social Networks Analysis, Management and Security (SNAMS), pp. 95–98 (2018). https://doi.org/10.1109/SNAMS.2018.8554619

19. Mutanga, M.B.,Abayomi, A.: Tweeting on COVID-19 pandemic in South Africa: LDA-based topic modelling approach. Afr. J. Sci. Technol. Innov. Dev. **14**, 163–172 (2022). https://doi.org/10.1080/20421338.2020.1817262
20. Nazir, Ambreen and Rao, Yuan and Wu, Lianwei and Sun, Ling.: Issues and Challenges of Aspect-based Sentiment Analysis: A Comprehensive Survey. In: IEEE Transactions on Affective Computing. vol. 13, pp. 845-86https://doi.org/10.1109/TAFFC.2020.2970399. (2022)
21. Vasanthi, A., Harish Kumar, B., Karanraj, R.: AN RL approach for ABSA using transformers. In: 2022 6th International Conference on Trends in Electronics and Informatics (ICOEI), pp. 354–366 (2022). https://doi.org/10.1109/ICOEI53556.2022.9776915
22. Maier, D.: Applying LDA topic modeling in communication research: toward a valid and reliable methodology. In: Communication Methods and Measures, vol. 12, pp. 93–118 (2018). https://doi.org/10.1080/19312458.2018.1430754
23. Bouma, G.: Normalized (Pointwise) mutual information in collocation extraction. In: Proceedings of the Biennial GSCL Conference 2009 (2009)
24. Qi, Y., Shabrina, Z.: Sentiment analysis using Twitter data: a comparative application of lexicon- and machine-learning-based approach. In: Social Network Analysis and Mining, vol.13, p. 31. (2023). https://doi.org/10.1007/s13278-023-01030-x
25. Kaur, P., Edalati, M.: Sentiment analysis on electricity twitter posts (2022). https://arxiv.org/abs/2206.05042
26. Wang, Y., Guo, J., Yuan, C., Li, B.: Sentiment analysis of Twitter data. Appl. Sci. **12**, 11775 (2022). https://www.mdpi.com/2076-3417/12/22/11775
27. Rodrigues, A., et al.: Real-time twitter spam detection and sentiment analysis using machine learning and deep learning techniques. In: Computational Intelligence and Neuroscience, vol. 2022, p. 1 (2022). https://doi.org/10.1155/2022/5211949
28. Saif, H., He, Y., Fernandez, M., Alani, H.: Contextual semantics for sentiment analysis of Twitter. Inf. Process. Manag. **52**, 5–19 (2016). https://www.sciencedirect.com/science/article/pii/S0306457315000242
29. Godin, F., Slavkovikj, V., De Neve, W., Schrauwen, B., Van de Walle, R.: Using topic models for twitter hashtag recommendation. In: Proceedings of the 22nd International Conference on World Wide Web, pp. 593–596 (2013). https://doi.org/10.1145/2487788.2488002
30. Kraemer, H.C.: Kappa coefficient. In: Wiley StatsRef: Statistics Reference Online, pp. 1–4 (2014). https://doi.org/10.1002/9781118445112.stat00365.pub2
31. Bergstra, J., Bengio, Y.: Random search for hyper-parameter optimization. J. Mach. Learn. Res. **13**, 2 (2012)

Item Response Theory in Sample Reweighting to Build Fairer Classifiers

Diego Minatel[(✉)], Nícolas Roque dos Santos, Vinícius Ferreira da Silva,
Mariana Cúri, and Alneu de Andrade Lopes

Institute of Mathematics and Computer Science, University of São Paulo,
São Carlos, Brazil
{dminatel,nrsantos,vfsilva}@usp.br, {mcuri,alneu}@icmc.usp.br

Abstract. Currently, one of the biggest challenges of Machine Learning
(ML) is to develop fairer models that do not propagate prejudices, stereotypes, social inequalities, and other types of discrimination in their decisions. Before ML faced the problem of unfair decision-making, the field
of educational testing developed several mathematical tools to decrease
bias in selections made by tests. Thus, the Item Response Theory is
one of these main tools, and its great power of evaluation helps make
fairer selections. Therefore, in this paper, we use the concepts of Item
Response Theory to propose a novel sample reweighting method named
IRT-SR. The IRT-SR method aims to assign weights to the most important instances to minimize discriminatory effects in binary classification
tasks. According to our results, IRT-SR guides classification algorithms
to fit fairer models, improving the main group fairness notions such as
demographic parity, equal opportunity, and equalized odds without significant performance loss.

Keywords: Data Bias · Fairness · IRT · Machine Learning ·
Preprocessing Algorithm

1 Introduction

Machine Learning (ML) algorithms significantly influence consequential decisions in various domains, including credit transactions, advertising targeting,
credit assessment, translation, and content recommendation [26]. As these algorithms possess the power to shape people's lives, it becomes imperative to
acknowledge the accompanying responsibilities. It is crucial to exercise caution
and ensure that these models do not perpetuate societal biases and discrimination that already exist within our society [23,24].

One notable example of discrimination arising from learning models is exemplified by the utilization of the COMPAS (Correctional Offender Management
Profiling for Alternative Sanctions) system to predict recidivism risk and aid
judges in determining sentences within the criminal justice system of the United
States. This case gained attention due to the identification of potential biases

J. A. Lossio-Ventura et al. (Eds.): SIMBig 2023, CCIS 2142, pp. 184–198, 2024.
https://doi.org/10.1007/978-3-031-63616-5_14

and adverse impacts on certain racial and socioeconomic groups, particularly against black defendants [2]. These biases resulted in a troubling outcome where low-risk black defendants were twice as likely to be misclassified as high-risk compared to their white counterparts, consequently depriving them of parole rights.

In this context, one of the biggest challenges in the field of ML is to develop fairer decision-making models, especially when these decisions involve people's futures [22]. An inherent challenge in this pursuit arises from the nature of data itself, as they often serve as a reflection of societal realities [3]. Thus, prejudices, stereotypes, and inequalities present in society are often contained in the data. As models are data-driven, training them on biased datasets unintentionally reproduces undesirable behaviors.

One way to minimize the biases contained in the data is through the preprocessing algorithms, which, when developed for this purpose, aim to transform the data set used in training, thereby incorporating some fairness notions or eliminating explicit discriminatory biases [25]. One of these preprocessing strategies is the sample reweighting method, the focus of this paper, which aims to assign weights to the instances used in model training. This helps to determine which instances are more important to be classified correctly to minimize the discriminatory effects of these models. Consequently, these weights support the classification algorithms' search for fairer solutions.

Before ML faced the problem of unfair decision-making, the educational testing field developed solutions to decrease bias in the applicant selection process. One of these solutions is the Item Response Theory (IRT), which has a great power of evaluation and is a fairer tool for evaluating tests than the Classical Test Theory [19]. IRT is used as an assessment model in some of the world's leading exams, such as the SAT[1], TOEFL[2], and ENEM[3]. Therefore, given its success in educational testing, IRT can be a promising path to developing fairer models [16].

In this scenario, we propose a novel sample reweighting method named IRT-SR based on Item Response Theory concepts to be applied in binary classification tasks. Our experimental results show that IRT-SR can improve key group fairness metrics, making classifiers fairer without significant performance loss. Complementarily, we highlight two main contributions of this paper. Firstly, it introduces Item Response Theory concepts into solutions to minimize discriminatory effects in machine learning models. Secondly, it introduces our IRT-SR sample reweighting method to guide classification algorithms to fit fairer models.

The remaining of this paper is divide as follows: Sect. 2 provides an overview of the background and related work about the topic. Section 3 presents our proposed methods and approaches. In Sect. 4, we detail the experimental settings

---

[1] The SAT is an educational exam given to high school students in the United States, which serves as a criterion for admission to American universities.

[2] TOEFL is the acronym for Test of English as a Foreign Language.

[3] ENEM is the exam that evaluates high school students in Brazil. The students use their ENEM scores to try to enter public and private universities in the country.

and methodology employed to evaluate our proposed methods. Section 5 outlines the results obtained from our experiments and analyzes their implications. Finally, in Sect. 6, we conclude the paper by summarizing our findings and discussing their significance.

2   Background

This section presents the key terms and fundamental concepts of group fairness analysis and item response theory necessary to understand our proposal.

2.1   Group Fairness Analysis

Protected attributes are characteristics that hold sensitive information, like gender, race, nationality, religion, and sexual orientation. These attributes should receive equal treatment, regardless of their value. A *group* is a collection of individuals who share the same protected attributes, such as males and females in the case of gender. Moreover, a *privileged group* refers to a group or set of groups historically receiving better treatment than *unprivileged groups*.

One form of discrimination is to use protected attributes in decision-making. This practice is called *adverse treatment* and is typically forbidden by law in democratic countries. However, *adverse impact* occurs when certain groups are either advantaged or disadvantaged by outcomes, irrespective of whether adverse treatment is present or not [3]. In machine learning, adverse treatment arises when protected attributes are incorporated into model training, while adverse impact pertains to uneven results (*e.g.*, F1-score) across various groups.

Group fairness analysis aims to identify any potential unfair outcomes between different groups, with a particular focus on identifying adverse impacts. Three group fairness notions are discussed when we want to ensure that the adverse impact does not occur: demographic parity, equal opportunity, and equalized odds. *Demographic parity* means that every group has an equal chance of receiving a positive label [13]. *Equal opportunity* ensures that each group has an equal true positive rate [15]. Finally, *equalized odds* ensure all groups share the same true and false positive rates [15].

Therefore, group fairness analysis is determined by comparing group outcomes. This implies that any performance metric can be analyzed as group fairness. However, achieving equal rates is sometimes infeasible. Thus, we typically calculate the score ratio between privileged and unprivileged groups to determine any disparities in results based on these group fairness notions.

2.2   Item Response Theory

Item Response Theory (IRT) is a collection of mathematical models that are utilized in test evaluation, primarily in educational and psychometric applications. These models depict the relationship between the responses to test items and the abilities of the examinees, which enhances the assessment's effectiveness [10].

The IRT models stand out for their evaluation power and can be considered a fairer form of evaluation since they are able to detect unwanted behaviors of an examinee, such as correct answers by guessing.

Dichotomous item response models are characterized by evaluating tests in which the correctness of the test questions is in the right and wrong format, regardless of the number of answer options. This form of evaluation resembles the evaluations of binary classifiers, where to calculate the metrics derived from the confusion matrix, the correct and incorrect classifications of the classifier are used. For this reason, we use dichotomous item response models in this work, specifically the two-parameter logistic model. Table 1 shows an example of the modeling of dichotomous items, where the data structure U represents a test with k items (columns) and n examinees (rows), where $U_{ij} = 1$ indicates that examinee i correctly answered question j, and $U_{ij} = 0$ indicates an incorrect answer.

Table 1. Data structure for modeling dichotomous items.

Individual	Item 1	Item 2	Item 3	$\cdots$	Item k
Examinee 1	1	1	0	$\cdots$	1
Examinee 2	0	0	0	$\cdots$	1
Examinee 3	0	1	1	$\cdots$	0
$\vdots$	$\vdots$	$\vdots$	$\vdots$	$\vdots$	$\vdots$
Examinee n	1	1	0	$\cdots$	1

The two-parameter logistic model (2PL) is formulated by Eq. 1. If we have a data structure U that contains k items and n examinees, then $P(U_{ij} = 1 \mid \theta_i)$ represents the probability of examinee i answering item j correctly, which depends on their ability θ_i. The parameters a_j and b_j define the logistic curve associated with item j, known as the Item Characteristic Curve (ICC).

$$P(U_{ij} = 1 \mid \theta_i) = \frac{1}{1 + e^{-a_j(\theta_i - b_j)}} \tag{1}$$

Figure 1 shows examples of ICCs, where the y-axis represents the probability of correctly answering the item and the x-axis represents the ability θ. Figure 1a shows the influence of parameter a, and it can be seen that parameter a acts directly on the ICC slope. Therefore, the parameter a is proportional to the derivative of the logistic curve at its inflection point. In contrast, Fig. 1b shows an example with three items, each with a different b-value. The b-value indicates the location of the ICCs on the ability scale, at which the probability of providing a correct answer is 50%. As the value of b increases, θ's ability to answer the item correctly increases. In general, ability values are commonly assumed to follow a normal distribution with an average of 0 and a standard deviation of 1.

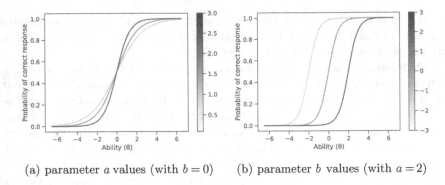

(a) parameter a values (with $b=0$)   (b) parameter b values (with $a=2$)

Fig. 1. Example of Item Characteristic Curves

Therefore, the θ values typically fall within the range of -4 to $+4$, and b values fall between -2 and $+2$ [14].

In the context of ML, IRT has already been applied in classification tasks. In [20,21], the authors find a strong correlation between the abilities (θ value) of the classifiers and their accuracy; with this result, they suggest some applications for IRT in ML, such as model selection and classifier evaluation. Another application is [9], in which the authors proposed a new weighted voting in an ensemble of classifiers. Thus, the voting weight of a classifier is given by its θ values. These works use the same item modeling, with classifiers modeled as examinees and instances as items. However, this work inverts this modeling, modeling classifiers as items and instances as examinees, to make it possible to assign one θ value to each instance and thus formulate our sample reweighting method.

3 Proposal

This section presents our sample reweighting method, IRT Sample Reweighting (IRT-SR), based on Item Response Theory concepts. In order to transpose them to the domain of ML, we model a set of base classifiers as items and the sample as examinees. Then, we can define the weight of each instance by calibrating IRT parameters. The underlying idea of this method is that as the IRT is a fairer evaluation method, the weights defined using this mathematical model can contribute to developing fairer classifiers. Our proposed method comprises four stages, which we discuss in detail in the subsequent sections.

3.1 Stage 1: Base Classifiers Predictions

In the first stage of our method, we train a set of k base classifiers using the training sample. Next, we perform predictions on that same sample with the same k classifiers. This step is necessary as it allows us to model this set of predictions as a dichotomous test problem for using Item Response Theory, as described in Sect. 2.2.

As we model the set of classifiers as items in the next stage, the number k of base classifiers must satisfy the following condition $k > 2$ [10]. Thus, we need more than two items to estimate the parameters a and b of the ICCs. We selected the following four classifiers from the k-Nearest Neighbors (kNN) classification algorithm: 1NN, 3NN, 5NN, and 7NN, which use 1, 3, 5, and 7 as the value of the hyperparameter of nearest neighbors, respectively. We opted for kNN in this stage due to its simplicity, performance, and ease of interpreting its decisions. Upon the completion of this stage, given a sample D_m with m instances, we have the following set of predictions $[\hat{Y}_{1NN}, \hat{Y}_{3NN}, \hat{Y}_{5NN}, \hat{Y}_{7NN}]$.

3.2   Stage 2: Item Modeling

Since we want to include a weight for each instance of the training sample, we model in this stage the training sample as examinees and the set of base classifiers as items. Thus, we are able to associate one θ value for each instance, which can be used to determine the weight of the instance. Therefore, to transform the classifier predictions $[\hat{Y}_{1NN}, \hat{Y}_{3NN}, \hat{Y}_{5NN}, \hat{Y}_{7NN}]$ into items $[I_{1NN}, I_{3NN}, I_{5NN}, I_{7NN}]$, we have the modeling of items U, where $U_{ij} = 1$ indicates a correct prediction of classifier i in instance j and 0 otherwise.

Table 2 illustrates the functioning of the item modeling matrix U. Each entry U_{ij} indicates if a specific instance i is correctly classified by the classifier j. A value of 1 in the table indicates a correct classification, while a value of 0 indicates the opposite. For example, the item I_{7NN} shows that the 7NN correctly classified instances 1, 2, and 5 and misclassified instances 3 and 4.

Table 2. The classifier's predictions are modeled as a right or wrong test. The value of cell ij indicates correct (equal to 1) or incorrect (equal to 0) prediction of instance i by the classifier in column j.

Instances	I_{1NN}	I_{3NN}	I_{5NN}	I_{7NN}
Instance 1	1	1	0	1
Instance 2	0	0	0	1
Instance 3	0	1	1	0
Instance 4	0	1	0	0
Instance 5	1	1	0	1

3.3   Stage 3: IRT Parameters Calibration

In the third stage, we employ the 2PL model in the item modeling matrix U to estimate the θ values of the instances and the ICCs associated with the trained base classifiers. To calibrate these parameters, we utilize the expectation-maximization (EM) algorithm [5].

To better understand the behavior of an ICC, Fig. 2 presents an illustrative example with parameters $a = 2$ and $b = 0$ within the classification context.

Notably, the classifier has a high probability of misclassifying instances with θ values lower than the value of its parameter b, as exemplified by the red vertical line. Conversely, instances with θ values greater than parameter b (indicated by the green vertical line) are more likely to be correctly classified by the classifier. Moreover, instances with θ values equal to parameter b are characterized by the vertical gray line, signifying a 50% probability of being classified correctly.

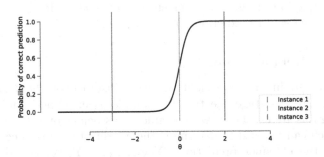

Fig. 2. Example of the Item Characteristic Curve, with $a = 2$ and $b = 0$, associated with a classifier. Note that instance 3 (green line) has a high probability of being correctly predicted by the classifier, while instance 1 (red line) has a high probability of being incorrectly predicted by the classifier. Finally, instance 2 (gray line) has a 50% probability of being predicted correctly. (Color figure online)

3.4   Stage 4: Sample Reweighting

Lastly, we can assign the sample weight with the estimated θ values for each instance. However, as seen in Fig. 2, the smaller the θ value of an instance, the more difficult it is to predict it correctly. Thus, these instances should have greater weight in the sample reweighting. Therefore, we rescaled the θ values to a range between 1 and 5. We use this new scale to maintain the tradeoff between improvement in group fairness measures without significant performance losses. Finally, the sample weight of IRT-SR is given by Eq. 2, where $\theta_{rescaled}$ is the θ value translated to the new value scale.

$$Sample\,Weight = \frac{1}{\theta_{rescaled}} \tag{2}$$

4   Experimental Settings

This experiment evaluates IRT-SR's capacity to aid the selected classification algorithms to fit fairer classifiers. The first step of the experiment is to separate the dataset into a training set (80%) and a test set (20%). We employ 5-fold cross-validation on the training set. This configuration was chosen because some selected datasets have few instances, as shown in Table 3. Moreover, we apply the selected sample reweighting methods for each training fold and use the sample weight generated in the selected classification algorithms. We also apply the classification algorithms without using sample reweighting methods to have a benchmark for comparison.

At the end of the validation step, based on the demographic parity, equal opportunity, and equalized odds fairness measures, we select the best configuration for each type of classification algorithm of each sample reweighting method tested. Then we reapply the sample reweighting methods and retrain the classifiers with the entire training set and its best settings. Thus, in the end, we can compare the sample reweighting methods on the test set, verifying which method best guides the classification algorithms to develop fairer classifiers. An overview of the experiment we performed can be seen in Fig. 3.

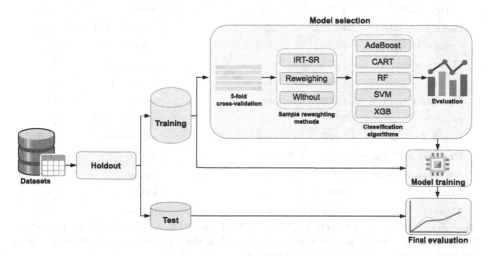

Fig. 3. Overview of the performed analysis. Initially, we split the dataset into training and testing sets. In sequence, we use 5-fold cross-validation and apply sample reweighting methods to each training fold to assess fairness metrics using five classification algorithms to identify the best hyperparameters for each classifier. Thus, we then trained the classifiers with the entire training set using the obtained hyperparameters. Finally, we assess the discriminatory effects of each classifier on the test set.

The source code and benchmark datasets utilized in the evaluation process are available in a public code repository[4]. The experiments were conducted using Python and R programming languages, with the help of the following libraries: scikit-learn (classification algorithms) [6], xgboost [8], aif360 (fairness metrics and Reweighing method) [4], and mirt (IRT calibration) [7]. In the remainder of this section, we detail the datasets, algorithms, and the evaluation approach used in the experiments.

---

[4] https://github.com/diegominatel/irt-sample-reweighting-method.

4.1 Datasets

For this work, we selected the relevant binary classification benchmark datasets used in the Fairness in Machine Learning research community. Table 3 summarizes the datasets, showing their amount of instances (#I), number m of attributes (#A), which protected attributes are analyzed, the privileged group of each task related to the dataset, and reference.

Table 3. Dataset information. Here #I denotes amount of instances and #A represents the number of attributes

Dataset	#I	#A	Protected Attributes	Privileged Group	Ref.
Arrhythmia[a,b]	452	278	sex	male	[12]
Bank Marketing	45,211	42	age	over 25 years old	[12]
Census Income	48,842	76	race and sex	white-male	[12]
Contraceptive[a,c]	1,473	10	religion	non-islam	[12]
Crack[d]	1,885	11	race	non-white	[12]
German Credit	1,000	36	sex	male	[12]
Heart[a]	303	13	age	middle-aged	[12]
Heroin[d]	1,885	11	race	non-white	[12]
Recidivism[e] Female	1,395	176	race	white	[18]
Recidivism Male[e]	5,819	375	race	white	[18]
Student	480	46	sex	male	[1]
Titanic	1309	6	sex	female[f]	[27]

[a]Age and gender are protected attributes that can play a crucial role in predicting health datasets, which is why they are included in class prediction. Nevertheless, does not preclude the analysis of adverse impact.
[b]We binarize the output between the absence and presence of cardiac arrhythmia, ignoring the different arrhythmia groups.
[c]We binarize the output to predict whether or not a woman uses contraception.
[d] It is the Drug Consumption dataset just changing the target class.
[e]We split this dataset into two: Recidivism Female (female examples) and Recidivism Male (male examples).
[f]There was selection bias in the rescue operation during the Titanic disaster, as women and children were given priority. As a result, the protected attribute is utilized in making predictions using the Titanic dataset.

4.2 Algorithms

We used the following classification algorithms that allow the application of sample reweighting for the experiment: AdaBoost (ADA), Classification Trees (CART), Random Forest (RF), Support Vector Machines (SVM), and XGBoost (XGB). We tested fifteen parameterization settings for each of them. Table 4 shows each classification algorithm and the numerical variation range for their hyperparameters used in this experiment.

Table 4. Algorithms and ranges of numeric variation defined for their hyperparameters.

Algorithm	Hyperparameter	Variation Range (initial : final : step)
ADA	Number of trees	100 : 500 : 25
CART	Minimum number of samples to be a leaf node	2 : 30 : 2
RF	Number of trees	100 : 500 : 25
SVM	Gamma	0.0025 : 1.075 : 0.075
XGB	Number of trees	100 : 500 : 25

In addition to comparing the results without using sample reweighting, we used the well-known Reweighing [17] method in our experiment. This method aims to enhance fairness in classification tasks by assigning appropriate sample weights W. Specifically, Reweighing computes:

$$W(A = i, Y = j) = \frac{P(A = i)P(Y = j)}{P(A = i, Y = j)}, \tag{3}$$

where $P(A = i)$ is the probability of occurrence of group i and $P(Y = j)$ is the probability of occurrence of class j. Additionally, $P(A = i, Y = j)$ is the probability of occurrence of group i with class j in dataset D. The underlying idea of this method is to assign greater weight to instances with less frequent (group, class) pairs.

4.3 Evaluation

As previously mentioned, we use the fairness measures of demographic parity, equal opportunity, and equalized odds to select the best hyperparameters of each classification algorithm. Also, we use these measures in the final evaluation to compare the effectiveness of the reweighting methods. Furthermore, due to the class imbalance of some datasets, we use the macro F1-score to analyze the performance of the selected classifiers.

To simplify the categorization process of fairness metrics, we use the highest score as the denominator for calculating the ratio between privileged and unprivileged groups of a specific fairness metric, as described in Sect. 2.1. As a result, the ratio of group fairness metrics, such as the demographic parity ratio, will always be in the interval $[0, 1]$, with the ideal outcome being a score of 1.

5   Results

In this section, we present the results obtained in our experiments, as explained in Sect. 4. We provide a summary of fairness metrics results on the test set for selected models with or without applying reweighting method. Additionally, we discuss the macro F1-score results.

Table 5 shows the average result of the demographic parity ratio on the test set applying demographic parity as a criterion for model selection. The "Without" column indicates the results without using the sample reweighting method. Bold values indicate the best score by datasets, and the value in parentheses indicates the standard deviation. IRT-SR performed best in 7 of the 12 datasets and also had the best average demographic parity ratio, being more than 5% ahead of the second-best average. Reweighing performed better in 4 of the 12 datasets, while not using sample reweighting had better results in only one dataset.

Table 5. Average demographic parity ratio results on the test set.

Dataset	Without	IRT-SR	Reweighing
Arrhythmia	70.75% (19.80%)	**82.31% (12.91%)**	75.97% (15.09%)
Bank Marketing	50.57% (8.89%)	56.31% (16.51%)	**61.81% (5.73%)**
Census Income	31.83% (2.02%)	36.48% (4.01%)	**36.53% (3.45%)**
Contraceptive	94.73% (4.61%)	**94.83% (3.94%)**	92.01% (4.35%)
Crack	52.49% (39.93%)	**59.21% (34.13%)**	23.40% (21.47%)
German Credit	**83.61% (9.46%)**	83.41% (10.33%)	82.78% (10.78%)
Heart	53.40% (13.82%)	52.21% (5.28%)	**63.15% (16.83%)**
Heroin	56.55% (19.08%)	**77.04% (15.03%)**	46.23% (14.66%)
Recidivism Female	82.44% (22.03%)	**85.64% (5.31%)**	80.71% (17.37%)
Recidivism Male	72.36% (5.89%)	**83.59% (11.03%)**	76.39% (6.43%)
Student	86.82% (6.46%)	**88.01% (4.88%)**	86.82% (6.46%)
Titanic	19.59% (4.55%)	28.58% (12.15%)	**36.92% (19.69%)**
Average	62.93% (26.73%)	**68.97% (24.44%)**	63.56% (25.04%)

Table 6 shows the average equal opportunity ratio on the test set applying equal opportunity as a criterion for model selection. Reweighing performed best on 7 out of 12 datasets in this assessment criteria. However, IRT-SR had a better average performance and the best performance on 4 datasets. It is important to note that in the Crack dataset, not using sample reweighting methods obtained a result almost three times better than the selected methods.

Table 6. Average equal opportunity ratio results on the test set.

Dataset	Without	IRT-SR	Reweighing
Arrhythmia	81.17% (10.29%)	85.61% (6.42%)	**87.77% (3.48%)**
Bank Marketing	88.34% (11.40%)	**93.92% (6.42%)**	82.36% (9.08%)
Census Income	86.19% (1.89%)	90.25% (4.34%)	**91.08% (2.97)**
Contraceptive	93.35% (5.99%)	91.45% (5.39%)	**95.69% (5.02%)**
Crack	**59.80% (42.80%)**	21.08% (29.54%)	16.72% (37.40%)
German Credit	90.33% (5.83%)	90.86% (6.10%)	**91.91% (6.94%)**
Heart	78.72% (9.33%)	77.59% (3.12%)	**85.16% (5.76%)**
Heroin	9.80% (15.10%)	**50.65% (33.72%)**	26.14% (21.02%)
Recidivism Female	83.69% (22.09%)	**96.15% (3.19%)**	82.08% (23.17%)
Recidivism Male	78.62% (3.77%)	**88.56% (8.20%)**	80.89% (3.58%)
Student	98.32% (1.62%)	98.52% (1.72%)	**98.76% (0.94%)**
Titanic	51.52% (3.60%)	57.31% (19.88%)	**71.02% (21.85%)**
Average	74.99% (27.57%)	**78.50% (26.35%)**	75.80% (29.41%)

The last group fairness metric evaluated is equalized odds, shown in Table 7. Once again, IRT-SR had the best average performance, in addition to having the best performance in 7 of the 12 datasets. Reweighing obtained the best performance of the five datasets. In contrast, not using reweighting method did not perform better in any of the datasets. We highlight that the IRT-SR obtained better average results for equalized odds in all datasets when compared to not using the reweighting method.

Table 7. Average equalized odds ratio results on the test set.

Dataset	Without	IRT-SR	Reweighing
Arrhythmia	67.67% (16.05%)	**78.35% (9.29%)**	74.87% (16.33%)
Bank Marketing	65.53% (4.13%)	72.68% (6.09%)	**79.11% (10.77%)**
Census Income	54.02% (2.78%)	60.41% (4.34%)	**61.10% (4.64%)**
Contraceptive	88.09% (0.35%)	**91.37% (13.89%)**	88.61% (3.63%)
Crack	38.85% (40.02%)	**44.18% (29.54%)**	23.68% (23.82%)
German Credit	76.64% (14.87%)	80.29% (11.99%)	**81.89% (10.65%)**
Heart	53.00% (5.83%)	**56.67% (6.10%)**	55.31% (11.67%)
Heroin	51.19% (26.37%)	**60.12% (29.06%)**	42.72% (17.57%)
Recidivism Female	81.71% (16.18%)	**81.86% (9.74%)**	78.39% (20.61%)
Recidivism Male	77.66% (6.84%)	**85.90% (7.92%)**	82.67% (7.04%)
Student	91.38% (10.64%)	92.93% (6.52%)	**93.13% (8.43%)**
Titanic	33.38% (2.92%)	43.90% (13.53%)	**58.14% (25.75%)**
Average	64.93% (23.58%)	**70.72% (21.31%)**	68.30% (24.10%)

We apply a Nemenyi posthoc test [11] to verify if there is a statistically significant difference in the results of demographic parity, equal opportunity, and equalized odds. For the Nemenyi posthoc test, we consider all classifiers selected with better hyperparameters per classification algorithm. Figure 4 shows the results of the Nemenyi posthoc test. The top of the diagram indicates the critical difference (CD), and the horizontal axes indicate the average ranks of the group fairness metric, with the best-ranked algorithms to the left. A black line connects the algorithms when it is not detected a significant difference between them. For this experiment, with a significance level of 5% (p-value < 0.05), the critical difference is 0.4278.

The IRT-SR method ranked first in the three evaluated group fairness metrics, as illustrated in Fig. 4. Reweighing was ranked second in all group fairness metrics. Figures 4a and 4c show that IRT-SR and Reweighing with statistically significant differences compared to using no sample reweighting method on demographic parity and equalized odds metrics. Finally, the non-use of the sample reweighting method was ranked last in all fairness metrics tested.

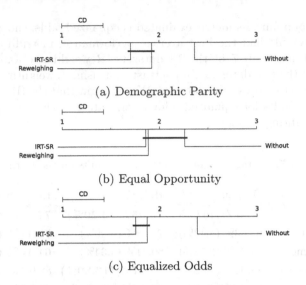

(a) Demographic Parity

(b) Equal Opportunity

(c) Equalized Odds

Fig. 4. Nemenyi posthoc test applied to the results of demographic parity, equal opportunity, and equalized odds.

Table 8 shows the macro F1-score averages for each group fairness metrics used in model selection. As expected, not using the sample reweighting method has the best macro F1-score averages. In contrast, the models developed with IRT-SR had the worst performance in the macro F1-score. IRT-SR had only a maximum mean difference of 1.50% for the best means. However, this small performance loss is compensated by improving fairness metrics.

Table 8. Macro F1-score averages on the test set for each criterion used in model selection.

Group fairness metric	Without	IRT-SR	Reweighing
Demographic parity	**69.53% (11.98%)**	68.09% (11.64%)	68.42% (11.74%)
Equal opportunity	**69.36% (11.85%)**	68.23% (11.68%)	68.69% (12.09%)
Equalized odds	**69.83% (11.76%)**	68.23% (11.26%)	68.86% (11.92%)

The results demonstrate that using the IRT-SR can be a great option to improve demographic parity, equal opportunity, and equalized odds. This is without a significant performance loss, as shown in Table 8. We note that both for average results (Tables 5, 6, and 7) and for methods ranking (Fig. 4) of the three group fairness metrics, IRT-SR stood out as the best option among the options tested in this experiment. Finally, experimental results indicate that our IRT-SR sample reweighting method can guide classification algorithms to fit fairer models.

6   Conclusion

This paper introduced a novel sample reweighting method named IRT-SR that uses concepts from the Item Response Theory. We aimed to model the sample reweighting problem as a test to benefit from the IRT's evaluative power and use it to improve the group fairness notions through sample reweighting. The experimental results indicate that our method is more effective in maximizing demographic parity, equal opportunity, and equalized odds metrics than not using sample reweighting and the Reweighing method. In conclusion, the findings of this study highlight that IRT-SR effectively guides the classification algorithms to fit fairer classifiers.

In future work, we intend to optimize the hyperparameters of the base classifiers set and also test other classification algorithms in this set, which enables the merging of classifiers from different paradigms. With this, we aim to improve further the group fairness notions presented in this work.

Acknowledgments. This study was financed in part by the Coordenação de Aperfeiçoamento de Pessoal de Nível Superior – Brasil (CAPES) – Finance Code 001; the São Paulo Research Foundation [grants #20/09835-1 and #22/09091-8]; and the Brazilian National Council for Scientific and Technological Development [grant #303588/2022-5].

References

1. Amrieh, E.A., Hamtini, T., Aljarah, I.: Preprocessing and analyzing educational data set using x-api for improving student's performance. In: 2015 IEEE Jordan Conference on Applied Electrical Engineering and Computing Technologies (AEECT), pp. 1–5. IEEE (2015)
2. Angwin, J., Larson, J., Mattu, S., Kirchner, L.: Machine bias: risk assessments in criminal sentencing (2016). https://www.propublica.org/article/machine-bias-risk-assessments-in-criminal-sentencing
3. Barocas, S., Selbst, A.D.: Big data's disparate impact. Calif. L. Rev. **104**, 671 (2016)
4. Bellamy, R.K.E., et al.: AI Fairness 360: An extensible toolkit for detecting, understanding, and mitigating unwanted algorithmic bias, October 2018
5. Bock, R.D., Aitkin, M.: Marginal maximum likelihood estimation of item parameters: application of an EM algorithm. Psychometrika **46**(4), 443–459 (1981)
6. Buitinck, L., et al.: API design for machine learning software: experiences from the Scikit-learn project. In: ECML PKDD Workshop: Languages for Data Mining and Machine Learning, pp. 108–122 (2013)
7. Chalmers, R.P.: MIRT: a multidimensional item response theory package for the R environment. J. Statist. Softw. **48**(6), 1–29 (2012). https://doi.org/10.18637/jss.v048.i06
8. Chen, T., Guestrin, C.: XGBoost: a scalable tree boosting system. In: Proceedings of the 22nd ACM SIGKDD International Conference on Knowledge Discovery and Data Mining, pp. 785–794. KDD 2016, ACM, New York, NY, USA (2016). https://doi.org/10.1145/2939672.2939785, http://doi.acm.org/10.1145/2939672.2939785

9. Chen, Z., Ahn, H.: Item response theory based ensemble in machine learning. Int. J. Autom. Comput. **17**(5), 621–636 (2020)
10. De Ayala, R.J.: The Theory and Practice of Item Response Theory. Guilford Publications, New York City (2013)
11. Demšar, J.: Statistical comparisons of classifiers over multiple data sets. J. Mach. Learn. Res. **7**, 1–30 (2006). http://dl.acm.org/citation.cfm?id=1248547.1248548
12. Dua, D., Graff, C.: UCI machine learning repository (2017). http://archive.ics.uci.edu/ml
13. Dwork, C., Hardt, M., Pitassi, T., Reingold, O., Zemel, R.: Fairness through awareness. In: Proceedings of the 3rd Innovations in Theoretical Computer Science Conference, pp. 214–226 (2012)
14. Hambleton, R.K., Swaminathan, H., Rogers, H.J.: Fundamentals of Item Response Theory, vol. 2. SAGE Publications, Thousand Oaks (1991)
15. Hardt, M., Price, E., Srebro, N.: Equality of opportunity in supervised learning. Adv. Neural. Inf. Process. Syst. **29**, 3315–3323 (2016)
16. Hutchinson, B., Mitchell, M.: 50 years of test (un) fairness: lessons for machine learning. In: Proceedings of the Conference on Fairness, Accountability, and Transparency, pp. 49–58 (2019)
17. Kamiran, F., Calders, T.: Data preprocessing techniques for classification without discrimination. Knowl. Inf. Syst. **33**(1), 1–33 (2012). https://doi.org/10.1007/s10115-011-0463-8
18. Larson, J., Mattu, S., Kirchner, L., Angwin, J.: How we analyzed the compas recidivism algorithm (2016). https://www.propublica.org/article/how-we-analyzed-the-compas-recidivism-algorithm
19. van der Linden, W.J., Hambleton, R.K.: Handbook of Modern Item Response Theory. Springer Science & Business Media, New York (2013). https://doi.org/10.1007/978-1-4757-2691-6
20. Martínez-Plumed, F., Prudêncio, R.B., Martínez-Usó, A., Hernández-Orallo, J.: Making sense of item response theory in machine learning. In: Proceedings of the Twenty-Second European Conference on Artificial Intelligence, pp. 1140–1148 (2016)
21. Martínez-Plumed, F., Prudêncio, R.B., Martínez-Usó, A., Hernández-Orallo, J.: Item response theory in AI: analysing machine learning classifiers at the instance level. Artif. Intell. **271**, 18–42 (2019)
22. Mehrabi, N., Morstatter, F., Saxena, N., Lerman, K., Galstyan, A.: A survey on bias and fairness in machine learning. ACM Comput. Surv. (CSUR) **54**(6), 1–35 (2021)
23. Minatel, D., dos Santos, N.R., da Silva, A.C.M., Cúri, M., Marcacini, R.M., Lopes, A.A.: Unfairness in machine learning for web systems applications. In: Proceedings of the 29th Brazilian Symposium on Multimedia and the Web, pp. 144–153 (2023)
24. Minatel, D., da Silva, A.C.M., dos Santos, N.R., Curi, M., Marcacini, R.M., de Andrade Lopes, A.: Data stratification analysis on the propagation of discriminatory effects in binary classification. In: XI Symposium on Knowledge Discovery, Mining and Learning, pp. 73–80. SBC (2023)
25. Pessach, D., Shmueli, E.: A review on fairness in machine learning. ACM Comput. Surv. (CSUR) **55**(3), 1–44 (2022)
26. Sarker, I.H.: Machine learning: algorithms, real-world applications and research directions. SN Comput. Sci. **2**(3), 160 (2021)
27. Vanschoren, J., van Rijn, J.N., Bischl, B., Torgo, L.: OpenML: networked science in machine learning. SIGKDD Explor. **15**(2), 49–60 (2013). https://doi.org/10.1145/2641190.2641198

Predicting Course Performance on a Massive Open Online Course Platform: A Natural Language Processing Approach

Grant Alphenaar[iD] and Rahat Ibn Rafiq[✉][iD]

Grand Valley State University, Allendale, MI 49401-9403, USA
{alphengr,rafiqr}@gvsu.edu

Abstract. Massively open online courses (MOOCs) and platforms such as Udemy have proliferated in recent years. These courses run the gamut from highly successful and high-rated to courses with very low ratings and little engagement. This research aims to address the challenge of preemptively identifying potentially low-rated courses by leveraging instructor-provided textual information. Our approach involves a two-stage process. First, we employ transformer-based Large Language Models (LLMs) to extract semantic information from the text provided by the instructors on the Udemy platform. In the second stage, we incorporate the extracted information as additional features into an upstream predictive model. To the best of our knowledge, this is the first attempt to use extracted semantic information from MOOC courses as features in a predictive model. In general, we find that existing consumer research findings hold and identify three key takeaways. First, we find that an instructor's prior performance is a strong indicator of future ratings. Second, we see that including semantic information contained in instructor-provided text can have an additive effect on model performance. Finally, we demonstrate that fine-tuning language models on Udemy-specific text have an appreciable positive effect on upstream model performance.

Keywords: Natural Language Processing · MOOC · Education Data Mining · Data Analysis

1 Introduction

Udemy has recently emerged as a prominent commercial Massive Open Online Course (MOOC) platform, hosting over $200,000$ courses offered by $70,000$ instructors and taken by almost 59 million learners [29]. One of the challenges that instructors face on a commercial MOOC platform such as Udemy is: *How to effectively market my course among a plethora of similar offerings by other instructors to maximize enrollments?* However, prospective learners often struggle to judge the relative quality of seemingly similar course offerings in a vacuum and suffer from information overload [10]. Instructors can provide additional textual information – examples include attention-grabbing titles and headlines

J. A. Lossio-Ventura et al. (Eds.): SIMBig 2023, CCIS 2142, pp. 199–216, 2024.
https://doi.org/10.1007/978-3-031-63616-5_15

or detailed personal biographies highlighting career achievements and credentials on the topic taught – to encourage enrollment of potential learners. Although instructors have complete control over the textual course information they publish on Udemy, the course's textual reviews and ratings are influenced indirectly by instructors. Consequently, the quality of such textual information may indicate overall course ratings, enabling early identification of potentially low-rated courses.

Existing research into consumer psychology suggests that prior product ratings are among the most influential factors in consumer decision-making and that early ratings and reviews may predict later ratings and reviews [14,34]. Text-based descriptions have also been found to be an effective secondary factor influencing purchase decisions [16]. We build off of this research and attempt to use instructor-provided textual information such as biographical details, job descriptions, and details about instructors' courses in a predictive model. Throughout this paper, we will refer to such instructor-provided textual information as *IPTs: Instructor-Provided Texts*. We implement the predictive model through a two-stage model process. In the first stage, we leverage transformer-based Large Language Models (LLMs) [31] to extract semantic information from IPTs. We also employ LLM fine-tuning to give the models a greater understanding of Udemy-specific language. In the second stage, we engineer features from the semantic information extracted in the first stage in order to use in an upstream classifier model. We attempt to identify courses in the bottom 25th percentile of courses by rating as a weak proxy for overall course quality, as course quality is subjective and abstract. We also account for the effect of prior ratings on consumer decision-making by including instructors' recent ratings in our model. Ultimately, this paper seeks to answer the following research question: *To what extent can important semantic meaning be extracted from instructor-provided textual information and used to help identify and flag courses likely to be low-rated on the Udemy platform?*

To our knowledge, this is the first attempt to preemptively identify potentially low-rated courses on an MOOC platform by extracting and leveraging semantic features from IPTs. This is a unique contribution as the vast amount of research into MOOCs has been on learner-focused elements such as learner outcomes and retention rates rather than on instructor perspectives [37]. We organize the rest of the paper as follows. First, we present a broad review of relevant literature, including MOOC-specific research and consumer psychology research. Then, we present an overview of our collected dataset. Next, we outline our experiment, including model selection and fine-tuning. Finally, we present our results and findings, including pertinent limitations to our study.

2   Related Work

2.1   MOOC Research

Most MOOC research has historically focused on learner-based metrics such as learner experiences, outcomes, and retention [37]. Instructor-focused MOOC research has largely concentrated in educational theory and pedagogy, instructional design, and online learning [7]. Additionally, even recent research applying machine learning techniques to MOOC data focuses on learner perspectives and experiences rather than instructor-centered analyses [21,37]. A prevalent theme observed in MOOC research is that high dropout rates among learners can be attributed to the considerable learner heterogeneity [21]. This indicates the inadequacy of a uniform approach for MOOC content creation [24]. Low barriers to entry, both for learners and instructors, may also contribute to this issue. However, while MOOC learners may be heterogeneous [12], the courses themselves may be more homogeneous in nature [32]. For example, many similar courses purport to teach basic programming concepts, but potential learners may be from vastly different educational, cultural, or socioeconomic backgrounds. Therefore, MOOC learner behavior may often mimic a herding pattern in which learners "follow the crowd" to highly-rated courses without better information. Herding behavior most commonly happens with inexperienced learners as they need more knowledge to distinguish high-quality courses from low-quality courses compared to their more experienced peers [32].

Recent research on MOOC delivery from an instructor's perspective highlights several challenges for instructors. In addition to the aforementioned difficulties regarding assessment and learner participation [21], MOOC instructors also struggle with learner heterogeneity and limited access to data. This results in an environment in which instructors have little ability to adapt to learners' diverse needs in an ad-hoc manner [5]. We intend to fill part of the gap in this research by focusing on course ratings as a weak proxy for course quality from an instructor's perspective, using contemporary machine learning techniques to make course rating classifications.

2.2 Consumer Psychology

Existing MOOC research indicates that consumer psychology plays a crucial role in prospective learners' course enrollment decisions. However, the abundance of seemingly homogeneous courses often leads to information overload and difficulties in decision-making [10]. In consumer behavior and psychology research, product ratings are considered a significant factor, particularly when products are similar. Ratings and reviews are often prioritized over product descriptions of similar products, allowing consumers to narrow down choices and reduce perceived risk [14,34]. Review balance, the ratio of low-rating to high-rating reviews, is also important, as excessive negative reviews can increase perceived risk [34]. Similarly, rating variance holds more significance than the number of ratings, with consistently high ratings counteracting negative associations with higher prices [14,18]. Recent and helpful reviews have a considerable influence on consumer purchasing behavior, highlighting the importance of accessible, relevant, and objective information in decision-making [13].

Textual information such as product titles and descriptions are also crucial in Internet shopping and e-commerce, despite the large influence of reviews and ratings [16]. Positively presenting textual information, known in consumer psychology discourse as positive framing, can influence purchasing decisions [15].

This suggests IPTs, such as a good, attention-grabbing course title or headline, could significantly attract prospective learners. Positive framing has also been found to reduce uncertainty and perceived risk and makes potential customers more likely to purchase [15]. Finally, research into international commerce indicates that accurate textual descriptions are vital as consumers' levels of information tend to be low, and items tend to be highly homogeneous [22]. This is similar to MOOC courses in that learners come from a diverse, international, and heterogeneous market, while individual courses are relatively homogeneous from a learner's perspective.

2.3 Udemy Review Process

Udemy learners can provide course reviews after a short video viewing of only twelve minutes [28]. In contrast, some MOOC providers require learners to complete a course before leaving reviews, which excludes valuable feedback from those who drop out and can impact ratings [10]. Udemy learners can update their ratings and reviews at any time, and there is no obligation to provide review text. Recent average ratings for individual Udemy instructors are calculated based on a rolling average over the past ninety days or the ten most recent ratings, prioritizing input from the most engaged students [28]. Previous research indicates that around 25% of Udemy courses lack ratings or reviews, and course ratings tend to skew towards higher scores, with an average rating of 4.0 or higher out of 5.0 [10]. Our analysis confirms this positive bias towards higher scores.

3 Data Description

3.1 Data Collection and Feature Selection

We collected these data in the summer of 2021 using the Udemy API [30]. The collected dataset consists of the most recent information on $45,177$ courses and $21,463$ instructors. These courses are represented by fourteen distinct categories. We begin by enumerating the six numeric and five textual features used in our analysis, as shown in Table 1. These features are selected because they represent course information immediately available to a prospective learner when browsing courses on the Udemy site. Our dataset also includes a preliminary outcome feature in each course's rating on a scale of 0.0 to 5.0.

3.2 Dataset Statistics

We create our Full Course Sample (FCS) from the collected dataset by removing all non-English courses, removing any courses with missing features, and excluding any courses with missing rating information. This leaves us with a sample of $43,725$ courses from $21,463$ distinct instructors. Next, we further restrict our analysis sample to instructors teaching three or fewer courses to reduce the influence of prolific and likely very experienced instructors. This results in an

Table 1. Data Features

Course-specific numeric features	Total number of instructional video minutes, total number of downloadable resources, course price (in USD), total number of students
Course-specific textual features	Course title, course headline, course category
Instructor-specific numeric features	Recent average course rating, total number of students taught
Instructor-specific textual features	Biography, job title

Analysis Sample (*AS*) dataset of 22,856 courses from 17,598 unique instructors. We find that both the FCS and AS datasets exhibit similar course distribution across the fourteen categories, as shown in Table 2.

Table 2. Course category distribution for the full course sample

Full Dataset		Sample Dataset	
Course Category	% of Sample	Course Category	% of Sample
Other	16.6%	Other	20.3%
Teaching & Academics	11.8%	Teaching & Academics	12.5%
Business	10.1%	Business	10.4%
Personal Development	8.5%	Personal Development	9.6%
Development	8.0%	Development	7.1%
Design	7.1%	Health & Fitness	5.9%
Marketing	6.9%	Marketing	5.8%
Lifestyle	5.3%	Design	5.8%
Finance & Accounting	5.2%	Lifestyle	5.0%
Health & Fitness	5.1%	IT & Software	4.8%
IT & Software	4.4%	Finance & Accounting	4.3%
Photography & Video	4.1%	Music	3.4%
Music	4.1%	Photography & Video	3.2%
Office Productivity	3.0%	Office Productivity	2.0%

Next, we examine the ratings distribution for the two datasets. Figure 1 demonstrates that both the FCS and AS are remarkably similar in rating distribution, with both samples exhibiting a top-heavy distribution. In other words, courses in both the FCS and AS tend to have high ratings. The average course rating in the FCS is 3.60, with a median of 4.20. The average course rating in the AS is 3.67 with a median of 4.20.

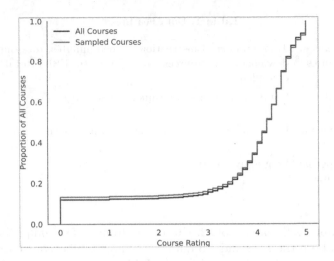

Fig. 1. Cumulative Rating Distribution: FCS and AS

Finally, *we construct a binary outcome identifying courses with a rating at or below the 25th percentile by course rating*. This outcome serves as a proxy for course quality; due to the skewed distribution of course ratings, we posit that a rating below the 25th percentile is indicative of low course quality. In the AS, this cutoff is a rating of 3.7 or lower and is comprised of 5,661 courses.

4   Methodology

Next, we describe our core experiment, in which we make use of a two-stage pipeline. In the first stage, we use LLMs to extract the semantic meaning and context from IPTs and fine-tune our LLMs on a Udemy-specific corpus in parallel for additional upstream predictive power. In the second stage, we make use of upstream gradient-boosted tree models for course classification.

4.1   Experimental Setup

We now describe the process and setup of our experiment. Broadly, our experiment has seven main steps across two parallel branches as shown in Fig. 2.
Step 1 consists of data collection and text preprocessing tasks described in Sect. 3. We further remove data collection artifacts such as HTML formatting, escape characters, hexadecimal characters, and excess whitespace as part of these text preprocessing tasks. *Step 2* consists of text tokenization. We use cased tokenizers for both BERT and DistilBERT [33] because an instructor's use of case (for example, "I will teach *you*" compared to "I will teach *YOU*") may have legitimate semantic meaning. *Step 3* consists of numeric feature normalization prior to use in the upstream model. In *Step 4*, we fine-tune the LLMs to give them a greater understanding of Udemy-specific linguistic context. In *Steps 5a*

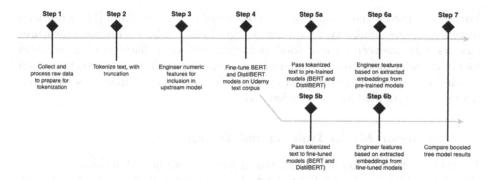

Fig. 2. Experiment steps and workflow

and *5b*, we diverge into two parallel workflows, passing tokenized text features to the pre-trained and fine-tuned LLMs, respectively. In *Steps 6a* and *6b*, we engineer additional features using embedding vectors extracted from the pre-trained and fine-tuned language models. Finally, we pass all features to the upstream boosted tree models and compare results in *Step 7*.

4.2 Feature Engineering

We pass each of the following five tokenized IPT features as inputs to the BERT and DistilBERT models: instructor's biography ("biography"), instructor's job title ("job"), course title ("title"), course headline ("headline"), course category ("category"). Each input follows the form CSL ... [SEP], with the text in question prepended by a special CLS token and appended by another special [SEP] token [6]. We then extract the embedding vector of the initial [CLS] input token. This special token is prepended to each input in BERT-family models and represents the overall semantic meaning of the following text [6]. The embedding vector of the [CLS] token has been demonstrated to provide a reasonable [4] if imperfect [17] semantic representation of the CSL ... [SEP] context. Each of these five embedding vectors has a length of 768 for a combined total of 3,840 features extracted from the raw embeddings.

We first attempt to reduce the number of features present in our models by performing principal component analysis (PCA) on these features such that the reduced principal components explain 95% of the variance within the raw embedding features. This results in an approximately 75% reduction in the number of features. We then engineer text similarity features by combining the previously calculated text embedding vectors. Specifically, we create eight text similarity features: headline × biography, title × biography, job × biography, headline × title, headline × job, headline × category, title × job, and title × category. These features leverage the idea that high similarity between embedding vectors suggests an instructor's expertise in the taught material. For instance, if an instructor's biography, job title, and course category exhibit semantic similarity, it likely indicates their knowledge and experience in that specific area.

We employ three vector similarity metrics based on F-score from [11]: Euclidean distance, cosine similarity, and inner dot product. Euclidean distance measures the distance between two vectors' endpoints, where a distance of 0 indicates identical endpoints. Cosine similarity measures the angle between vectors, with a value of 1 denoting perfect parallelism. The dot product measures the angle between vectors relative to their lengths.

4.3   Upstream Model Training and Tuning

For training the upstream boosted tree models [3], we partition the dataset into 70% for training and 30% for testing. The training sample consists of 15,999 observations, with 12,023 above the 25th percentile and 3,976 at or below. The test sample comprises 6,857 observations, with 5,172 above the 25th percentile and 1,685 at or below. To address the imbalanced nature of the 25th percentile outcome, we oversample the underrepresented class in the training sample, while the test sample remains unchanged [19]. After oversampling, the training sample consists of 12,023 outcomes above the 25th percentile and 12,023 randomly oversampled outcomes at or below, totaling 24,046 training observations. We perform hyperparameter tuning [23] using five-fold cross-validation and 100 random searches, resulting in 500 model fittings. The model hyperparameters yielding the best F_1 score are selected after the random hyperparameter search and cross-validation. Each experiment may have slightly different hyperparameters, leading to a better-fit model compared to using default or uniform hyperparameters across models [35].

4.4   LLM Fine Tuning

We perform fine-tuning on the pre-trained BERT and DistilBERT models to enhance their domain-specific semantic understanding of Udemy text. We chose BERT due its widespread use and ubiquity [26] and DistilBERT as a smaller and faster but otherwise similar model to BERT [27]. The fine-tuning process utilizes only the 15,999-observation training sample mentioned earlier, ensuring the exclusion of test sample data to maintain the integrity of the fine-tuned models. The training sample is further divided into a 70% training partition and a 30% validation partition. We concatenate the five textual features separated by the special [SEP] tokens that BERT-family LLMs use to preserve semantic differences [6] into a single document per course to create input documents for fine-tuning. The concatenation of instructor biographies is done last to prioritize preserving their content while allowing truncation to occur if necessary. Truncation is common due to the increased length of the concatenated document and the models' limitation of 512 tokens [6,31]. For fine-tuning, we train the models for the task of course classification using the same 25th percentile outcome as the upstream model, employing 10 training epochs. Our subsequent analysis demonstrates that fine-tuning enhances the models' comprehension of domain-specific Udemy semantic context compared to their pre-trained counterparts.

4.5 Gradient-Boosted Tree Models

We employ gradient-boosted tree models, based on the concept of additive learning, as our upstream classifier [9]. These models consist of an ensemble of random forest trees, with new trees added to the forest to correct errors from existing trees. The goal is to move the loss gradient towards zero and minimize overall model loss. These trees, known as "weak learners," have limited predictive power individually, and the final classification is determined by a weighted sum of these trees that minimizes loss [8]. In our experiments, we utilize the GPU-based gradient boosting machine provided by the XGBoost library [3], referring to it as the "boosted tree model" or "upstream model" for simplicity. Recently, gradient boosted tree models have found success in a wide variety of applications [2,25], from public health [20] to business modeling [36], with XGBoost in particular providing a strong balance between predictive power and training time [1].

5 Results

We now present our findings on the impact of adding semantic features from fine-tuned LLMs on the performance of upstream models. We structure this section as follows: first, we describe the baseline models for performance comparison. Then, we present the metrics and findings from upstream boosted tree models using pre-trained BERT and DistilBERT LLMs. Next, we showcase the metrics and findings from upstream boosted tree models using fine-tuned BERT and DistilBERT models. Finally, we analyze misclassified courses and highlight significant findings for chronically-misclassified courses.

First, we start with a comparison of two boosted tree models using baseline feature sets consisting of only numeric features present in the analysis sample with no additional embedding engineering, shown in Table 3.

Table 3. Baseline models and their features

Baseline Models (BM)	Features
BM1	Instructors' average recent ratings only (one feature)
BM2	Features from model 1 + total video minutes, total downloadable resources, course price, total students per course, total students per instructor (5 additional features)

We compare the performance of upstream models using additional features engineered from LLM embeddings. We consider five feature sets for each of pre-trained BERT, pre-trained DistilBERT, fine-tuned BERT, and fine-tuned DistilBERT. This yields a total of twenty different models, in addition to the two baseline comparison models. Note that although the base boosted tree model is the same for all experiments, hyperparameters will differ slightly between

Table 4. Additional Feature Sets

Feature Engineering	Feature Set
Cosine Similarity	All features from BM2 + cosine vector similarities (8 additional features)
Euclidean Distance	All features from BM2 + Euclidean distance vector similarities (8 additional features)
Inner (Dot) Product	All features from BM2 + inner (dot) product vector similarities (8 additional features)
Principal Components	All features from BM2 + reduced principal components ($\approx$ 1,000 additional features)
Raw Embeddings	All features from BM2 + unprocessed raw extracted embeddings (3,840 additional features)

models due to hyperparameter tuning [1]. Our additional feature sets are shown in Table 4.

We evaluate models based on accuracy, precision, recall, and F_1 score. Precision and recall receive special attention as we aim to minimize false negatives and false positives. This means reducing the misclassification of low-rated courses (emphasizing recall) while maintaining accurate low-rated course classifications (emphasizing precision). The F_1 score enables us to strike a balance between precision and recall priorities.

5.1 Baseline Models

We begin by presenting two baseline models for comparison purposes, illustrated in Table 5. We can see that an instructor's average recent ratings alone are already a very strong predictor of course performance before adding any engineered features, with an overall accuracy of 88.86%. *BM1* beats *BM2* by 10% points in precision, but has a lower recall by nearly 16% points. Overall accuracy is similar between the two models, but *BM2*'s higher recall compared to precision gives it an overall F_1 score approximately 3% points higher than *BM1*.

In the tables that follow, the best metric across all models in the comparison group is highlighted, an * indicates metrics that are better than the best baseline metric, and an ↑ indicates metrics that have improved after fine-tuning.

Table 5. Baseline Metrics

	BM1	BM2
Accuracy	***88.86%***	88.13%
Precision	***82.21%***	72.10%
Recall	68.84%	***84.33%***
F_1 Score	74.94%	***77.74%***

5.2 Pre-trained BERT Embeddings

In general, the upstream models using feature sets with engineered similarity features tend to perform better on recall but worse on precision that the feature sets using either principal components or raw embeddings. The upstream models using engineered similarity feature sets have precision of approximately 71% and recall of approximately 82%. On the other hand, the *Principal Components* and *Raw Embeddings* models have similar precision and recall of around 78%. Overall, the *Principal Components* and *Raw Embeddings* boosted tree models perform very similarly, and both outperform the best baseline model in overall accuracy. Out of all five feature sets, *Raw Embeddings* from the pre-trained BERT model has the best metrics in all but recall, where it is beaten by approximately 4% points by the *Euclidean Distance* model. The metrics statistics are presented in Table 6.

Table 6. Model Metrics Using Features Extracted From Pre-Trained BERT

	Cosine Similarity	Euclidean Distance	Inner Product	Principal Components	Raw Embeddings
Accuracy	87.04%	87.21%	86.90%	88.93%*	*89.00%**
Precision	70.56%	70.93%	70.30%	77.59%	*77.66%*
Recall	81.74%	*81.92%*	81.57%	77.27%	77.57%
F_1 Score	75.74%	76.03%	75.52%	77.43%	*77.61%*

5.3 Pre-trained DistilBERT Embeddings

The upstream models using features engineered from pre-trained DistilBERT perform similarly to their BERT counterparts. Interestingly, the models using engineered vector similarities tend to perform slightly worse than their BERT counterparts, while the *Principal Components* and *Raw Embeddings* models perform slightly better. The *Principal Components* and *Raw Embeddings* models also beat the best baseline models in accuracy and F_1 score. Finally, we note that the *Raw Embeddings* model has the best overall accuracy and precision, while the *Cosine Similarity* model has the best recall and the *Principal Components* model has the best overall F_1 score, as shown in Table 7.

Table 7. Model Metrics Using Features Extracted From Pre-Trained DistilBERT

	Cosine Similarity	Euclidean Distance	Inner (Dot) Product	Principal Components	Raw Embeddings
Accuracy	86.67%	86.64%	86.89%	89.15%*	*89.22%**
Precision	69.82%	70.09%	70.54%	77.40%	*78.63%*
Recall	*81.33%*	80.33%	80.80%	78.87%	77.75%
F_1 Score	77.74%	74.86%	75.32%	*78.13%**	77.96%*

5.4 Fine-Tuned BERT Embeddings

Every upstream model sees performance gains compared to their pre-trained counterparts when using the extracted embeddings from a fine-tuned BERT model, shown in Table 8. The *Raw Embeddings* model sees impressive gains in precision and recall of approximately five and eight percentage point respectively and an associated increase in F_1-score. Here, the *Raw Embeddings* model has the best overall accuracy, precision, and F_1 score, just barely losing out to the *Principal Components* model in recall. The *Raw Embeddings* model also beats the best baseline model metrics across all metrics. Interestingly, all models have very similar recall while the *Principal Components* and *Raw Embeddings* models outperform the models using engineered similarities in recall.

5.5 Fine-Tuned DistilBERT Embeddings

In general, the upstream models using embeddings extracted from fine-tuned DistilBERT models do not perform as well as their fine-tuned BERT counterparts, shown in Table 9. Intuitively, this makes sense, as DistilBERT is a smaller and more limited LLM compared to BERT and is similar to what we observed with pre-trained BERT and DistilBERT models. Interestingly, the models using embeddings from fine-tuned DistilBERT generally perform worse than their counterparts using embeddings from pre-trained BERT except for the *Raw Embeddings* model. This suggests that a larger pre-trained model may still be more performant than a fine-tuned but more limited model. This also suggests that the raw embedding vectors from a fine-tuned model impart significant additional predictive power to the upstream model. The *Inner (Dot) Product* and *Raw Embeddings* models see performance gains for all metrics, and the *Cosine Similarity* model sees an increase in precision. Otherwise, all other model metrics performed slightly worse than their pre-trained counterparts. This set of models is unique, however, in that the *Raw Embeddings* model is the strictly-best model out of all fine-tuned DistilBERT models. However, we note that only overall accuracy and F_1 score for the *Raw Embeddings* model were better than the best baseline metrics.

Table 8. Model Metrics Using Features Extracted From Fine-Tuned BERT

	Cosine Similarity	Euclidean Distance	Inner (Dot) Product	Principal Components	Raw Embeddings
Accuracy	88.83%↑	88.81%*↑	88.93%*↑	91.21%*↑	*91.83%*↑
Precision	73.97%↑	73.91%↑	74.14%↑	80.26%↑	*82.50%*↑
Recall	84.69%*↑	84.75%*↑	84.92%*↑	*85.16%*↑	84.75%*↑
F_1 Score	78.97%*↑	78.96%*↑	79.17%*↑	82.62%*↑	*83.61%*↑

Table 9. Model Metrics Using Features Extracted From Fine-Tuned DistilBERT

	Cosine Similarity	Euclidean Distance	Inner (Dot) Product	Principal Components	Raw Embeddings
Accuracy	86.55%	86.52%	88.95%*↑	86.23%	*89.98%*↑
Precision	69.94%↑	69.95%	73.96%↑	71.25%	*79.68%↑*
Recall	80.04%	79.92%	85.92%*↑	74.44%	*81.25%↑*
F_1 Score	74.65%	74.60%	79.38%*↑	72.81%	*79.94%*↑

5.6 Best Model Analysis

The upstream model using raw embeddings extracted from a fine-tuned BERT model is the best overall model, with the globally-highest accuracy, precision, and F_1 score. Compared to *BM1*, this represents a 2.97 percentage point increase in accuracy, a 0.29 percentage point increase in precision, a 15.91 percentage point increase in recall, and a 6.69 percentage point increase in overall F-score. Compared to *BM2*, this represents a 3.7 percentage point increase in accuracy, 10.4 percentage point increase in precision, a 0.42 percentage point increase in recall, and a 5.87 percentage point increase in F-score. These findings suggest that there is significant predictive power in semantic information extracted from models fine-tuned on a domain-specific corpus.

5.7 Misclassification Analysis

The *Raw Embeddings* model using fine-tuned BERT misclassified 560 observations in the test sample, with 257 false negatives and 303 false positives. A false negative in this case is a low-rated course that is not correctly flagged, and a false positive is high-rated course incorrectly classified as low-rated. From Table 10, we see that courses in the "Other" category comprise a significant proportion (just under 30%) of all false positives. Courses in the next three most commonly misclassified course categories make up 10.1%, 8.9%, and 8.6% of all misclassified observations, respectively. However, we notice that while the "Other" category makes up nearly 25% of all false negatives, courses in the next three most commonly misclassified course categories make up 13.2%, 10.9%, and 10.9% of all misclassified observations, respectively. This suggests that there may be common elements among courses in the "Other" category that make them more prone to false positive misclassification.

Table 10. Misclassification Statistics

False Negatives		False Positives	
Category	% Misclassified	Category	% Misclassified
Other	29.6%	Other	24.8%
Business	10.1%	Teaching & Academics	13.2%
Teaching & Academics	8.9%	Development	10.9%
Personal Development	8.6%	Business	10.9%
Development	7.0%	IT & Software	7.9%
Design	7.0%	Marketing	6.6%
IT & Software	5.4%	Finance & Accounting	5.3%
Health & Fitness	4.7%	Design	5.0%
Lifestyle	4.7%	Personal Development	5.0%
Marketing	4.7%	Lifestyle	4.0%
Finance & Accounting	4.3%	Health & Fitness	3.6%
Photography & Video	2.3%	4.3% Photography & Video	2.0%
Music	1.6%	Office Productivity	1.0%
Office Productivity	1.2%		

A granular analysis of misclassified courses reveals that courses with ambiguous titles, terse and factual headlines, and a third-person biography tended to be frequently represented among the misclassified courses, but it should also be noted that many similar courses were correctly classified. Further qualitative analysis is needed to identify trends among misclassified courses.

6 Limitations

The limitations of our study primarily concern the strong co-variation between an instructor's recent average overall rating and the recent average ratings of that instructor's specific courses, which reduces the independent predictive power of our engineered outcome variable. This results in a model that risks ascribing too much importance to an instructor's history and may be less effective for new instructors with no prior performance information; while adding embedding features improves model performance, instructors' recent ratings remain the primary predictor. Moreover, using an instructor's course count as a proxy for experience may not accurately reflect their expertise. Additionally, we lacked detailed course descriptions, information on course materials and syllabuses, and data on new courses, thereby limiting the depth of our analysis. Furthermore, we have limitations in capturing the whole semantic meaning from short passages such as course titles and course categories, posing challenges in extracting comprehensive information.

7 Future Works

Future work can address these limitations by conducting a study on new Udemy courses and tracking their performance over time. This would provide insights into the impact of early ratings on learner behavior. Collecting more detailed course information and incorporating sentiment or emotion analysis from written reviews as features in the upstream classifier model could be another research direction. A more granular approach to course outcomes may explore different 25th percentile rating cutoffs per course category to account for variations in rating distributions between course categories. Exploring individual sentence-level embedding extraction may be valuable for improving the analysis and, conversely, exploring a single concatenated text document of IPTs for each instructor may also have value. Further work might also experiment with using the concatenated IPT documents as inputs to our existing fine-tuned BERT-family models using a final linear layer for classification.

8 Conclusion

This study aimed to assess the effectiveness of instructor-provided textual information in identifying low-rated courses. The baseline results confirmed that an instructor's prior performance serves as a strong predictor of future ratings. The inclusion of semantic information from IPTs demonstrated an improvement in the performance of upstream models. However, simplistic text similarity measures alone did not contribute significantly to the predictive power of baseline models. Notably, fine-tuning the downstream language models using Udemy-specific text yielded a substantial positive impact on model performance.

This research contributes to the existing body of knowledge on MOOCs by emphasizing the significance of considering instructor-focused information in evaluating course quality. The findings underscore the importance of an instructor's prior ratings as the most reliable predictor of future ratings, suggesting a pattern of prior success leading to future success. Moreover, the results suggest that IPTs may indirectly influence course ratings. However, while extracting semantic meaning from IPTs proves valuable and enhances model performance, it is evident that capturing the complete semantic context cannot be achieved through simplified metrics without sacrificing predictive power.

Acknowledgement. This research was partially supported by grants from NVIDIA and utilized an NVIDIA A100 for model training and inference.

References

1. Bentéjac, C., Csörgo, A., Martínez-Muñoz, G.: A comparative analysis of xgboost (2019)
2. Bentéjac, C., Csörgo, A., Martínez-Muñoz, G.: A comparative analysis of gradient boosting algorithms. Artif. Intell. Rev. **54**(3), 1937–1967 (8 2020). https://doi.org/10.1007/s10462-020-09896-5, https://doi.org/10.1007%2Fs10462-020-09896-5

3. Chen, T., Guestrin, C.: XGBoost. In: Proceedings of the 22nd ACM SIGKDD International Conference on Knowledge Discovery and Data Mining. ACM (8 2016). https://doi.org/10.1145/2939672.2939785

4. Choi, H., Kim, J., Joe, S., Gwon, Y.: Evaluation of Bert and albert sentence embedding performance on downstream nlp tasks. In: 2020 25th International Conference on Pattern Recognition (ICPR), pp. 5482–5487 (2021).https://doi.org/10.1109/ICPR48806.2021.9412102

5. Daradoumis, T., Bassi, R., Xhafa, F., Caballé, S.: A review on massive e-learning (MOOC) design, delivery and assessment. In: 2013 Eighth International Conference on P2P, Parallel, Grid, Cloud and Internet Computing, pp. 208–213 (2013). https://doi.org/10.1109/3PGCIC.2013.37

6. Devlin, J., Chang, M.W., Lee, K., Toutanova, K.: Bert: pre-training of deep bidirectional transformers for language understanding (2018). https://doi.org/10.48550/ARXIV.1810.04805, https://arxiv.org/abs/1810.04805

7. Ebben, M., Murphy, J.S.: Unpacking MOOC scholarly discourse: a review of nascent MOOC scholarship. Learn. Media Technol. **39**(3), 328–345 (2014). https://doi.org/10.1080/17439884.2013.878352

8. Friedman, J.H.: Greedy function approximation: a gradient boosting machine. Ann. Stat. **29**(5), 1189–1232 (2001). https://doi.org/10.1214/aos/1013203451

9. Friedman, J.H.: Stochastic gradient boosting. Comput. Stat. Data Anal. **38**(4), 367–378 (2002). https://doi.org/10.1016/S0167-9473(01)00065-2, https://www.sciencedirect.com/science/article/pii/S0167947301000652, nonlinear Methods and Data Mining

10. Gomez, M.J., Calderón, M., Sánchez, V., Clemente, F.J.G., Ruipérez-Valiente, J.A.: Large scale analysis of open MOOC reviews to support learners' course selection. Expert Syst. Appl. **210**, 118400 (2022)

11. Hajeer, S.: Comparison on the effectiveness of different statistical similarity measures. Int. J. Comput. Appl. **53**, 14–19 (09 2012). https://doi.org/10.5120/8440-2224

12. Hou, Y., Zhou, P., Xu, J., Wu, D.O.: Course recommendation of MOOC with big data support: a contextual online learning approach. In: IEEE INFOCOM 2018 - IEEE Conference on Computer Communications Workshops (INFOCOM WKSHPS), pp. 106–111 (2018). https://doi.org/10.1109/INFOCOMW.2018.8406936

13. Hu, N., Koh, N.S., Reddy, S.K.: Ratings lead you to the product, reviews help you clinch it? the mediating role of online review sentiments on product sales. Decis. Support Syst. **57**, 42–53 (2014). https://doi.org/10.1016/j.dss.2013.07.009

14. Jang, S., Prasad, A., Ratchford, B.: How consumers use product reviews in the purchase decision process. Marketing Letters **23** (01 2013). https://doi.org/10.1007/s11002-012-9191-4

15. Jin, J., Zhang, W., Chen, M.: How consumers are affected by product descriptions in online shopping: event-related potentials evidence of the attribute framing effect. Neurosci. Res. **125**, 21–28 (2017). https://doi.org/10.1016/j.neures.2017.07.006

16. Kim, M., Lennon, S.: The effects of visual and verbal information on attitudes and purchase intentions in internet shopping. Psychol. Market. **25**, 146 – 178 (02 2008). https://doi.org/10.1002/mar.20204

17. Ma, X., Wang, Z., Ng, P., Nallapati, R., Xiang, B.: Universal text representation from BERT: an empirical study. CoRR **abs/1910.07973** (2019). http://arxiv.org/abs/1910.07973

18. Maslowska, E., Malthouse, E.C., Viswanathan, V.: Do customer reviews drive purchase decisions? the moderating roles of review exposure and price. Decis. Support Syst. **98**, 1–9 (2017). https://doi.org/10.1016/j.dss.2017.03.010
19. Mohammed, R., Rawashdeh, J., Abdullah, M.: Machine learning with oversampling and undersampling techniques: overview study and experimental results (04 2020). https://doi.org/10.1109/ICICS49469.2020.239556
20. Montomoli, J., e.a.: Machine learning using the extreme gradient boosting (xgboost) algorithm predicts 5-day delta of sofa score at icu admission in covid-19 patients. J. Intensive Med. **1**(2), 110–116 (2021). https://doi.org/10.1016/j.jointm.2021.09.002, https://www.sciencedirect.com/science/article/pii/S2667100X21000323
21. Moore, R.L., Blackmon, S.J.: From the learner's perspective: a systematic review of MOOC learner experiences (2008–2021). Comput. Educ. **190**, 104596 (2022)
22. Mou, J., Zhu, W., Benyoucef, M.: Impact of product description and involvement on purchase intention in cross-border e-commerce. Indust. Manage. Data Syst. (12 2019). https://doi.org/10.1108/IMDS-05-2019-0280
23. Pedregosa, F., et al.: Scikit-learn: Machine learning in Python. J. Mach. Learn. Res. **12**, 2825–2830 (2011)
24. Qiu, L., Liu, Y., Liu, Y.: An integrated framework with feature selection for dropout prediction in massive open online courses. IEEE Access **6**, 71474–71484 (2018). https://doi.org/10.1109/ACCESS.2018.2881275
25. Shyam, R., Ayachit, S.S., Patil, V., Singh, A.: Competitive analysis of the top gradient boosting machine learning algorithms. In: 2020 2nd International Conference on Advances in Computing, Communication Control and Networking (ICACCCN), pp. 191–196 (2020). https://doi.org/10.1109/ICACCCN51052.2020.9362840
26. Rogers, A., Kovaleva, O., Rumshisky, A.: A primer in BERTology: what we know about how BERT works. Trans. Assoc. Comput. Linguist. **8**, 842–866 (2020). https://doi.org/10.1162/tacl_a_00349, https://aclanthology.org/2020.tacl-1.54
27. Sanh, V., Debut, L., Chaumond, J., Wolf, T.: DistilBERT, a distilled version of BERT: smaller, faster, cheaper and lighter (2019). https://doi.org/10.48550/ARXIV.1910.01108, https://arxiv.org/abs/1910.01108
28. Udemy: Course Reviews FAQ. https://teach.udemy.com/course-reviews-101/. Accessed 20 Sept 2022
29. Udemy: Learn about Udemy culture, mission, and careers — About Us. https://about.udemy.com/. Accessed 20 Sept 2022
30. Udemy: Udemy Affiliate API Documentation (v2.0). https://www.udemy.com/developers/instructor/models/course_review/. Accessed 23 Jan 2023
31. Vaswani, A., et al.: Attention is all you need (2017).https://doi.org/10.48550/ARXIV.1706.03762, https://arxiv.org/abs/1706.03762
32. Wang, W., Guo, L., Sun, R.: Rational herd behavior in online learning: insights from MOOC. Comput. Hum. Behav. **92**, 660–669 (2019). https://doi.org/10.1016/j.chb.2017.10.009
33. Wolf, T., et al.: HuggingFace's transformers: State-of-the-art natural language processing (2020)
34. Yang, J., Sarathy, R., Lee, J.: The effect of product review balance and volume on online shoppers' risk perception and purchase intention. Decis. Support Syst. **89**, 66–76 (2016). https://doi.org/10.1016/j.dss.2016.06.009
35. Yang, L., Shami, A.: On hyperparameter optimization of machine learning algorithms: theory and practice. Neurocomputing **415**, 295–316 (2020). https://doi.org/10.1016/j.neucom.2020.07.061

36. Zhao, Y., Hryniewicki, M., Cheng, F., Fu, B., Zhu, X.: Employee turnover prediction with machine learning: a reliable approach (09 2018). https://doi.org/10.1007/978-3-030-01057-7
37. Zhu, M., Sari, A., Lee, M.: A comprehensive systematic review of MOOC research: Research techniques, topics, and trends from 2009 to 2019. Educ. Technol. Res. Develop. **68** (06 2020). https://doi.org/10.1007/s11423-020-09798-x

The Study of Human Action Recognition in Videos with Long Short-Term Memory Model

Hussan Khan[1], Sammra Habib[2], Amna Qasim[3], Nisar Hussain[4],
Muhammad Usman[4], Ahmad Mahmood[5], Zainab Shaukat[5], Asghar Afzal[5(✉)],
and Muhammad Zain[2]

[1] National College of Business Administration and Economics, Lahore, Pakistan
[2] Minhaj University, Lahore, Pakistan
[3] Instituto Politécnico Nacional, Centro de Investigación en Computación,
Mexico, Mexico
[4] Instituto Politécnico Nacional (IPN), Centro de Investigación en Computación
(CIC), Mexico, Mexico
[5] Comsats University Islamabad, Lahore, Pakistan
asgharafzal7696@gmail.com

Abstract. Human Action Recognition (HAR) requires tracking diverse fields of human activities in healthcare, education, entertainment, visual monitoring, video collection, and irregular behavior identification. Machine learning techniques are widely used to identify an action. These techniques have their limitations; they do not provide automatic feature selection for this purpose. This paper presents a deep learning algorithm, the Long Short Term Memory Model (LSTM) combined with the pre-trained Convolutional Neural Network (CNN) VGG16 that will provide a completely automatic feature selection. Firstly, the features in the video sequence are extracted using a VGG16 convolutional neural network. The video is then classified using an LSTM algorithm. The well-known benchmark, UCF101, which includes all 101 classes, is used to test the network. This research will propose an improved approach for identifying an action from multiple videos using the deep learning method. The presented method for an automated system for recognition of human action classification presents 99% accuracy.

Keywords: Human Action Recognition · LSTM · VGG16 · UCF101 · Long Short Term Memory Model

1 Introduction

The realm of video content in today's digital landscape has burgeoned, presenting a vast reservoir of information. Embedded within these videos lie intricate human actions, a rich tapestry of behavior that holds immense value across diverse applications. Understanding and deciphering these actions within videos

Supported by organization x.

stand as a critical pursuit, leading to the emergence of sophisticated technological solutions. Among these, the Long Short-Term Memory (LSTM) model has garnered significant attention and acclaim for its prowess in unraveling temporal patterns and sequences within video data [1]. "The Study of Human Action Recognition in Videos with Long Short-Term Memory Model" delves into the realm of video analysis with a focus on deciphering human actions. This research embarks on a journey to explore the potential and efficacy of LSTM, a specialized form of recurrent neural network, in comprehending and recognizing nuanced human behaviors depicted in videos [2]. Traditional Machine Learning (ML) approaches face limitations when dealing with the complexities of large-scale activities in challenging environments [3]. Handling imbalanced data and sluggish learning rates further compound these challenges [4]. While supervised ML-based Human Activity Recognition (HAR) methods hold promise, they often demand substantial labor for comprehensive activity identification [5]. Also, the surge in multimedia device usage has resulted in a deluge of video content, making manual retrieval a daunting and time-consuming task [6].

This backdrop sets the stage for the exploration of the CNN model VGG16 + LSTM as a solution for human action recognition within videos. Deep learning methodologies present an enticing alternative to traditional feature engineering, minimizing the reliance on massive datasets for training [7]. In our approach, we convert videos into frames and train models based on this frame-level data. Then a promising pathway is needed to emerge in the quest for efficient, effective video processing techniques [8]. By leveraging the advanced model, this study aspires to contribute significantly to the fields of computer vision and human behavior analysis [9]. It aims to clarify the strengths and weaknesses of LSTM in the context of action recognition through rigorous testing and validation, opening the door for improved techniques in video processing and comprehending human behavior in dynamic visual environments [10].

2 Literature Review

Researchers have spent a great deal of time in recent years investigating various sensing technologies, and many alternative approaches have been put forth for modeling and identifying human activity. Lightweight deep neural network-based action recognition architecture only uses RGB data. CNN units, LSTM units, and a temporal-wise attention model are used in the suggested design. First, CNN is used to extract spatial characteristics that may be used to distinguish objects from the context utilizing local and semantic attributes. Secondly, spatial function maps from different CNN layers are used (the pooling layer and the fully connected layer) two types of LSTM networks are executed to extract temporal motion characteristics. Then, following the LSTM, a temporary care model is developed to know which components are more vital in certain frames. The last thing to do is to examine inherent relations between two types of LSTM features using a combined optimization module. The efficiency of the suggested approach is shown by experimental findings [11]. Recognize human activities, and develop a multi-stream architecture for the Convolutional Neural Network (CNN). In addition, human areas with the most informative characteristics are considered. First, the area of interest matching the look and the character movement may be reliably recognized in actual circumstances by enhancing foreground detection. We build one aspect and one movement stream based on the complete observed human body. Moreover, we pick a secondary zone that comprises the key movements of an actor based on movement. By merging the standard streams with new streams relating to human beings, we present an architecture linked to human CNN (HR-MSCNN), which encompasses the look, movement, and tubes caught in human regions. A comparative assessment of JHMDB, HMDB51, UCF Sports, and UCF101 data sets shows the streams that include complementary characteristics. On these four datasets, the suggested multi-stream architecture delivers cutting-edge results [12]. Spatial-temporal domain analysis simultaneously on both domains of action-related hidden data sources inside input data. We suggest further a more powerful tree-structure-based traversal technique the human skeleton is influenced by its aesthetic structure. Present a new gating system inside LSTM for managing 3D skeleton noise and occlusion data to learn the trustworthiness of sequence input data, and therefore to alter their influence on the memory cell's long-term context information. Our approach delivers cutting-edge performance on 4 difficult 3D human action analysis benchmark data sets [13].

A new 3D action recognition class of the LSTM Global Context-Aware Attention (GCALSTM) network that may, by selection and with global contextual information, focus on informative joint sequences. We are additionally proposing a recurring method for the attention of our GCA-LSTM network to ensure a reliable depiction of the action sequence. Experiments that in each sequence, the most informative joints can be consistently focused on our edge network. In addition, our network delivers state-of-the-art results for 3D action detection in three demanding datasets [14]. Fully linked LSTM deep all-the-time action recognition network on a skeleton basis. Inspired by the fact that the coincidence of the joint inherently characterizes human activities, the skeleton is used for input every time, and a new regularization technique is introduced to understand the skeletal joints' co-occurrence properties. We present a new drop-out method, which concurrently runs on the doors, cells, and output responses of the LSTM neurons, to train the LSTM deep network efficiently. The efficacy of the proposed approach is consistently demonstrated by experimental findings from three human actions recognition datasets [15]. Time pattern descriptors suggested for joint positions are designed to provide precise and robust action identification using the popular long short-term memory (LSTM) system. Given that actions are mostly made up of tiny sub-actions to extract temporal pattern descriptors for each subaction in the frequency domain. First, we use a two-dimensional wavelet transformation. We then construct a new LSTM structure, which models a long-term spatial time connection between bodily components, for deep characteristics. Because temporal design descriptors and LSTM's deep functions are seen as multimodal representations for actions, they are fused with a network of autoencoders for a more efficient recognition action descriptor. The efficiency of the suggested 3-dimensional recognition action approach is demonstrated by experimental findings on three demanding data sets using different comparison approaches [16].

Various frames play various roles in human action identification in video-based feature learning. Most profound models, however, in the parameter training stage use the same weights on different visual and temporal indicators which adversely affect the differentiation between features. To solve the problem, the visual focus mechanism is used and a two-stream LSTM focus network is proposed. It may concentrate on the effective characteristics of the original photos and pay multiple kinds of attention to the deeper outputs characteristic map. A deep functional correlation layer is presented for adjusting deep network learning parameters based on the assessment of correlations because of the correlation between two deep functional streams. Finally, our technique is assessed using three different data sets, and the results of our experiment demonstrate that the latest achievements in the typical scenarios may be achieved by our proposal [17]. Video sequence recognition has several applications for health surveillance, supporting living, surveillance, and intelligent homes. Despite progress in sensing, particularly concerning 3D video, research remains on the techniques for processing data. A system that blends recurrent neural networks with convolutionary neural networks in an electoral approach demonstrates improved outcomes. The non-recurring unit networks are especially suitable for distinguishing activities from long-term optical tracking data based on long-term information. The 3D-CNNs are focused on comprehensive recent video data. The resultant characteristics are combined into an SVM classifying the motion. Our technique increases 14% standard data set the detection rates of state-of-the-art methods in this architecture [18]. A focus on learning spatial characteristics using a CNN and graphing their temporal relationships connected with the aid of Long-short–Term-Memory (LSTM) networks. The deep fusion framework uses spatial characteristics of CNNs with temporal information in LSTM models more efficiently. Evaluation of their strengths and flaws is very comprehensive. Find out that the completely linked features function as an attention mechanism by integrating both feature sets and directing the LSTM towards intriguing sections of the convolutional sequence of features. The importance of the fusion process in contrast to other cutting-edge technologies is its simplicity and efficiency. The assessment findings show that this Hierarchical Multi-Stream Fusion Approach offers a high level of performance in three frequently used databases: UCF11, UCF Sports, jHMDB, and more. In this case, the method is superior to single-stream mapping methods [19].

A novel model has been suggested. To increase model generality, first pre-train 3D CNN using an immense video recognition dataset, Kinetics. Long short-term memory (LSTM) will next be introduced to create a high-level temporal model characteristic of the Kinetics 3D model CNN. Our tests have shown that the pre-trained kinetics model usually can exceed the pre-trained ImageNet model. And lastly, our planned network is leading the way with UCF-101 data sets [20]. Offered the comprehensive design of a convolutional neural network-long short-term memory network (CNN-LSTM). This technique CNN-LSTM not only increases human prediction accuracy from raw data but decreases the model's complexity while eliminating the requirement for the latest feature technology. The network CNNLSTM is both deep in space and in time. The 99% accuracy of our suggested model about the iSPL, an internal dataset, and 92% exactness of the public UCI HAR dataset is achieved. It has also been compared to other techniques. We evaluated their performance with other techniques as well. It competes with various architectures of the Deep Neural Network (DNN) that have been suggested in the past and with machine learning models that rely on manual data [21].

3 Materials and Methods

3.1 Dataset

With 101 action categories, UCF101 is an action recognition data set of realistic action videos that were gathered from YouTube. There are 13320 video clips of 101 activity types in the collection. The videos are organized into 25 groups in 101 categories, with 4-7 movies of action available for each group. Some characteristics are shared, such as a similar mindset, and comparable viewpoints might be shared by movies of the same group. These categories have five types:

- The Interaction of Human-Object
- The Interaction of Human-Human
- Instrument that Playing Music
- Body-Motion Only
- Physical Activity

3.2 Proposed Approach

Deep neural networks are used in an innovative way to classify human action using the UCF101 dataset. Deep neural networks are an improved branch of artificial neural networks that can categorize high-dimensional and large datasets accurately. Each data set is trained and tested in groups and is classified using a deep neural network model. In this paper, convert the videos into frames. Every frame in a video can be tagged as belonging to the same video category. We then utilize the CNN + LSTM model with these frameworks, we use them. Every frame of a video is predicted as a video category in test mode.

The pre-trained CNN with LSTM architecture employs CNN layers for feature extraction on frames as well as LSTMs for sequence prediction. The feature extraction is done with the VGG16 model that has been pre-trained. The CNN model's spatial characteristics of the LSTM architecture are deployed, which extracts time data to provide an experienced action model categorization. Spatial-temporal data are activity videos that are made up of image frames with a defined size that are concatenated along the time axis. The spatial and temporal components of video can be organically separated. The spatial component, which has a frame-by-frame look, gives knowledge about the video's pictures and objects. The time component that moves across the frames gives information on the movement of the observer, camera, and objects. The extraction of spatial and temporal features is a crucial step in visual recognition. For image categorization, CNNs are the primary source. CNNs are traditional deep models that can extract local characteristics straight from the raw inputs. Convolution layers are constructed using kernel numbers and an appropriate step for local characteristics. The layers of normalization must increase the generalization of data and lessen its overlay [17]. Swimming pools, such as medium pooling, and max pooling reduce the complexity of the local characteristics. In addition, all previous layer neurons that combine local and world representation features have been fully integrated into the connected layers. The conceptual characteristics of each layer in the network are high-end.

The frames were split into training and testing. 75% used for training and 25% for testing. Then, for each frame, a VGG16 ConvNet is performed, and the final ConvNet output is used as a feature extraction of the frame. These extraction representations are used as input to the classification model, with video categories serving as predicted labels. The spatial features of the convolutional neural network model are transferred to the long-term memory architecture that collects temporal data to create a trained model for the categorization of activity. A detailed workflow of the proposed model is shown in Fig. 1:

VGG16. The design input is a dimension image (224 * 224 * 3). It begins with 2 layers with 64 filter-size channels of 3×3 and the same padding with a maximum stride layer (2, 2). The following two levels are 128-channel convolution layers with a filter size of (3, 3). (2, 2). The first set is made up of 256 filter channels (3, 3), and the other 2 contain 512 (3, 3) filters with the same padding size. Afterward, there are 3 sets of 3 convolution layers and one max pond layer. We have a feature map (7, 7, 512) after the convolution stack and the max-pool layer. Fully connected layers follow. These top layers are removed for feature extraction [18, 20].

LSTM. To tackle the problem of the disappearance gradient created by long input sequences, a variety of recurrent neural networks termed LSTM units were suggested. For applications in which there are terrible gaps of infinite lengths between important occurrences, LSTM is highly appropriate. Long-short-term model network models are a kind of RNN that can detect and record extended input sequences. They are intended for use with extended data sequences, up to 200 to 400 time steps [19,21]. In Python, the LSTM is a special type of RNN supplied by Keras. Finally, a Softmax classifier is used to create high-level feature predictions [23]. Developed a long-term model with a 256-neuron LSTM layer [22]. As an input for the layer LSTM, the feature map is employed. The LSTM layer output is sent to a 256-unit FC dense layer [24]. We have utilized the activation "Softmax" which mainly provides an output category. The optimizer utilized was "Nadam" and the rate of learning was 0.002 with 1e-08 decay, which was utilized as a loss measure for "categorical_crossentropy." The model fits with batch size 32 and epochs 5. After completing the training, the model is saved for future video classification [25].

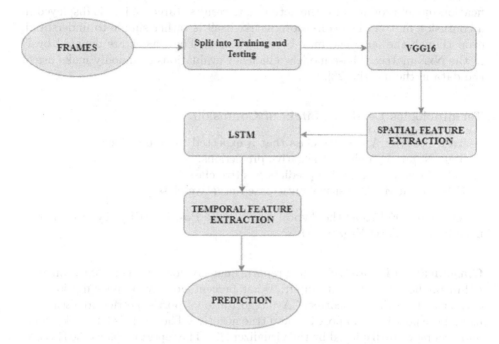

Fig. 1. Detail Workflow of the Proposed Model

4   Results and Discussion

4.1   Model Evaluation Parameter

A crucial stage in the process of creating a model is model evaluation. It helps determine which model best represents our data and how well the selected model will function going forward. Hyper-parameters control the form of the model, whereas model parameters control how input data is converted into suitable outputs. Before the model can be trained, hyperparameter properties are present in almost all common learning techniques. Numerous measures have been employed for process evaluation, including the F1-score, accuracy, recall, and confusion matrix.

Confusion Matrix. Generally referred to as a matching matrix in unsupervised learning, a confusion matrix, also called an error function, is a unique table arrangement that provides an image of the performance of an algorithm typical of supervised learning, especially for statistical classification. Each row in the matrix denotes the actual class, whereas each column shows the projected class's occurrences [27]. The number of accurate and inaccurate predictions the classification model produced for the actual data results (target value) is displayed in a confusion matrix. The confusion matrix itself is rather simple to understand, even though the language may be complicated. The classes are denoted by N in the NxN matrix. These models' efficiency evaluations commonly make use of the data in the matrix [28].

Terminologies Used in Matrix of Confusion.

- True Positive: A positive class that is expected to be positive.
- True Negative: a class of negative predictions.
- False Positive: a negative predicts positive class.
- False Negative: A positive, anticipated negative class.

Often referred to as the Type I Error, False Positive (FP). Type II error is usually called False Negative (FN).

Classification Report. Grading reports quantify how well a classification algorithm predicts based on its input. What percentage of your presumptions are correct and which are incorrect? A categorization report's metrics are estimated using false positive, real positive, and true negative. The model's F1 mark, recall, and accuracy are displayed by the visualizer [30]. The report displays the f1 score, accuracy, and reminder of the primary classification factors on a per-class basis. Both true and false negative results as well as true and false positive results are used to construct the measurements. Positive and negative are the generic terms for the anticipated classes in this instance [31].

Recall. The percentage of Positive samples that were correctly classified as Positive to the total number of Positive samples is used to calculate the recall [33]. The recall measure evaluates how well the model detects positive samples. The number of positive samples found increases with recollection [41]. The recall formula is presented in Eq. 1 [41].

$$Recall = \frac{TP}{TP + FN} \tag{1}$$

Precision. The ratio of correctly identified positive samples to the total number of correctly or incorrectly categorized positive samples is used to calculate accuracy. The model's accuracy in classifying a sample as positive is evaluated by the precision metric [37]. Equation 2 [37] presents the precision formula:

$$Recall = \frac{TP}{TP + FP} \tag{2}$$

F1-Score. F1-Score is medium accuracy and reminder weighted. Both false negatives and incorrect positives are taken into account in this way. In situations where there is an uneven distribution of classes, F1 is frequently more advantageous than precision. Additionally, it is not as simple as accuracy [38]. Reminder and harmonic mean accuracy form the basis of the F1-Score. Another name for the F measure is the F score. In other words, the F1 scoring is an exact and accurate balancing [35]. False-positive and false-negative results are the main focus of F1 Score. We are interested in learning about the false-positive and false-negative distributions for different models. The F1-Score is used to evaluate these models' performance [40]. We can see the F1-Score format in Eq. 3 [40].

$$Recall = 2 * \frac{Precision - Recall}{Precision + Recall} \tag{3}$$

Support. The number of actual class instances in the provided dataset is known as support. It may be necessary to use equalization or stratified sampling to uncover underlying problems in the reported classification scores if the training data is given unfair support [36].

5   Experiment and Result

5.1   Experiment I

We used the 40-class UCF101 dataset for the experiment. The proposed deep transfer learning method with the VGG 16 + LSTM for the classification of action recognition presents each UCF 101 class, 96 percent grade accuracy for each class of UCF 101 data sets, and 96 percent value for grade metrics with parameters Remembrance, Precision, F1score, macro, and Weighted medium for each grace. Performance is also measured using the accuracy and entropy loss graph for training, testing, and validation sets. The train and validation accuracies and validation loss that we observed in the experiment depicted in Fig. 2 are displayed in the graphs below.

5.2   Experiment II

The UCF101 dataset with 101 classes was used in Experiment II. The proposed deep transfer learning method with the VGG 16 + LSTM for the classification of action recognition presents each UCF 101 class, 99 percent grade accuracy for each class of UCF 101 data sets, and 99 percent value for grade metrics with parameters Remembrance, Precision, F1-score, macro, and Weighted medium for each grace. The entropy loss graph and accuracy for training and testing a The train and validation accuracies and validation loss that I observed in the experiment depicted in Fig. 3 are displayed in the graphs below.

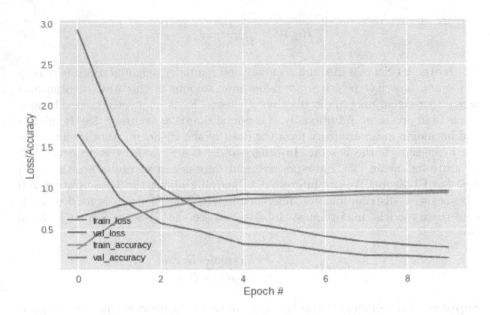

Fig. 2. Loss and Accuracy for 40 Classes of UCF 101

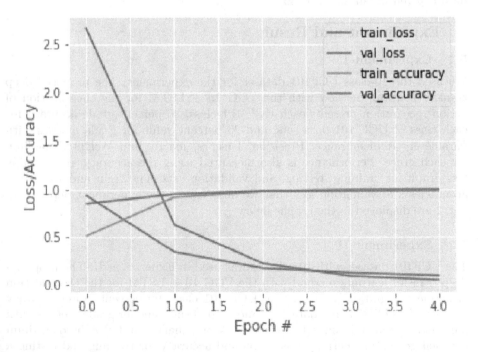

Fig. 3. Loss and Accuracy for 101 Classes of UCF 101

6   Discussion

An automated deep transfer learning technique of VGG16 + LSTM architecture for human action recognition is proposed in the experiment. The UCF101 dataset's forty different class types are used to recognize human actions. The three sections of these classes are used to identify activity using the suggested methodology. The training, validation, and testing sets are the components that make up the dataset. Use the UCF101 dataset to train the network according to the suggested method. First, create frames from each class's videos, assessment of the recommended method's effectiveness using each class's test set of frames. An automated deep transfer learning method of VGG16 + LSTM architecture for human action recognition was proposed in Experiment II. The UCF101 dataset's 101 types of classes are used to recognize human actions. I used all classes in the UCF101 dataset in Experiment II by reducing the number of frames, and my results were better than those of Experiment I. The three sections of these classes are used to identify activity using the suggested methodology. The training, validation, and testing sets are the components that make up the dataset.

Use the UCF101 dataset to train the network according to the suggested method. First, create frames from each class's videos, assessment of the recommended method's effectiveness using each class's test set of frames. Following the execution of both experiments, our suggested model attains the maximum accuracy. My suggested model's accuracy is 99%. The best possible ratio is indicated by the precision value of 99%. 99% of the recall is better than in Experiment I. The model's test accuracy is 99%, as indicated by the F1-Score result.

The method for recognising human actions is implemented on the Python platform with GPU on "Google Colab". Since GPU operates more quickly than CPU, it is utilised instead of CPU. They perform better and produce the best classification outcomes.

7   Conclusion

Deep transfer learning techniques underpin the UCF101 dataset, which comprises 101 distinct classes, as shown by an automated system in that study. The suggested approach used the VGG16 + LSTM model's deep transfer learning technique to extract features from the UCF101 dataset. For improved performance, the features were incorporated into the classifier model. Comparing the proposed method to earlier related work, the classification accuracy is the best. Better results, including 99% accuracy in terms of precision, recall, F1-score, macro-average, and weighted average for each class of UCF 101, are presented by the automated system for human action classification recognition that is being presented. Additionally, it displays the entropy loss graph and accuracy for every class in the UCF101 dataset. This study aids in the recognition and detection of human behavior.

8 Future Work

The proposed method will be used in the future for automated action classification of numerous other kinds. This architecture will continue to function in the future when deep transfer learning models are used, perhaps with additional tuning and data augmentation.

Acknowledgment. A1-S-47854 of CONACYT, Mexico, grants 20232138, 20232080, and 20231567 of the Secretara de Investigación y Posgrado of the Instituto Politécnico Nacional, Mexico, and other grants provided partial funding for the work. The authors acknowledge Microsoft's support through the Microsoft Latin America PhD Award and thank CONACYT for providing computing resources through the Laboratorio de Supercómputo of the INAOE, Mexico's Plataforma de Aprendizaje Profundo para Tecnologas del Lenguaje.

References

1. Ma, M., Marturi, N., Li, Y., Leonardis, A., Stolkin, R.: Region-sequence-based six-stream CNN features for general and fine-grained human action recognition in videos. Pattern Recogn. **76**, 506–521 (2018)
2. Poppe, R.: A survey on vision-based human action recognition. Image Vis. Comput. **28**(6), 976–999 (2010)
3. Masoud, O., Papanikolopoulos, N.: A method for human action recognition. Image Vis. Comput. **21**(8), 729–743 (2003)
4. Kong, Y., Fu, Y.: Human action recognition and prediction: a survey. arXiv preprint arXiv:1806.11230 (2018)
5. Yao, B., Jiang, X., Khosla, A., Lin, A.L., Guibas, L., Fei-Fei, L.: Human Action Recognition by Learning Bases of Action Attributes and Parts, pp. 1331–1338. IEEE (2011)
6. Parameswaran, V., Chellappa, R.: View invariance for human action recognition. Int. J. Comput. Vision **66**(1), 83–101 (2006)
7. Zhang, Z., Hu, Y., Chan, S., Chia, L.-T.: Motion context: a new representation for human action recognition. In: Forsyth, D., Torr, P., Zisserman, A. (eds.) ECCV 2008. LNCS, vol. 5305, pp. 817–829. Springer, Heidelberg (2008). https://doi.org/10.1007/978-3-540-88693-8_60
8. Cho, S., Foroosh, H.: A Temporal Sequence Learning for Action Recognition and Prediction, pp. 352–361. IEEE (2018)
9. Singh, S., Velastin, S.A., Ragheb, H.: Muhavi: A Multicamera Human Action Video Dataset for the Evaluation of Action Recognition Methods, pp. 48–55. IEEE (2010)
10. Aslan, M.F., Durdu, A., Sabanci, K.: Human action recognition with bag of visual words using different machine learning methods and hyperparameter optimization. Neural Comput. Appl. **32**(12), 8585–8597 (2020)
11. Sargano, A.B., Wang, X., Angelov, P., Habib, Z.: Human Action Recognition Using Transfer Learning with Deep Representations, p. 463469. IEEE (2017)
12. Chenarlogh, V.A., Razzazi, F.: Multi-stream 3D CNN structure for human action recognition trained by limited data. IET Comput. Vision **13**(3), 338–344 (2019)
13. Ijjina, E.P., Chalavadi, K.M.: Human action recognition using genetic algorithms and convolutional neural networks. Pattern Recogn. **59**, 199–212 (2016)

14. Ji, S., Xu, W., Yang, M., Yu, K.: 3D convolutional neural networks for human action recognition. IEEE Trans. Pattern Anal. Mach. Intell. **35**(1), 221–231 (2012)
15. Wang, L., Xu, Y., Cheng, J., Xia, H., Yin, J., Wu, J.: Human action recognition by learning spatio-temporal features with deep neural networks. IEEE Access **6**, 17913–17922 (2018)
16. Ravanbakhsh, M., Mousavi, H., Rastegari, M., Murino, V., Davis, L.S.: Action Recognition with Image Based CNN Features (2015)
17. Jin, C.-B., Li, S., Do, T.D., Kim, H.: Real-time human action recognition using CNN over temporal images for static video surveillance cameras. In: Ho, Y.-S., Sang, J., Ro, Y.M., Kim, J., Wu, F. (eds.) PCM 2015. LNCS, vol. 9315, pp. 330–339. Springer, Cham (2015). https://doi.org/10.1007/978-3-319-24078-7_33
18. Sun, L., Jia, K., Yeung, D.-Y., Shi, B.E.: Human Action Recognition Using Factorized Spatio-Temporal Convolutional Networks, p. 45974605 (2015)
19. Mishra, S.R., Mishra, T.K., Sanyal, G., Sarkar, A., Satapathy, S.C.: Real time human action recognition using triggered frame extraction and a typical CNN heuristic. Pattern Recogn. Lett. **135**, 329–336 (2020)
20. Ahmad, Z., Khan, N.: CNN-based multistage gated average fusion (MGAF) for human action recognition using depth and inertial sensors. IEEE Sens. J. **21**(3), 3623–3634 (2020)
21. Tu, Z., et al.: Multi-stream CNN: learning representations based on human-related regions for action recognition. Pattern Recogn. **79**, 32–43 (2018)
22. Liu, J., Shahroudy, A., Xu, D., Wang, G.: Spatio-temporal LSTM with trust gates for 3D human action recognition. In: Leibe, B., Matas, J., Sebe, N., Welling, M. (eds.) ECCV 2016. LNCS, vol. 9907, pp. 816–833. Springer, Cham (2016). https://doi.org/10.1007/978-3-319-46487-9_50
23. Liu, J., Wang, G., Hu, P., Duan, L.-Y., Kot, A.C.: Global Context-Aware Attention LSTM Networks for 3d Action Recognition, pp. 1647–1656 (2017)
24. Zhu, W., et al.: Co-occurrence feature learning for skeleton based action recognition using regularized deep LSTM networks **30** (2016)
25. Li, W., Nie, W., Su, Y.: Human action recognition based on selected spatio-temporal features via bidirectional LSTM. IEEE Access **6**, 44211–44220 (2018)
26. Song, S., Lan, C., Xing, J., Zeng, W., Liu, J.: Spatio-temporal attention-based LSTM networks for 3D action recognition and detection. IEEE Trans. Image Process. **27**(7), 3459–3471 (2018)
27. Song, S., Lan, C., Xing, J., Zeng, W., Liu, J.: An end-to-end spatio-temporal attention model for human action recognition from skeleton data. **31** (2017)
28. Wu, Y., Wei, L., Duan, Y.: Deep spatiotemporal LSTM network with temporal pattern feature for 3D human action recognition. Comput. Intell. **35**(3), 535–554 (2019)
29. Dai, C., Liu, X., Lai, J.: Human action recognition using two-stream attention based LSTM networks. Appl. Soft Comput. **86**(105820), 69 (2020)
30. Zhao, R., Ali, H., Van der Smagt, P.: Two Stream RNN/CNN for Action Recognition in 3D Videos, pp. 4260–4267. IEEE (2017)
31. Zhang, Z., Lv, Z., Gan, C., Zhu, Q.: Human action recognition using convolutional LSTM and fully-connected LSTM with different attentions. Neurocomputing **410**, 304–316 (2020)
32. Jaouedi, N., Boujnah, N., Bouhlel, M.S.: A new hybrid deep learning model for human action recognition. J. King Saud Univ.-Comput. Inf. Sci. **32**(4), 447–453 (2020)

33. Khan, M.A., Sharif, M., Akram, T., Raza, M., Saba, T., Rehman, A.: Hand-crafted and deep convolutional neural network features fusion and selection strategy: an application to intelligent human action recognition. Appl. Soft Comput. **87**, 568–4946 (2020)

34. Thurau, C., Hlaváč, V.: Pose Primitive Based Human Action Recognition in Videos or Still Images, p. 8. IEEE (2008)

35. Lv, F., Nevatia, R.: Single View Human Action Recognition Uing Key Pose Matching and Viterbi Path Searching, pp. 1–8. IEEE (2007)

36. Russakovsky, O., et al.: Imagenet large scale visual recognition challenge. Int. J. Comput. Vision **115**(3), 211–252 (2015)

37. Wan, Y., Yu, Z., Wang, Y., Li, X.: Action recognition based on two-stream convolutional networks with long-short-term spatiotemporal features. IEEE Access **8**, 85284–85293 (2020)

38. Han, Y., Chung, S.-L., Xiao, Q., Lin, W.Y., Su, S.-F.: Global spatio-temporal attention for action recognition based on 3D human skeleton data. IEEE Access **8**, 88604–88616 (2020)

39. Xiao, J., Cui, X., Li, F.: Human action recognition based on convolutional neural network and spatial pyramid representation. J. Vis. Commun. Image Represent. **71**, 102722 (2020)

40. Wang, L., Ding, Z., Tao, Z., Liu, Y., Fu, Y.: Generative multi-view human action recognition. In: Proceedings of the IEEE International Conference on Computer Vision, pp. 6212–6221 (2019)

41. Karpathy, A., Johnson, J., Fei-Fei, L.: Visualizing and Understanding Recurrent Networks (2015)

Novel Algorithm to Predict Electoral Trends, Case in Mexico

Mauricio Flores-Geronimo[1]([✉]) [iD], Ulises Cruz-Valencia[2] [iD],
Manuel Alejandro Guerrero Martínez[3] [iD], Renato García-González[4] [iD],
and A. Daniela Grave-Aragón[5]

[1] Department of Engineering Studies for Innovation,
Universidad Iberoamericana Ciudad de México, Mexico, Mexico
mauricio.flores@ibero.mx
[2] Institute of Applied Research and Technology,
Universidad Iberoamericana Ciudad de México, Mexico, Mexico
ulises.cruz@ibero.mx
[3] Social and Political Sciences, Universidad Iberoamericana Ciudad de México,
Mexico, Mexico
alejandro.guerrero@ibero.mx
[4] Department of Philosophy, Universidad Autónoma de Puebla, Puebla, Mexico
renato.garciago@correo.buap.mx
[5] Universidad Nacional Autónoma de México, UNAM, Mexico, Mexico

Abstract. The purpose of this research work is to investigate whether
the natural language expressed on social networks, in addition to traditional surveys, can be a factor in anticipating the winner of a presidential
election in Mexico. To achieve this, our research team has developed an
algorithm that aims to differentiate the explicit and implicit manifesta-
tions of users' electoral preferences based on the grammatical structure
of Twitter comments. After conducting a systematic search for argument
structures, we identified a set of verbal words that allowed us to infer
voting intentions and program the algorithm accordingly. Subsequently,
we applied the tool to a sample of 10,000 tweets during the 2018 presidential elections. The results obtained by the algorithm proposed in
this research show similarity in trend with the results obtained by the
National Electoral Institute of Mexico.

Keywords: Natural language process · machine learning · algorithm ·
case study · presidential elections

1 Introduction

Knowing the opinion of citizens through the application of surveys is increasingly difficult and costly. This can be attributed to problems associated with
survey design, data collection, and processing, as well as the growing distrust or
disinterest of citizens in responding to them. Conversely, social networks have
emerged as a viable, cost-effective, and easily accessible option for analyzing
electoral preferences. When reviewing the prior knowledge on predicting voter

© The Author(s), under exclusive license to Springer Nature Switzerland AG 2024
J. A. Lossio-Ventura et al. (Eds.): SIMBig 2023, CCIS 2142, pp. 231–237, 2024.
https://doi.org/10.1007/978-3-031-63616-5_17

preference on Twitter, it has been found that studies have mainly focused on two broad aspects: volume-based analysis or volumetric models and content-based analysis or sentiment analysis [3, 7, 10].

Bermingham and Smeaton found that volume-based analysis not only allowed for predicting election results but also enhanced predictive quality when combined with sentiment analysis [1]. Counter and Faruquie [4], utilizing a regression model based on the volume of bigrams mentioned by supporters of US presidential candidates in 2012, achieved similar results by predicting Barack Obama's victory over Mitt Romney. Other volume-based investigations with favorable results are shown in [5, 6, 11]. An important aspect in the analysis of electoral trends involves analyzing the grammatical content of user comments on social networks to determine their preference towards specific candidates or parties. Pioneering work in this area was conducted by O'Connor et al. [9], they evaluated the approval of the Obama administration on Twitter in 2009 and found that the textual sequences in tweets were associated with opinions expressed in surveys, research related to grammatical analysis is shown in [2, 8].

This work consists of the development and implementation of an algorithm that allows identifying voting trends in text messages on Twitter. This will be done by searching for syntactic and grammatical structures, defined by a team of three linguists in the context of the language of Mexicans. That is, each tweet will be classified to assign voting preference to a target candidate. This represents something new in the text classification process, since the algorithm is designed and focused for a specific language and context. The results obtained from the design and implementation process are favorable, since the results obtained are very close to the results of the electoral process in Mexico in 2018.

2   Tweet Classification Methodology

The development of the algorithm proposed in this work was done in collaboration with a group of linguists who conducted a linguistic analysis of tweets in the context of the 2018 Mexican elections to identify voting trends. A systematic search for plot structures was conducted, identifying a set of verbal words from which an intention to vote can be inferred using syntactic-semantic criteria.

2.1   Explicit Tweet (EX)

An explicit tweet is closely linked to contextual elements of the election, such as the names of political parties, candidates, phrases, and forms of reference to the candidates i.e. #YoConAMLO (#IsupportAMLO) or puns that arise during the political situation and campaign. Examples are provided in the repository[1] in the file exTweetEXIM.txt

2.2   Implicit Tweet (IM)

Tweets with an implicit voting tendency are those that imply an interpretive process. Bags of words were created to capture these indirect references. Following

---

[1] https://github.com/maufloresg/TendenciasElectoral2018.

a systematic search for argument structures, a set of verbal words was identified from which an intention to vote can be inferred using syntactic-semantic criteria. Examples of these words or phrases are shown in file exTweetEXIM.txt in the repository.

Once the tweets were classified as EX or IM, the labeling and categorization process to identify voting tendency was using the system based on rules, which were defined by the group of linguists, grammatical and syntactic structures were established for each electoral candidate. This version of the algorithm only classifies voting tendency, however in a later stage the analysis of emotions based on a linguistic analysis will be included.

3 Input Data

Set of tweets analyzed to identify voting trends. This set is recovered based on a group of 400 phrases or words defined by the team of linguists. Examples of these are shown in the repository, flie searchPhrases. Using the search criteria, 3,384 tweets were recovered. The team of linguists developed a set of approximately 200 phrases or words for each candidate, which assign voting preference. Examples of voting trend phrases are shown in the repository: Andrés Manuel López Obrador (trendAMLO), Ricardo Anaya (trendANAYA), Jose Antonio Meade (trendMEADE).

4 Classification Algorithm

4.1 Flowchart

The general representation of the algorithm proposed in this work is depicted in Fig. 1. An important aspect to highlight is that the text classification process for tweets is based on the syntactic-semantic criteria identified by linguists within the context of the Mexican language, examples are shown in Sect. 3. The algorithm was implemented in an object-oriented language (Java). It is worth mentioning that the main steps of natural language processing were performed, including tweet cleaning, removal of special symbols, emojis, and so on.

Once this is done, the algorithm classifies the tweets as **EX** (explicit) and **IM** (implicit) based on the grammatical structures proposed by the team of linguists, examples of phrases to classify a tweet as explicit are shown in repository in file (Explicit), it is worth mentioning that these are different from those used to search for tweets to analyze and these explicit tweets are common for all candidates. Once they are classified as explicit, they are compared with a predefined bag of words associated with each candidate to classify the tweets and determine the voting trend, examples were mentioned in Sect. 3 (trendAMLO, trendANAYA, trendMEADE). For implicit tweets, each tweet is segmented into individual words, and a series of processes are applied based on grammar rules to classify the tweets for each candidate and determine their respective voting trend.

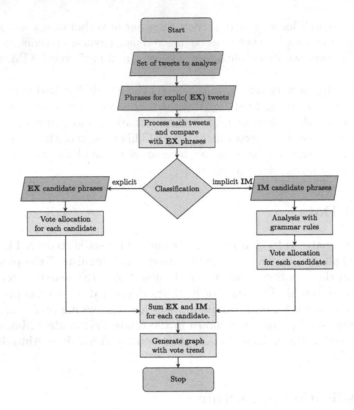

Fig. 1. Flowchart of the proposed algorithm for electoral trends

4.2   K-Nearest Neighbors (k-NN)

To compare the results of the model proposed in this paper, the k-nearest neighbors (k-NN) algorithm was used, which can be used for classification tasks. As previously mentioned, the algorithm proposed in this work classifies tweets with a voting tendency for a certain candidate. This classification process allowed the tweets to be labeled (AMLO, ANAYA, MEADE). Examples of tagged tweets are shown in repository[2] (classified tweets). An approximate of 2500 tweets were classified by the algorithm proposed in this work, which were used as input for the use of the algorithm K-NN, assigning 70% for training and 30% for testing. The main steps are shown in Algorithm 1. Initially, a set of pre-classified tweets is read and subjected to the aforementioned structural and grammar rules. Subsequently, the tweets are cleaned and transformed for analysis, including the tokenization process, stpowrod removal, etc. To later carry out the vectorization process. The k-NN algorithm is then applied using the Scikit Learn library. The results obtained are explained in more detail in the Sect. 5.3 and are shown in Fig. 3.

---

[2] https://github.com/maufloresg/TendenciasElectoral2018.

Algorithm 1. Algorithm use of k-nearest neighbors

Require: file csv with classified tweets
1: data frame *(df)* is generated
2: **for** each line of *df* **do**
3:     cleaning and tokenization
4:     remove stopword   ▷ defined by linguists
5: **end for**
6: Process of splitting *df*
7: Vectorization of tweets tf-idf
8: Use of k-nearest neighbors
9: Set value of k
10: Training process
11: Get classification graphs

---

5   Results

5.1   Manual Classification of Tweets

Initially, linguists generated a code-book according to syntactic-semantic criteria, based on it, a first "manual" classification was carried out from a total of 3,384, the classification obtained from the tweets (EX, IM and unclassified) was: 1234 explicit voting position, 1622 implicit IM voting stance and 1028 left out because they did not offer information on. Once it has distinguished between EX and IM tweets, for both cases, all the syntactic-semantic rules are applied, as well as the search for words associated with each candidate, this will allow to classify the tweets and obtain the voting preferences. The final result obtained is shown in Fig. 2a, emphasizing that these results were obtained by a manual classification process by linguists.

5.2   Using Proposed Algorithm

The algorithm proposed in Fig. 1 was coded with their respective syntactic-semantic analysis rules. The results obtained after the classification process and obtaining electoral trends are shown in Fig. 2b, similarity is observed in voting tendency with respect to Fig. 2a, where the classification was carried out manually by the linguists. The graph shows that the voting trend favors AMLO with 45.6%, ANAYA (37.1%) and MEADE with (17.3)%.

5.3   Using K-NN

To validate the results obtained in Sect. 5.2, with respect to the electoral vote trend, the algorithm called nearby neighbors was used, through the Scikit Learn library. The results obtained from the simulation are shown in Fig. 3, the decision limits for each candidate are, AMLO (red), ANAYA (blue) and MEADE (green).

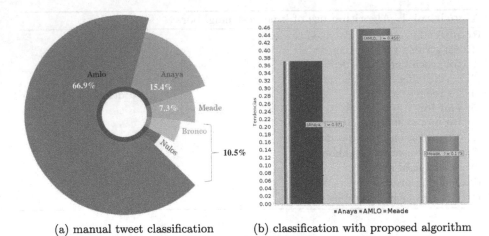

(a) manual tweet classification   (b) classification with proposed algorithm

Fig. 2. Comparison between manual classification and the algorithm proposed

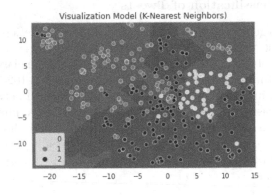

Fig. 3. Simulation result using K-NN (Color figure online)

6   Conclusions

According to the results obtained from the algorithm proposed in this study, it is possible to predict the electoral outcome of an election based on the natural language expressed on Twitter. The algorithm, when applied to the test set, showed a similar trend to the final result of the 2018 presidential election in Mexico. However, due to the limited number of tweets used in the analysis, the accuracy of the predictions showed variations, the accuracy for AMLO was -7.6%, while for ANAYA it was $+14.4\%$ and MEADE $+.9\%$. It is important to note that while there was overrepresentation and underrepresentation of the first two places, there is no probable winner bias (AMLO).

Additionally, it was observed that the convergence of explicit and implicit tweets contributed to increasing the number of units analyzed. However, due to the limitations of the research, it was not possible to significantly increase the number of tweets, which is considered crucial for improving the accuracy of predictions, as suggested by previous literature. Furthermore, the algorithm was applied post hoc rather than in real-time, as proposed by other researchers. Therefore, it is recommended to explore the future research agenda by applying the algorithm in real-time during key moments of an election.

References

1. Bermingham, A., Smeaton, A.: On using twitter to monitor political sentiment and predict election results. In: Bandyopadhyay, S., Okumura, M. (eds.) Proceedings of the Workshop on Sentiment Analysis where AI meets Psychology (SAAIP 2011), pp. 2–10. Asian Federation of Natural Language Processing (2011). https://aclanthology.org/W11-3702
2. Ceron, A., Curini, L., Iacus, S.M.: Using sentiment analysis to monitor electoral campaigns: method matters—evidence from the United States and Italy. Soc. Sci. Comput. Rev. **33**(1), 3–20 (2015). https://doi.org/10.1177/0894439314521983
3. Coletto, M., Lucchese, C., Orlando, S., Perego, R.: Electoral predictions with twitter: a machine-learning approach. http://ceur-ws.org/Vol-1404/paper_19.pdf
4. Contractor, D., Faruquie, T.A.: Understanding election candidate approval ratings using social media data. In: Proceedings of the 22nd International Conference on World Wide Web (WWW 2013 Companion), pp. 189–190. Association for Computing Machine (2013). https://doi.org/10.1145/2487788.2487883
5. Deltell, L., Claes, F., Osteso, J.M.: Predicción de tendencia política por twitter: elecciones andaluzas 2012 (22) (2013). https://revistascientificas.us.es/index.php/Ambitos/article/view/10892
6. Gaurav, M., Srivastava, A., Kumar, A., Miller, S.: Leveraging candidate popularity on twitter to predict election outcome. In: Proceedings of the 7th Workshop on Social Network Mining and Analysis (SNAKDD 2013), pp. 1–8. Association for Computing Machine (2013). https://doi.org/10.1145/2501025.2501038
7. Gayo-Avello, D.: A meta-analysis of state-of-the-art electoral prediction from Twitter data. Soc. Sci. Comput. Rev. **31**(6), 649–679 (2013). https://doi.org/10.1177/0894439313493979
8. Hopkins, D.J., King, G.: A method of automated nonparametric content analysis for social science. Am. J. Politic. Sci. **54**(1), 229–247 (2010). https://doi.org/10.1111/j.1540-5907.2009.00428.x
9. O'Connor, B., Balasubramanyan, R., Routledge, B., Smith, N.: From tweets to polls: linking text sentiment to public opinion time series. Proc. Int. AAAI Conf. Web Soc. Media **4**(1), 122–129 (2010). https://doi.org/10.1609/icwsm.v4i1.14031
10. Shi, L., Agarwal, N., Garg, R., Spoelstra, J.: Predicting US primary elections with twitter. https://www.semanticscholar.org/paper/Predicting-US-Primary-Elections-with-Twitter-Shi-Agarwal/564f64407587db38018c92322777ce6197b547c6
11. Zhou, Z., Makse, H.A.: Artificial intelligence for elections: the case of 2019 Argentina primary and presidential election (2019). https://doi.org/10.48550/arXiv.1910.11227

A Bayesian Machine Learning Model for Predicting Uncontrolled Type 2 Diabetes Mellitus

Joana Itzel Ríos-Barba[1] , Adriana Robles-Cabrera[2,3] , Romel Calero-Ramos[3] ,
Areli Monserrat Ríos-Vázquez[2], and Christopher R. Stephens[3,4(✉)]

[1] Software and Database Engineering, Instituto de Investigaciones en Matemáticas Aplicadas y en Sistemas (IIMAS), Universidad Nacional Autónoma de México (UNAM), Mexico City, Mexico

[2] Facultad de Medicina, Universidad Nacional Autónoma de México (UNAM), Mexico City, Mexico

[3] Centro de Ciencias de la Complejidad, Universidad Nacional Autónoma de México (UNAM), Mexico City, Mexico
stephens@nucleares.unam.mx

[4] Instituto de Ciencias Nucleares, Universidad Nacional Autónoma de México (UNAM), Mexico City, Mexico

Abstract. Type 2 diabetes mellitus (T2DM) is a chronic disease with multiple causes that represents a health and social problem. In the early stages, it may not be symptomatic, and late diagnosis and inadequate management can lead to severe complications, such as vision loss, heart attack, kidney failure, and limb amputation. Those complications, that impact the quality of life and cause premature death in patients, are highly related to their T2DM being uncontrolled. Although there is evidence on the physiopathology of metabolic imbalance, little is known about the many potential external variables, such as socioeconomic status, lifestyle, health knowledge and beliefs and environmental influences that are related to hyperglycemia. Therefore, this study aims to use a simple machine learning model applied to a dataset generated from a highly multi-factorial, multi-disciplinary questionnaire applied to a group of diabetics to predict the profiles of those patients most likely, or at risk, of having uncontrolled T2DM. As a result of our research, we propose an exploratory framework which could help in evaluating and predicting complications related to inadequate management of T2DM. These insights indicate that, by providing clear information and adequate education, patients can be helped to understand the importance of adopting a holistic approach in managing diabetes, incorporating both pharmacological treatment and lifestyle changes. This will enable them to have greater control over their health and improve their long-term quality of life.

Keywords: Uncontrolled T2DM · Data mining · Naive Bayes · metabolic control in diabetes

J. A. Lossio-Ventura et al. (Eds.): SIMBig 2023, CCIS 2142, pp. 238–248, 2024.
https://doi.org/10.1007/978-3-031-63616-5_18

1 Introduction

One of the diseases with the highest prevalence worldwide is type 2 diabetes mellitus (T2DM). In Mexico, it is the second leading cause of death, with 59,996 cases/year. According to the National Health and Nutrition Survey (Ensanut), 12.4 million people have T2DM [1]. Maintaining appropriate sugar levels is crucial to delay the onset and reduce the risk of adverse consequences of T2DM, such as micro and macrovascular complications [2]. The cost of T2DM for healthcare systems is enormous. In Mexico estimates vary widely, with 5% to 14% of healthcare expenditure allocated to the management of this disease and its complications. This investment, according to the International Diabetes Federation, is directly related to the mortality rate associated with T2DM [3]. Despite a large investment in prevention, T2DM has been increasing, both in Mexico and globally. The principal challenge in understanding and potentially reverting this trend is the high degree of multi-factoriality of the disease, with risk factors from genetics to politics.

Machine Learning techniques have proven to be an important and effective tool in the field of medicine to predict diseases and reduce their morbidity and mortality [4, 5]. In the area of disease prevention, explainable classifiers are particularly important, as they help to identify and quantify potentially causal and/or actionable risk factors. This paper uses a Naïve Bayes classifier to explore, from among a large set of potential predictors, those profiles of T2DM patients who exhibit inadequate disease control and who are most at risk of suffering its adverse consequences. By so doing we hope to contribute to the development of programs aimed at enhancing T2DM management and in reducing disease costs.

2 Methodology

Our overall goal was to predictively classify patients according to their status of having uncontrolled versus controlled T2DM, considered as our class of interest, C, and using a set of predictor variables $X = (X_1, X_2, X_3, ...X_N)$, by determining $P(C|X)$, the probability to have uncontrolled diabetes conditioned on the "risk" variables X. We will compare the posterior probability $P(C|X)$ to a Bayesian prior $P(C)$ through Bayes theorem

$$P(C|X) = \frac{P(X|C) * P(C)}{P(X)} \tag{1}$$

where $P(X|C)$ is the likelihood to see the data X given the class C and $P(X)$ is the evidence. Although many different machine learning techniques are available to calculate $P(C|X)$, we will use the Naive Bayes approximation which possesses several advantages: i) its transparency, where the contributions from each variable to the overall classification are transparent; ii) as a Bayesian framework, it is possible to include in subjective priors as well as quantitative evidence; iii) it is computationally very efficient, where new or updated data can be very easily included; iv) it is robust in the face of scarce data. In the Naive Bayes approximation, we assume independence of the X_i with respect to the class C. Although this may seem to be an extreme approximation, its robust performance has been demonstrated across a wide variety of problems and explained in [6], where it was shown that, as correlations can be positive or negative, cancellations can, and generally will occur [6]. To dispense with the evidence function it is customary to consider the score function:

$$S(C|X) = ln(P(C|X)/P(\neg C|X)) \qquad (2)$$

where $\neg C$ is the set complement of C and $S(C|X)$ is a monotonic function of $P(C|X)$. Writing the likelihood as: $P(X|C) = \prod_{i=1}^{N} P(X_i|C)$ we have

$$S(C|X) = \sum_{i=1}^{N} s(X_i) + s_0 \qquad (3)$$

where $s(X_i) = ln\frac{P(X_i|C)}{P(X_i|\neg C)}$ and $s_0 = ln(P(C)/P(\neg C))$. As $s(X_i)$ is a ratio of probabilities, an important question is whether the correlation between C and X_i is statistically significant. To answer this, as our classification task is binary, we use a binomial test:

$$\varepsilon(X_i) = \frac{NX_i[P(C|X_i) - P(C)]}{[NX_i P(C)(1 - P(C))]^{1/2}} \qquad (4)$$

where NX_i is the number of elements with feature X_i. When the binomial distribution can be approximated by a normal distribution, $|\varepsilon(X_i)| > 1.96$ is equivalent to the standard 95% confidence interval. Calculation of $s(X_i)$, $\varepsilon(X_i)$ and $P(C|X_i)$ gives a comprehensive view of how each variable contributes to the overall probability and allows for feature selection for model optimization by a choice of statistical weight, $s(X_i)$, and statistical significance, $\varepsilon(X_i)$. Note that the more positive/negative the score, $s(X_i)$, the more it is a risk/protective factor with respect to T2DM control. Equally, for $S(C|X)$ the more positive/negative it is the higher/lower the probability that the patient described by the profile X has uncontrolled diabetes. Although our chief goal was to determine and interpret the most important risk factors for uncontrolled T2DM, we also evaluated the performance of the overall classifier using a Confusion Matrix.

3   Data Collection

Data was obtained via a questionnaire, administered over a period of 2 months (Jan. to Mar. 2019) at the "Gral. Ignacio Zaragoza" Regional Hospital of the ISSSTE in Mexico. Participants were patients previously diagnosed with T2DM. The questionnaire was classified into sections: a) Personal Information, b) Family Medical History, c) Personal Medical History, d) Self-evaluation of health status, e) Nutrition, f) Lifestyle, g) Health Information and h) Opinions about their T2DM condition. It contained 305 questions with 1911 possible responses which, in the Naïve Bayes formalism, correspond to 1911 potential predictors. A total of 99 completed questionnaires were collected and analyzed to identify characteristics of those patients who have experienced uncontrolled diabetes and those who have not.

4 Results and Interpretation

In the following, unless explicitly stated, only those statistically significant items ($|\varepsilon(X_i)| > 1.96$, $p < 0.05$) are shown. With the current population $P(C) = 51/99 = 0.515$ which represents the null hypothesis against which the impact of a particular predictive factor will be measured. The profile of the uncontrolled diabetics can be categorized as shown below.

a) Personal Medical History
Considering factors from the category "Personal medical history", in Table 1 we see those statistically significant responses ($p < 0.05$) to the question: "Has a doctor told you that you have any of the following chronic conditions?" As insulin resistance can increase the production of cholesterol and triglycerides in the liver, which leads to maintaining high levels of them in the blood, we hypothesize that a person with uncontrolled diabetes is more likely to have elevated blood cholesterol levels, 72.4%, compared to a person whose diabetes is controlled, 42.9%.

Table 1. Chronic conditions correlated ($p < 0.05$) with uncontrolled T2DM.

Disease	Response	$s(X_i)$	$P(C \mid X_i)$	$P(C)$	Epsilon
High cholesterol	Yes	0.90	0.724	0.515	2.32
High cholesterol	No	−0.35	0.429	0.515	−1.49
High triglycerides	Yes	0.88	0.719	0.515	2.38
High triglycerides	No	−0.39	0.418	0.515	−1.64
Retinopathy	Yes	1.24	0.786	0.515	2.09
Retinopathy	No	−0.16	0.476	0.515	−0.74
Neuropathy	Yes	1.55	0.833	0.515	2.78
Neuropathy	No	−0.28	0.444	0.515	−1.31
Renal insufficiency	Yes	1.89	0.875	0.515	2.10
Renal insufficiency	No	−0.13	0.484	0.515	−0.62

Importantly, we also see the consequences of having uncontrolled diabetes wherein the probabilities for retinopathy, neuropathy and renal insufficiency (three very serious complications of diabetes) are much higher, 78.6%/47.6%, 83.3%/44.4% and 87.5%/48.4% respectively, for uncontrolled versus controlled patients. Further evidence of the strong correlation between uncontrolled diabetes and adverse consequences can be seen in Tables 2, where we see answers to the questions "How many episodes of diabetic coma have you had?", "Have you been hospitalized before?" and "When was your last blood test?". Results speak to the strong relationship between uncontrolled diabetes and adverse outcomes, with the incidence of diabetic coma only occurring in the uncontrolled group. Similarly, we see that those who have been hospitalized are twice as likely to come from the uncontrolled group – 76.1% versus 30.8% ($p < 0.05$).

Table 2. Personal medical history profile

Question	Response	$s(X_i)$	$P(C \mid X_i)$	$P(C)$	Epsilon
How many episodes of diabetic coma have you had?	More than zero	5.00	1.000	0.515	1.73
	None	−0.06	0.500	0.515	−0.31
Have you been hospitalized before?	Yes	1.10	0.761	0.515	3.44
	No	−0.87	0.308	0.515	−3.09
When was your last blood test?	Less than a month	−0.59	0.370	0.515	−2.19
	1–6 months	0.89	0.722	0.515	2.56
	>6 months	1.04	0.750	0.515	0.97

As well as the consequences of uncontrolled diabetes we can also see how important it is for the patient to actively participate in the control of their condition. For those who attend blood tests much less frequently - 1–6 months or >6 months - the probability of being in the uncontrolled group - 72% and 75% respectively - is twice the probability of being in the controlled group and having a frequency <1 month (see Table 2).

b) Lifestyle

Lifestyle covers many different, important facets, such as nutrition and physical activity. Several lifestyle factors were found to be predictive. In Table 3 we see responses to several questions about patients' lifestyle. In the case of "Do you like exercise?", for those who do not like exercise, 83% are uncontrolled ($p < 0.05$).

For the question "Have you changed your exercise habits over time?", we see that only 32% of those who haven't changed their habits are uncontrolled, while 72% of those who have been sedentary all their life are uncontrolled and only 37% of those who exercise more now than before are uncontrolled. Note that in the case of "I have not changed my habits over time" this could also encompass those who have kept up a good habit. The question "If you have changed your habits (nutrition, exercise, lifestyle...) why did you change them?" was geared to a wider set of lifestyle factors. We see now that a lack of change in this context is associated with a propensity to be uncontrolled, with 77% of those who hadn't changed their habits being uncontrolled. In general, most reasons given are indicative of being a controlled diabetic, with "Medical advice" being statistically significant ($p < 0.05$). In response to the question: "How many units of alcohol do you consume per week?", every single patient who reported consuming alcohol ($N = 10$) was in the uncontrolled group. Furthermore, all those reporting alcohol consumption also reported that they were long term consumers (>10 years). Turning now to the question "When you eat, do you like to eat...?", we see that the probability to be in the control group if they eat "a lot" is 74% compared to only 38% of those who report eating normal portions.

Table 3. Lifestyle profile

Question	Response	$s(X_i)$	$P(C \mid X_i)$	$P(C)$	Epsilon
Do you like exercise?	No	1.55	0.833	0.515	2.27
	Yes	−0.18	0.471	0.515	−0.85
Have you changed your exercise habits over time?	I haven't changed my habits over time	−0.81	0.320	0.515	−2.01
	I don't exercise now	0.37	0.607	0.515	1.00
	I exercise more than before	−0.60	0.368	0.515	−1.32
	I've been sedentary all my life	0.89	0.722	0.515	1.81
	Other	0.63	0.667	0.515	0.94
If you have changed your habits (nutrition, exercise, lifestyle…) why did you change them?	Medical advice	−0.75	0.333	0.515	−2.60
	Diagnosed with diabetes	−0.38	0.420	0.515	−1.63
	Diagnosed with another disease	0.86	0.714	0.515	1.54
	Family member died was diagnosed or died with a disease	−0.06	0.500	0.515	−0.08
	Own decision	−0.47	0.400	0.515	−1.41
	For reasons of work	0.00	0.000	0.515	−1.06
	For a personal or family situation	0.63	0.667	0.515	0.54
	I haven't changed my habits	1.14	0.769	0.515	2.67
	Television	−1.04	0.273	0.515	−1.66
	Family advice	−0.75	0.333	0.515	−1.30
	Diagnosed with obesity	0.09	0.538	0.515	0.17
	Friends' advice	−0.06	0.500	0.515	−0.04
	Health campaigns of the ISSSTE	0.00	1.000	0.515	1.41
	Magazines, books, newspapers	0.00	0.000	0.515	−2.13
How many units of alcohol do you consume per week?	More than 1	5.00	1.000	0.515	3.16
	None	−0.18	0.470	0.515	−0.85

(*continued*)

Table 3. (*continued*)

Question	Response	$s(X_i)$	$P(C \mid X_i)$	$P(C)$	Epsilon
When you eat, do you like to eat…?	Little	−0.06	0.500	0.515	−0.13
	Normal	−0.53	0.385	0.515	−1.94
	A lot	1.00	0.742	0.515	2.60

c) Health Information

The impact of health information is hugely important as it is something that can be controlled directly by the health authorities. In this regard there is a question of "just what information can make a difference?" Here, we will deviate slightly from the stated goal of showing those factors that distinguish between uncontrolled and controlled diabetics and consider responses to the questions: "How important is exercise for good health?" and "How important is a healthy diet for good health?" The results are shown below in Table 4. Although we can see that the responses do not distinguish between uncontrolled and controlled, i.e. the two groups have the same opinions on the relative importance of exercise and healthy eating, we see that basically everyone - 95% and 94% - believe that exercise and healthy eating are either important or very important for good health. In other words, although both groups are aware of their importance, this does not lead to positive actions.

Table 4. Attitude towards exercise, healthy eating and obesity knowledge

Question	Response	Nx_i	$s(X_i)$	$P(C \mid X_i)$	$P(C)$	Epsilon
How important is exercise for good health?	Unimportant	1	0.00	0.000	0.515	−1.06
	Important	15	−0.19	0.470	0.515	−0.39
	Very important	81	0.06	0.530	0.515	0.29
how important is a healthy diet for good health?	Unimportant	2	0.00	1.000	0.515	1.41
	Relatively unimportant	1	0.00	0.000	0.515	−1.06
	Important	15	0.07	0.530	0.515	0.15
	Very important	79	0.02	0.520	0.515	0.07
Do you know the range of BMI that corresponds to a normal person?	Less than 23	2	0.00	0.000	0.515	−1.50
	Don't know	97	0.04	0.526	0.515	0.22
Obesity is defined as BMI > what value?	Don't know	96	0.06	0.531	0.515	0.33
	>25	3	0.00	0.000	0.515	−1.84

In contrast, we see that 97% do not know the correct answers to: "Do you know the range of BMI that corresponds to a normal person?" and "Obesity is defined as BMI > what value?". This means that if they are told their own BMI that they would not be able to make some correspondence with whether the value was good or bad, although neither question distinguishes between uncontrolled and controlled. We also studied how accurate was the population's knowledge of the extent of the obesity epidemic in Mexico, as well as their knowledge of how much exercise is necessary for a healthy life, asking: "What percentage of Mexicans suffer from obesity?" and "How many hours of exercise per week are necessary for good health?" The results are shown in Table 5. Interestingly, over 80% either wildly overestimated it ($>80\%$) or wildly underestimated it ($<5\%$). Moreover, those who overestimated it were much more likely (83%, $p < 0.05$) to be in the uncontrolled group, while those who underestimated it were much more likely to be in the controlled group. For exercise, again, we see wild overestimates, with a substantial group ($N = 18$) saying >12 h, with those with such estimates being in the uncontrolled group. We may hypothesize that this could be a significant barrier to exercise if they believe that a healthy life is not possible without dedicating such many hours.

Table 5. Knowledge of frequency of obesity in Mexico

Question	Responses	Nx_i	$s(X_i)$	$P(C \mid X_i)$	$P(C)$	Epsilon
What percentage of Mexicans suffer from obesity?	40–49%	2	−0.06	0.500	0.515	−0.04
	50–60%	5	1.33	0.800	0.515	1.31
	70–79%	5	−0.47	0.400	0.515	−0.53
	Up to 39%	2	−0.06	0.500	0.515	−0.04
	More than 80%	18	1.55	0.833	0.515	2.78
	Less than 5%	67	−0.39	0.418	0.515	−1.64
How many hours of exercise per week are necessary for good health?	More than 24	13	1.14	0.769	0.515	1.89
	21–24	1	5.00	1.000	0.515	1.00
	13–16	4	5.00	1.000	0.515	2.00
	9–12	4	−1.16	0.250	0.515	−1.09
	4–8	56	−0.20	0.464	0.515	−0.79
	Don't know	21	−0.35	0.429	0.515	−0.82

Finally, in the category of health information we asked: "What are your principal sources of information about obesity, diabetes and your health? The results can be seen below in Table 6. Interestingly, there is a strong divide between the uncontrolled and controlled as to their use of "subjective" direct-contact sources, such as work colleagues, family and friends, versus media, such as television, internet and books, magazines and newspapers, with the uncontrolled preferentially using the former. Information from the ISSSTE itself did not discriminate between one group and another.

d) Regarding Their condition, Diabetes Mellitus
Based on the provided information, the hypothesis is proposed that some patients with diabetes consider medication to be sufficient for controlling the disease, without giving

Table 6. Sources of health information

Source	Nx$_i$	s(X$_i$)	P(C I X$_i$)	P(C)	Epsilon
Your doctor	89	0.01	0.517	0.515	0.03
Internet	29	−0.70	0.345	0.515	−1.89
Other source	7	−0.35	0.429	0.515	−0.47
Television	37	−3.64	0.027	0.515	−6.12
Family	22	0.31	0.591	0.515	0.73
Work colleagues	5	5.00	1.000	0.515	2.24
Information from the ISSSTE	32	0.06	0.531	0.515	0.19
Information from the Seguro Popular	3	−0.75	0.333	0.515	−0.65
Books, magazines and newspapers	16	−0.57	0.375	0.515	−1.16
Social media	9	−0.75	0.333	0.515	−1.13
Friends	8	0.45	0.625	0.515	0.64
Information from the IMSS	1	−5.00	1.000	0.515	1.00

the same attention to the importance of adopting healthy eating habits and engaging in regular physical activity. We asked the patients: "What percentage do you think that your lifestyle contributed to the development of your disease?" The results can be seen in Table 7. There is a very interesting pattern: a strong tendency for the uncontrolled group to assign a very low percentage 0–10 of the development of their disease to lifestyle, with 87% of those who assigned such a low percentage belonging to that group. However, there was another, smaller group (N = 10) who attributed a very large percentage (91–100) to lifestyle. Similarly, to the results in questions related to BMI and obesity in Mexico, the uncontrolled patients are associated with very unrealistic views of both their disease, the frequency of related disease - obesity - and the requirements for having healthy exercise patterns.

Table 7. Reported attribution of lifestyle to disease development

Percentage responsible	Nx$_i$	s(X$_i$)	P(C I X$_i$)	P(C)	Epsilon
0–10	23	1.84	0.870	0.515	3.51
11–20	2	0.00	0.000	0.515	−1.50
21–30	7	−0.35	0.430	0.515	−0.47
31–40	12	−1.67	0.170	0.515	−2.49
41–50	15	−0.47	0.400	0.515	−0.92
51–60	13	−0.21	0.460	0.515	−0.40

(*continued*)

Table 7. (*continued*)

Percentage responsible	Nx$_i$	s(X$_i$)	P(C | X$_i$)	P(C)	Epsilon
61–70	6	−1.67	0.170	0.515	−1.76
71–80	5	0.34	0.600	0.515	0.39
81–90	2	0.00	0.000	0.515	−1.50
91–100	10	2.14	0.900	0.515	2.51

5 Model Performance

In the previous section we reviewed the most significant predictors of uncontrolled diabetes. This is important from the perspective of examining each variable that exhibits a significant degree of correlation, that might also represent a causal relationship, and to decide whether a particular variable may be "actionable" or not, i.e., is it a variable that might be changed through a suitable intervention. However, to use the full model as a prediction model, for each patient we calculate their total score according to their profile X using Eq. (3), ranking patients from the maximum to minimum of $S(C|X)$ and assigning a class label - C = uncontrolled - to those patients with $S(C|X) > 0$. To measure model performance, we constructed a confusion matrix. In Table 8 we see the model's performance in terms of the standard metrics.

Table 8. Confusion Matrix statistics: accuracy, error, sensitivity and specificity.

Name	Formula	%
Accuracy	(TP + TN)/(TP + FP + FN + TN)	86%
Precision	TP/(TP + FP)	84%
Sensitivity	TP/(TP + FN)	88%
Specificity	TN/(TN + FP)	84%
F-measure	2 * ((precision*sensitivity)/(precision + sensitivity))	86%
Error	FP + FN/(TP + TN + FP + FN)	14%

6 Conclusion

Uncontrolled diabetes is a generator of huge burdens on health systems, far more than controlled diabetes. It is therefore important to understand its predictive drivers. As we have shown, there are many factors involved that span a significant number of categories. We believe that our results show however, the feasibility of using multifactorial, multidisciplinary datasets in combination with machine learning techniques to model important healthcare problems such as uncontrolled diabetes. Beyond identifying significant predictors, it is important to determine their causal relationship and whether they are actionable. With respect to causality: retinopathy, neuropathy and renal disease are all important consequences of uncontrolled diabetes, as are diabetic coma and hospitalizations. It is important to explain to diabetic patients how their risk of these grave consequences is increased by not controlling their T2DM. In terms of lifestyle, we saw that alcohol consumption, overconsumption of food and attitudes towards exercise were all significant predictors, and most likely causes of uncontrolled T2DM. Health information was shown to be an important element but that there were significant differences according to the type of information, with information that is typically promoted, such as the importance of exercise and healthy eating, being widely acknowledged but not being predictive of better health outcomes. Interestingly, uncontrolled diabetics had several health beliefs that were very different to reality. The most notable was how little they attributed their condition to their lifestyle. Finally, we noted that as a prediction model to predict uncontrolled diabetics using the considered profiles the model's performance was very satisfactory.

Acknowledgments. We would like to thank Dr Gloria Maldonado from ISSSTE in Mexico City. This study was funded by DGAPA PAPIIT (IG101520).

References

1. Ramírez-Hinojosa, J.P., Zacarías-Castillo, R., Torres-Tamayo, M., Tenorio-Aguirre, E.K., Torres-Viloria, A.: Costos económicos en el tratamiento farmacológico del paciente con diabetes mellitus tipo 2. Estudio de pacientes en consulta externa de medicina interna de un hospital de segundo nivel de la Ciudad de México. Salud Pública de México **59**(1), 6 (2017). https://doi.org/10.21149/7944
2. Secretaria de Salud: Comunicado de Prensa "En México, 12.4 millones de personas viven con diabetes" (2022). https://www.gob.mx/salud/prensa/547-en-mexico-12-4-millones-de-per sonas-viven-con-diabetes?idiom=es
3. Esparza-Romero, J.: Prevalencia y factores asociados a diabetes mellitus tipo 2 en población indígena de México: revisión sistemática. Revista Médica Del Instituto Mexicano Del Seguro Social **58**(3) (2021). https://www.redalyc.org/journal/4577/457768136014/
4. Raikomar, A., Dean, J., Kohane, I.: Machine learning in medicine. N. Engl. J. Med. **380**, 1347–1358 (2019). https://doi.org/10.1056/NEJMra1814259
5. Aishwarya, M., Vaidehi, V.: Diabetes prediction using machine learning algorithms. Procedia Comput. Sci. **165**, 292–299 (2019)
6. Stephens, C.R., Huerta, H.F., Linares, A.R.: When is the Naive Bayes approximation not so naive? Mach. Learn. **107**(2), 397–441 (2018)

Reviewer 2 Must Be Stopped: Transformer-Based Approaches for Predicting Paper Acceptance

Lukas Rimkus, Jonas Verbickas, and Riza Batista-Navarro[✉]

Department of Computer Science, University of Manchester,
Manchester M13 9PL, UK
riza.batista@manchester.ac.uk

Abstract. Peer review is a fundamental process in assessing the quality of papers for publication in academic settings. However, peer review is reported to be often highly subjective leading to undesirable decisions being made. Studies demonstrated that two independent review boards would accept and reject the same paper 50% of the time. In an attempt to support paper authors in assessing their chances of getting their paper accepted, previous work proposed traditional machine learning-based approaches (e.g., decision trees with handcrafted features) to predict whether a paper will be accepted or rejected. To the best of our knowledge, state-of-the-art pre-trained language models, i.e., transformers, have not been explored for this problem as of yet. To address this gap, we developed transformer models for the above-mentioned classification problem, and compared their performance with support vector machine (SVM) and multilayer perceptron (MLP) models. Specifically, we fine-tuned BERT, RoBERTa and Longformer transformer models on the ASAP-Review dataset, and compared their performance with traditional machine learning-based models trained on handcrafted features. Among the transformer models, Longformer obtained the highest accuracy of 76.92% on the test set. Overall, MLP obtained the best accuracy of 78.37%. We believe that our proposed classification system can support conference participants, helping them in assessing their papers before submission.

Keywords: Long Document Classification · Paper Acceptance Prediction · Transformers · Natural Language Processing · AI Conferences

1 Introduction

Peer review is a process used in academic publishing to ensure the quality and validity of research articles. It involves the evaluation of a manuscript by experts in the same field as the authors, who provide feedback and recommendations for improvement before the article is accepted for publication. Despite its widespread use, it is far from perfect. In 2014, the NeurIPS conference conducted a study of consistency between two review boards and found that when one of the groups

© The Author(s), under exclusive license to Springer Nature Switzerland AG 2024
J. A. Lossio-Ventura et al. (Eds.): SIMBig 2023, CCIS 2142, pp. 249–260, 2024.
https://doi.org/10.1007/978-3-031-63616-5_19

decided to accept a paper, the other would reject the same paper 50% of the time [7]. Cortes and Lawrence [3] analysed papers submitted to NeurIPS 2014 and showed that reviewers could identify low-quality papers but struggle to distinguish between average and high-quality papers since reviewer scores do not necessarily correlate with the number of citations a paper will receive. The contradictory views between reviewers are well-known within the scientific community. The reviewer who gives a negative or harsh review is often mockingly called 'Reviewer 2'. Online communities[1] where people can discuss their academic hardships have been named after such a reviewer. The issue of unfair reviews might become more prominent since submissions to AI conferences are growing exponentially [10].

We developed binary classification models to take the paper and predict if the conference would accept it. Papers from the International Conference on Learning Representations (ICLR) were utilised for this study as all papers including rejected ones are uploaded to the OpenReview platform, and hence can be used for training models for classification. As previous research mainly focussed on machine learning-based models trained on handcrafted features [5,14], we sought to compare their performance with that of transformers [16], which now underpin most of the state-of-the-art approaches to natural language processing (NLP) tasks. The following models, most often used by the previous research, took handcrafted features as input: support vector machines (SVM), k-nearest neighbours (k-NN), random forests, decision trees, naïve Bayes and multilayer perceptrons (MLP). These were then compared with the following transformer models: BERT [4], RoBERTa [8] and Longformer [1]. Additionally, a Bagging (**B**ootstrap **Agg**regat**ing**) ensemble of transformers was explored [2].

These models can be used by participants as a loose indicator of whether their paper would be accepted by the ICLR conference. It should be noted that they may be more reliable for assessing word choice, clarity and fluency than the quality of research and novelty criteria.

2   Related Work

Due to various existing problems in the peer review process, researchers started to analyse and try to improve it using Machine Learning (ML). Kang et al. [5] introduced the first dataset of public papers, PeerRead, with accept or reject decisions from top-tier venues like the Association for Computational Linguistics (ACL) conference and ICLR. The dataset also includes pre-prints from arXiv. They experimented with different traditional ML classifiers (e.g., SVMs, decision trees, naïve Bayes) using 22 handcrafted features (e.g., the length of the title, the number of authors, the number of sections), which achieved an accuracy of 65.3% for the ICLR 2017 dataset. However, the authors did not specify which model performed best. Meanwhile, Skorikov and Momen [14] achieved an accuracy of 81% using a random forest classifier on the whole PeerRead dataset. It is worth noting though that their study did not attempt to balance the dataset as there

---

[1] For example: https://facebook.com/groups/reviewer2.

were 9029 rejected and 5570 accepted papers in the dataset that they used, which could have skewed the results.

Yuan et al. [17] updated the PeerRead dataset by including ICLR submissions throughout 2018–2020 and named it the **A**spect-enhanced **P**eer (ASAP)-Review dataset,[2] which we utilised in our study. Kumar et al. [6] modified the task and designed a deep neural architecture that uses the reviews (rather than the papers themselves), review aspect categories and sentiments to predict whether a paper will be accepted. Their results show that the model achieves up to 76.67% accuracy on the ASAP-Review dataset. However, this architecture assumes the existence of reviews in predicting acceptance or rejection. Therefore this system is not suitable for our use case of allowing participants of a conference to assess their paper and obtain a predicted decision.

To the best of our knowledge, no pre-trained transformer-based approaches, which take the textual content of a paper for predicting the decision, have been attempted yet.

3 Methodology

In this section, we describe the dataset that was utilised in developing and evaluating our approaches, and present details of how different models were trained.

3.1 The ASAP-Review Dataset

Our chosen dataset, ASAP-Review, contains papers, their metadata and reviews in JSON format. Taking the ICLR submissions from 2017 to 2020 (5192 papers) [17], we obtained 1859 accepted papers and 3333 rejected ones. Although ASAP-Review also contains papers from the NeurIPS conference from 2016 to 2019, it was decided to discard those as they correspond to accepted papers only.

Our dataset contains about twice more rejected papers than accepted ones from ICLR. Therefore, it was decided to subsample the dataset to prevent models from being biased towards rejected papers. We randomly discarded rejected papers to match the number of accepted papers. The dataset was then randomly partitioned into 80% and 20% stratified splits for training and testing models. To allow for validation of model performance in the way of choosing optimal hyperparameters, 20% of the training set was set aside as our validation set. We used seeds in splitting the data to ensure reproducibility of the data partitions.

3.2 Models with Handcrafted Features

Data Preprocessing. Prior to training traditional machine learning-based models, the lexical features listed in Table 1 were extracted from the samples in our dataset. These were inspired by the features used by Kang et al. [5] and were extracted with the help of their codebase.[3]

---

[2] Available at https://drive.google.com/file/d/1nJdljy468roUcKLbVwWUhMs7teira h75/.

[3] Available at https://github.com/allenai/PeerRead.

Table 1. Handcrafted features for traditional machine learning-based models

Feature	Data Type
Whether abstract contains keywords: "deep", "neural", "embedding", "outperform", "novel", "state of the art"	boolean
Length of title	integer
Number of authors	integer
Most recent reference year	integer
Number of references	integer
Number of references mentioned	integer
Average length of references mentioned	float
Number of figures, tables, sections, equations and theorems	integer
Number of sections	integer
Average sentence length	float
Whether an appendix is provided or not	boolean

Selection and Training of Models. The extracted features were fed as input to the following models: SVM, decision trees, random forests, k-NN, naïve Bayes and MLP. Their training required the tuning of specific hyperparameters, which are discussed in Sect. 4.1.

3.3   Transformer-Based Models

Data Preprocessing. In training transformer models, the input text from the papers does not need any pre-processing as the complete sequence of tokens (including stopwords) is needed for context comprehension.

However, since transformer models are limited to a fixed number of tokens they can take as input, the original text needed to be shortened. To this end, we experimented with different text splitting configurations for selecting certain sections of the paper only, which would then serve as input text. It is worth noting that irrespective of the splitting method, the number of tokens stays the same for a certain model. The following configurations were considered:

- **Introduction with Abstract (IwA)**: the text from the Introduction of the paper including the Abstract.
- **Introduction without Abstract (IwoA)**: the text from the Introduction of the paper, but without the Abstract.
- **Tail**: the last section(s) at the end of the paper (including the Conclusion but not any appendices).
- **Middle**: the middle part of the text of the paper without the Abstract, Introduction and the Tail.
- **Abstract with Tail (AwT)**: the combined text of the Abstract and the Tail of the paper.

Furthermore, we experimented with prepending some metadata about the paper at the beginning of the input text, to give the model access to more information. Namely, the following metadata were added: the title of the paper, whether the paper includes any appendices, the number of sections and references. The inclusion of this metadata was enabled using a hyperparameter that allowed us to observe whether it leads to improved model performance. Kang et al. [5] generated these features manually as input to traditional machine learning-based models, which inspired us to use them with transformer models as well.

Fine-Tuning of Pre-trained Models. Three pre-trained language models, i.e., BERT, RoBERTa and Longformer, were fine-tuned for the binary classification task of predicting paper acceptance. Specifically, we fine-tuned the base BERT, RoBERTa and Longformer models available from Huggingface.[4] The pre-processed text is tokenised by the corresponding model's tokeniser. Binary cross-entropy was used as the loss function with AdamW as optimiser [9].

These models were selected to observe how results differ depending on the architecture. We consider BERT to be the baseline transformer-based model. RoBERTa shares the same architecture as BERT but differs by having an improved pre-training procedure which often results in better performance [8]. Both models have a limit of 512 tokens.

Additionally, Longformer, which can be given longer text of up to 4096 tokens, was chosen for this task as papers tend to be long documents with more than 512 tokens. Longformer solves a problem of BERT-like models, namely, the quadratic growth of memory and computational requirements of self-attention, with sequence length making it often infeasible and expensive to process long sequences. The architecture of Longformer scales linearly and utilises a combination of local and global attention information [1]. Such an architecture allowed us to confirm if using longer input could result in better performance for a transformer model, as was reported in previous work comparing the performance of Longformer with that of RoBERTa on long document processing tasks [1].

Bagging Ensemble. A Bootstrap Aggregating (Bagging) ensemble of transformer models was also built to observe if it can outperform any of the single models. An illustration of how a Bagging ensemble is constructed is shown in Fig. 1. The rationale for combining multiple models is that errors made by a single model trained on a subset of bootstrapped data, could possibly be corrected by the other models that were trained on other bootstrapped subsets of data [13]. To aggregate predictions, we averaged the probabilities of individual models for each class.

Hyperparameter Optimisation. The hyperparameters for model training that were considered are learning rate, the text sections included and whether or

---

[4] Available in Huggingface (https://huggingface.co/) as `bert-base-cased`, `roberta-base` and `allenai/longformer-base-4096`.

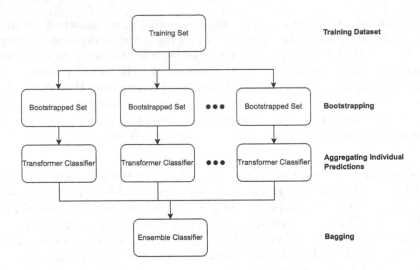

Fig. 1. A Bagging ensemble of a number of transformer-based models

not metadata is included. The Weights & Biases (W&B) platform[5] was employed to conduct hyperparameter optimisation, whereby randomly selected values from provided ranges were applied to maximise accuracy on the validation set.

4   Evaluation and Discussion

4.1   Experimental Setup for Models with Handcrafted Features

As mentioned above, SVM, decision trees, random forests, k-NN, naïve Bayes and MLP were trained on handcrafted features. For SVM, the kernel type was radial basis function (RBF) and the regularisation parameter was tuned with values between $[0, 1]$. For decision trees, the Gini index for splitting the tree was used and the maximum depth was varied between $[1, 20]$. For random forests, the Gini index was also used and the number of trees in the forest was varied between $[100, 1000]$. For k-NN, we used different values between $[1, 21]$ as the number of neighbours. Lastly, for MLP, the alpha score determining the strength of L2 regularisation was tuned using values between $[0.05, 1]$, whereas the learning rate was set to 0.001 with the stochastic gradient descent (SGD) optimiser.

4.2   Experimental Setup for Transformer-Based Models

We utilised base transformer models since their large counterparts require a large amount of memory and long training times, making the training (and testing) process significantly longer and resource-intensive.

---

[5] Available at https://wandb.ai/site.

For AdamW weight decay, we used the default value of 0.01. For BERT and RoBERTa, we used 10 as the number of epochs and a batch size of 16 as a trade-off between performance and required resources. For Longformer, we utilised 2 epochs due to this model requiring longer training times for text inputs with more tokens. We experimented with limiting the text input to 2048 and 4096 tokens, to observe if there is a noticeable difference in performance considering that the former has the advantage of requiring less amount of computing resources. We utilised a combination of 2048 tokens with a batch size of 2 and 4096 tokens with a batch size of 4. We anticipated that Longformer would outperform both BERT and RoBERTa due to its ability to process longer inputs, which should enable the model to gain a deeper understanding of the papers and better distinguish between accepted and rejected submissions. Furthermore, BERT was expected to perform worse than RoBERTa as the latter was designed to enhance BERT with a more sophisticated training procedure [8].

Furthermore, Sun et al. [15] achieved the highest accuracy by joining the Abstract and Tail of papers, so we expected the AwT text splitting configuration to perform the best. The Abstract and the Conclusion of a paper often provide a summary of achievements and a reflection on the work, which may form the basis of its acceptance. In contrast, the Middle part of a paper was expected to perform the worst. Moreover, it was hypothesised that models would produce better results using metadata as features, as previous research by Kang et al. [5] and Skorikov and Momen [14] successfully utilised them as input to models like decision trees.

Due to the long training times and resources required by Longformer, we utilised the parameters of the best-performing RoBERTa model to construct a Bagging ensemble. An ensemble of RoBERTa models should increase the performance compared to a single model. However, that may not be the case if the individual models trained on bootstrapped data do not discover patterns in data, i.e., they may predict randomly or only the same class.

4.3 Results

Table 2 presents the results of traditional ML models trained on handcrafted features. The hyperparameter optimisation on the parameters discussed in Sect. 4.1 was carried out to identify the best combination of parameter values for each model on the validation dataset. These models were then tested on the test set to obtain a value for accuracy, the primary performance metric for classification models. However, SVM, k-NN and naïve Bayes performed poorly, obtaining only around 50% accuracy on the binary classification problem. Possibly more data samples and a more extensive list of features might increase the performance for these models. Nevertheless, the others, i.e., random forest, decision trees and MLP, obtained significantly higher than 50% accuracy. Overall, MLP trained on hand-crafted features reached the highest accuracy of 78.37% on the test set.

Table 2. Accuracies obtained by models trained on handcrafted features

Model Name	Validation Accuracy	Test Accuracy
SVM	50.09%	49.93%
KNN	49.91%	50.07%
Naïve Bayes	50.09%	50.51%
Random Forest	57.71%	61.54%
Decision Tree	64.25%	67.34%
MLP	**71.33%**	**78.37%**

Figure 2 depicts the results on the validation set for each transformer model architecture, with hyperparameters set to values selected from those shown in Table 3 for each run. The validation accuracy was essential in understanding if the models were either underfitting or overfitting. The figure shows that more than half of the runs did not find meaningful patterns in deducing what makes a paper accepted or rejected. Therefore many ended up predicting only one class or selecting labels at random. This evidently shows that this classification task is difficult even for transformers. Throughout our experimentation, it was observed that the model often found it challenging to learn from the textual content alone. Satisfactory performance was obtained only when metadata is prepended at the beginning of the input. The inclusion of metadata features positively correlated with higher accuracy.

Table 3. Range of hyperparameter values

Parameter	Values
Learning Rate	[1e−5, 9e−5]
Text Splitting Configuration	IwA, IwoA, AwT, Middle, Tail
Model Architecture	BERT, RoBERTa, Longformer
Metadata Included	False, True

As expected, taking only the Middle part of a paper did not attain state-of-the-art results. The AwT (Abstract with Tail) configuration did not achieve superior accuracy either (contrary to what we anticipated), whereas taking the Introduction with or without the Abstract (i.e., the IwA and IwoA configurations, respectively) performed better. The truncation methods were used for all papers as the token limits were smaller for the models than the length of papers.

Table 4 presents the results of the best performing model for each transformer architecture, when evaluated on each of the validation and test sets. The

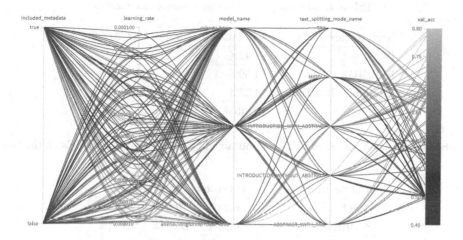

Fig. 2. Visualisation of hyperparameter search results on the validation set using Weights & Biases (W&B). Each line represents one run with different selected hyperparameter values shown on the vertical lines. The aim was to maximise validation accuracy. High values of accuracy are represented as yellow, whereas darker shades of purple correspond to lower accuracy. (Color figure online)

validation accuracy is maximised through hyperparameter search to find the optimal values for such parameters. Table 4 presents the highest attained validation accuracy for each transformer architecture and the corresponding test accuracy using the same hyperparameters. BERT, RoBERTa and Longformer achieved these results based on the Tail, IwoA and IwA text splitting configurations, respectively. The best-performing models for each transformer architecture utilised the metadata features, which we expected as it provides models with more characterising information which may help models in making a prediction. RoBERTa outperformed BERT, which is unsurprising due to the fact that RoBERTa's architecture was designed to improve upon BERT. Moreover, as anticipated, Longformer surpassed the performance of other architectures with 76.92% accuracy on the test set. As depicted in Table 5, the precision and recall of the best-performing transformer model are 82.69% and 68.02% respectively, indicating that the model tends to reject good papers as Reviewer 2 does. This finding can be attributed to the model potentially suffering from the Reviewer 2 problem (described in Sect. 1) that is very likely to be inherent in the dataset.

The best results for Longformer were obtained based on imposing a limit of 2048 tokens on the input text. Contrary to our expectation that giving Longformer models access to longer inputs will lead to better performance, the highest accuracy obtained when using inputs with 4096 tokens is only 71.28%. This can be explained by the fact that training ran for only 2 epochs (due to prohibitive training times otherwise).

Table 4. Accuracy obtained by transformer models

Architecture	Validation Accuracy	Test Accuracy
BERT	68.42%	70.39%
RoBERTa	74.59%	74.89%
Ensemble (RoBERTa)	74.23%	73.44%
Longformer	**78.95%**	**76.92%**

Table 5. Precision, recall and F1-score obtained by the transformer models on the test set

Architecture	Precision	Recall	F1-score
BERT	70.23%	70.64%	70.43%
RoBERTa	80.21%	65.99%	72.41%
Ensemble (RoBERTa)	76.74%	67.15%	71.63%
Longformer	**82.69%**	**68.02%**	**74.64%**

It was also found that the best model that was not trained on metadata features is Longformer; it obtained a test accuracy of 75.47%; this is lower than that of the best-performing transformer model (76.92%), which made use of metadata features. This supports our hypothesis that metadata features can enhance a model's predictive capabilities for determining paper outcomes.

An ensemble of ten RoBERTa models attained a test accuracy of 73.44%, about 1% point lower than a single RoBERTa model trained on the entire training data. It can be observed that some models did not manage to learn sufficiently from the data, i.e., they either made arbitrary decisions or guessed one class all the time, which decreased the combined predictive abilities of the ensemble. More data might be required to allow models to comprehend the data better. Also, other architectures capable of processing longer inputs could potentially increase ensemble performance, and other ensemble methodologies might outperform bagging.

Among the transformer-based models, the best test accuracy found through hyperparameter search is 76.92%, which can be regarded as competitive performance compared to previous studies on this task. However, overall, the highest performance on the test set is 78.37%, which was obtained by extracting handcrafted features and using them as input to the MLP model. This outcome indicates that the accuracy of training traditional ML models on extracted features and that of feeding raw text to transformer models are comparable. Nevertheless, transformers have the clear advantage of not requiring to extract features manually, making it more scalable. More complex transformer-based models could potentially surpass the performance of models trained on handcrafted features.

In previous work, Kang et al. [5] obtained 65.3% accuracy on the ICLR 2017 subset of PeerRead, using traditional ML models trained on handcrafted features. More recently, Kumar et al. [6] obtained an accuracy of 76.67% but instead used the reviews and aspect scores for ICLR and NeurIPS papers in the ASAP-review dataset as input. Our solution produced comparable (if not higher) accuracy in relation to previous studies. However, previous work utilised slightly different datasets, therefore our results cannot be directly compared with them.

5   Conclusion

In this paper, we developed different types of models for predicting paper acceptance: traditional machine learning-based and transformer-based ones. Longformer obtained an accuracy of 76.92%, outperforming BERT, RoBERTa and a Bagging ensemble of RoBERTa models, in distinguishing between accepted and rejected papers. The inclusion of metadata features, e.g., the existence of appendices, assisted in improving the models' prediction quality. Meanwhile, handcrafted features were extracted as input for SVM, decision trees, random forests, k-NN, naïve Bayes and MLP, where MLP attained an accuracy of 78.37% which slightly surpassed the performance of the transformer models.

Improved results may be obtained by using large transformer models, longer text inputs, and a more extensive hyperparameter search. Future research could also focus on increasing token limits by employing hierarchical transformers without the need for truncation methods [12], and collecting a larger training dataset that considers different conferences. An improved system using an instruction-tuned large language model (LLM) like GPT4 [11] could produce the reasoning and arguments for why the paper should be accepted or rejected.

References

1. Beltagy, I., Peters, M.E., Cohan, A.: Longformer: the long-document transformer. arXiv preprint arXiv:2004.05150 [cs] (2020)
2. Breiman, L.: Bagging predictors. Mach. Learn. **24**(2), 123–140 (1996). https://doi.org/10.1007/BF00058655
3. Cortes, C., Lawrence, N.D.: Inconsistency in conference peer review: revisiting the 2014 NeurIPS experiment. arXiv preprint arXiv:2109.09774 [cs] (2021)
4. Devlin, J., Chang, M.W., Lee, K., Toutanova, K.: BERT: pre-training of deep bidirectional transformers for language understanding. In: Proceedings of the 2019 Conference of the North American Chapter of the Association for Computational Linguistics: Human Language Technologies, Volume 1 (Long and Short Papers), pp. 4171–4186. Association for Computational Linguistics, Minneapolis (2019). https://doi.org/10.18653/v1/N19-1423
5. Kang, D., et al.: A dataset of peer reviews (PeerRead): collection, insights and NLP applications. In: Proceedings of the 2018 Conference of the North American Chapter of the Association for Computational Linguistics: Human Language Technologies, Volume 1 (Long Papers), pp. 1647–1661. Association for Computational Linguistics, New Orleans (2018).https://doi.org/10.18653/v1/N18-1149

6. Kumar, S., Arora, H., Ghosal, T., Ekbal, A.: DeepASPeer: towards an aspect-level sentiment controllable framework for decision prediction from academic peer reviews. In: Proceedings of the 22nd ACM/IEEE Joint Conference on Digital Libraries (JCDL 2022), pp. 1–11. Association for Computing Machinery, New York (2022).https://doi.org/10.1145/3529372.3530937

7. Langford, J., Guzdial, M.: The arbitrariness of reviews, and advice for school administrators. Commun. ACM **58**(4), 12–13 (2015). https://doi.org/10.1145/2732417

8. Liu, Y., et al.: Roberta: a robustly optimized bert pretraining approach (2019)

9. Loshchilov, I., Hutter, F.: Decoupled Weight Decay Regularization (2019). https://openreview.net/forum?id=Bkg6RiCqY7

10. Nature. Growth in AI and robotics research accelerates. Nature **610**(7931), S9 (2022). https://doi.org/10.1038/d41586-022-03210-9

11. OpenAI. GPT-4 Technical Report. arXiv preprint arXiv:2303.08774 [cs] (2023)

12. Pappagari, R., Zelasko, P., Villalba, J., Carmiel, Y., Dehak, N.: Hierarchical transformers for long document classification. In: 2019 IEEE Automatic Speech Recognition and Understanding Workshop (ASRU), pp. 838–844 (2019).https://doi.org/10.1109/ASRU46091.2019.9003958

13. Sagi, O., Rokach, L.: Ensemble learning: a survey. WIREs Data Min. Knowl. Discov. **8**(4), e1249 (2018). https://doi.org/10.1002/widm.1249

14. Skorikov, M., Momen, S.: Machine learning approach to predicting the acceptance of academic papers. In: 2020 IEEE International Conference on Industry 4.0, Artificial Intelligence, and Communications Technology (IAICT), pp. 113–117 (2020).https://doi.org/10.1109/IAICT50021.2020.9172011

15. Sun, C., Qiu, X., Xu, Y., Huang, X.: How to fine-tune BERT for text classification? In: Sun, M., Huang, X., Ji, H., Liu, Z., Liu, Y. (eds.) CCL 2019. LNCS (LNAI), vol. 11856, pp. 194–206. Springer, Cham (2019). https://doi.org/10.1007/978-3-030-32381-3_16

16. Vaswani, A., et al.: Attention is all you need. In: Guyon, I., et al. (eds.) Advances in Neural Information Processing Systems, vol. 30. Curran Associates, Inc. (2017). https://proceedings.neurips.cc/paper/2017/file/3f5ee243547dee91fbd053c1c4a845aa-Paper.pdf

17. Yuan, W., Liu, P., Neubig, G.: Can we automate scientific reviewing? J. Artif. Intell. Res. **75**, 171–212 (2022).https://doi.org/10.1613/jair.1.12862

Corporate Event Prediction Using Earning Call Transcripts

Zhaomin Xiao[1](✉)(iD), Yachen Cui[1](✉)(iD), Zhelu Mai[2](✉)(iD), Zhuoer Xu[3](✉)(iD), and Jiancheng Li[1](✉)(iD)

[1] University of North Texas, Denton, USA
{zhaominxiao,jianchengli}@my.unt.edu, yachen.cui@unt.edu
[2] I-66 Express Mobility Partners, Manassas, USA
zhelumai@my.unt.edu
[3] Hewlett Packard Enterprise, Houston, USA
patrick.xu.work@gmail.com

Abstract. This paper addresses the task of predicting the occurrence of corporate events based on earning call transcripts. We introduce a novel dataset of earning call transcripts specifically curated for corporate event prediction. Through a comprehensive analysis, we explore what kind of information is presented in the transcripts that can be utilized for event prediction. Our experimental results with various machine learning models demonstrate the feasibility of automating this challenging task.

Keywords: Natural Language Processing · Machine Learning · Corporate Events

1 Introduction

Information is the most precious asset in the capital market due to the fact that any new information disclosure would change the stock price, which is tightly related to investors. This information can be documented in a company's financial reports and verbally communicated during any public conference call. Generally, an earning call conference can be divided into two parts, with the interaction among companies' managers, hosts, and analysts. One part is a presentation where company managers actively talk about the information they intend to share, while the other part is a Q&A section where managers answer questions asked by analysts and investors. Earnings calls are more informative than highly formatted and similar financial reports such as 10K or 10Q [19] because the dialogues are more flexible, powerful, and purposeful, especially during the Q&A portion where there is no prepared direct communication. In this way, stakeholders can efficiently learn contemporary operating activities, industry competitions, market guidance, strategic insight, and future perspectives and address their concerns through interaction with executives; meanwhile,

---

Z. Xiao and Y. Cui—Contributed equally to this work.

executives could treat earning call conference as a disclosure chance to reduce information asymmetry and maintain investor relationships in the long term [8]. Because earning call conference is one of the most meaningful resources of new information [2], extracting information from earnings call transcripts to predict corporate event occurrence would assist investors in jumping into potential trading opportunities before events actually occur to end up with a better return.

While utilizing NLP techniques for analyzing earning call transcripts is a well-established practice, the focus of previous studies has primarily been on predicting stock trends [29]. Unlike them, in this paper, we use earning call transcripts to predict whether or not corporate events will happen in the future. Corporate events play an important role in the financial market. Any financial and strategic decision requires time, diligence, cautious consideration, and funding and has a significant effect on investors' wealth. For instance, announcements related to Merger & Acquisition and Seasoned Equity Offerings can lead to negative abnormal returns, whereas buyback announcements may result in positive returns. By extracting relevant cues about corporate events from earning calls, investors gain the advantage of taking preemptive action (e.g., making informed decisions and mitigating risks associated with corporate events) before these events unfold. Bearing this in mind, we create a new dataset and propose machine learning models to automate the task of corporate event prediction.

The works on corporate event prediction presented in this paper open the door to many applications. For example, corporate events can provide insights into the potential impact on stock prices. Going beyond stock price prediction, the understanding of corporate events can also provide insights into the management of financial risk and the supply chain of the related companies. Furthermore, investors can respond strategically, identify market opportunities, and stay ahead of other investors by gathering event information.

The main contributions of this paper are: (a) a dataset of 7,058 earning call transcripts annotated with occurrences of three corporate events[1], (b) detailed dataset analyses showing what kind of information can be utilized to predict corporate events, (c) experiments with machine learning models to automatically predict whether or not the corporate events will happen, and (d) results showing that this challenging task can be automated.

2 Related Work

Most publicly traded companies host earning call conferences to control their information, stand out from competitors, and promote transparency in an era of financial turmoil and public distrust in large corporations [15,40,43]. Previous works on the effect of earning calls on the financial market can be on either participant analysis or transcript sentiment analysis. Regarding participants, expertise, ethnicity, and gender of insider executives influence market response to executive earnings call communication and investor sentiment [7,18,46]. In addition, evidence from analysts' attendances at earnings call conferences sheds light

---

[1] Data is available at https://zhaomin1995.github.io/.

on the accuracy of their earnings estimation and their career development [12]. Regarding the latter, earnings call tone and sentiment play an important role in predicting stock price movement and volatility [37]. Company-level culture measurement and political sentiment, manager-specific optimism, and company ethics can also be derived from earning call transcripts [9,16,17,27].

Utilizing NLP techniques to process earning call transcripts is not new. Previous studies have explored the use of semantic and pragmatic features to analyze analysts' decision-making behavior [23]. One benchmark, DigiCall [36], has been introduced to assess the digital strategy maturity of companies. Additionally, the application of AutoAI for Text [14] with earning call transcripts has been utilized to predict stock price volatility [35]. Unlike these efforts, we are aiming at corporate event prediction.

Event information extract has been extensively explored since decades ago. Bilingual structure projection is used to learn event expressions [25]. Going beyond the explicit expression, spatiotemporal information about events is also active research since decades ago, such as event localization [38], event ordering [10,13], and event duration [33,45]. More recently and comprehensively, MCTACO [48], is proposed to study the problem of temporal commonsense understanding which includes stationary, frequency, and typical time of events, in addition to ordering and duration. Unlike the previous efforts on general event information extraction, we aim to extract information about corporate events.

More relatedly, a corporate event detector at low-level and high-level is proposed to investigate the role of corporate events in the task of stock prediction [49]. To approach their proposed problem, they create a new dataset, EDT, containing 2,266 English news articles mentioning at least one corporate event. Unlike their works, we are targeting event occurrence, rather than event expression.

3   A Dataset for Corporate Event Prediction

Our main goal is to understand the relationship between earning calls and corporate events. To the best of our knowledge, we are the first to tackle this challenging problem, so we create a new dataset. This allows us to delve into the potential utilization of earning call transcripts in predicting the occurrence of future corporate events.

3.1   Transcript Collection

We download the earning call transcripts from the website seeking-alpha[2]. We use spaCy[3] to extract the conference information (e.g., company name, stock ticker, and timestamp) from the transcripts. Since we focus on English transcripts, we only consider the companies listed on the American stock exchangse (i.e., NYSE, AMEX, and NASDAQ). This process results in approximately 30,000 earning call transcripts.

---

[2] https://seekingalpha.com/.
[3] https://spacy.io/.

3.2 Event Collection

We focus on three corporate events: Acquisition, Corporate Bond Issuance (CBI), and Seasoned Equity Offering (SEO). We collect all of this event data from Refinitiv Securities Data Company (SEC) to match our transcript data coverage.

Acquisitions involve one company acquiring the assets of another company, effectively becoming the new owner while the acquired company ceases to exist. Acquisitions can bring various benefits to the acquiring company, including innovation acquisition, integration of human capital, cost savings, diversification, and increased market power [24,28,31,42,44]. Predicting acquisitions can help stakeholders gauge companies' plans and prepare for potential market impacts. Corporate bond issuances are a means for companies to raise capital by issuing bonds to public investors. Compared to bank loans, corporate bonds offer advantages such as flexibility, favorable terms, access to a larger investor pool, and reduced creditor monitoring compared to bank loans [3,4,34]. Detecting corporate bond issuances can assist investors in managing risk and making informed investment decisions. SEOs occur when a public company sells additional equity shares to raise capital on the stock market [21]. The decision to conduct an SEO and the resulting ownership dilution [1] can significantly impact existing shareholders and creditors, leading to reactions in the bond and stock markets [20,22]. Information about SEOs extracted from earning call conferences is beneficial for investors to plan and adjust their investment strategies accordingly.

3.3 Data Matching

The earning call transcripts do not always correspond to our event data because they are collected from two data sources (i.e., seeking-alpha and SEC), we follow a two-step methodology to align earning call transcripts and our event data.

1. We use stock tickers to align transcripts and events. If stock tickers are not available, we move to the second step.
2. We use manually defined rules[4] to normalize companies' names and use normalized names to align transcripts and events.

Consequently, with the original 30,000 transcripts on hand, after filtering out the transcripts which do not correspond to all three corporate events (acquisitions, corporate bond issuances, and seasoned equity offerings), the final dataset consists of only 7,058 transcripts. It can be seen that we discard a large proportion of transcripts because most companies are not identifiable in our event data due to the presence of noisy and inconsistent company names used on the seeking-alpha website. For each event with each earning call, we use **yes** and **no** to denote that the event occurs and does not occur within one quarter (3 months) after the earning call, respectively. We set the time window as 3 months because earning calls are usually held quarterly.

---

[4] For example, we remove parentheses, brackets, commas, periods, leading/trailing white spaces, and commonly used terms such as Inc, Co, LLC, and Ltd. In addition to the removal, we also convert all letters to lowercase so that normalized names can be better utilized to align transcripts and our event data.

Table 1. Dataset statistics (left) and label distribution for each event (right).

#Calls	7,058
#Companies	1,058
#Sentences per transcript	430.7
Max sentences per transcript	1,650
#Words per transcript	8,277.8
Max words per transcript	32,563

	yes	no
Acquisition	22%	78%
SEO	15%	85%
CBI	28%	72%

3.4 Ethics

In this section, we address the potential risks associated with our dataset and outline the best practices we implement to protect data privacy. The dataset might contain personal information such as names and positions, which can be found in the original earnings conference calls of public companies in the United States. These calls are mandated to be publicly available under U.S. law. However, we argue that the personal information within the earnings call dataset pertains to legal persons rather than natural persons. Also, we will replace all identifiable names in the earnings call transcripts with '¡UNK¿' before making it public. By doing so, our dataset will be anonymized, and the privacy concerns are mitigated.

4 Dataset Analyses

Table 1 shows the essential statistics of our dataset. Our dataset includes the transcripts of 7,058 earning calls, hosted by 1,058 companies. The lengths of transcripts vary greatly, as the average transcript length is 430 sentences or 8,278 tokens, while some transcripts are much longer than this—the maximum number of sentences and tokens are 1,650 and 32,563, respectively. Examining the label distribution of each event, we find that the problem of class imbalance is severe in all three events. For Acquisition and CBI, approximately one-quarter of the instances is labeled as **yes**, indicating that the corporate event will not occur within three months after the earning call, and the remaining three-quarter is labeled as **no**, indicating the opposite. The label distribution of SEO is even more skewed—only 15% is labeled as **yes**. Figure 1 presents the most frequently occurring nouns and verbs in the transcripts. Conference-related keywords, such as *year*, *quarter*, and *question*, along with business-related terms, such as *growth*, *market*, and *customer*, highlight the primary topics of the conferences. In terms of verb usage, in addition to verbs specific to the conference such as *thank* and *continue*, business-related verbs like *increased* and *expect*, shed light on the speakers' tone. Interestingly, verbs in the past tense are equally prevalent as their present

Fig. 1. Most frequent nouns (left) and verbs (right).

continuous counterparts. For example, *look* is as large as *looking*, and *going* is just a bit larger than *go*, suggesting that many companies discuss their ongoing plans during these conferences.

Figure 2 illustrates which kind of information we can extract from the earning call transcript to predict the occurrence of different corporate events. For instance, *"near-term debt maturity"* indicates that the company will likely issue corporate bonds to replace old debt to maintain its leverage ratio. Additionally, a high borrowing capacity (i.e., *3.2 billion*) indicates the potential for issuing more company bonds. The blue text, *"expect to see [...] the end of the year,"* corresponds to the explicit mention in the analyst's question about larger-scale M&A (i.e., *"Any thoughts around larger-scale M&A?"*), indicating that their acquisition plan is undergoing. Furthermore, the blue text at the end, *"use those proceeds from our tax refund to repay [...] maturity,"* indicates that the company is currently short on cash and is likely to raise external funding through SEO(s).

5   Experiments and Results

Armed with our dataset consisting of 7,058 earning call transcripts, we conduct experiments to automatically determine whether specific corporate events will occur within one quarter (3 months) after earning calls. We reduce this problem to a classification task. The input to the model is a (transcript, event) pair, and the output is a label indicating whether or not the event will occur within the next quarter after the earning call. To reduce the effect of randomness, we conduct experiments following the procedure of stratified 5-fold cross-validation.

CFO: [...] As of June 30, our total liquidity inclusive of cash, cash equivalents and short-term investments and combined with **borrowing capacity was approximately $3.2 billion** with **the only near-term debt maturity** being $250 million senior notes maturing this month.

Analyst: Thank you. Can you just give us an update on your capital allocation thoughts both in terms of capital returns? **Any thoughts around larger-scale M&A?** Thanks.

CEO: [...] We've benefited from this tax refund that we received of $254 million and we will turn around and **use those proceeds from our tax refund to repay the $250 million of maturities** in August. [...] That's been more than made up for by select service and full-service signings across the globe and full service and resorts in the Americas [...] and we do **expect to see some real progression and positive developments in the select service area between now and the end of the year.**

Fig. 2. An example showing what kind of explicit and implicit clues in the earning call transcript can be used to predict the occurrence of corporate events. The text in **blue**, yellow, and green contains implicit or explicit clues about Acquisition, SEO, and CBI, respectively. (Color figure online)

5.1 Experiments

We use TFIDF to vectorize the raw text data and make it suitable for model consumption. For tokenization, we utilize the NLTK tokenizer [5][5]. To enhance the model's performance, we remove stopwords, as they do not provide much information for our task. Only unigrams are considered during the vectorization process. However, due to computational constraints, we only take into account the 50,000 most frequent unigrams. Additionally, we apply L2-normalization [32] to ensure that differences in the value ranges do not distort the importance of features.

Baseline. The baseline model (i.e., random baseline) serves as a reference point, and its purpose is to establish a performance benchmark. The baseline model makes predictions based on the distribution of ground truth.

Machine Learning Models. We perform experiments using a total of six machine learning models. For assessing linear models, we utilize Logistic Regression (LR), Naive Bayes (NB), and Decision Tree (DT). In addition to these, we also employ Random Forest (RF) to evaluate ensemble learning techniques. To evaluate non-linear models, we incorporate Support Vector Machine (SVM) and k-nearest-neighbor (kNN) into our experiments. In our decision tree-based models (i.e., DT and RF), we utilize the Gini index [6] as the metric to determine how to split the nodes during the tree construction process. In the case of kNN, we rely on the Minkowski distance metric to measure the distances between data points and identify the nearest neighbors. For SVM, we employ the radial basis function [41] to calculate the distances between different classes.

---

[5] https://www.nltk.org/.

Table 2. Performance of different machine learning models, where the results are averaged over 5-fold cross-validation. The standard deviations are also reported below the averaged results. DT, RF, LR, SVM, NB, and kNN denote Decision Tree, Random Forest, Logistic Regression, Support Vector Machine, Naive Bayes, and k Nearest Neighbor, respectively. kNN outperforms other models on Acquisition and SEO. The best performance on CBI is obtained by Naive Bayes.

	Acquisition			SEO			CBI		
	P	R	F1	P	R	F1	P	R	F1
Baseline	0.661	0.661	0.661	0.752	0.752	0.752	0.592	0.592	0.592
	(0.000)	(0.000)	(0.000)	(0.000)	(0.000)	(0.000)	(0.000)	(0.000)	(0.000)
DT	0.638	0.603	0.614	0.73	0.646	0.679	0.625	0.613	0.617
	(0.047)	(0.110)	(0.085)	(0.028)	(0.105)	(0.073)	(0.016)	(0.040)	(0.031)
RF	0.705	0.742	0.679	0.735	0.788	0.753	0.717	0.734	0.666
	(0.065)	(0.053)	(0.025)	(0.021)	(0.090)	(0.05)	(0.020)	(0.008)	(0.012)
LR	0.699	0.779	0.689	0.741	0.852	0.784	0.719	0.735	0.664
	(0.068)	(0.004)	(0.006)	(0.030)	(0.000)	(0.001)	(0.014)	(0.00)	(0.009)
SVM	0.762	0.781	0.698	0.748	0.849	0.784	0.726	0.742	0.684
	(0.054)	(0.007)	(0.008)	(0.014)	(0.002)	(0.001)	(0.011)	(0.006)	(0.011)
NB	0.693	0.706	0.698	0.75	0.788	0.766	0.693	0.703	**0.695**
	(0.027)	(0.016)	(0.020)	(0.016)	(0.029)	(0.017)	(0.020)	(0.026)	(0.020)
kNN	0.711	0.751	**0.718**	0.768	0.831	**0.787**	0.674	0.697	0.681
	(0.015)	(0.018)	(0.005)	(0.016)	(0.012)	(0.005)	(0.010)	(0.010)	(0.009)

5.2 Results

Table 2 shows that averaged experimental results over 5 stratified test splits. The standard deviations are also shown below the averaged results to provide insights into the stability of each model. We observe that all of the machine learning models outperform the random baseline, except that Decision Tree cannot beat the random baseline on Acquisition and SEO. The fact that Random Forest outperforms Decision Tree on all events shows the strength of the ensemble model. kNN outperforms all other models on Acquisition and SEO, indicating that the non-linearity brought by its decision boundary is beneficial when the dimensionality is high (i.e., the number of distinct unigrams is high). Notably, Naive Bayes outperforms the other models on CBI. We attribute this to the validation of its feature independence assumption. Given that the model's inputs consist of numerous independent unigrams, the independence assumption allows Naive Bayes to achieve the best performance while maintaining its naturally fast learning speed.

6   Conclusions and Future Works

We have introduced the task of determining whether or not corporate events will happen within the next quarter (3 months) of the earning call. Going beyond event detection, this problem is about determining occurrences of events. Our new dataset (size: 7,058 transcripts) shows that this task is challenging because there are few explicit textual cues in the transcripts, and our experimental results show that the task can be automated, although our models obtain modest results.

Our research agenda includes the multimodal extension of the current work. The information carried by different modalities has been proven in many NLP tasks, such as spatial information extraction [47], sentiment analysis [30], sarcasm detection [11]. Toward the combination of NLP and finance, financial risk prediction [26] and stock volatility prediction [39] have brought the attention since years ago.

References

1. Asquith, P., Mullins, D.W., Jr.: Equity issues and offering dilution. J. Financ. Econ. **15**(1–2), 61–89 (1986)
2. Basu, S., Duong, T.X., Markov, S., Tan, E.J.: How important are earnings announcements as an information source? Eur. Account. Rev. **22**(2), 221–256 (2013)
3. Berlin, M., Loeys, J.: The choice between bonds and bank loans. Tech. rep, Federal Reserve Bank of Philadelphia (1986)
4. Berlin, M., Loeys, J.: Bond covenants and delegated monitoring. J. Financ. **43**(2), 397–412 (1988)
5. Bird, S., Loper, E.: NLTK: the natural language toolkit. In: Proceedings of the ACL Interactive Poster and Demonstration Sessions, pp. 214–217. Association for Computational Linguistics, Barcelona (2004). https://aclanthology.org/P04-3031
6. Breiman, L., Friedman, J.H., Olshen, R.A., Stone, C.J.: Classification and Regression Trees. Routledge (2017)
7. Brown, N.C., Francis, B.B., Hu, W., Shohfi, T., Zhang, T., Xin, D.: Gender and Earnings Conference Calls. Available at SSRN 3473266 (2023)
8. Brown, S., Hillegeist, S.A., Lo, K.: Conference calls and information asymmetry. J. Account. Econ. **37**(3), 343–366 (2004)
9. Cao, C.X., Chen, C.: Political sentiment and stock crash risk. J. Risk Financ. (2022)
10. Cassidy, T., McDowell, B., Chambers, N., Bethard, S.: An annotation framework for dense event ordering. In: Proceedings of the 52nd Annual Meeting of the Association for Computational Linguistics (Volume 2: Short Papers), pp. 501–506. Association for Computational Linguistics, Baltimore (2014). https://doi.org/10.3115/v1/P14-2082
11. Castro, S., Hazarika, D., Pérez-Rosas, V., Zimmermann, R., Mihalcea, R., Poria, S.: Towards multimodal sarcasm detection (an _Obviously_ perfect paper). In: Proceedings of the 57th Annual Meeting of the Association for Computational Linguistics, pp. 4619–4629. Association for Computational Linguistics, Florence (2019). https://doi.org/10.18653/v1/P19-1455

12. Cen, L., Chen, J., Dasgupta, S., Ragunathan, V.: Do analysts and their employers value access to management? evidence from earnings conference call participation. J. Financ. Quantit. Anal. **56**(3), 745–787 (2021)

13. Chambers, N., Cassidy, T., McDowell, B., Bethard, S.: Dense event ordering with a multi-pass architecture. Trans. Assoc. Comput. Linguist. **2**, 273–284 (2014). https://doi.org/10.1162/tacl_a_00182

14. Chaudhary, A., et al.: Autotext: an end-to-end auto AI framework for text. In: Proceedings of the AAAI Conference on Artificial Intelligence **35**(18), 16001–16003 (2021). https://doi.org/10.1609/aaai.v35i18.17993

15. Clark Williams, C.: Toward a taxonomy of corporate reporting strategies. J. Bus. Commun. (1973) **45**(3), 232–264 (2008)

16. Crawford Camiciottoli, B.: Ethics and ethos in financial reporting: analyzing persuasive language in earnings calls. Bus. Commun. Q. **74**(3), 298–312 (2011)

17. Davis, A.K., Ge, W., Matsumoto, D., Zhang, J.L.: The effect of manager-specific optimism on the tone of earnings conference calls. Rev. Acc. Stud. **20**, 639–673 (2015)

18. De Amicis, C., Falconieri, S., Tastan, M.: Sentiment analysis and gender differences in earnings conference calls. J. Corp. Finan. **71**, 101809 (2021)

19. De Franco, G., Fogel-Yaari, H., Li, H.: Md&a textual similarity and auditors. Audit.: J. Pract. Theory **39**(3), 105–131 (2020)

20. Elliott, W.B., Prevost, A.K., Rao, R.P.: The announcement impact of seasoned equity offerings on bondholder wealth. J. Bank. Financ. **33**(8), 1472–1480 (2009)

21. Geddes, R.: IPOs and Equity Offerings. Elsevier (2003)

22. Hull, R.M., Kwak, S., Walker, R.L.: Explanation for market response to seasoned equity offerings. J. Econ. Financ. **36**, 634–661 (2012)

23. Keith, K., Stent, A.: Modeling financial analysts' decision making via the pragmatics and semantics of earnings calls. In: Proceedings of the 57th Annual Meeting of the Association for Computational Linguistics, pp. 493–503. Association for Computational Linguistics, Florence (2019). https://doi.org/10.18653/v1/P19-1047

24. Kling, G., Ghobadian, A., Hitt, M.A., Weitzel, U., O'Regan, N.: The effects of cross-border and cross-industry mergers and acquisitions on home-region and global multinational enterprises. Br. J. Manag. **25**, S116–S132 (2014)

25. Li, F., Huang, R., Xiong, D., Zhang, M.: Learning event expressions via bilingual structure projection. In: Proceedings of COLING 2016, the 26th International Conference on Computational Linguistics: Technical Papers, pp. 1441–1450. The COLING 2016 Organizing Committee, Osaka (2016). https://aclanthology.org/C16-1136

26. Li, J., Yang, L., Smyth, B., Dong, R.: Maec: a multimodal aligned earnings conference call dataset for financial risk prediction. In: Proceedings of the 29th ACM International Conference on Information Knowledge Management (CIKM 2020), pp. 3063–3070. Association for Computing Machinery, New York (2020). https://doi.org/10.1145/3340531.3412879

27. Li, K., Mai, F., Shen, R., Yan, X.: Measuring corporate culture using machine learning. Rev. Financ. Stud. **34**(7), 3265–3315 (2021)

28. Lin, B.W., Hung, S.C., Li, P.C.: Mergers and acquisitions as a human resource strategy: evidence from us banking firms. Int. J. Manpow. **27**(2), 126–142 (2006)

29. Mathur, P., et al.: DocFin: multimodal financial prediction and bias mitigation using semi-structured documents. In: Findings of the Association for Computational Linguistics: EMNLP 2022, pp. 1933–1940. Association for Computational Linguistics, Abu Dhabi (2022). https://aclanthology.org/2022.findings-emnlp.139

30. Mihalcea, R.: Multimodal sentiment analysis. In: Proceedings of the 3rd Workshop in Computational Approaches to Subjectivity and Sentiment Analysis, p. 1. Association for Computational Linguistics, Jeju (2012). https://aclanthology.org/W12-3701

31. Motis, J., et al.: Mergers and Acquisitions Motives, pp. 1–31. Toulouse School of Economics, University of Crete (2007)

32. Ng, A.Y.: Feature selection, l1 vs. l2 regularization, and rotational invariance. In: Proceedings of the Twenty-First International Conference on Machine Learning (ICML 2004), p. 78. Association for Computing Machinery, New York (2004). https://doi.org/10.1145/1015330.1015435

33. Pan, F., Mulkar-Mehta, R., Hobbs, J.R.: Annotating and learning event durations in text. Comput. Linguist. 37(4), 727–752 (2011). https://doi.org/10.1162/COLI_a_00075

34. Park, C.: Monitoring and structure of debt contracts. J. Financ. 55(5), 2157–2195 (2000)

35. Pataci, H., Li, Y., Katsis, Y., Zhu, Y., Popa, L.: Stock price volatility prediction: a case study with AutoML. In: Proceedings of the Fourth Workshop on Financial Technology and Natural Language Processing (FinNLP), pp. 48–57. Association for Computational Linguistics, Abu Dhabi (Hybrid) (2022). https://aclanthology.org/2022.finnlp-1.6

36. Pataci, H., Sun, K., Ravichandran, T.: DigiCall: a benchmark for measuring the maturity of digital strategy through company earning calls. In: Proceedings of the Fourth Workshop on Financial Technology and Natural Language Processing (FinNLP), pp. 58–67. Association for Computational Linguistics, Abu Dhabi (Hybrid) (2022). https://aclanthology.org/2022.finnlp-1.7

37. Price, S.M., Doran, J.S., Peterson, D.R., Bliss, B.A.: Earnings conference calls and stock returns: the incremental informativeness of textual tone. J. Bank. Financ. 36(4), 992–1011 (2012)

38. Pustejovsky, J.: Where things happen: on the semantics of event localization. In: Proceedings of the IWCS 2013 Workshop on Computational Models of Spatial Language Interpretation and Generation (CoSLI-3), pp. 29–39. Association for Computational Linguistics, Potsdam (2013). https://aclanthology.org/W13-0705

39. Qin, Y., Yang, Y.: What you say and how you say it matters: predicting stock volatility using verbal and vocal cues. In: Proceedings of the 57th Annual Meeting of the Association for Computational Linguistics, pp. 390–401. Association for Computational Linguistics, Florence (2019). https://doi.org/10.18653/v1/P19-1038

40. Saatchi, E.: The discourse of voluntary disclosures in quarterly conference calls: implications for investor relations. In: Discourse and Identity in Specialized Communication (2007)

41. Schölkopf, B., Tsuda, K., Vert, J.P.: A primer on Kernel methods. In: Kernel Methods in Computational Biology. The MIT Press (2004). https://doi.org/10.7551/mitpress/4057.003.0004

42. Sevilir, M., Tian, X.: Acquiring innovation. In: AFA 2012 Chicago Meetings Paper (2012)

43. Tasker, S.C.: Bridging the information gap: quarterly conference calls as a medium for voluntary disclosure. Rev. Acc. Stud. 3, 137–167 (1998)

44. Vander Vennet, R.: The effect of mergers and acquisitions on the efficiency and profitability of EC credit institutions. J. Bank. Financ. 20(9), 1531–1558 (1996)

45. Vempala, A., Blanco, E., Palmer, A.: Determining event durations: Models and error analysis. In: Proceedings of the 2018 Conference of the North American Chapter of the Association for Computational Linguistics: Human Language Technologies, Volume 2 (Short Papers), pp. 164–168. Association for Computational Linguistics, New Orleans (2018). https://doi.org/10.18653/v1/N18-2026

46. Xiao, L., Ye, Y., Luo, R.: The diligent effect of investor relation officers in conference calls: Evidence from china. Int. Rev. Financ. Anal. **87**, 102619 (2023)

47. Xiao, Z., Blanco, E.: Are people located in the places they mention in their tweets? a multimodal approach. In: Proceedings of the 29th International Conference on Computational Linguistics, pp. 2561–2571. International Committee on Computational Linguistics, Gyeongju (2022). https://aclanthology.org/2022.coling-1.226

48. Zhou, B., Khashabi, D., Ning, Q., Roth, D.: "Going on a vacation" takes longer than "Going for a walk": a study of temporal commonsense understanding. In: Proceedings of the 2019 Conference on Empirical Methods in Natural Language Processing and the 9th International Joint Conference on Natural Language Processing (EMNLP-IJCNLP), pp. 3363–3369. Association for Computational Linguistics, Hong Kong (2019).https://doi.org/10.18653/v1/D19-1332

49. Zhou, Z., Ma, L., Liu, H.: Trade the event: corporate events detection for news-based event-driven trading. In: Findings of the Association for Computational Linguistics: ACL-IJCNLP 2021, pp. 2114–2124. Association for Computational Linguistics (2021). https://doi.org/10.18653/v1/2021.findings-acl.186

A Framework to Transform Metadata and Document-Level Tabular Spatial Information and Measurements to Marine Geology Gazetteer

Muhammad Asif Suryani[1,2]([✉]) [ID], Christian Beth[1] [ID], Klaus Wallmann[2] [ID], and Matthias Renz[1] [ID]

[1] Institute of Informatik, Christian -Albrechts -Universität zu Kiel, Kiel, Germany
{mas,cbe,mr}@informatik.uni-kiel.de
[2] GEOMAR Helmholtz Centre for Ocean Research Kiel, Kiel, Germany
kwallmann@geomar.de

Abstract. In many natural science domains, scientific documents provide a very important source for fundamental measurements that have been recorded at various geo-spatial locations. Manually extracting these reported measurements and their location information from these documents is extremely tedious and expensive, necessitating an automatic approach. These documents, primarily accessible in PDF format, are designed for platform-independent viewing and printing rather than presenting content in a conveniently accessible structure, which poses a significant challenge for automatic extraction. Relevant records of measurements and location information are often provided in tables that are structured quite diversely regarding the number of (nested) rows and columns, table orientation and depend on the article template and the author's style of presentation. In this paper, we propose a framework that, to the best of our knowledge, is the first generic approach that focuses on automatic location information and measurement extraction from tables in PDF documents. Based on various publications of arbitrary format from Marine Geology, we showcase how to segregate both spatial and quantitative measurement information, which alongside respective metadata could answer numerous pertinent questions about values of SR (Sedimentation Rate) and MAR (Mass Accumulation Rate) at specific locations, who measured these values, and referenced information (identifier) to these locations. Our proposed framework also validates the extracted information from scientific publications. Finally, all the aggregated information constitutes a novel Marine Geology Gazetteer and offers an interactive visualization.

Keywords: Information Extraction · Tabular Data · Spatial Information · Marine Geology Gazetteer

© The Author(s), under exclusive license to Springer Nature Switzerland AG 2024
J. A. Lossio-Ventura et al. (Eds.): SIMBig 2023, CCIS 2142, pp. 273–287, 2024.
https://doi.org/10.1007/978-3-031-63616-5_21

1   Introduction

Scientific publications are a rich source of valuable information, presenting text, tables, and figures. These publications are generally in the portable document format (PDF), providing readers access to relevant information in a stream-lined reading experience. However, due to the continuously growing number of publications, the broad extraction of spatial and quantitative information, while desirable for many studies [12,17,22] is infeasible when performed manually. At the same time, the complex internal PDF structure makes the automatic extraction of these components challenging since PDFs are designed with platform-independent viewing and printing in mind and not for structured representation of data. Most spatial and quantitative information in these publications is provided in tables (cf. Fig. 1) on which we take our main focus in this research. Thereby, we have to overcome the problem that tables are structured quite diversely regarding the number of (nested) rows and columns, table orientation and depend on the article template and the author's style of presentation [7].

Sample	Latitude	Longitude	Date Collected	*Porites* Species[a]	Extension Rate (mm/yr)
Orpheus-1, GBR[b]	−18.750	146.483	Feb 1995	*lobata*	12.5
Orpheus-2, GBR[b]	−18.750	146.483	Feb 1995	*lobata*	22
Ningaloo Reef, WA	−21.900	113.917	Apr 1993	*australiensis*	12
Nusa Barung, Java[b]	−8.517	113.367	Jul 1994	*solida*	24
Samar, Philippines	+11.487	125.513	Apr 2004	*lutea*	18
10h-4	n/a[c]	n/a	n/a	n/d[c]	5.6
12h-4	n/a	n/a	n/a	*lobata*	4.5

Fig. 1. Sample table snippet adapted from [11].

In Marine Geology, researchers perform extensive experiments to record mea-surements at different oceanographic locations. Specifically, the extraction of Sedimentation Rate (SR) and Mass Accumulation Rate (MAR) at the seafloor is an excellent example [8]. Marine geologists have recorded these measurements for over one hundred years and typically reported them in tables of scientific pub-lications (e.g. as in Fig. 1). This proper representation of quantitative information would be tremendously helpful for both readers and for the automatic extraction process to acquire relevant information [7,12,17,22]. It is worth mentioning that every extracted measurement must be associated with spatial coordinates and carry unique identifiers [16]. Specifically, we strive to answer certain questions automatically i.e.,

- Where have these measurements been measured?
- What are the identifiers for these locations?
- What are the reported values and units of SR and MAR?

The first column in Fig. 1 represents the unique identifiers for the oceanographic locations where the potential measurements were recorded. The latitude and longitude columns provide spatial information, and the sedimentation rate values for each oceanographic location are presented in the last column with the unit in the header. Access to respective spatial information of these measurements would provide marine geologists with broader insights and benefit them by having convenient access to their desired information and could greatly accelerate the knowledge discovery process [26]. It is also worth highlighting that these targeted measurements and their corresponding spatial information have never been compiled in any repository yet but were reported primarily in written publications.

Hence, to identify and extract relevant spatial and quantitative information automatically from tables, additional factors besides the PDF format need to be considered, e.g. no standardized guidelines, formats exist to represent measurement identifiers or their associated latitude and longitude information, that could facilitate the automatic information extraction. Hence, information representation generally relies on the author's choice or apparatus used in the experimentation. Further, MAR and SR are not defined in the International System of Units (SI), which makes their extraction task additionally challenging [11, 26].

This paper introduces a framework that extracts spatial and quantitative information from tables of marine geology publications and performs validation. Finally, the extracted information alongside respective metadata is being exploited to constitute a novel Marine Geology Gazetteer. The visualization module further illustrates the extracted information in an interactive map view.

2   Related Work

Gazetteers play a crucial role in research by providing specialized, authoritative indexes of geographical information, which facilitate the retrieval of geospatial data. The primary function of Gazetteers is to obtain explanatory information about geographical locations and maintain additional information for each respective entity. Gazetteers are valuable sources to provide geographical knowledge about the past and structure the relevant interconnected data, which could be a step towards FAIR data principles and research data management [10].

Marine Geologists mainly report scientific measurements such as Mass Accumulation Rate (MAR) and Sedimentation Rate (SR) in publications, represented in various structures, i.e. text and tables. These documents do not support a fully automatic information extraction from these structural components. Contrarily, various individual studies were focused previously but to some extent

Metadata Extraction. Metadata extraction has evolved over time and various approaches are available, the most prominent being Grobid, which is used in numerous studies [15]. Other metadata-related studies have focused on collaboration networks, citation analysis and publication trends [19, 27].

Table Extraction. Tabula is an open-source library that allows users to extract tables from PDFs into CSVs [5]. Camelot is another open-source Python library which extracts tables from PDFs in CSVs. In addition, camelot offers modularity and allows to make it adaptable in any extraction pipeline [4]. Recently, measurement extraction from tabular data was carried out using Quantulum3, a community-maintained Python library, which focuses on extraction of volumetric units, i.e. liter and pints from the tabular data. However, the extraction was only performed on spreadsheets instead of PDFs [7]. ExtracTable is an approach recently proposed that extracts tabular data from text files and CSVs by detecting the row patterns and separating the columns accordingly [14]. However, this approach does also not address table extraction from raw PDFs.

NER. Named entity recognition (NER) focuses on extracting locational entities (e.g. "Black Sea") from plain text. spaCy is an open-source library that efficiently supports NER that spawns various customized adaptations, such as the ScispaCy module that specifically targets scientific entities in the text [13,20]. In medical domain, humongous amount of data is available which could be explored, recently a hybrid based approach is proposed to identify named entity from the medical literature documents. New dictionary has been built for route of administration, dosage forms and symptoms to annotate the entities in the medical documents. The annotated entities are fine-tuned by focusing base spaCy model. The fine-tuned model provide a decent accuracy when compared with the existing model [23].

In biomedical domain, content mining has become a pivotal area of research, driven by the rapid growth of textual data. The proposed approach presents a ArRaNER model, a named entity recognition (NER) system employing rule-based approach. The ArRaNER model demonstrates better accuracy in extracting named entities from life science literature encompassing PubMed and Wikipedia articles [24]. A recent study in the field of archaeology has focused on Dutch Named Entity Recognition (NER) task. The resulting dataset includes six entity types and serves the purpose of enhancing semantic search capabilities within Dutch archaeology by enabling structured information retrieval from excavation reports [6].

Furthermore, the locational entities still require appropriate geo-coding to obtain the precise location information, *e.g.* the Black Sea would be geo-coded to its latitude and longitude coordinates. GeoPy provides a Python client to access the spatial coordinates and the global address and Geoparsepy also provides the coordinate information from the GeoNames gazetteer [2,25].

In this regard, the cited approaches may address the proposed problem individually to some extent. However, no known system can automatically parse scientific publications to extract metadata and tables to transform into a domain-specific gazetteer.

3   Spatial Entity Extraction System

The section describes the proposed framework and discusses the insights into individual components. The framework mainly focuses on tasks of component extraction, Entities Extraction, Information Parser, Marine Geology Gazetteer and Visualization, as shown in Fig. 2. Generally, PDF is the primary format for scientific publications, so we focus on extracting metadata and tabular information from raw PDF documents.

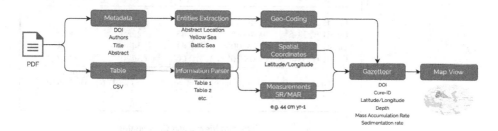

Fig. 2. Proposed Framework

3.1   Component Extraction

The component extraction module takes on scientific publications to perform two crucial tasks, i.e. metadata extraction and table extraction.

Metadata extraction focuses on retrieving significant features of scientific publication, i.e. DOIs, authors, titles, and abstracts. This process is facilitated through the Python module PDFminer.six and Tika, both of them are community maintained [9, 21]. Moreover, metadata extraction was conducted using PDFDataExtractor, but due to template dependencies, this method was restricted to only a subset of the files from Elsevier publications [28]. The extracted metadata is pivotal in supporting the subsequent information extraction module for the Marine Geology Gazetteer.

The table extraction module aims to extract tables from scientific publications and transforms them machine readable formats i.e. comma-separated files. This task is intricate due to the diverse orientations in which tables are presented within scientific publications. Due to the template dependency of publications, tables can appear anywhere and in varying orientations. Hence, the table extraction module is designed to execute two sequential sub-processes: first, the identification of tables and, subsequently, the extraction of these identified tables.

Camelot, a Python module, stimulates table extraction from general PDF documents but cannot identify the tables efficiently from scientific publications, as shown in the results. So we introduced additional steps to support the table identification process. Initially, the PDF document is transformed into a coordinates file as shown in Fig. 3 by using PDFminer.six. The process involves identifying table captions, typically situated at the top of the tables, which serve as initial reference points. These captions are then followed by the corresponding table content.

Actual Document View

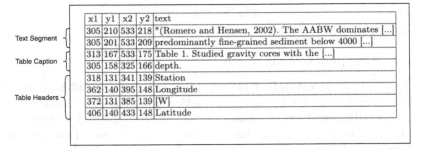

Text Segment { (Romero and Hensen, 2002). The AABW dominates the transport of predominantly fine-grained sediment below 4000 m water depth. The

Caption as Text Segment { Table 1. Studied gravity cores with the location and water depth.

Table Headers as Text Segment

Station	Longitude [W]	Latitude [S]	Water Depth [m]	Core Length [m]
GeoB 6223-6	49°40.86′	35°44.42′	4280	8.67
GeoB 6223-5[a]	49°40.86′	35°44.43′	4280	8.15
GeoB 6229-6	52°39.00′	37°12.41′	3446	9.50
GeoB 6308-4	53°08.70′	39°10.00′	3620	11.66

[a] Core GeoB 6223-5 is the parallel core at site GeoB 6223 subjected to magnetic analysis.

Extracted View using Coordinates

Text Segment

Table Caption

Table Headers

x1	y1	x2	y2	text
305	210	533	218	"(Romero and Hensen, 2002). The AABW dominates [...]
305	201	533	209	predominantly fine-grained sediment below 4000 [...]
313	167	533	175	Table 1. Studied gravity cores with the [...]
305	158	325	166	depth.
318	131	341	139	Station
362	140	395	148	Longitude
372	131	385	139	[W]
406	140	433	148	Latitude

Fig. 3. Snippet of Coordinate File [11]

At first, we looked for the case-sensitive expressions for the tables e.g. "Table" and recorded all the occurrences. This procedure will provide all table captions as well as the mentions within the plain-text. Furthermore, we expanded each token with the table expression by concatenating it with its adjacent token towards right to form a bi-gram. Afterward, we excluded all bi-grams not positioned at the beginning of sentences. For each remaining bi-gram, we calculated the word count within the subsequent five lines and neglected the instances where the line length exceeded the average words per line. Additionally, we omitted bi-grams where a number was not present after the table expressions. These filters generated a list of lines containing table captions, thereby serving as potential starting points for the tables respectively, therefore these respective coordinates are passed to Camelot module for the extraction of tables.

3.2   Information Extraction

The information extraction module consist of two significant sub-tasks: Entity Extraction and Information Parser. The proposed entity extraction module performs two distinct tasks. Firstly, it extracts locational named entities from the titles and abstracts of each publication. Moreover, each extracted entity is geocoded to determine its corresponding latitude and longitude. Given that the oceanographic locational entities we are interested in are not commonly identified by existing NER models, hence we fine-tuned the large spaCy Named Entity Recognition module by incorporating oceanographic location-specific examples that hold relevance within the realm of relevant oceanographic locations.

The outcome of this effort is a specialized NER module capable of extracting oceanographic locations from the plain-text. But in this study, only titles and abstracts of each publication were considered. Furthermore, every extracted locational entity is geo-coded to acquire pair of coordinates, which also performs entity disambiguation task. The Python module GeoPy, a wrapper for various geo-coding services, facilitates the geo-coding task. Within this wrapper, we are using the Nominatim service, which allows us to geo-code locations within the data of the OpenStreetMap database [2,3,13]. Thus extracted oceanographic locational entities could act as an abstract validator for extracted spatial information.

The information parser module plays a crucial role in the proposed framework, table processing, which involves information detection and correction, segregation tasks. The information parser module is specifically designed to handle tables within the context of Marine Geology publications, confining the following essential attributes:

- Core-IDs: Distinct identifiers associated with each oceanographic location.
- Latitude and Longitude: Expressed in Degree/Decimal
- Mass Accumulation Rate (MAR) and Sedimentation Rate (SR) expressed in Mass/Area/Time and Length/Time respectively: Conveying essential sedimentary information.
- Depth Values expressed in meter: Offering insights into the vertical position within the marine environment.

Due to the specific nature of our problem, we studied more than 100 relevant papers to have an overview of possible information representation cases for each of the targeted features. To address this, we carefully compiled an extensive dictionary encompassing a multitude of potential variants for each relevant feature. Particularly, we identified twelve distinct variants for Core-IDs, eleven variations for location data, sixteen alternatives for MAR and SR headers, and seven diverse representations for depth measurements.

Later, each pre-processed table is parsed to extract relevant features while maintaining internal relationships. Core-IDs often lack a fixed pattern, encompassing alphanumeric strings, numbers, or arbitrary names. So for Core-IDs, the parser references our dictionary and tracks the relevant column. A similar

nan	nan	nan	nan	nan	Extension	Tissue
nan	nan	nan	nan	Porites	Rate	Thickness
Sample	Latitude	Longitude	Date Collected	Speciesa	(mm/yr)	(mm)
Orpheus-1, GBRb	-18.750	146.483	Feb 1995	lobata	12.5	6.5
Orpheus-2, GBRb	-18.750	146.483	Feb 1995	lobata	22	6.5
Ningaloo Reef, WA	-21.900	113.917	Apr 1993	australiensis	12	5.5
Nusa Barung, Javab	-8.517	113.367	Jul 1994	solida	24	6.0
Samar, Philippines	11.487	125.513	Apr 2004	lutea	18	5.0
10h-4	n/ac	nan	nan	n/dc	5.6	3.0
12h-4	nan	nan	nan	lobata	4.5	5.7

Fig. 4. Snippet of Extracted Table [11].

approach is employed for identifying depth columns, though their presence is sporadic.

Parsing latitude and longitude from tables presents complicated challenges. Coordinates expressed initially in degrees and minutes encounter encoding abnormalities, such as "°" becoming "8" and "'" turning into "1", such complexities are not much in numbers and are not addressed in this version, the sample of extracted and parsed table is shown in Fig. 4 and Fig. 5 respectively. Additionally, measurement columns like MAR and SR are cross-referenced with dedicated headers and units dictionaries respectively.

	Sample	Latitude	Longitude	Date Collected	Porites Speciesa	Extension Rate (mm/yr)	Tissue Thickness (mm)
0	Orpheus-1, GBRb	-18.750	146.483	Feb 1995	lobata	12.5	6.5
1	Orpheus-2, GBRb	-18.750	146.483	Feb 1995	lobata	22.0	6.5
2	Ningaloo Reef, WA	-21.900	113.917	Apr 1993	australiensis	12.0	5.5
3	Nusa Barung, Javab	-8.517	113.367	Jul 1994	solida	24.0	6.0
4	Samar, Philippines	11.487	125.513	Apr 2004	lutea	18.0	5.0
5	10h-4	n/ac			n/dc	5.6	3.0
6	12h-4				lobata	4.5	5.7

Fig. 5. Snippet of Parsed Table [11].

3.3   Marine Geology Gazetteer

The Gazetteer module constructs an extensive Marine Geology Gazetteer by integrating appropriate metadata, DOI, authors and available abstract locations. From Information Parser, it encompasses core-ids, latitude, longitude, MAR/SR and depth values. The DOI of every publication is used to backtrack to the respective publication. This initiative is the first in Marine Geology and will likely empower research data management and support open data initiatives.

3.4 Visualization

The visualization module populates the data from the Marine Geology Gazetteer to generate an interactive map view. This map showcases location instances as markers and showcases available information for each marker is presented such as, DOI, authors, measurements, depth etc. The map view is built on the top of the Python library folium [1]. Folium exploits the leaflet.js library and incorporates data manipulation approaches from Python. Moreover, the library has several built-in tilesets from OpenStreetMap and also supports both Image, Video, GeoJSON and TopoJSON overlays. The visualization module can draw logical boundaries using GeoJSON for each abstract location (such as the "Baltic Sea"). This approach enhances the visualization of marine geological data and provides better insights, as shown in Fig. 8.

4 Experimental Setup

This section provides an detailed exploration of the experimental setup employed for the proposed framework, followed by a brief discussion on the gathered results.

4.1 Data Description

In this study, scientific publications from Marine Geology were considered for diverse collective/individual tasks. A comprehensive exploration of over 300 full articles was conducted, serving various purposes, such as exploratory study for potential cases, annotation process for the Named Entity Recognition (NER) module and testing. The selection criteria for sourcing these publications was centred around an important requirement. Each publication must contain location coordinates and relevant measurements i.e. mass accumulation rate and sedimentation rate data in tables. Moreover, it is important to mention that the problem, we are addressing here is not explored before, so the search for relevant data take much efforts. Furthermore, an evaluation of the overall framework was undertaken on twenty-seven full papers comprising of 36 relevant tables, and test set that adhered to the same criteria mentioned above.

4.2 Annotation Process

The annotation process plays a pivotal role in enhancing the functionality of the extraction module. As explained in the previous section, spaCy is the module used for locational entity extraction. So base spaCy module needs to be fine-tuned in a way that could extract our targeted locational entities. For location entities, the large pre-trained spaCy model is fine-tuned. The annotation of relevant data was carried out using the Prodigy tool [18]. The corpus used for this process consists of over 10000 text chunks extracted from Marine Geology publications by domain experts.

4.3   Experimental Results

This section presents the detailed results obtained to showcase the efficacy of our proposed framework. The outcomes of the metadata extraction process are summarized in Table 1. The results demonstrate the performance of our component extraction module. In particular metadata extraction was compared with the results from the PDFDataExtractor framework. However, due to template restrictions, the module was only able to process a limited number of documents. Here one important factor needs to be presented. In this scope of study, we tailored the approaches to be generic and did not assume any template dependency of the publications, which may have an impact on the results. Here for simplicity, precision, recall and f1-score is denoted by "P", "R" and "F1" respectively.

Table 1. Evaluation and Comparison of Metadata Extraction.

Framework	DOI			Title			Abstract			Authors		
	P	R	F1	P	R	F1	P	R	F1	P	R	F1
PDFDataExtractor	1.0	0.52	0.68	0.71	0.43	0.54	1.0	0.48	0.65	0.97	0.24	0.38
This Study	1.0	0.89	0.94	0.93	1.0	0.96	0.89	1.0	0.94	0.98	0.86	0.92

Furthermore, to assess the effectiveness of the table extraction approach, we initially review all the documents and count the actual number of tables within these publications. Later, we process all the files using the base Camelot module to determine the tables it detects. We repeat the process with our coordinate-based approach, and the results are shown in Table 2. However, the results indicate that our proposed way of handling tabular extraction performs better and it is streamlined with the actual number of tables exist in the publications.

Table 2. Evaluation for Table Extraction

Details	Number of Tables
Actual Number of Tables	72
Base Camelot without Coordinates	152
Camelot with Coordinates	82

To evaluate the information extraction module, we process all the extracted tables with our information parser and counted the correctly parsed instances in this regard. Beside, the actual number of instances were also counted and reported in the Table 3. To count an instance as correctly extracted, if must satisfy that it carry valid location information, core-ids followed by targeted measurement values. The results clearly indicates that our information extraction approach for tables is capable of extracting locational information besides its quantitative information from tables.

Table 3. Information Extraction from Tables

Details	Location Instances with Measurements
Total Number of Location Instances	669
Extracted Location Instances	631

To evaluate the Named Entities Extraction approach for oceanographic locational entities extraction, we process titles and abstracts to very scientific publications with our customized spaCy module. Moreover, to remove any disambiguation, we also geo-coded each locational entity, this approach will remove the entities with no location coordinates. However, we also counted the actual relevant location entities from titles and abstracts to further evaluate both methods. The results showcase the effectiveness of our trained NER module for locational entities. The results for titles and abstracts are depicted in Figs. 6 and 7, respectively, showcasing the effectiveness of our approach.

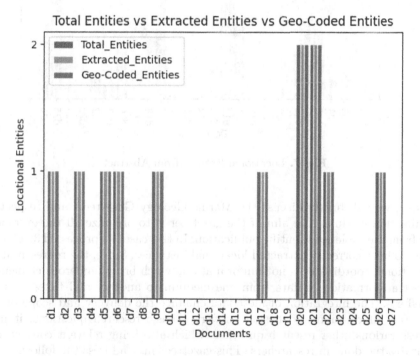

Fig. 6. Locational Entities from Title

The results provide valuable insights, by indicating that the NER module excels in extracting locational entities from document titles, likely due to their concise nature. However, in the case of document abstracts, certain instances arise where our module extracts general locational entities such as "ocean" and "northern sea" as relevant locational entities. But, these cases can be effectively filtered out by the use of geo-coding approach, which could serve as a disambiguation step to refine the extracted locational entities.

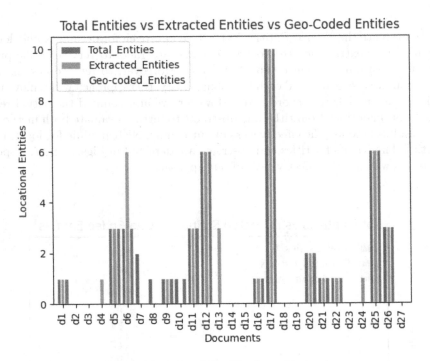

Fig. 7. Locational Entities from Abstract

Now, we will briefly discuss the Marine Geology Gazetteers and respective visualization module. The aim of the gazetteer is to organize all the extracted data from the tables of scientific publication. In this case, we processed 36 diverse tables to have correctly extracted locational instances. Since, the representation of locational coordinates is not uniform at all, which bring numerous challenges while transformation of data from one medium to another and takes most of the efforts. The integration of metadata enhance the delivery and scope of the extracted information and beside answering basic research questions, it may address various other research questions which also bring relevant context and facilitates the domain researchers. This gazetteer may address the following set of questions:

- What are locational information against targeted measurements.
- What are the identifiers to targeted locations?
- Who measured these values?
- What are regions explored in the previous studies considering timeline?

- What are future possible destinations for the experimentation?
- What are future possible collaborations based on focused geographical regions?
- Indication of information dense and sparse areas.

At present, our publication selection process does not prioritize specific regions. However, the introduction of querying language is expected to shed more light on insights within distinct geographical contexts. Finally, we showcase all the extracted information in an interactive map view as shown in the Fig. 8. The map view comprehensively provides the insights into our Marine Geology Gazetteer. Here the each marker represented a geographical location, where the experiment has been conducted. Beside it indicates the importance of spatial characteristics in respective domain.

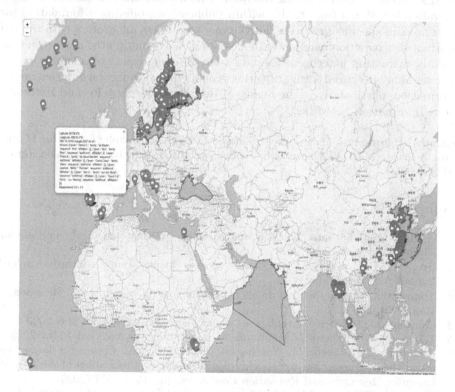

Fig. 8. Interactive Map View

5   Conclusion

The proposed framework tackles the challenging problem of extracting spatial and corresponding quantitative data from tables within the raw PDF files. In contrast to prevalent approaches primarily centered around textual data, our framework delves into tables, generating precise insights previously unavailable to domain scientists. The potential output of the framework is the creation of a Marine Geology Gazetteer. This innovative resource marks a significant stride forward in research data management within Marine Geology and may play a pivotal role in shaping the future Marine environment. The visualization module further enhances the usefulness of the proposed framework, enabling researchers to visualize information-dense and sparse regions and presenting a map of measurements. Furthermore, the lack of standardized guidelines for representing such diverse data in marine geology publications is notable. The introduction of our proposed framework has the potential to stimulate empirical investigations, shed light on insights and enhanced overall research and development. It could also contribute to the increased feasibility of automated data discovery.

Beyond Marine Geology, the framework holds potential as a versatile solution suitable across various scientific disciplines. Its adaptability extends to extracting valuable insights from tables within publications, offering a foundation for other domain-specific gazetteers. Furthermore, seamless integration with textual information extraction culminates in a comprehensive automated approach, proficiently extracting heterogeneous data from all components of scientific publications. Many potential future directions could emerge to leverage the extracted information, particularly in the realms of Recommender Systems and Heterogeneous Information Networks.

Acknowledgements. This work was supported by the Helmholtz School for Marine Data Science (MarDATA) partially funded by the Helmholtz Association (grant HIDSS-0005).

References

1. Folium - python data, leaflet.js maps. https://python-visualization.github.io/folium/. Accessed 4 May 2023
2. Geopy - python wrapper for geocoding services. https://geopy.readthedocs.io/en/stable/. Accessed 4 May 2023
3. Nominatim. https://nominatim.openstreetmap.org/ui/search.html. Accessed 4 May 2023
4. Camelot (2022). https://github.com/atlanhq/camelot. Accessed 4 May 2023
5. Tabula-py (2022). https://github.com/chezou/tabula-py. Accessed 4 May 2023
6. Brandsen, A., Verberne, S., Wansleeben, M., Lambers, K.: Creating a dataset for named entity recognition in the archaeology domain. In: Proceedings of the Twelfth Language Resources and Evaluation Conference, pp. 4573–4577 (2020)
7. Ceritli, T., Williams, C.K.: Identifying the units of measurement in tabular data. arXiv preprint arXiv:2111.11959 (2021)
8. Chuang, P.C., et al.: Carbon isotope exchange during anaerobic oxidation of methane (AOM) in sediments of the northeastern south china sea. Geochim. Cosmochim. Acta **246**, 138–155 (2019)
9. Contributors, G.: Apache tika - a content analysis toolkit. https://tika.apache.org/. Accessed 4 May 2023
10. Ducatteeuw, V.: Developing an urban gazetteer: a semantic web database for humanities data. In: Proceedings of the 5th ACM SIGSPATIAL International Workshop on Geospatial Humanities, pp. 36–39 (2021)

11. Gagan, M.K., Dunbar, G.B., Suzuki, A.: The effect of skeletal mass accumulation in porites on coral sr/ca and δ18o paleothermometry. Paleoceanography **27**(1) (2012)

12. Göpfert, J., Kuckertz, P., Weinand, J., Kotzur, L., Stolten, D.: Measurement extraction with natural language processing: a review. Find. Assoc. Comput. Linguist.: EMNLP **2022**, 2191–2215 (2022)

13. Honnibal, M., Montani, I.: spacy 2: natural language understanding with bloom embeddings, convolutional neural networks and incremental parsing. To appear **7**(1), 411–420 (2017)

14. Hübscher, L., Jiang, L., Naumann, F.: Extractable: Extracting tables from raw data files. BTW 2023 (2023)

15. Lopez, P.: GROBID: combining automatic bibliographic data recognition and term extraction for scholarship publications. In: Agosti, M., Borbinha, J., Kapidakis, S., Papatheodorou, C., Tsakonas, G. (eds.) ECDL 2009. LNCS, vol. 5714, pp. 473–474. Springer, Heidelberg (2009). https://doi.org/10.1007/978-3-642-04346-8_62

16. Luo, M., Gieskes, J., Chen, L., Shi, X., Chen, D.: Provenances, distribution, and accumulation of organic matter in the southern Mariana trench rim and slope: Implication for carbon cycle and burial in hadal trenches. Mar. Geol. **386**, 98–106 (2017)

17. Martinez-Rodriguez, J.L., Hogan, A., Lopez-Arevalo, I.: Information extraction meets the semantic web: a survey. Semantic Web **11**(2), 255–335 (2020)

18. Montani, I., Honnibal, M.: Prodigy: A new annotation tool for radically efficient machine teaching. Artificial Intelligence to appear (2018)

19. Moulin, T.C., Amaral, O.B.: Using collaboration networks to identify authorship dependence in meta-analysis results. Res. Syn. Methods **11**(5), 655–668 (2020)

20. Neumann, M., King, D., Beltagy, I., Ammar, W.: Scispacy: fast and robust models for biomedical natural language processing. arXiv preprint arXiv:1902.07669 (2019)

21. PDFminer: pdfminer.six. https://github.com/pdfminer/pdfminer.six. Accessed 20 Mar 2023

22. Petersen, T., Suryani, M.A., Beth, C., Patel, H., Wallmann, K., Renz, M.: Geoquantities: A framework for automatic extraction of measurements and spatial context from scientific documents. In: 17th International Symposium on Spatial and Temporal Databases, pp. 166–169 (2021)

23. Ramachandran, R., Arutchelvan, K.: Named entity recognition on bio-medical literature documents using hybrid based approach. J. Ambient Intell. Human. Comput. 1–10 (2021). https://doi.org/10.1007/s12652-021-03078-z

24. Ramachandran, R., Arutchelvan, K.: Arraner: a novel named entity recognition model for biomedical literature documents. J. Supercomput. **78**(14), 16498–16511 (2022)

25. of Southampton, U.: Geoparsepy. https://pypi.org/project/geoparsepy/ (2022). Accessed 4 May 2023

26. Suryani, M.A., Wölker, Y., Sharma, D., Beth, C., Wallmann, K., Renz, M.: A framework for extracting scientific measurements and geo-spatial information from scientific literature. In: 2022 IEEE 18th International Conference on e-Science (e-Science), pp. 236–245. IEEE (2022)

27. Wahle, J.P., Ruas, T., Mohammad, S.M., Gipp, B.: D3: A massive dataset of scholarly metadata for analyzing the state of computer science research. arXiv preprint arXiv:2204.13384 (2022)

28. Zhu, M., Cole, J.M.: Pdfdataextractor:a tool for reading scientific text and interpreting metadata from the typeset literature in the portable document format. J. Chem. Inf. Model. **62**(7), 1633–1643 (2022)

Visualizing Software Test Requirements Using NLP and HITL Approach

S. M. Azizul Hakim[1] , Rahat Ibn Rafiq[1]([✉]) , and Michael Lingg[2]

[1] Grand Valley State University, Allendale, MI 49401, USA
`hakims@mail.gvsu.edu`,
`rafiqr@gvsu.edu`
[2] Array of Engineers, Grand Rapids, USA
`michael.lingg@arrayofengineers.com`
`https://www.arrayofengineers.com/`

Abstract. This research paper presents an innovative approach for capturing and representing system specifications through structured requirements and their visualization using knowledge graphs. We introduce a formalized syntax and structure to define system behavior, conditions, and actions to achieve precision and eliminate ambiguities. The proposed solution encompasses a multi-panel web application featuring a knowledge graph panel, a semistructured requirements panel, a structured requirements panel, and a feedback panel. Users can conveniently edit and save requirements in the semistructured panel, automatically propagating changes to the other panels. Additionally, we fine-tune the CodeT5 language model to effectively convert semistructured requirements into structured ones, facilitating the regeneration of the knowledge graph. This process significantly enhances the intuitive visualization of required dependencies among system components. This methodology enables effective collaboration, validation, and refinement of requirements, thereby substantially improving the quality and accuracy of the software testing process.

Keywords: Software Test Generation · NLP · Human-In-Tha-Loop · Knowledge Graph

1 Introduction

Software testing is one of the most important components of the software development lifecycle [5]. Efficiently generating comprehensive test cases is crucial for ensuring the reliability and quality of software systems in the field of software testing, especially for safety-critical software systems [12]. For these reasons, software testing is often time-consuming, and resource-intensive. Recent advancements in NLP also resulted in several attempts [19] to convert the natural language directly to test cases. While full automation is still out of our reach, these attempts are partially automated and do not have any room for generalization. Moreover, manual approaches to software testing itself can be prone to human error. Therefore a tool to help software test engineers interact and visualize test requirements in a structured way can be a crucial step toward full automation.

To address these challenges, our work introduces a unique contribution to the field by developing a pipeline that starts with naturally typed semistructured requirements obtained from various sources. We finetune a Code-T5 transformer model to produce structured requirements from semistructured requirements. This transformation enables a more precise and standardized specification of system behavior, paving the way for effective test generation. To facilitate comprehension and collaboration, we present a knowledge graph-like structure that visually represents the structured requirements. This graph allows users to intuitively navigate and explore different requirements, providing a holistic view of the system under test. Additionally, we have developed an interactable multipanel tool with a feedback loop that enhances the visualization experience. Changes made in any panel, be it the semistructured requirements, structured requirements, or the knowledge graph, are dynamically reflected in real-time across the other two panels, ensuring synchronization and coherence. The feedback loop makes the system improve gradually allowing it to be more generalized over time. This work is the first step towards our goal to fully automate the software test generation process.

We organize the rest of the paper as follows. First, we provide a review of the related previous works. Then, in Sect. 3, we present an overview of the system architecture. Then in Sects. 4 and 5, we detail how we implemented the NLP and system components of the system. Finally, we conclude our paper in Sect. 7 by summarizing our contribution and exploring future research directions.

2 Related Works

In recent years, significant advancements in Natural Language Processing have led to its widespread application in various domains, including software testing. A recent study [19] discusses the role of NLP in software testing as well as the challenges in light of recent LLM advancement. (LLMs generate text based on the data they were trained on. If a specific concept or software domain isn't adequately covered during training, the model may produce incomplete or incorrect information when applied to testing tasks [22]. LLMs struggle with handling ambiguity [15]. Software requirements and test cases often contain vague or ambiguous language, and LLMs may not provide precise or accurate interpretations, leading to potential misunderstandings and incorrect test results. Sharing sensitive code or test data with external NLP models can raise data privacy and security concerns, especially in industries where proprietary or confidential information is involved [18]. Another work [8] conducted a systematic literature overview on 67 papers identifying various NLP approaches and tools for software testing and their limitations. Also, Ahsan et al. [4] conducted a systematic review of 16 research works on NLP techniques to generate test cases from preliminary requirements documents.

Several distinct methods have been proposed to assist automated test generation. Kähkönen et al. [11] uses dynamic symbolic execution for generating test cases for software components. Keyvanpour et al. [13] tried to efficiently find a small set of cases that allow an adequacy criterion to be fulfilled. Esnaashari et al. [7] proposed a memetic algorithm that uses reinforcement learning as a local search method for test data generation. Candea et al. [6] discussed various methods like random testing and input fuzzing, symbolic execution and its challenges in practices, whitebox fuzzing, selective symbolic execution, etc. Varshney et al. [20] proposed a genetic algorithm-based novel method to generate test data for a program.

The current emphasis on software testing largely overlooks the development of interactive tools. For instance, Marculescu et al. [17] introduced a search-based interactive software testing system that capitalizes on the expertise of domain professionals while demanding minimal software testing proficiency. Although their work is well-suited for software testing scenarios reliant on domain-specific knowledge, it doesn't endeavor to automate the test generation process from the initial requirement phase.

Our research endeavors to serve as an intermediary step towards achieving full automation, starting from natural language requirement specifications and culminating in software test generation. We address the limitations of Language Model Models (LLMs) by selecting an in-house hosted model, effectively mitigating concerns related to privacy and data leakage. Through fine-tuning the model via active learning, we empower our system to adeptly handle ambiguity and better equip it for tests that necessitate domain-specific expertise.

3   System Overview

We now present a brief overview of all the system architecture components and entities, as specified in Fig. 1.

(1) Semistructured Requirements: We start from naturally typed semistructured requirements. These requirements occupy a unique space between unstructured natural language and highly structured formal specifications, offering a harmonious balance of comprehensibility for human understanding and clarity for system development. By incorporating structured elements like states, events, actions, and conditions, these requirements achieve enhanced clarity while remaining easily accessible to non-technical stakeholders. This approach facilitates effective communication and collaboration among diverse teams, fostering a deeper comprehension of the system's intricacies. An example is given below:

> *When the Display State is Radio Summary and Button 2 is pressed, the Display State shall transition to DME Radio.*

(2) CodeT5 Converter: Semistructured requirements go through the CodeT5 converter to be transformed into structured requirements. The CodeT5 converter is a CodeT5 transformer [21] model finetuned to convert the unpredictable semistructured requirements into a predefined structured format, specified in [14].

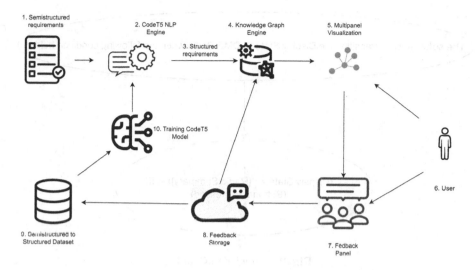

Fig. 1. System Architecture

(3) Structured Requirements: Structured requirements provide a systematic approach to representing system specifications. They utilize a predefined syntax to define behavior, conditions, and actions precisely. Our approach defines structured requirements as a combination of setting and conditional statements. This methodology enhances clarity, consistency, and knowledge graph generation for semistructured requirements. We leverage [14] as the basis of forming the structured requirements. The following is an instance of a structured converted version of the requirement presented above.

```
The software shall transition the
Display State to DME Radio when
the following condition holds:
(
    (Display State == [Radio Summary]) AND
    (Button 2 is pressed)
)
```

(4) Knowledge Graph Engine: A knowledge graph serves as a valuable tool for visually representing structured requirements and facilitating their analysis, offering a clear and interactive visualization that allows users to grasp the intricate relationships between various requirements. Within the knowledge graph, each structured requirement is depicted through two distinct sub-components as nodes: the setting statement and the conditional statement. The generation of nodes and edges within the knowledge graph is carried out by the knowledge graph engine, which derives this information directly from the structured

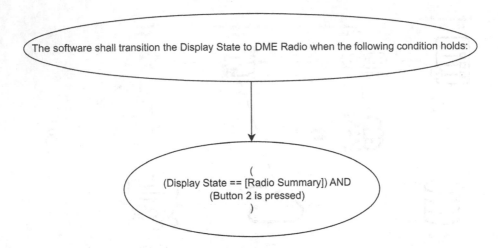

Fig. 2. Knowledge Graph

requirements. As a result, the knowledge graph not only provides a comprehensive overview of the requirements but also enhances the understanding and exploration of the underlying connections among them.

Figure 2 shows the aforementioned structured requirement's corresponding knowledge graph conversion.

(5) Multipanel Visualization: The Multipanel Visualization Tool is a comprehensive software application designed to assist software test engineers and domain knowledge experts in their critical roles of evaluating and validating software and device requirements. This tool offers a multifaceted approach to enhancing the understanding and management of requirements and their associated knowledge graphs.

(6) User: Our primary user base comprises software test engineers and domain knowledge experts who are intimately involved in the rigorous testing of software applications or electronic devices. These professionals rely on the Multipanel Visualization Tool to gain deeper insights into the intricacies of requirements and their relationships within complex systems.

(7) Feedback Panel: At the core of the Multipanel Visualization Tool is the Feedback Panel, an interactive component that empowers users to actively participate in the refinement and improvement of the system. Users can readily report any inconsistencies or errors they encounter during their interactions with the tool.

(8) Feedback Storage: The Feedback Storage module serves as a secure and efficient repository for all user-generated feedback. This meticulously collected feedback is invaluable, as it fuels an iterative process aimed at enhancing both the semistructured to structured requirement conversion and the knowledge graph engine.

(9) Semistructured to Structured Dataset: One of the vital functions of the system is the conversion of semistructured requirements into structured, actionable data. This process relies on a specialized dataset, which acts as the foundation for this conversion. Periodically, the system reviews user feedback stored in the Feedback Storage module to identify instances where conversions have been incorrect or suboptimal. This user-provided feedback is then harnessed to refine and expand the semistructured to the structured dataset. Consequently, the system becomes more adept at converting requirements accurately and effectively.

(10) Retraining the CodeT5: The culmination of this iterative refinement process involves the retraining of the CodeT5 model. This powerful machine learning model is the driving force behind the conversion of semistructured requirements into structured formats. By integrating the knowledge gleaned from user feedback and the enhanced semistructured to the structured dataset, the CodeT5 model undergoes continuous improvement. This updated model represents a more proficient and reliable converter, capable of transforming requirements with precision.

4 Semistructured to Structured Requirement Converter

4.1 Generating Dataset with ChatGPT

We began with a dataset of 40 semi-structured requirements from the aviation and aeronautics domain, generously provided by Array of Engineers [1]. To expand our data pool, we utilized ChatGPT [16] to generate approximately 160 synthetic requirements. For the structured requirements, we followed a standardized setting statement-condition format [14]. The setting statement comprises a concise one-line sentence that commences with "The software shall....", followed by one or more combinations of output variable or state being set and the value being set to. The condition portion consists of one or multiple logical statements connected using logical operators like AND, OR, XOR, or others enclosed within parentheses. This structured format proves instrumental in the creation of a knowledge graph, offering a powerful visualization tool for our analysis and exploration of the requirements.

4.2 Finetuning CodeT5

To transform semistructured requirements into structured formats, we leverage the capabilities of the CodeT5 model, an encoder-decoder-based transformer renowned for its proficiency in code generation and comprehension tasks, as it has been trained on CodeSearchNet [10]. Given that our structured requirements closely resembled pseudo-code, CodeT5 emerged as the natural choice for our conversion engine. We leverage the Google Colab free tier environment, a cloud-based, cost-effective platform that provides ample computing resources for machine learning tasks. Our training journey began with an augmented

dataset comprising 160 semistructured requirements and their structured counterparts. The finetuning process unfolded over a span of 10 epochs, allowing the
CodeT5 model enough exposure to the nuances and intricacies of our requirements dataset. We imposed a token length constraint of 256, keeping in mind
the computational efficiency with the imperative of optimal model performance.
After fine-tuning CodeT5 for the task of converting semistructured requirements
into structured formats, we seamlessly integrated the model into our Multipanel
Visualization Tool using a REST API built with Flask, a well-established Python
web framework.

5   System Implementation

5.1   Interactive Multipanel Tool

Our multipanel tool, shown in Fig. 3 is a web application featuring four panels in
a 2 by 2 grid layout. Developed with React and Flask, it includes the knowledge
graph panel, semistructured requirements panel, structured requirements panel,
and feedback panel. Flask [9] was chosen as the backend framework, offering
flexibility and efficiency for development and deployment. React [2], a popular
JavaScript library provides a dynamic and interactive frontend experience with
its component-based architecture. This integration of Flask and React enables
a powerful and user-friendly tool for visualizing and generating software test
requirements, enhancing comprehension and usability.

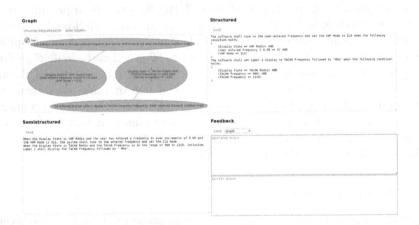

Fig. 3. Overview of our system

5.2   Knowledge Graph Panel

The knowledge graph panel, shown in Fig. 4 displays generated graphs for
requirements, with each requirement represented as a disconnected graph. An

Graph

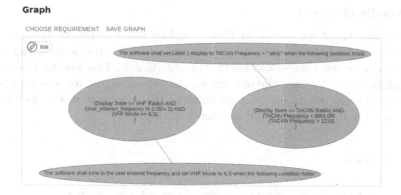

Fig. 4. Knowledge Graph Panel

edit button at the top left corner allows for adding and editing nodes and edges, facilitating easy feedback from the user.

Two modules handle the generation and conversion of knowledge graphs. The structured2graph module converts structured requirement text into nodes and edges using string matching. The graph2structured module converts nodes and edges back into structured requirement text using breadth-first search.

To visualize the knowledge graph and enable interactive manipulation, we employ the widely adopted open-source JavaScript library, Vis.js [3]. This library integrates seamlessly with React, the JavaScript framework used for the front-end development of our tool. Leveraging Vis.js within the React environment allows for the convenient addition, deletion, and modification of nodes and edges within the knowledge graph panel by the user.

5.3   Structured and Semistructured Requirement Panel

Clicking the save button in the semistructured panel will take the current text in the panel and call the semistructured2structured module which is responsible for converting the semistructured requirements into structured requirements using the CodeT5 transformer model, described in Sect. 4. After that, the structured requirements will be used to regenerate the knowledge graph using the structured2graph module.

Both newly generated knowledge graphs and structured requirements will then replace the existing contents of the respective panels. Modifying the structured requirements and clicking the save button will only result in updating the knowledge graph. As semistructured requirements are the base of generating structured requirements and the knowledge graph, they only are changed manually through the semistructured requirements panel of the source file.

5.4   Feedback Panel

The feedback panel, presented in Fig. 5, enables users to report system errors and inconsistencies. Users can select the relevant panel, provide both the generated and correct outcomes, and submit their feedback. Two feedback boxes are distinguished by color cues, the red box for the generated and incorrect outcomes and the green one for the correct outcome of the requirement The feedback is stored in a Firebase database for human verification.

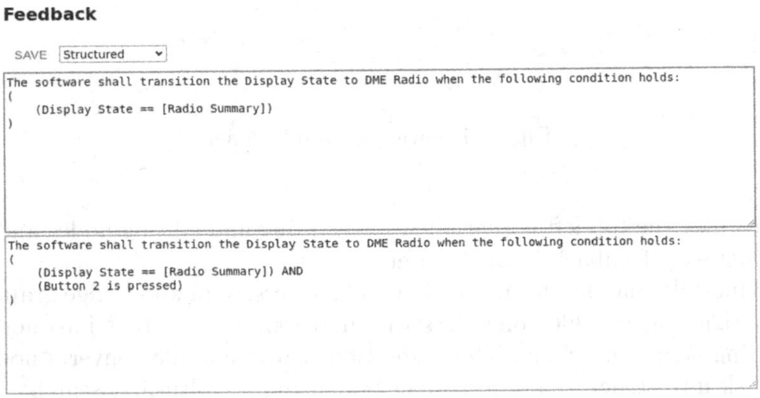

Feedback

SAVE   Structured   ▾

The software shall transition the Display State to DME Radio when the following condition holds:
(
    (Display State == [Radio Summary])
)

The software shall transition the Display State to DME Radio when the following condition holds:
(
    (Display State == [Radio Summary]) AND
    (Button 2 is pressed)
)

Fig. 5. Feedback Panel

It is then utilized to enhance the system's performance, either through retraining the converter or modifying the graph generation process. This feedback loop facilitates continuous improvement of the system through an active learning cycle.

6   Active Learning and Human in the Loop

Owing to the confidentiality surrounding software testing data in the aviation and aeronautics domain, generating a substantial dataset presents challenges. To tackle this, we devised an active learning feedback loop within our system. This feedback loop incorporates iterative improvement over time, capitalizing on the periodically received limited data from the users. Central to this feedback mechanism is the pivotal role played by the feedback panel, allowing users to identify errors and inconsistencies in our system in real time. This user-collected feedback plays a crucial role in retraining the semistructured to structured converter model. Additionally, it contributes to enhancing the consistency of the structured2graph module, ultimately refining the visualization and analysis of requirements within the knowledge graph. By actively leveraging user feedback and continuously updating our system, our ultimate objective is to create a more generalized and highly effective tool for analyzing software test requirements.

7   Conclusion and Future Work

In this paper, we present an interactive software test visualization framework that harnesses the power of human-in-the-loop active learning and natural language processing. We presented the details of our approach, including the methodology employed for the conversion process, the architecture of our codeT5 transformer model, and the design of our interactive multi-panel visualization tool. However, we acknowledge that, due to the confidential nature of the test requirement dataset in the aerospace industry, our system is overfitted to the available dataset. With the active learning feedback loop in our system, we can make a generalized system as new data comes in.

From a software standpoint, incorporating features such as user login, registration, and the capability to handle multiple systems requirements while preserving user progress would significantly enhance the system's user-friendliness. Presently, the generated knowledge graph derived from the requirements is rather rudimentary, comprising solely two nodes: one for the condition and another for the setting statement. In our future development roadmap, we plan to create a hierarchical knowledge graph that generates nodes for each of the individual statements interconnected by arithmetic operators. This envisioned enhancement will furnish users with a substantially more comprehensive and detailed insight into the intricacies of the requirements.

Overall, our work demonstrates the potential of NLP-driven techniques in transforming the software testing landscape, enhancing efficiency, accuracy, and collaboration throughout the software development lifecycle.

References

1. Array of engineers (2022). https://www.arrayofengineers.com
2. React (2022). https://react.dev
3. Vis.js (2022). https://almende.github.io/vis
4. Ahsan, I., Butt, W.H., Ahmed, M.A., Anwar, M.W.: A comprehensive investigation of natural language processing techniques and tools to generate automated test cases. In: Proceedings of the Second International Conference on Internet of things, Data and Cloud Computing, pp. 1–10 (2017)
5. Bassil, Y.: A simulation model for the waterfall software development life cycle. arXiv preprint arXiv:1205.6904 (2012)
6. Candea, G., Godefroid, P.: Automated software test generation: some challenges, solutions, and recent advances. Computing and Software Science: State of the Art and Perspectives, pp. 505–531 (2019)
7. Esnaashari, M., Damia, A.H.: Automation of software test data generation using genetic algorithm and reinforcement learning. Expert Syst. Appl. **183**, 115446 (2021)
8. Garousi, V., Bauer, S., Felderer, M.: Nlp-assisted software testing: a systematic mapping of the literature. Inf. Softw. Technol. **126**, 106321 (2020)
9. Grinberg, M.: Flask web development: developing web applications with python. " O'Reilly Media, Inc." (2018)

10. Husain, H., Wu, H.H., Gazit, T., Allamanis, M., Brockschmidt, M.: Codesearch-net challenge: Evaluating the state of semantic code search. arXiv preprint arXiv:1909.09436 (2019)

11. Kähkönen, K., et al.: Automated test generation for software components (2009)

12. Kassab, M.: Testing practices of software in safety critical systems: Industrial survey. In: ICEIS, vol. 2, pp. 359–367 (2018)

13. Keyvanpour, M.R., Homayouni, H., Shirazee, H.: Automatic software test case generation: an analytical classification framework. Int. J. Softw. Eng. Appl. **6**(4), 1–16 (2012)

14. Lingg, M., Paul, H., Kushwaha, S., Ortiz, J.: Automation of test case generation and software system modelling. In: DEVCOM GVSC SEC (2022)

15. Liu, A., et al.: We're afraid language models aren't modeling ambiguity. arXiv preprint arXiv:2304.14399 (2023)

16. Liu, Y., et al.: Summary of chatgpt/gpt-4 research and perspective towards the future of large language models. arXiv preprint arXiv:2304.01852 (2023)

17. Marculescu, B., Feldt, R., Torkar, R.: A concept for an interactive search-based software testing system. In: Fraser, G., Teixeira de Souza, J. (eds.) SSBSE 2012. LNCS, vol. 7515, pp. 273–278. Springer, Heidelberg (2012). https://doi.org/10.1007/978-3-642-33119-0_21

18. Montagna, S., Ferretti, S., Klopfenstein, L.C., Florio, A., Pengo, M.F.: Data decentralisation of llm-based chatbot systems in chronic disease self-management. In: Proceedings of the 2023 ACM Conference on Information Technology for Social Good, pp. 205–212 (2023)

19. Pham, K., Nguyen, V., Nguyen, T.: Application of natural language processing towards autonomous software testing. In: Proceedings of the 37th IEEE/ACM International Conference on Automated Software Engineering, pp. 1–4 (2022)

20. Varshney, S., Mehrotra, M.: Automated software test data generation for data flow dependencies using genetic algorithm. Int. J. Adv. Res. Comput. Sci. Softw. Eng. **4**(2), 472–479 (2014)

21. Wang, Y., Wang, W., Joty, S., Hoi, S.C.: Codet5: Identifier-aware unified pretrained encoder-decoder models for code understanding and generation. arXiv preprint arXiv:2109.00859 (2021)

22. Wen, H., et al.: Empowering llm to use smartphone for intelligent task automation. arXiv preprint arXiv:2308.15272 (2023)

Improvement of EduBPMN Transformation Rules from an Empirical Validation

Eduardo Díaz[1(⊠)] and Jose Ignacio Panach[2]

[1] Universidad Peruana de Ciencias Aplicadas, Prolongación Primavera 2390, Lima 15023, Peru
pcsijord@upc.edu.pe
[2] Escola Tècnica Superior d'Enginyeria, Departament d'Informàtica, Universitat de València,
Avenida de la Universidad, s/n, 46100 Burjassot, València, Spain
joigpana@uv.es

Abstract. EduBPMN method allows the generation of graphical components from a BPMN model complemented with the UML class diagram. This article proposes the improvement of five transformation rules of the EduBPMN method from an experiment developed in 2019, with the improved transformation rules an experiment was developed that was executed by 31 subjects where the results of two metrics were obtained, (i) the correctness of the rules, where the subjects had to map BPMN to graphic components intuitively through an experimental problem, had a positive result (87.50%), (ii) the satisfaction of the generalization of the rules, had a positive result in its Perceived Ease of Use (93%), Perceived Usefulness (95%), and Intention to Use (96%). This article provides positive results on the five new improved rules of the EduBPMN method, which is used to map BPMN to graphical components.

Keywords: BPMN · Transformation rules · Graphic components · Experiment

1 Introduction

Currently, the generation of graphical components from a conceptual model has taken prominence based on the Model Driven Software Development (MDD) paradigm [1]. There are different methods that work in this paradigm such as the EduBPMN method [2–7], MoCaDiX [28], OO-METHOD [8] and others. It must be taken into account that MDD improves the productivity and quality of the development process, applying an approach that uses models at different levels of abstraction and transformations between said models. The EduBPMN method allows generating graphical components from a Business Process Model and Notation (BPMN) model complemented with a UML class diagram. The BPMN model allows understanding the business procedures of organizations [9]. BPMN is a widely used model to elicit simple and complex business process requirements, furthermore, it is complemented by the UML class diagram [10] to use the attributes with their data types. EduBPMN contains a set of transformation rules that involves a set of graphic components, where for each graphic component a stereotype was assigned to avoid ambiguities in the automatic generation of a graphic component,

J. A. Lossio-Ventura et al. (Eds.): SIMBig 2023, CCIS 2142, pp. 299–315, 2024.
https://doi.org/10.1007/978-3-031-63616-5_23

the method was based on the study of BPMN patterns (sequence pattern, exclusive decision pattern, synchronization pattern, implicit decision pattern, and union pattern and synchronized structure) and on the analysis of Bizagi projects [11] that correspond to a business, health, administrative and academic context. EduBPMN can perform the extension of a BPMN model with stereotypes, these models are developed in the Visual Paradigm v 15.0 application [12] where it can be exported in an XML file, through a web compiler, so that it can automatically generate graphical components.

The contribution of this work is to provide the improvement of five transformation rules of the EduBPMN method, these transformation rules were improved from the validation of transformation rules of an experiment in 2019, where in this experiment nine transformation rules of the EduBPMN were validated with students from the University of Valencia (Spain). With the five improved EduBPMN rules, a new experiment was carried out based on two metrics: (i) correctness of the transformation rules and (ii) satisfaction of the generalization of transformation rules to map BPMN to graphical components. The subjects of this experiment are students of the Software Engineering career of the Peruvian University of Applied Sciences (Peru) where they know the design of graphic components, UML class diagram, and they were trained on the elements of BPMN so that they can develop the experiment. For the correctness of the transformation rules, the subjects subjectively had to draw graphic components from a BPMN complemented with a UML class diagram. The results were compared with the graphic components of the transformation rules proposed in this article, where positive results were obtained with 87.50% correctness. For the satisfaction of the generalization of the rules, the subjects had to fill out a questionnaire based on a Moody's framework [13], based on the work of Lindland's [14]. The questionnaire was based on 16 questions, where it was measured in terms of Perceived Ease of Use (FUP) with 6 questions, Perceived Utility (UP) with 8 questions, and Intention to Use (UI) with 2 questions. The questionnaire is based on questions where the existence of whether it would be useful is evaluated and if there is an intention to use transformation rules in a general way to map BPMN to graphical components, the results were positive with 93% in FUP, 95% in UP, and 96% in UI.

This paper is structured as follows: Sect. 2 reviews the literature related to the generation of graphical components from BPMN. Section 3 shows EduBPMN. Section 4 presents how the rules of EduBPMN were improved. Section 5 defines the planning and definition of the experiment with the new graphic components for the transformation rules. Section 6 shows the results of the experiment. Section 7 shows the discussions of the work. Section 8 shows the threats to validity where they might affect the experiment. Section 9 presents the conclusions and future work.

2   State of the Art

In this section we review work related to the generation of graphical component design alternatives using a Directed Literature Review (TLR), an in-depth, informative, non-systematic literature review aimed at retaining only significant references to minimize selection bias. The search string in this work was carried out in the Scopus digital library (see https://www.scopus.com/home.uri): ("BPMN" AND "user interface" OR

"GUIs" OR "extension" AND "experiment"). The inclusion criteria are: (1) generation of graphical components from a BPMN model, (2) extensions of BPMN models. The exclusion criteria are: (1) models other than the BPMN model, (2) approaches that do not generate design alternatives for graphical components from a BPMN model. The first search shows 110 scientific articles. After applying inclusion and exclusion criteria, the sample of 9 articles has been considered. The articles accepted in the search are shown below:

2.1 Generation of Graphical User Interfaces from a BPMN Model

Bouchelligua et al. [15] defined an approach with a design methodology supported by a set of transformations based on Model Driven Engineering (MDE) [16]. These transformations allow you to derive design alternatives for graphical workflow components, and the interaction of the BPMN model as the task model, and other models. Torres et al. [17] propose an extension to the OOWS Web Engineering method for the development of web applications based on business processes such as BPMN, this extension contains the existence of manual tasks in a B2B, using the executable specification in WS-BPEL. Brambilla et al. [18] describe a BPMN model extended with information on task assignment, policies, activity semantics, and written data flows. The proposal is based on WebRatio, a model-driven web application that allows you to edit BPMN models and automatically transform them into running JEE applications. Sousa et al. [19] proposed an approach to unifying a business process with graphical components, (1) defining associations between business processes and graphical component, and (2) presenting a tool for model transformation that addresses traceability. LeiHan et al. [20] defined an approach for the derivation of graphical components from BPMN models. This is based on a role-enriched business process model developed with task descriptions and associated data, thereby extending the BPMN model. A set of control flow and data flow patterns are identified for the derivation of the graphical components. A complete set of restrictions and recommendations is specified to support the generation and update of the graphical components.

As a conclusion on works considered in this sub-section deal with a set of transformations to generate graphical components from BPMN [17, 19, 21], while others integrate the specifications in the BPMN models [18, 20, 22]. On the contrary, this paper proposes the use of transformation rules that allow the use of a single model to generate graphical components from BPMN.

2.2 Extended BPMN Model

In the work of Rodríguez et al. [23] extended BPMN to incorporate security requirements into business process diagrams in accordance with a Model Driven Architecture (MDA). The extension allows the business analyst to express the security requirements from his own perspective. Stroppi et al. [24] presented an extension of the BPMN model, using the extension mechanisms provided by the BPMN 2.0 meta-model. They focused on 3 main aspects of the resource perspective [25], resource structure, authorization, and work distribution, thus improving the communication of resource perspective requirements between analysts and technical developers. Abouzid et al. [26] defined a set of BPMN extensions that represent some crucial manufacturing domain concepts for business process improvement. BPMN extensions allow you to incorporate information into the process model, from a manufacturing point of view, it makes the process more complete. Intrigila et al. [27] propose a lightweight BPMN extension that specifically addresses data properties in terms of constraints, preconditions, and postconditions that business process activities must satisfy. The model allows software analysts and developers to provide information to easily assign updates to the software implementation.

To summarize related works considered in this sub-section, we can state that some use a design framework with extensions of the BPMN [23, 24, 26, 27], to capture relevant information. Therefore, the use of BPMN extension mechanisms is remarkable, taking into account that in our proposal it is for the automatic generation of graphical components.

3 EduBPMN Method

This section shows the EduBPMN method [2–7] which consists of 15 transformation rules, each rule contains a set of graphical components, where each graphical component is represented by a stereotype from a BPMN model complemented with the UML class diagram in order to use the attributes. The transformation rules were extracted from the analysis of 14 Bizagi BPMN projects [11]. EduBPMN was based on 5 BPMN patterns (sequence pattern, exclusive decision pattern, synchronization pattern, implicit decision pattern, and synchronization structured join pattern) [29]. EduBPMN allows you to develop an extended BPMN model in the Visual Paradigm v. 15.0 [12], the stereotypes were configured so that they can be added to the extended BPMN model. This modeler allows exporting to an XML format file where a web compiler developed in the PHP and HTML5 programming languages can automatically generate graphical components in HTML5. Next, an example of the R0 transformation rule that corresponds to the UML class diagram will be shown, and an example of the R2 transformation rule that corresponds to the BPMN model with the sequence pattern: (i) the R0 transformation rule is used for three data attributes (text string, integers and booleans) of the UML class diagram, each attribute is represented with a graphic component depending on its data type: (1) Text box, for any text string; (2) List box or Combo box for any enum with simple option, (3) Radio button or Check box for any boolean value. For each graphic component a stereotype was assigned to avoid ambiguities in the generation of graphic components. (ii) the R2 transformation rule is used when the sequence pattern appears, this pattern indicates that when there are sequential user-type tasks they have to be developed in an orderly manner one after the other. Figure 1 shows the R2 transformation rule, where from two user-type tasks three graphic component design alternatives can be generated, such as: Wizard (Navigation Assistant) where each user-type task is a form, Tabbed dialog box (Dialog with tabs) where a form contains tabs, one tab for each user-type task, or Group box (group of boxes) where each user-type task is a group. It must be taken into account that transformation rule 2 is complemented by transformation rule R0 in order to be able to use the attributes of the UML class diagram and convert them into graphical components such as text box, combo box, list box, etc.

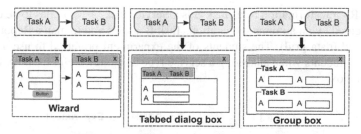

Fig. 1. R2 transformation rule example.

4   Definition of Improved Transformation Rules

This section shows the transformation rules that were improved in the EduBPMN method. In order to improve these rules, the results of the transformation rules that obtained the worst results in an experiment in 2019 have been considered. For this experiment, nine transformation rules of the EduBPMN method were evaluated with students from the University of Valencia (Spain) [4]. These worse results are due to the fact that the students used other graphical components that were not similar to the graphical components of the transformation rules of the EduBPMN method (these transformation rules are R2 and R3 (sequence pattern), R7 (implicit decision pattern) and R8 (generic transformation rule for any pattern)). To improve the transformation rules for this article, we will use the graphical components that the students voluntarily preferred to draw in the validated experiment.

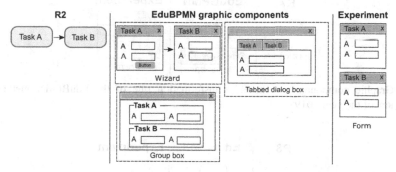

Fig. 2. Graphic components of the R2 transformation rule of the EduBPMN method and Experiment of the year 2019.

Figure 2 shows the R2 transformation rule used with the sequential pattern, where BPMN User type tasks are displayed sequentially. For each user type task (Task A and Task B) they allow mapping a Wizard (navigation assistant), where each user type task is a form, Tabbed dialog box (dialog box with tabs) where each user type task is a tab, or Group box, where each user type task is a group. The students, when analyzing the sequence of two user-type tasks in the experiment, preferred to use simple Forms, this must be because the students considered that using forms is more intuitive. Figure 3 shows the R3 transformation rule, Task B is a Service task. A result has to be displayed that is executed by an automatic operation. Task B allows you to map a Report (report) or a Datagrid (data grid). The students of the experiment preferred to use a Message box, but the students when analyzing a service type task, they prefer to show the results in Message box.

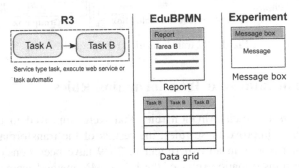

Fig. 3. Graphic components of the R3 transformation rule of the EduBPMN method and Experiment of the year 2019.

Figure 4 shows the R7 transformation rule that is used in the simple type event, this event allows to map a Hyperlink or Menu bar, but most of the students when analyzing the simple type event in the experiment preferred to use a Form.

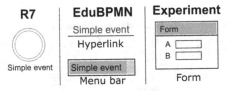

Fig. 4. Graphic components of the R7 transformation rule of the EduBPMN method and Experiment of the year 2019

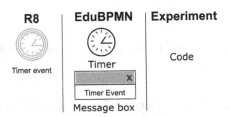

Fig. 5. Graphic components of the R8 transformation rule of the EduBPMN method and Experiment of the year 2019

Figure 5 shows the R8 transformation rule that uses a timer event, which allows mapping a Timer (clock) or Message box (message box). The students, when analyzing the timer event in the experiment, preferred not to use any graphic component, and only use code (textual description), which for them is very common to represent time in code. In addition, for the R0 transformation rule that consists of three attributes of the UML class diagram, more graphic components were assigned for five attributes according to the data type, these data types are: (Date, Char, Real, Media, URL). This was based on the analysis of Bizagi projects that contain UML class diagrams and we verified which graphical components map from the data attributes. Table 1 shows the incorporation of more attributes mapped to graphic components. It has been considered that a stereotype is assigned to each graphic component to avoid ambiguity in the extension of the BPMN model:

Table 1. R0 transformation rule with Data type and Graphics components.

Rules of EduBPMN Method	Date type	Graphics Components
R0	String	Text box
	Boolean	Check box
	Int	Combo box List box Acummulator Slider
	Date	Text box
	Char	Text box
	Real	Text box
	Media	Push button, linked to the media manager
	URL	Link

Table 2 shows a summary of the improved rules of EduBPMN with its graphic components. Each graphic component was assigned a stereotype by the researchers, taking into account that in this document a new experiment will be carried out with these transformation rules. For the R2 and R7 transformation rules, the <<form>> stereotype is used to generate a form, for the R3 transformation rule the <<message>> stereotype is used to generate a Message box, only for the R8 transformation rule the stereotype will not be used since the code will have to be done manually, for the R0 rule the following stereotypes will be used: (i) << text>> stereotype to generate a Text box, (ii) <<stereotype check>> to generate a Check box, (iii) stereotype <<combo>> to generate a Combo box, (iv) stereotype <<list>> to generate a List box, (v) stereotype <<accumulator>> to generate an Accumulator, (vi) stereotype <<slider>> to generate a Slider, (vii) stereotype <<media>> to generate a Push button, (viii) stereotype <<link>> to generate a links.

Table 2. Summary of improved transformation rules.

Transformation rules	Graphics components	Stereotypes
R2	Form	<<form>>
R3	Message box	<<message>>
R7	Form	<<form>>
R8	Code	–
R0	Text box	<<text>>
	Check box	<<check>>
	List box	<<list>>
	Accumulator	<<accumulator>>
	Slider	<<slider>>
	Push button	<<media>>
	Link	<<link>>

5 Planning and Definition of the Experiment

This section describes the experiment to be able to validate EduBPMN rules that were modified by the 2019 experiment for the R2, R3, R7 and R8, in addition to the R0 rule. This section is structured as follows: first it shows the research questions with their hypotheses, then the experimental design that is detailed with its results.

5.1 Research Questions and Hypotheses

This section shows the research questions with the prefix name (PI).

PI1: What is the correctness of the transformation rules regarding how subjects design graphical components from a BPMN model supplemented with a UML class diagram? Correctness is defined as the degree to which a system or component is free from faults in its specification, design and implementation according to the IEEE [30]. To address this property, we want to analyze the hypothesis H1: The rules used by the subjects are similar to the proposed rules.

PI2: What is the satisfaction of the transformation rules by the subjects to map BPMN to graphical components? Satisfaction is defined as satisfaction and positive attitudes towards the use of a product [31]. We measure satisfaction in terms of how comfortable developers feel while building a system. To address this research question, we want to analyze hypothesis H2: Subjects perceive as useful the use of any transformation rule to map BPMN to graphical components.

5.2 Experiment Method

Response Variables and Their Metrics. The experiment uses two response variables: one variable to evaluate the correctness of the transformation rules of the EduBPMN method (PI1), and another variable to measure the satisfaction of the subjects regarding the mapping of BPMN to graphical components (PI2). The correctness of the transformation rules (PI1) is measured as the percentage of the transformation rule mapping that the subjects would use of our rules without knowing it. For example, if a subject maps the rules R2, R3 of the provided model, while our proposal is to use R2, R4, this means that they agree on a rule that is proposed, therefore, the correctness for the subjects is: $1/2 \times 100\% = 50\%$, the value close to 100% means that the subjects apply the same rules that we propose.

Rule correctness = Number of rules used by a subject of the reference set × 100%/Total number of rules used by a subject.

The satisfaction of the transformation rules (PI2) is measured as the numerical sum of the assigned values of the sixteen definitions of the Moody's framework [13] based on the work of Lindland's [14] which is a widely used and validated framework. Each definition contains a response group based on a Likert scale: 1 = Totally disagree, 2 = Fairly disagree, 3 = Neutral, 4 = Fairly agree, 5 = Totally agree. The result of the sum of the values is measured in the following ranking: 1–16 = Totally disagree, 17–32 = Fairly disagree, 33–48 = Neutral, 49–64 = Fairly agree, 65–80 = Totally agree. For this variable, we do not measure the satisfaction of the subjects with respect to our proposed rules, but what is the satisfaction on the part of the subjects if, in general, the concept of using transformation rules to map from BPMN to graphical components existed, this is important to know if the use of transformation rules is necessary. For example, a subject answers 10 questions with Totally agree = 5, and 6 with Fairly agree = 4, the total result is: $(10 \times 5) + (6 \times 4) = 74$ (Totally agree).

Experiment Problems. The experiment has an experimental problem, this problem is small to avoid fatigue of the subjects and limit the experiment with a duration of one hour. The experimental problem is described below. The BPMN model is structured in four sections, where each section intends to generate a graphic component, where the subject does not know these proposed graphic components.

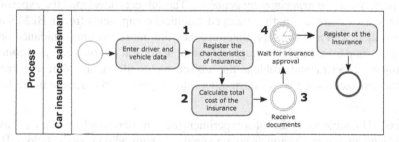

Fig. 6. BPMN model of the experiment problem

Figure 6 shows the four sections: Section 1, are the user type tasks "Enter driver and vehicle data" and "Register the characteristics of the insurance", Section 2, is the service type task "Calculate total cost of the insurance", Section 3 is the simple type event "Receive documents", Section 4 is the timer type event "Wait for insurance approval".

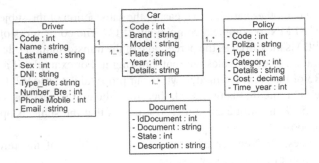

Fig. 7. UML class diagram of the Experimental Problem

Figure 7 shows the UML class diagram of the experimental problem, the classes are Driver, Vehicle, Policy and Document, each class has its attributes and data types.

Experiment Procedure. The procedure for the experiment was structured in a one hour session.

Introduction to BPMN: Before the subjects carried out the experiment, they were given a document about the elements of the BPMN model two weeks in advance. In addition, before the experiment, an explanation was given to the subjects about this document with a duration of 10 min. *Fill in a test: Before developing the experiment*: the subjects filled out a test about questions from the BPMN model. This serves so that only subjects with knowledge of the BPMN model can develop the experiment. The test consists of eight questions about the BPMN model with four answer alternatives, and one possible correct answer. Each correct question is worth one point, and each wrong question is worth 0 points. We consider that subjects with a score greater than 6 points could carry out the experiment. All 31 subjects exceeded a score of 6 points, therefore, all subjects were considered fit for the experiment. *Fill out a demographic questionnaire*: Each subject recorded their data such as mail, age, sex and signed a consent form to carry out the experiment. *Solve the experimental problem:* The subjects developed the experimental problem in a 40-min session, they mapped graphical components from a BPMN model complemented with a UML class diagram, they did not receive any guidance on how they should map from BPMN to graphical components. *Fill out the post-questionnaire:* Finishing the experimental problem, the subjects had to fill out an online questionnaire about the satisfaction of the transformation rules in general, the questionnaire lasts 10 min.

Subjects. The subjects for the rules experiment are considered end users, it was based on subjects who are not professionals but university students who know the field of Human Computer Interaction (HCI). In this experiment, the objective is to evaluate subjects so that they can map from BPMN to graphical components, the subjects were students, because experiments with real designers are expensive to involve. Furthermore, using visual editors would also be expensive and would have a different visual appearance with respect to the objective of our experiment. The sample of students was from the Software Engineering Degree of the Peruvian University of Applied Sciences. There were 31 subjects (25 men and 6 women, 28 with ages in the range of 17–20, 3 with ages in the range of 21–24, M = 19, SD = 1.39) with low knowledge in BPMN models, but with high knowledge in graphic component design. All participated voluntarily, they were instructed to develop the experiment and draw the graphical components with paper and pencil from a BPMN model and a UML class diagram. Table 3 shows the results of the subjects about the knowledge of the BPMN model, UML Class Diagram and Graphic Components, where we can say that the subjects before the experiment had basic knowledge about the BPMN model, for which they were trained. It must be taken into account that they did have medium and high knowledge of the UML class diagram and the design of the graphic components.

Table 3. Knowledge of BPMN, UML Class diagram, and Graphical Components

Knowledge of	Nothing	Low	Half	High
BPMN model	0	20	9	2
UML Class diagram	0	13	17	1
Design of graphics components	0	2	13	16

6   Results

The metrics were calculated through a Microsoft Office Excel 2020 sheet in an anonymous format so that the subjects could not be identified.

6.1   Correctness of Transformation Rules

The subjects drew graphical components from a BPMN model and a UML class diagram, where they were compared with the transformation rules of the EduBPMN method.

Table 4. Correctness percentage of transformation rules

Experiment Problem	Correctness percentage
Section 1	100%
Section 2	50%
Section 3	100%
Section 4	100%
Average	87.50%

Table 4 shows the percentage of correctness of each of the four sections of the experimental problem, the sections of the experimental problem that had the best results were Sections 1, 3 and 4, with a value of 100% correctness. This suggests that the graphical components that the subjects mapped are the same graphical components that we propose in the improved transformation rules of EduBPMN. For Section 1, most of the subjects used a Form similar to the one proposed by the R2 that is complemented with the fields of the attributes of the UML class diagram using the R0. Section 3, most of the subjects use a Form, being a graphic component similar to the one we propose that is complemented by R0. For Section 4, the subjects did not use any graphic component but used code (textual description). The rule that obtained the worst results was Section 2 with a value of 50% correctness. This suggests that for the subjects, this section was not very intuitive to generate a graphic component similar to the one we propose with our rules. Subjects prefer to use a Form instead of a Message box, as proposed in our proposal. This suggests that the result of the correctness of the transformation rules is positive with 87.50%. Therefore, most of the subjects used the same improved rules that we have proposed.

Table 5 shows the frequency of the transformation rules that the subjects used in each section of the experimental problem and the proposal of the transformation rules of EduBPMN of the document. For Section 1 they agree with the two proposed transformation rules R0 and R2, for Section 2 they only agree with one transformation rule R0, the subjects used Another Rule (OR), for Section 3 they agree with the two transformation rules R0 and R7, for Section 4 the subjects prefer to use code where they agree with the transformation rule R8.

Table 5. Correctness percentage of transformation rules

Section	Rules used by subjects	Proposed rules EduBPMN Method
Section 1	R0 (31), R2 (31)	R0–R2
Section 2	OR (31), R0 (31), R3(0)	R0–R3
Section 3	R0 (31), R7 (31)	R0–R7
Section 4	R8 (31)	R8

6.2 Satisfaction of Transformation Rules

Satisfaction is measured in terms of Perceived Ease of Use (FUP), Perceived Utility (UP) and Intention to Use (UI), on a 5-point Likert scale (the higher the score on the scale, the greater the satisfaction). It is measured through a questionnaire structured as follows (6 questions for FUP, 8 questions for UP, 2 questions for UI).

Figure 8 shows a divergent stacked bar of the answers provided by the subjects to the transformation rules questionnaire, regarding the Perceived Ease of Use (FUP) approximately 36% totally agree and 57% quite agree (93% total). Therefore, most of the subjects consider that the existence of transformation rules is important where they can be useful and easy to use to map from BPMN to graphical components. Regarding Perceived Utility (UP), approximately 26% fully agree and 69% quite agree (95% total).

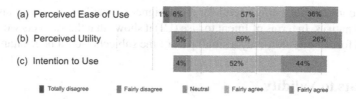

(a) Perceived Ease of Use   1% 6%   57%   36%

(b) Perceived Utility   5%   69%   26%

(c) Intention to Use   4%   52%   44%

■ Totally disagree   ■ Fairly disagree   ■ Neutral   ■ Fairly agree   ■ Fairly agree

Fig. 8. Distribution of the results of the questionnaire questions.

Therefore, most of the subjects find the use of transformation rules to map BPMN to graphical components useful. Regarding the Intention of Use (UI), approximately 44% fully agree and 52% quite agree (96% in total). Therefore, most of the subjects consider that they would intend to use transformation rules to map BPMN to graphical components. It must be taken into account that in FUP (6% neutral), UP (5% neutral) and UI (4% neutral), only a minimum percentage consider that the use of transformation rules would be indifferent. We conclude that the subjects perceive as useful the use of any transformation rule to map BPMN to graphical components.

7   Discussion

This section reviews the results of the experiment, for each variable the results are discussed. The results of the Correctness of the transformation rules show that the subjects use the same rules that are proposed in this article. The transformation rules that yielded the best results are the R2, R7 and R8. For the R2, most of the subjects consider that from a set of user-type tasks in a sequential manner it must be transformed into simple forms, with the fields that are extracted from the UML class diagram, unlike using Wizard, Tabbed dialog box, or Group bx as proposed above, this suggests that the subjects with sider that it is more common and intuitive to use a form for the rule. For the R7, most of the subjects prefer that from a simple event type it be transformed into a form because this allows data to be recorded, this suggests that the subjects do not intend to use Hyperlink or Menu bar as previously proposed, but rather a form with its data fields. For the R8, most of the subjects prefer that from a timer event the representation must be in code using time intervals so that it can perform an action, taking into account that the use of time intervals as a graphic component is not frequent except in the code. The transformation rule that obtained the worst results was the R3, this because it is ambiguous and interpretation is needed to represent it in a specific graphic component. For this R3, most of the subjects prefer that from a service type task it is transformed into a form, because this allows to display a result that is processed in the service type task, this suggests that the subjects do not intend to use a Message box as proposed in this article, so it is not very intuitive. The results with the Satisfaction of the generalization of the rules show that the subjects consider that in terms of Perceived Ease of Use (FUP), the existence of transformation rules to map BPMN to graphic components with easy-to-use and subject-friendly characteristics would be very important, the majority chose quite agree and totally agree. In terms of Perceived Utility (UP) it shows that the majority of the subjects consider that the transformation rules would improve the development of graphic components, being useful for the designer so that he can choose and modify design alternatives. In terms of Intent to Use (UI) it shows that the subjects would intend to use transformation rules, only a small part of the subjects would be hesitant to use.

8   Threats to Validity

This section shows the validation of the threats that could affect the development of the subjects in the experiment. Threats are described according to Wohlin's classification [32]. For each group of threats they will be described according to the classification of the group of threats within four types:

Validity at Conclusion. This type of threat refers to the ability to draw the correct conclusion about treatment and outcome relationships. The experiment can suffer from the following threats of this type: Random heterogeneity subjects, which means that there is always heterogeneity in a study group. To minimize this threat, we have recruited subjects who are students of the Software Engineering career who have the same profile where they took courses on Human-Computer Interaction and graphic components. The subjects had to register a demographic questionnaire where we can know that they have similar profiles. **Internal validity.** This type of threats analyzes the influences that can affect the causality factor. The experiment may suffer from the following threats of this type: History, which means that differences may arise when treatments are applied at different times. To minimize this threat, the experiment was carried out in one session lasting one hour. Another threat that can appear is Subjects' Experience, which means that the subjects' experience is not enough to perform the experiment. To minimize this threat, subjects have a year and a half practice programming graphic components. Regarding the BPMN model, the subjects were trained with a guide document and training before starting the experiment. **Construct validity.** This type of threat refers to generalizing the result of the experiment to the concept or theory behind the experiment. The experiment can suffer from the following threats of this type: Hypothesis Guessing, which means that when people participate in the experiment, they can try to figure out the purpose of the experiment and act to improve its results. To minimize this threat, the researchers did not mention any data about the experiment's research questions. **External Validity.** This type of threat refers to conditions that limit our ability to generalize the results of our experiments to industrial practice. The experiment can suffer the following threats of this type: Interaction of the environment and the treatment, this means that the effect of not having the experimental environment or material representative of industrial practice. The experiment is run in an academic setting and the results can only be generalized in such a setting. Another threat that can appear is the Interaction of the environment and the treatment, which means that the effect of having a population of subjects that is not representative of the population that we want to generalize. With results obtained from the subjects, it is not possible to generalize and guarantee that the results are valid for other experiments with subjects with a different profile.

9 Conclusions and Future Work

This article presents four improved transformation rules for EduBPMN that allows the generation of graphical components design alternatives from a BPMN model complemented with the UML class diagram. The transformation rules that were improved are the following: the transformation rules R2, R3, R7, R8 were improved from a 2019 experiment with students from the University of Valencia (Spain). The graphical components that most of the students have preferred in that experiment were used. The graphical components of the R0 transformation rule were extended based on Bizagi projects that have a UML class diagram. The new data attributes were identified to see what graphical components they generate. Using the five improved rules of EduBPMN, this article ran an experiment to test them. This experiment is based on two metrics: (i) correctness of the transformation rules and (ii) satisfaction of the generalization of the transformation rules. The result of the correctness of the transformation rules shows that most of the subjects have drawn graphical components from the BPMN complemented with the UML class diagram, where these graphical components are similar to the graphical components of the improved transformation rules proposed in this article. In addition, the satisfaction result shows positive results where the subjects consider that the existence would be useful and would intend to use transformation rules to map from BPMN to graphical components in a general way. The experiment suffers from the following limitations: (i) to develop experiments with more complex projects of companies with several processes, (ii) the other transformation rules of EduBPMN were improved from the results of the 2019 experiment. As future work, the following has been considered: (i) develop more experiments with various subjects in order to obtain a family of experiments and analyze their data; (ii) carry out experiments with more complex BPMN projects.

Acknowledgements. This work has been developed with the help of the Generalitat Valenciana through the GENI project (CIAICO/2022/229) and the PDC2021-121243-I00 project financed by the Spanish Ministry of Science and Innovation.

References

1. Mellor, S.J., Clark, T., Futagami, T.: Model-driven development: guest editors' introduction. IEEE Softw. **20**, 14–18 (2003)
2. Diaz, E., Panach, J.I., Rueda, S., Pastor, O.: Towards a method to generate GUI prototypes from BPMN. In: 2018 12th International Conference on Research Challenges in Information Science, (RCIS), pp. 1–12 (2018)
3. Diaz, E., Panach, J.I., Rueda, S., Pastor, O.: Generación de Interfaces de Usuario a partir de Modelos BPMN con Estereotipos. Presented at the Jornada de la Sociedad de Ingeniería de Software y Tecnologías de Desarrollo de Software (SISTEDES) (2018)
4. Díaz, E., Panach, J.I., Rueda, S., Vanderdonckt, J.: An empirical study of rules for mapping BPMN models to graphical user interfaces. Multimed. Tools Appl. **80**, 9813–9848 (2021)
5. Díaz, E., Panach, J.I., Rueda, S., Distante, D.: A family of experiments to generate graphical user interfaces from BPMN models with stereotypes. J. Syst. Softw. **173**, 110883 (2021)
6. Díaz, E., Panach, J.I.: New transformation rules for the EduBPMN method to generate graphical user interfaces from BPMN. In: 2022 Third International Conference on Information Systems and Software Technologies (ICI2ST), Quito, Ecuador, p. 164 (2022)

7. Díaz Suárez, J.E.: EduBPMN: Un método Basado en Reglas de Transformación para Generar Interfaces Gráficas de Usuario a partir de Modelos de Procesos de Negocio (BPMN) (2020)
8. Pastor, O., Insfrán, E., Pelechano, V., Romero, J., Merseguer, J.: OO-method: an OO software production environment combining conventional and formal methods. In: Olivé, A., Pastor, J.A. (eds.) CAiSE 1997. LNCS, vol. 1250, pp. 145–158. Springer, Heidelberg (1997). https:// doi.org/10.1007/3-540-63107-0_11
9. BPMN: Business Process Modeling Notation (2013). http://www.bpmn.org
10. Berardi, D., Calvanese, D., De Giacomo, G.: Reasoning on UML class diagrams. Artif. Intell. **168**, 70–118 (2005)
11. Bizagi: Bizagi (2002). https://www.bizagi.com/es
12. Paradigm, V.: Visual paradigm (2019)
13. Moody, D.L.: The method evaluation model: a theoretical model for validating information systems design methods. Presented at the European Conference on Information Systems (ECIS 2003), Naples, Italy (2003)
14. Lindland, O.I., Sindre, G., Solvberg, A.: Understanding quality in conceptual modeling. IEEE Softw. **11**, 42–49 (1994)
15. Bouchelligua, W., Mahfoudhi, A., Mezhoudi, N., Daassi, O., Abed, M.: User interfaces modelling of workflow information systems. In: Barjis, J. (ed.) EOMAS 2010. LNBIP, vol. 63, pp. 143–163. Springer, Heidelberg (2010). https://doi.org/10.1007/978-3-642-15723-3_10
16. Favre, J.-M., Estublier, J., Blay-Fornarino, M.: L'ingénierie dirigée par les modèles: au-delà du MDA: Hermes-Lavoisier (2006)
17. Torres, V., Pelechano, V.: Building business process driven web applications. In: Dustdar, S., Fiadeiro, J.L., Sheth, A.P. (eds.) BPM 2006. LNCS, vol. 4102, pp. 322–337. Springer, Heidelberg (2006). https://doi.org/10.1007/11841760_22
18. Lam, B.H., Nguyen, V.T.H., Phan, C.H., Truong, T.T.T.: An approach for application generation based on BPMN. In: 2020 12th International Conference on Knowledge and Systems Engineering, pp. 115–119 (KSE) (2020)
19. Sousa, K.S., Mendonça, H., Vanderdonckt, J.: A model-driven approach to align business processes with user interfaces. J. UCS **14**, 3236–3249 (2008)
20. Han, L., Zhao, W., Yang, J.: An approach towards user interface derivation from business process model. Commun. Comput. Inf. Sci. **602**, 19–28 (2016)
21. Brambilla, M., Butti, S., Fraternali, P.: WebRatio BPM: a tool for designing and deploying business processes on the web. In: Benatallah, B., Casati, F., Kappel, G., Rossi, G. (eds.) ICWE 2010. LNCS, vol. 6189, pp. 415–429. Springer, Heidelberg (2010). https://doi.org/10. 1007/978-3-642-13911-6_28
22. Cruz, E.F., da Cruz, A.M.R.: Deriving integrated software design models from BPMN business process models. In: ICSOFT, pp. 605–616 (2018)
23. Rodríguez, A., Fernández-Medina, E., Piattini, M.: A BPMN extension for the modeling of security requirements in business processes. IEICE Trans. Inf. Syst. **90**, 745–752 (2007)
24. Stroppi, L.J.R., Chiotti, O., Villarreal, P.D.: A BPMN 2.0 extension to define the resource perspective of business process models. In: XIV Congreso Iberoamericano en Software Engineering (2011)
25. Zur Muehlen, M.: Organizational management in workflow applications–issues and perspectives. Inf. Technol. Manag. **5**, 271–291 (2004)
26. Abouzid, I., Saidi, R.: Proposal of BPMN extensions for modelling manufacturing processes. In: 2019 5th International Conference on Optimization and Applications (ICOA), pp. 1–6 (2019)
27. Intrigila, B., Della Penna, G., D'Ambrogio, A.: A lightweight BPMN extension for business process-oriented requirements engineering. Computers **10**, 171 (2021)

28. Vanderdonckt, J., Nguyen, T.-D.: MoCaDiX: designing cross-device user interfaces of an information system based on its class diagram. Proc. ACM Hum. Comput. Interact. **3**, 1–40 (2019)
29. B. BPMN: Business model patterns (2017). http://resources.bizagi.com/docs/Workflow_Pat terns_using_BizAgi_Process_Modeler_Esp.pdf
30. ISO 9241-11: Guidance on Usability, ed (1998)
31. IEEE: Systems and software engineering – Vocabulary, ISO/IEC/IEEE 24765:2010(E), Ed., pp. 1–418 (2010)
32. Wohlin, C., Runeson, P., Höst, M., Ohlsson, M.C., Regnell, B., Wesslén, A.: Experimentation in Software Engineering: An Introduction: Springer, Heidelberg (2012). https://doi.org/10.1007/978-3-642-29044-2

Recommendations for the Development of Augmented Reality Video Games for Children with ADHD

Augusto Morante Castañeda, Omar Cahuana Rios, and Eduardo Díaz[(✉)]

Universidad Peruana de Ciencias Aplicadas, Prolongación Primavera 2390, Lima 15023, Peru
{U201912150,U20161C887,pcsijord}@upc.edu.pe

Abstract. Currently, the percentage of children with Attention-Deficit /Hyperactivity Disorder (ADHD) is between 7% in Peru. This is a problem for their development at an early age, since they would demonstrate poor academic performance compared to neurotypical children. This paper aim is to propose 10 recommendations to develop a video game with Augmented Reality for children with ADHD. The recommendations have been extracted from 25 research works. Specifically, the proposal is based on the extraction of recommendations for development video games with Augmented Reality for children with ADHD. The recommendations were divided into 2 categories: (i) Video game development recommendations with augmented reality, (ii) Video game components recommendations. For a better understanding, an illustrative example was developed with the use of the proposed recommendations. This work may be of interest to video game developers focused on children with ADHD.

Keywords: ADHD · Recommendations · Augmented Reality · Video game

1 Introduction

Currently one of the most common disorders in childhood is Attention Deficit/Hyperactivity Disorder (ADHD), it is characterized by symptoms of inattention, impulsivity and hyperactivity and in most cases, it is identified in the school environment. And family since children present multiple problems of cognitive, emotional and social development [1]. If not identified early or treated appropriately, it can lead to poor school performance and behavioral problems compared to their neurotypical study peers. This would have long-term consequences such as job failure, stress, low self-esteem, problems with relationships, depression or substance abuse [2].

In Peru, the accuracy of the percentage of infants who suffer from this disorder is unknown; however, it is estimated to be between 3% to 7% [2]. There are three types of ADHD [3]: (i) ADHD with a predominance of attention deficit, is more focused on lack of attention, continuous neglect, difficulty following instructions, and avoidance of tasks that require mental effort. (ii) ADHD with a predominance of hyperactivity, is more focused on nervous movements of the hands or legs, difficulty staying seated, running or climbing on things excessively, talking excessively, constantly interrupting

J. A. Lossio-Ventura et al. (Eds.): SIMBig 2023, CCIS 2142, pp. 316–330, 2024.
https://doi.org/10.1007/978-3-031-63616-5_24

people, difficulty waiting or wait, (iii) combined ADHD, which presents the symptoms of both cases.

The contribution of this work is the proposal of 10 recommendations for the development of video game applications with augmented reality for children with ADHD, the proposed recommendations were extracted from the analysis of 25 research works related to the use of video games with the use of Augmented Reality. The recommendations are divided into 2 categories: (i) recommendations on the development of augmented reality in mobile application video games, where different types of tools for the development of video games are explained, as well as patterns and methods to improve the experience of children; (ii) recommendations on video game components for children with ADHD, which indicates the impact of using video games on the approaches of patients with ADHD and their cognitive consequences of learning. These recommendations for the development of video games for children with ADHD are aimed at children between the ages of 4 and 10, so it is a stage where children can have their ADHD treated.

The scope of the research is applied to an illustrative example, which has the purpose of showing the use of the development of a video game that has implemented the set of recommendations regarding its graphic components or design patterns.

The rest of the paper is structured as follows. Section 2 reviews the literature related to the development of video games with augmented reality divided into 2 subgroups. Section 3 defines the recommendations for the development of the video game. Section 4 defines the illustrative example of the project based on the recommendations extracted from the articles. Finally, Sect. 5 presents the conclusions of the work, the limitations, as well as future work.

2   Related Works

In this section, we review works related to the development of video games with augmented reality for children with ADHD. This is achieved by performing a Targeted Literature Review (TLR), it is a non-systematic and informative literature review that aims to keep only the significant references to keep biases to a minimum.

The proposal of recommendations for the development of video games with augmented reality for children with ADHD is based on research work collected from the Scopus bibliographic repository (see https://www.scopus.com/home.uri).

The search string used in this work is the following: ("ADHD" AND "augmented reality" OR "rules" OR "mobile app" OR "design patterns").

The inclusion criteria are: (1) topics related to the use of mobile applications with augmented reality, (2) development of applications for neurodivergent children, qualification received by patients with neurological disorders. The exclusion criteria are: (1) topics not related to the use of Augmented Reality, (2) topics not linked to children with ADHD. The first search shows 38 scientific articles, therefore, with the established criteria, 10 scientific articles have been selected. The research works were divided into two groups: (i) Use of augmented reality in mobile application video games, and (ii) video games for children with ADHD.

2.1 Use of Augmented Reality in Mobile Application Video Games

Brun et al. [4] developed CartonEd, a complete and open kit designed for children that allows them to build their own Augmented Reality (AR) device. The study examines the usability of the guide application and the construction process, shows the main components of the CartonEd kit and the results of an evaluation carried out with 57 children and adolescents (from 8 to 16 years old), which show a positive result regarding your built device (all functional), your feelings and desires in relation to augmented reality.

Liu et al. [5] presented a bibliometric analysis and literature review on the Geo AR mobile game, a new form of video game enabled by geolocation and augmented reality technology. Furthermore, they mention that Geo AR mobile games be built as "full games", that is, with sensors and augmented reality to achieve sustainable success.

Bhadra et al. [6] presented a new ABC3D game developed with augmented reality, which allows improving the knowledge of literacy based on writing in preschool children. This video game takes advantage of the motivating power of interest and the possibilities of augmented reality to involve children in the practice of writing-based literacy. ABC3D is bimodal, consisting of: (i) a "scan" mode that allows children to scan drawn letters and view three-dimensional images of content starting with the same letter and (ii) a "vehicle" mode that challenges Children collect objects that begin with certain letters as specified by the software or the instructor.

Saleem et al. [7] investigated the influence of augmented reality mobile applications on consumers' behavioral intention to use this technology, using the technology acceptance model. Partial least squares structural equation modeling was applied to verify path relationships. The findings of the study indicated that the augmented reality application directly influences perceived usefulness, perceived ease of use, perceived enjoyment, and indirectly influences attitude toward use and behavioral intention to use.

Saragih & Suyoto [8] propose an interactive mobile application and augmented reality for the tourist sites of Batam. The interactive mobile application uses marker-based augmented reality and provides information and a map of the city's tourist sites. The studio uses Android Studio to develop the prototype of the mobile application called "Kudan AR SDK" for augmented reality and Adobe XD to create the interface design.

To summarize related work considered in this group, we can stat that they different methods of using augmented reality in video games [5–8] from the development of kits to biometric analysis evidencing a pattern of skill improvements in education including different methods such as usability evaluations, user testing, video game development and augmented reality acceptance models. Therefore, it's important to use recommendations that allow you to approach video games with augmented reality.

2.2 Video Games for Children with ADHD

Rodrigo-Yanguas et al. [9] analyzed the effectiveness of a virtual reality video game, "The Secret Trail of Moon" (TSTM) for children with ADHD. Comparing with an online chess training group and a control group, the aim is to demonstrate that both TSTM and online chess are effective in children with ADHD clinically stable on medication, and highlighting the advantages of serious video games in virtual reality.

Peñuelas-Calvo et al. [10] reviewed systematically the evidence on the use of video games as assessment tools and interventions for children with ADHD. It is suggested that gamification and cognitive training are key mechanisms in these interventions for children with ADHD. The need to optimize the software and promote collaboration between developers and health professionals for future research is emphasized.

Anae et al. [11] presented two exploratory studies carried out in children with ADHD and children without the disorder to illustrate behavioral patterns: excessive use and positive use of video games. One study investigates video game use using questionnaires, while the other is based on observing children's performance on video games. Pathological video game use may be a risk factor for the subsequent development of other addictive behaviors. However, in a playful and motivating context, children with ADHD are capable of mobilizing their attention capacities and achieving a performance equivalent to that of children without ADHD.

Faraone et al. [12] compared the diagnostic accuracy of the Conners Brief Rating Scale, Parent Version, the Conners Continuous Performance Test II, and the interactive game "Groundskeeper" in discriminating psychiatric patients from children with and without ADHD. The diagnostic accuracy of the Groundskeeper was found to be similar to the Conners Inattention Scale and superior to the CPT II. The combination of the three tests improved diagnostic accuracy. These preliminary findings suggest that computer games may be useful in the ADHD diagnostic process.

Cardona-Reyes et al. [1] propose the use of virtual reality environments as an alternative to support the learning process in children with special educational needs, such as ADHD and other associated disorders that children present. These proposed virtual reality environments are designed under a user-centered approach and their contents are in line with expert therapeutic guidelines. They developed a case study in which the child's experience is evaluated through the use of an interactive environment to support the special educational needs of primary school children in an educational institution in Mexico.

As a conclusion on works considered in this group, we can state that there are works focused on the development of video games with augmented reality [10–12] and virtual reality [1, 9] for children with ADHD. Among them, the effectiveness of a video game is analyzed, exploring approaches and methodologies, comparing it with other video games, improving the cognitive process. They focus on the use of assessment, treatment and educational support tools in these students with ADHD using different patterns and methodologies identified to improve the therapeutic approach to ADHD. This shows that video games are important for children with ADHD.

3 Definition of Recommendations for the Development of the Video Game

This section defines a set of ten recommendations for the development of video game applications with augmented reality for children with ADHD. The recommendations were based on the analysis of 25 research works that develop augmented reality video games for children with ADHD, to extract generic recommendations, each recommendation allows indicating that it should be used in the development of a video game with certain contexts such as: (i) the use of augmented reality, (ii) the design of software patterns, (iii) the number of sessions, (iv) cooperative games, (v) gamification techniques and others. For each recommendation, a prefix "R" with a number was used sequentially, for example, we have recommendations R1, R2, and so on. Next, we describe the recommendations for the development of the video game, that were identified in the 25 research works:

3.1 Video Game Development Recommendations

R1: Works that link the development of Augmented Reality (AR) in applications were analyzed: (i) Schmalstieg and Höllerer et al. [13] indicate that perception used by computers in the real world amplifies human perception and cognition in a notable way, and work in the field requires knowledge in different disciplines such as computer graphics or human-computer interaction. (ii) Liu et al. [14] developed The Go-Light, augmented reality is used for the safety and protection of children at home. The use of a friendly character such as an "elf" (creature from Norse mythology) stands out, which discourages children from approaching dangerous objects or areas through actions such as dancing or jumping. (iii) Blum et al. [15] developed TimeWarp, it is a game that takes place in the open air, set in a medieval context, in which the player must find elves within a stable area. In terms of scenarios, the player can experience a city in periods from times like the Roman era, or even contemporary Europe. In conclusion, the use of augmented reality in video games can provide an interactive and stimulating environment, mainly the use of fantasy characters and environments, being beneficial for children with ADHD.

R2: Works on design patterns for video game development was analyzed, the patterns analyzed are: (a) Model View Controller (MVC) design pattern, (b) Observer pattern. The Model View Controller design pattern is the most used according to: Gamma et al. [16] show the benefits of using this design pattern are determining multiple views towards a model to provide multiple presentations to the user. The architecture of this model is conceived by adopting three architectural principles; be thin client, be layered with MVC and be balanced between client side and server side. Notable works on mobile applications with this Controller View Model pattern are provided by (i) Zhang et al. [17] discuss about the implementation of a mobile augmented reality application (MAR Observer) and a server (MAR Server). For this implementation, a clear structure is demonstrated; by implementing the pattern, developers can have a more organized structure. The MVC Model would handle the business logic and data manipulation, the View would handle the presentation of augmented reality effects, and the Controller would be responsible for handling user input and coordinating the Model and View. (ii) Tenemaza et al. [18] presented the MVC pattern in their project Mobile Return, a mobile application that uses adaptive augmented reality to help people with mental disabilities in their daily route, it's architecture is composed of: (a) the model, which comprises the logic business and (b) the data model. Every time the application receives a new position from the user's GPS (Global Positioning System), it calculates the return route. If the user leaves the allowed radius, the application warns the caregivers and sends messages with the information necessary to locate them. The Observer pattern according to Gamma et al. [16] serves mainly for graphical interface tools and allows application data as well as presentations to be reused independently. Some works that use this pattern are: (i) Hamza et al. [19] present TCAIOSC, this is a solution that seeks to facilitate the development of cross-platform mobile applications, it is mentioned that the use of the Observer pattern within Android mobile applications allows responding to events by the user, such as clicking on a button. or in an image. (ii) Hornariu et al. [20] present ObDroid, it is an experimental application that uses the Observer pattern for events within the Android device itself, such as messages, calls and location. In this case, the established components act as observers, waiting for certain events or content changes to occur. When an event or change is detected, the observer receives a notification and a background service is started to collect the relevant data. This Observer pattern allows the application to be highly responsive to changes on the device, where data must be collected and sent to the server. In conclusion, the Model View Controller pattern is recommended, which facilitates modularity and separation of the responsibilities of the game logic, user interfaces, and data management. In addition, the Observer behavior pattern is recommended, it can be useful for handle events and actions in the game, which is relevant in an AR environment and even more so for detecting and receiving changes in data from ADHD patients.

R3: Works and applications were analyzed about the software development approaches that should be taken for the development of applications. (i) Young et al. [21] propose iterative design as one of the most relevant in their mHealth project, a mobile health application designed to perform cognitive evaluations on older adults. The authors consider it as an approach that allows constant improvement of the product or service to the long of the time. (ii) Hooglugt and Ludden [22] present MoveDaily, a mobile application that seeks to help people adopt healthier lifestyles and increase their physical activity and focuses on exploring how digital interventions can be designed to encourage change of behavior. (iii) The PuzzleWalk application, a mobile application designed to promote physical activity in adults with autism spectrum disorder. For the development of this application, the iterative development was divided into four phases, (a) defining the target user behavior, (b) conducting participatory sessions, (c) usability evaluation through test patients, and (d) evaluation of the effectiveness and viability of the system. In conclusion, it is recommended that video game development should focus on iterative development and continuous delivery to be able to adjust the game based on user feedback.

R4: Work on immediate feedback mechanisms was analyzed in the work of (i) Bång et al. [23] presented the Power Explorer project, a mobile video game that aims to transform the home into a persuasive environment where users can learn about household appliances and electricity consumption. The video game provides practically instantaneous feedback on the consumption of household appliances. This sets the feedback into an activity framework that can facilitate understanding of the energy consumption of household appliances. They also suggest that immediate feedback and contextualization can be means to change people's energy consumption patterns at home. (ii) Muis et al. [24] examined two studies about children's perceptions of technology use in the classroom and the effects of receiving immediate feedback while using this technology in the context of developing literacy skills. (iii) Cho and Castañeda [25] determined whether there were changes in students' motivational and affective engagement after participating in video game activities with a grammar-focused mobile application in

Spanish courses. With immediate feedback, students can instantly check whether their answers are correct or incorrect, allowing them to learn and improve at their own pace. In conclusion, immediate feedback is recommended allowing children with ADHD to make a direct connection between their actions and their results. This can help them develop a better understanding of the rules of the game and improve their ability to follow these rules. Additionally, providing this type of feedback in a fun and engaging format can help maintain the child's motivation and attention.

In summary, the recommendations extracted from this category result in using augmented reality, Model View Controller pattern, Observer pattern, iterative development and immediate feedback for the video game.

3.2   Video Game Component Recommendations

R5: Works related to gamification techniques that the video game must have were analyzed. (i) Ahmad et al. [26] designed a mobile video game based on existing literature on techniques used to retain attention and engage children with ADHD. They mention that rewards can be used to control the behavior of children with ADHD and how they can be used so that children can get involved in the video game. Rewards should be given frequently and should be withheld for tasks not completed or for not following instructions. (ii) Chen et al. [27] make it possible to help children with ADHD manage their medication, every time children report medication intake, parents are notified and the corresponding pending reward points appear for the approval of the parents. Parents can then send a brief message of encouragement along with approved reward points to reinforce children's positive behaviors. (iii) Said et al. [28] developed a mobile video game for children with ADHD. Although the document does not provide specific details on how the game uses rewards, it mentions that rewards are an important factor in engaging children with ADHD. Children with ADHD are more sensitive to rewards and providing some type of reward for each successful achievement can help engage them during the learning process. In conclusion, it is recommended to use gamification techniques as rewards in the video game, this allows children with ADHD to be involved and motivated. Rewards play a crucial role in encouraging positive behaviors and adherence to routines and tasks.

R6: Works about the concept of video game sessions were analyzed. In the work of (i) Morón et al. [29] focus on the use of a mobile application video game, which helps the rehabilitation of patients with acquired brain damage. The video game is part of an e-care and e-rehabilitation platform, and focuses on cognitive training. Short sessions are not explicitly detailed in the document, but it is mentioned that adjustments were made based on user feedback, which could mean shorter or longer game sessions. (ii) Choik and Paik [30] developed a virtual reality upper extremity rehabilitation program using video game applications. Patients in the intervention group received 30 min of conventional occupational therapy and 30 min of the virtual reality upper extremity rehabilitation program. Play sessions last 5 to 10 min and are carried out as part of a broader rehabilitation program that also includes conventional occupational therapy. (iii) Jung et al. [31] introduced Neuro-World, a set of six mobile video games designed to challenge visuospatial short-term memory and selective attention, allowing users to self-administer the assessment of their level of cognitive impairment. Patients played six video games on Neuro-World for a total of 30 min, or approximately five minutes per game. In addition, it is mentioned that patients can play up to 30 min a day, two days a week. In conclusion, the use of short sessions for the video game is recommended, with a maximum time of 30 min per game, which allows users to participate in therapy or evaluation in a way that adapts to their individual needs and abilities.

R7: Works about cooperative games were analyzed, in the work of. (i) Zheng et al. [32] focus on the use of serious video games (video games for educational or medical purposes) to help patients with ADHD. Cooperative video games promote communication with other users. Serious video games can improve the attention and suppress the impulse of ADHD patients, and also exercise the daily living skills and social skills of ADHD patients. (ii) De la Guía et al. [33], cooperative video games in this system involve the interaction of multiple users with distributed and tangible interfaces to improve their cognitive and communication skills. De la Guía et al. [34] present Sti-Cap, an interactive system that uses games and RFID (Radio Frequency Identification) and WiFi (Wireless Network Technology) technology for the distribution of user interfaces. Cooperative video games in this system improve the participation and integration of users, also improving their communication skills, self-confidence, self-awareness and ability to work with others. In conclusion, it is recommended to use cooperative video games as a tool to improve the cognitive and social skills of children with ADHD. Through interaction and collaboration, children can improve their attention, impulsivity, daily living skills, and social skills.

R8: Works about the concept of the integration of motion sensors and eye tracking in the development of augmented reality video games for children with ADHD is a promising strategy, supported by various research. These studies suggest that the use of eye-tracking technology and motion sensors can significantly enrich children's play and learning experience. For example, a study by Lee-Cultura et al. [35] on touchless motion-based games for children, "Motion-Based Touchless Games" (MBTG), highlights how children's digital avatars can efficiently communicate their motion-based interactivity, which is crucial in experiential learning. Additionally, games' ability to collect multimodal data through sensor technology allows for a deeper understanding of children's cognitive and affective states during play. Another of Lee-Culture et al. [36] studied, emphasizes the importance of varying degrees of avatar representation (ASR) and its impact on children's affective and behavioral processes, suggesting the need to adapt these elements in motion-based games to better support learning experiences. Together, these findings underscore the value of incorporating motion sensors and eye tracking into augmented reality video games for children with ADHD, offering a more personalized and effective approach to enhance their gaming experience and facilitate their learning and development.

R9: Works about the concept of the recommendation to use immersive and educational narratives in the development of augmented reality video games for children with ADHD is reinforced by recent research, which highlights the effectiveness of narratives in creating meaningful learning environments. In this work Pescarin et al. [37] and Fulmore et al. [38] presented the importance of intrinsically integrating narratives with educational content and personalizing the player's experience. These narratives not only increase engagement and motivation, but also improve learning outcomes by providing meaningful and relatable contexts for students. Naul & Liu [39] reinforce these findings, demonstrating that narrative distribution, endogenous fantasy, empathetic characters and adaptive and responsive narratives are key components that improve immersion, engagement and motivation, which in turn sometimes leads to greater learning. These studies collectively suggest that immersive and educational narratives are not just a complement to educational games, but an integral element that can transform the learning experience, making it more engaging, relevant, and effective for children with ADHD.

R10: Incorporating elements of mindfulness (meditation) and relaxation in the development of video games for children with ADHD can greatly benefit from the integration of interactive technologies and games. Studies such as those conducted by Weekly et al. [40] and Amon & Campbell [41] have shown that interactive electronic devices, such as mobile applications, can play a positive role in health by teaching relaxation techniques and physiologically monitoring the user's progress. Additionally, it has been found that regular practice of mindfulness techniques, such as yoga, mental work and biofeedbacks; which are effective in rebalancing the autonomic nervous system (ANS) in pediatric populations. Culbert's study [42] highlights that careful selection of technology can be useful for children to learn and practice mindfulness skills in more engaging and friendly ways. Furthermore, it is suggested that adapting these skills to children's interests and learning styles, and presenting them in a friendly manner, is effective for therapeutic interaction. This approach may include the use of biofeedback and relaxation-based techniques to treat a variety of conditions. Therefore, incorporating elements of mindfulness and relaxation into video games for children with ADHD using these technologies can offer a powerful and engaging method to improve their attention, concentration, and overall well-being.

In summary, the key recommendations for developing video games for children with ADHD include using gamification techniques, short gaming sessions, and cooperative play. Additionally, integrating motion sensors, eye tracking, and augmented reality enhances the learning experience. Immersive narratives within games improve engagement and educational outcomes. Finally, incorporating mindfulness and relaxation techniques, supported by interactive technologies, can significantly aid in the well-being and attention of children with ADHD.

4 Illustrative Example with the Proposed Recommendations

This section shows an example of a video game that contains 5 proposed recommendations (R1, R2, R5, R6, R7) for the development of a video game for children with ADHD. Next, we describe how these recommendations would be implemented in the design and functionality of the video game called "EducAR". It is an Augmented Reality video game that seeks to improve the participation and learning of children with ADHD through an interactive and motivating environment, which incorporates fantasy characters and environments in the educational processes. This video game will only have access to the rear camera of the mobile device and will generally consist of converting what is shown on the camera to a fantasy environment.

Figure 1 shows the use of the R1 recommendation with the use of a series of friendly characters in augmented reality, which vary according to the topic of study. These characters will guide children through educational content, helping them understand concepts in a fun and interactive way. Children will have the opportunity to learn in different fantasy environments. This can be especially useful for teaching history, geography and science, as children can "travel" to different times and places.

Fig. 1. Characters exploring the fantasy world with augmented reality.

Figure 2 shows that the video game contains recommendation R5 on gamification techniques that involves rewards, the video game is divided into modules, where each module has an interactive activity that reinforces the learned content and where children, when completing these modules, receive as gold score rewards, this will keep kids motivated. These activities may include treasure hunts, puzzles, and role-playing. To keep children motivated and engaged, the application will have a rewards system. Kids will earn points for completing tasks, which they can then redeem for virtual rewards. Children will receive instant feedback on their performance, which can help improve their self-esteem and motivation.

Figure 3 shows that the video game contains recommendation R6 where it is essential to take into account the duration of the game sessions to maintain the attention and interest of children with ADHD. For this reason, the application will be designed to allow play sessions of 5 to 20 min, and children will be able to play multiple sessions. This will provide enough time for interaction and learning, but will also limit overload and allow children to take regular breaks.

Figure 4 shows that the video game contains recommendation R7 that mentions the cooperative video game. The video game will include cooperative video game features, allowing children to interact with their friends or family, encouraging collaboration and communication. These cooperative game elements could involve solving challenges together, competing in mini-games, or collaborating to achieve common goals. The video game will be compatible with most mobile devices and will comply with all privacy and safety regulations to protect children.

Fig. 2. Choice of modules where gold reward score is displayed

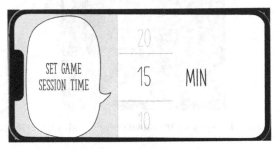

Fig. 3. Minute selection menu

Fig. 4. Link with other video game users

Figure 5 shows the video game that contains recommendation R2, where it will be based on the MVC design pattern to provide a clear and organized structure. The Model component will handle the business logic and data manipulation. For example, the child's playing progress in the video game, information about rewards earned, and lessons to be presented based on previous performance. The View component will be responsible for the presentation of augmented reality effects. It will present visual information of the fantasy environment and characters, as well as the results of user interactions. The controller component will handle user input and coordinate the Model and View. It will translate user interactions, such as touching or moving virtual objects, into commands that the Model and View can understand and respond to.

Fig. 5. Child's progress, in this case how the fantasy town improves according to the user's progress.

5 Conclusions and Future Work

This paper summarizes a set of ten recommendations for the development of a video game with augmented reality for children with ADHD. We have analyzed 25 research works about of augmented reality of mobile application video games and design patterns to identify recommendations. The recommendations have been focused on the use development of a video game for children with ADHD. Recommendation R1 indicates the use of augmented reality in the video game, recommendation R2 emphasizes the use of design patterns such as the Model View Controller design and the Observer pattern. Recommendation R3 proposes using iterative design in the video game. Recommendation R4 considers using feedback immediately. Recommendation R5 considers gamification techniques such as the use of rewards for children in the video game. Recommendation R6 considers the use of short sessions in the video game. Recommendation R7 considers that the video game must contain cooperative games. Recommendation R8 integrates motion sensors and eye-tracking to enrich learning experiences. Recommendation R9 includes immersive and educational narratives to enhance engagement and learning. Recommendation R10 considers mindfulness and relaxation elements to improve attention and well-being.

As future work, the following have been considered: (i) develop experiments with children with ADHD using a video game with the proposed recommendations, (ii) deepen the understanding of the specific challenges faced by children with ADHD and explore new strategies to address their needs in the context of video games, (iii) analyze applications that provide emotional support, offering relaxation activities, breathing exercises, interactive games to manage stress and activities to promote self-esteem in children with ADHD; (iv) identify and incorporate new patterns, set goals, and measure progress over time with apps that help track symptoms and skills; (v) develop an experiment with the proposed recommendations with children with ADHD.

References

1. Cardona-Reyes, H., Ortiz-Aguinaga, G., Barba-Gonzalez, M.L., Munoz-Arteaga, J.: User-centered virtual reality environments to support the educational needs of children with ADHD in the COVID-19 Pandemic. Revista Iberoamericana de Tecnologias Del Aprendizaje **16**(4), 400–409 (2021). https://doi.org/10.1109/RITA.2021.3135194
2. Manchego Meléndez, M.A.: El Rol del docente que atiende a niños con TDAH de nivel inicial (2021). https://repositorio.pucp.edu.pe/index/handle/123456789/179238
3. Home page | ADHD Institute (n.d.). https://adhd-institute.com/. Accessed 18 June 2023
4. Brun, D., Ruer, P., Gouin-Vallerand, C., George, S.: A toolkit for exploring augmented reality through construction with children. In: Proceedings - 2018 20th Symposium on Virtual and Augmented Reality, SVR 2018, pp. 106–113 (2018). https://doi.org/10.1109/SVR.2018.00026
5. Liu, H.X.: Building the "complete game": an overview study of a development strategy for geo AR mobile games. In: Meiselwitz, G., et al. (eds.) HCII 2022. LNCS, vol. 13517, pp. 604–622. Springer, Cham (2022). https://doi.org/10.1007/978-3-031-22131-6_45
6. Bhadra, A., et al.: ABC3D - using an augmented reality mobile game to enhance literacy in early childhood. In: 2016 IEEE International Conference on Pervasive Computing and Communication Workshops, PerCom Workshops 2016 (2016). https://doi.org/10.1109/PERCOMW.2016.7457067
7. Saleem, M., Kamarudin, S., Shoaib, H.M., Nasar, A.: Retail consumers' behavioral intention to use augmented reality mobile apps in Pakistan. J. Internet Commer. **21**(4), 497–525 (2022). https://doi.org/10.1080/15332861.2021.1975427
8. Saragih, R.E., Suyoto: Development of interactive mobile application with augmented reality for tourism sites in Batam. In: Proceedings of the World Conference on Smart Trends in Systems, Security and Sustainability, WS4 2020, pp. 512–517 (2020). https://doi.org/10.1109/WORLDS450073.2020.9210300
9. Rodrigo-Yanguas, M., et al.: A virtual reality serious videogame versus online chess augmentation in patients with attention deficit hyperactivity disorder: a randomized clinical trial. Games Health J. **10**(4) (2021). https://doi.org/10.1089/g4h.2021.0073
10. Peñuelas-Calvo, I., et al.: Video games for the assessment and treatment of attention-deficit/hyperactivity disorder: a systematic review. Eur. Child Adolesc. Psychiatry **31**(1) (2022). https://doi.org/10.1007/s00787-020-01557-w

11. Scopus - Document details - ADD/ADHD children and video games: Between excessive consumption and positive vidéo game use (n.d.)
12. Faraone, S.V., Newcorn, J.H., Antshel, K.M., Adler, L., Roots, K., Heller, M.: The groundskeeper gaming platform as a diagnostic tool for attention-deficit/hyperactivity disorder: sensitivity, specificity, and relation to other measures **26**(8), 672–685 (2016). https://doi.org/10.1089/CAP.2015.0174.https://Home.Liebertpub.Com/Cap
13. Schmalstieg, D., Hollerer, T.: Augmented reality: principles and practice. Proc. IEEE Virtual Real. **425–426** (2017). https://doi.org/10.1109/VR.2017.7892358
14. Liu, W., Lee, K.P., Gray, C.M., Toombs, A.L., Chen, K.H., Leifer, L.: Transdisciplinary teaching and learning in UX design: a program review and AR case studies. Appl. Sci. **11**(22), 10648 (2021). https://doi.org/10.3390/APP112210648
15. Blum, L., Wetzel, R., McCall, R., Oppermann, L., Broll, W.: The final TimeWarp: using form and content to support player experience and presence when designing location-aware mobile augmented reality games. In: Proceedings of the Designing Interactive Systems Conference, DIS 2012, pp. 711–720 (2012). https://doi.org/10.1145/2317956.2318064
16. Gamma, E., Helm, R., Johnson, R., Vlissides, J.: Design patterns: abstraction and reuse of object-oriented design. In: Nierstrasz, O.M. (ed.) ECOOP 1993. LNCS, vol. 707, pp. 406–431. Springer, Heidelberg (1993). https://doi.org/10.1007/3-540-47910-4_21
17. Zhang, H., Li, W., Ding, H., Yi, C., Wan, X.: Observer-pattern modeling and nonlinear modal analysis of two-stage boost inverter. IEEE Trans. Power Electron. **33**(8), 6822–6836 (2018). https://doi.org/10.1109/TPEL.2017.2756090
18. Majchrzak, T.A., Traverso, P., Monfort, V., Krempels, K.-H. (eds.): Proceedings of the 12th International Conference on Web Information Systems and Technologies, WEBIST 2016, vol. 1, Rome, Italy, 23–25 April 2016 (2016)
19. Hamza, R.B., Salama, D.I., Kamel, M.I., Yousef, A.H.: TCAIOSC: application code conversion. In: NILES 2019 - Novel Intelligent and Leading Emerging Sciences Conference, pp. 230–234 (2019). https://doi.org/10.1109/NILES.2019.8909207
20. Hornariu, M., Butean, A.: ObDroid: an Android permanent monitoring application using the observer pattern. Revista Romana de Interactiune Om-Calculator **10**(1), 25–38 (2017)
21. Young, S.R., et al.: Remote cognitive screening of healthy older adults for primary care with the MyCog mobile app: iterative design and usability evaluation. JMIR Form Res. **7**(1), e42416 (2023). https://doi.org/10.2196/42416.https://Formative.Jmir.Org/2023/1/E42416
22. Hooglugt, F., Ludden, G.D.S.: A mobile app adopting an identity focus to promote physical activity (MoveDaily): iterative design study. JMIR MHealth UHealth **8**(6) (2020). https://doi.org/10.2196/16720
23. Bång, M., Svahn, M., Gustafsson, A.: Persuasive design of a mobile energy conservation game with direct feedback and social cues (2009). https://urn.kb.se/resolve?urn=urn:nbn:se:ri:diva-23696
24. Muis, K.R., Ranellucci, J., Trevors, G., Duffy, M.C.: The effects of technology-mediated immediate feedback on kindergarten students' attitudes, emotions, engagement and learning outcomes during literacy skills development. Learn. Instr. **38**, 1–13 (2015). https://doi.org/10.1016/J.LEARNINSTRUC.2015.02.001
25. Cho, M.H., Castañeda, D.A.: Motivational and affective engagement in learning Spanish with a mobile application. System **81**, 90–99 (2019). https://doi.org/10.1016/J.SYSTEM.2019.01.008
26. Ahmad, I.S., Parhizkar, B., Pillay, S.O.: Engaging children with ADHD using mobile based games (n.d.)
27. Chen, H. et al.: Medbuddy: a mobile medicinal management system for children with ADD/ADHD. In: Donnelly, M., Paggetti, C., Nugent, C., Mokhtari, M. (eds.) ICOST 2012. LNCS, vol. 7251, pp. 286–290. Springer, Heidelberg (2012). https://doi.org/10.1007/978-3-642-30779-9_46

28. Ahmad, I.S., Ahmad, H.K., Aliyu, S.M., Ahmad, A.M.: Mathefunic: a mobile based game for engaging children with ADHD. Int. J. Perceptive Cognit. Comput. **6**(2), 60–66 (2020). https://doi.org/10.31436/IJPCC.V6I2.158

29. Moron, M.J., Yanez, R., Cascado, D., Suarez-Mejias, C., Sevillano, J.L.: A mobile memory game for patients with acquired brain damage: a preliminary usability study. In: 2014 IEEE-EMBS International Conference on Biomedical and Health Informatics, BHI 2014, pp. 302–305 (2014). https://doi.org/10.1109/BHI.2014.6864363

30. Choi, Y.H., Paik, N.J.: Mobile game-based virtual reality program for upper extremity stroke rehabilitation. J. Vis. Exp. JoVE **2018**(133) (2018). https://doi.org/10.3791/56241

31. Jung, H.T., et al.: Remote assessment of cognitive impairment level based on serious mobile game performance: an initial proof of concept. IEEE J. Biomed. Health Inform. **23**(3), 1269–1277 (2019). https://doi.org/10.1109/JBHI.2019.2893897

32. Zheng, Y., Li, R., Li, S., Zhang, Y., Yang, S., Ning, H.: A review on serious games for ADHD (2021). https://arxiv.org/abs/2105.02970v1

33. de La Guía, E., Lozano, M.D., Penichet, V.M.R.: Educational games based on distributed and tangible user interfaces to stimulate cognitive abilities in children with ADHD. Br. J. Edu. Technol. **46**(3), 664–678 (2015). https://doi.org/10.1111/BJET.12165

34. de La Guía, E., Lozano, M.D., Penichet, V.R.: Co-StiCap: system based on distributed and tangible user interfaces to improve skills in children with ADHD (n.d.). https://doi.org/10.5220/0004602800640073

35. Lee-Cultura, S., Sharma, K., Papavlasopoulou, S., Cosentino S., Giannakos, M.: Children's play and problem solving in motion-based educational games: synergies between human annotations and multi-modal data (2021). https://doi.org/10.1145/3459990.3460702

36. Lee-Cultura, S., Sharma, K., Papavlasopoulou, S., Retalis S., Giannakos, M.: Using sensing technologies to explain children's self-representation in motion-based educational games (2020). https://doi.org/10.1145/3392063.3394419

37. Pescarin, S., Fanini, B., Ferdani, D., Mifsud, K., Hamilton, A.: Optimising environmental educational narrative videogames: the case of 'a night in the forum' (2020). https://doi.org/10.1145/3424952

38. Fulmore, Y.: Video games and the customization of learning: interactive narratives as a promising design framework for crafting inclusive educational environments (2015).https://dl.acm.org/doi/10.1145/2807565.2807710

39. Naul. E., Liu, M.: Why story matters: a review of narrative in serious games (2019). https://journals.sagepub.com/doi/10.1177/0735633119859904

40. Weekly, T., Walker, N., Beck, J., Akers, S., Weaver, M.: A review of apps for calming, relaxation, and mindfulness interventions for pediatric palliative care patients (2018). https://pubmed.ncbi.nlm.nih.gov/29373515/

41. Amon, K.L., Campbell, A.: Can children with AD/HD learn relaxation and breathing techniques through biofeedback video games? (2008) https://files.eric.ed.gov/fulltext/EJ815662.pdf

42. Culbert, T.: Perspectives on technology-assisted relaxation approaches to support mind-body skills practice in children and teens: clinical experience and commentary (2017). https://pubmed.ncbi.nlm.nih.gov/28375179/

Comparative Analysis of GPT Models for Detecting Cyberbullying in Social Media Platforms Threads

Mohammad Shafiqul Islam[ID] and Rahat Ibn Rafiq[✉][ID]

Grand Valley State University, Allendale, MI 49401, USA
{islammo,rafiqr}@mail.gvsu.edu

Abstract. The escalating issue of cyberbullying on online social platforms has raised serious concerns regarding individuals' mental well-being and emotional health. As Large Language Models (LLMs) gain popularity and prevalence, exploring their potential in detecting cyberbullying becomes crucial. This research conducts a comparative analysis between GPT-3.5 Turbo and Text-Davinci models to identify cyberbullying within Instagram conversation threads. The evaluation of accuracy, precision, recall, and F1 score against manually labeled data allows us to assess the performance and limitations of these models in the context of cyberbullying detection. Through our findings, we aim to shed light on the effectiveness of LLMs in addressing this pervasive issue and their impact on online safety and well-being.

Keywords: Benchmarking · Cyberbullying · Classification

1 Introduction

With the rapid growth of social media platforms [8], online communication has become an integral part of our daily lives. While these platforms offer numerous benefits, they also present unique challenges, such as cyberbullying [30], which can have detrimental effects on individuals' well-being and mental health [7,21]. Cyberbullying refers to the use of electronic communication to harass, intimidate, or harm others [30], and it has emerged as a prevalent issue in the digital age [2].

Detecting and preventing cyberbullying is of paramount importance to create safe and inclusive online environments [27]. However, the vast amount of user-generated content on social media makes manual monitoring and intervention impractical [31]. To address this challenge, there is a growing interest in leveraging artificial intelligence and natural language processing techniques to automatically identify and classify instances of cyberbullying [10].

Language models, such as OpenAI's GPT-3.5 Turbo and Text-davinci-003, have shown tremendous potential in understanding and generating human-like text [32]. These models have been successfully applied to various natural

J. A. Lossio-Ventura et al. (Eds.): SIMBig 2023, CCIS 2142, pp. 331–346, 2024.
https://doi.org/10.1007/978-3-031-63616-5_25

language processing tasks, including sentiment analysis, text generation, and machine translation. In recent years, researchers have started exploring their application in the domain of cyberbullying detection [36,39].

The objective of this study is to investigate the effectiveness of language models in detecting cyberbullying instances in Instagram conversation threads [15]. We aim to assess the performance of different prompt designs and learning approaches, including zero-shot and one-shot learning, using ChatGPT 3.5 Turbo and Text-davinci-003 models [33].

The contributions of this research are twofold. First, we provide insights into the capabilities of language models in detecting cyberbullying, shedding light on their potential utility in cyberbullying detection. Second, we evaluate the performance of different prompt designs and learning approaches, providing valuable guidance for researchers and practitioners working in the field of cyberbullying detection.

The rest of this paper is organized as follows. Section 2 provides a review of related work on cyberbullying detection and the use of language models. Section 3 describes the learning approaches in our study. Section 4 describes the experimental setup in our study including dataset collection, preprocessing steps, and the models used. Section 5 presents the prompts used in our experiments. Section 6 presents the results and analysis of our experiments. Section 7 discusses the limitations of our study and suggests avenues for future work. Finally, Sect. 8 concludes the paper, summarizing our findings and outlining the implications of our research in the context of cyberbullying detection in social media platforms.

2   Related Works

2.1   Cyberbullying Detection Techniques

The issue of cyberbullying has garnered immense academic attention due to its widespread prevalence and detrimental impact on individuals, necessitating effective detection and prevention measures [11,29]. Traditional research extensively utilized machine learning techniques for automated cyberbullying detection across diverse online platforms [15,38]. These methods, leveraging textual content, linguistic patterns, and social network structures as key features, provided foundational insights into the identifiable characteristics of cyberbullying [25]. However, these approaches often required manual feature engineering and struggled to capture nuanced contextual subtleties, crucial for precise cyberbullying identification.

Islam et al. [17] innovatively combined machine learning and natural language processing, utilizing Bag-of-Words and Term Frequency-Inverse Text Frequency features, achieving exceptional accuracy and precision in identifying abusive online posts. Addressing the intricacies of sarcasm in cyberbullying, Ali and Syed [3] employed the Support Vector Machine (SVM) classifier and ensemble algorithms, surpassing previous classifiers in detecting sarcasm within cyberbullying contexts.

In recent years, advancements in deep learning and natural language processing have led to the application of sophisticated models like Convolutional Neural Networks (CNNs) and Recurrent Neural Networks (RNNs). These models excel in modeling the sequential and contextual nuances of online text [38]. Further progress has been made with the integration of attention mechanisms and transformer models, enhancing the ability to capture semantic relationships and dependencies within conversations, crucial for comprehensive cyberbullying detection. However, these advanced models demand extensive labeled data for training, posing a challenge in the ever-evolving landscape of cyberbullying [10].

Mahmud, Mamun, and Abdelgawad [23] explored various machine learning models, including Light GBM, XGBoost, and Logistic Regression, achieving impressive accuracy rates. Focusing on Arabic language-specific detection, Kanan, Aldaaja, and Hawashin [19] employed Random Forest and Arabic Natural Language Processing technologies, effectively recognizing bullying textual acts in Arabic social media content. The study conducted by Husain [16] emphasized the advantages of ensemble machine learning approaches, with bagging demonstrating notable superiority in detecting foul language in Arabic social media text.

The integration of deep learning techniques has significantly transformed cyberbullying detection. Alotaibi, Alotaibi, and Razaque [4] combined Transformer blocks, Bidirectional Gated Recurrent Units (BiGRU), and Convolutional Neural Networks (CNN) to classify aggressive and non-aggressive Twitter comments with an impressive 89% accuracy. Ajlan and Ykhlef [1] introduced the CNN-CB algorithm, eliminating the need for feature engineering and outperforming traditional methods by 95% in cyberbullying detection. Iwendi et al. [18] explored various deep learning models, highlighting the efficacy of Bidirectional Long Short-Term Memory (BLSTM) in spotting insults in social commentary.

Furthermore, the research landscape in cyberbullying detection has seen a significant shift towards hybrid techniques. Shanto et al. [37] utilized GRU models on Bangla Facebook comments, achieving an 85% accuracy rate. Rezvani and Beheshti [35] fine-tuned a variant of BERT, yielding an 86% accuracy rate for English language datasets. Hani et al. [14] employed CNN, outperforming Support Vector Machine (SVM) and showcasing the competitive edge of machine learning models in specific contexts.

2.2 Language Models in Cyberbullying Detection

The emergence of proficient language models like GPT-3.5 Turbo and Text-davinci-003 marks a significant stride in natural language processing, with their ability to understand and mimic human-like text becoming increasingly sophisticated [32]. The large corpus of text these models pre-train on presents a versatile foundation for task-specific fine-tuning, notably the detection of cyberbullying instances. Researchers have examined the competency of these models in identifying cyberbullying across varied platforms, extending the scope of detection from social media networks to online forums [36,39].

An intriguing facet these models proffer is zero-shot and one-shot learning capabilities. Zero-shot learning, leveraging the model's ability to classify instances even without explicit examples supports generalized cyberbullying detection absent of labeled data [12,22]. One-shot learning, in contrast, provides the model with a single labeled example, capitalizing on its ability to recognize patterns and generalize knowledge for effective detection [9,22].

Despite the promising outcomes, there remains potential to further understand the application of these models in the detection of cyberbullying, particularly with respect to the performance of various prompt designs and learning approaches [36]. A comprehensive exploration into this domain can result in useful revelations for future deployment of AI models in the detection and prevention of cyberbullying incidents.

2.3   Challenges and Ethical Considerations in AI-Based Detection

Despite the progress made in AI-based cyberbullying detection, there are several challenges and ethical considerations to acknowledge. The rapidly evolving language and context of cyberbullying posts, along with the creative evasion techniques deployed by cyberbullies make detection a continuously moving target [26,34].

Additionally, there are concerns related to privacy and freedom of speech. The task of automated content moderation must balance the urge to prevent and mitigate damaging cyberbullying behavior, with the privacy rights of users and the possibility of censorship [5,13]. Finally, false positive detections can lead to unjust consequences for innocent users, while false negatives can allow harmful content to go undetected [15,24].

Furthermore, development of AI models introduces potential biases, where the models could treat certain demographics or topics unfairly. Unintended inclusion of bias or discriminatory patterns present in training data could lead to models that are unfair or prejudiced in their decision-making processes [6,40]. Thus, fairness, accountability, and transparency form key guiding principles for AI researchers and developers in this domain.

3   Learning Approaches

In this section, we delve into the two fundamental learning approaches central to our study: zero-shot learning and one-shot learning. These approaches harness the capabilities of pre-trained language models, specifically GPT-3.5 Turbo and Text-davinci-003, to identify instances of cyberbullying within Instagram conversation threads.

3.1   Zero-Shot Learning Approach

Our zero-shot learning approach capitalizes on the power of pre-trained language models, such as GPT-3.5 Turbo and Text-davinci-003. In this method, the model is not explicitly trained on labeled examples of cyberbullying. Instead, it relies on carefully constructed prompts to comprehend the task and make accurate predictions.

We formulated specialized prompts designed for zero-shot learning, guiding the language model in distinguishing cyberbullying conversations from non-cyberbullying ones. By providing informative instructions without direct exposure to labeled training data, we assessed the model's ability to generalize its understanding of cyberbullying and accurately classify instances.

3.2   One-Shot Learning Approach

The one-shot learning approach involves presenting a single labeled example of a cyberbullying conversation thread to the language model. By learning from this solitary instance, the model generalizes its knowledge to detect cyberbullying in unseen conversations.

In our study, both GPT-3.5 Turbo and Text-davinci-003 were employed for the one-shot learning approach. By exposing the model to a single labeled example, we evaluated its capability to infer underlying patterns and characteristics of cyberbullying instances. This approach empowers the model to identify cyberbullying even in the absence of an extensive labeled dataset.

By employing both zero-shot and one-shot learning approaches, we aimed to meticulously explore the strengths and limitations of the language models in detecting cyberbullying within Instagram conversation threads.

4   Experimental Setup

We outline the dataset collection and preprocessing steps undertaken to prepare the Instagram conversation threads for analysis. Additionally, we describe the training and evaluation process for both the zero-shot and one-shot learning approaches. Metrics such as accuracy, precision, recall, and F1 score are used to evaluate the models' performance.

4.1   Dataset

The dataset used in this study was obtained from the research conducted by Hosseinmardi et al. (2015) titled "Analyzing labeled cyberbullying incidents on the Instagram social network." The dataset consists of 2,218 conversation threads extracted from Instagram, which were manually labeled as either cyberbullying or non-cyberbullying instances. The dataset can be accessed upon request at the provided email address: cucybersafety@gmail.com.

For the purpose of this research, a subset of the dataset was selected, focusing on 1,475 conversation threads. The selection criterion was based on the total word count of the conversations, specifically including threads with a word count less than or equal to 500. This subset was chosen to ensure manageable data size while still providing sufficient instances for analysis.

Each conversation thread in the dataset represents an interaction on Instagram and includes multiple comments posted by different users. The comments within each conversation thread are expected to contribute to the overall context and dynamics of the conversation. The dataset provides ground truth labels for the presence or absence of cyberbullying in each conversation thread. This labeled information serves as the basis for evaluating the performance of the models in cyberbullying detection.

4.2   Data Preprocessing

To prepare the data for analysis, several preprocessing steps were performed. These steps aimed to ensure the data's cleanliness, structure, and suitability for subsequent analysis and model training.

Removal of HTML Tags. Since the Instagram conversation data was obtained from a web-based source, it contained HTML tags that are irrelevant to the analysis. To eliminate these tags, an HTML tag removal process was applied. This step involved parsing the text and removing any HTML tags present within the conversation threads.

Parsing Time in Comments. Each comment in the conversation threads was associated with a timestamp indicating the time it was posted. To enable chronological sorting of the comments, the timestamp information was extracted and parsed. This involved identifying the time-related components within the comments and separating them from the textual content. Parsing the time information allowed for subsequent sorting of the comments based on their posting time.

Sorting Comments. Once the time information was extracted, the comments within each conversation thread were sorted in increasing order based on the time they were posted. Sorting the comments chronologically ensured that the conversation flow was maintained during subsequent analysis. By arranging the comments in the correct temporal order, the context and dynamics of the conversations could be accurately captured and analyzed.

By applying these preprocessing steps, the Instagram conversation data was transformed into a structured and organized format suitable for further analysis. The removal of HTML tags and the parsing and sorting of the comments based on their posting time contributed to maintaining the integrity and coherence of the conversations within each thread. These preprocessing steps laid the foundation for subsequent analysis, model training, and the detection of cyberbullying instances in the conversation data.

It is important to note that these preprocessing steps were specifically tailored to the characteristics and requirements of the Instagram conversation data used in this study. Depending on the nature of the data and the specific research objectives, additional or alternative preprocessing steps may be necessary to ensure data quality and relevance.

4.3 Language Models

To analyze and classify the Instagram conversation threads for cyberbullying detection, we utilized two models provided by the OpenAI API: ChatGPT 3.5 Turbo and Text-davinci-003 [28]. These models are based on the GPT-3.5 architecture, which is a state-of-the-art language model trained on diverse and extensive text data.

ChatGPT 3.5 Turbo. The GPT-3.5-Turbo is an advanced language model developed by OpenAI, designed to generate human-like text based on prompts provided to it. As a variant of the powerful GPT-3 model, GPT-3.5-Turbo leverages a similar transformer architecture but comes with numerous enhancements that make it even more efficient and versatile.

The primary strength of the GPT-3.5-Turbo lies in its conversational capabilities. It can participate in in-depth discussions, comprehend contextual clues, and furnish responses that showcase a high level of understanding. Its applications are broad and varied, encompassing areas like drafting emails, writing code, creating written content, answering questions, tutoring, language translation, and simulating characters for video games.

Text-Davinci-003. The Text Da Vinci 003 model is another advanced conversational AI created by OpenAI. It is among the high-end models in the GPT-3 family, known as the "Da Vinci" tier. The Da Vinci models are often designated with proprietary sophistication and intellectual prowess.

The text-generation capacity of Text Da Vinci 003 is particularly impressive, supporting complex tasks encompassing language translation, sentence completion, text summarization, and even content generation in the form of essays, articles, or stories. Like other models of OpenAI, it operates through a method referred to as "transformative learning," a type of machine learning where the model learns to predict the next word in a sentence. By doing this, the model effectively trains itself to identify and replicate human-style conversation and writing.

Both models, ChatGPT 3.5 Turbo and Text-davinci-003, offer sophisticated natural language understanding capabilities. They have been trained on a diverse range of internet text, enabling them to comprehend and generate human-like responses. These models excel at various NLP tasks, including text classification, sentiment analysis, and language generation.

5 Prompt Design

In this section, we detail the prompts designed for classifying Instagram conversation threads as cyberbullying or non-cyberbullying using the ChatGPT

3.5 Turbo and Text-davinci-003 models provided by the OpenAI API. These prompts were carefully crafted to elicit responses from the models, determining their classification abilities without explicit examples (zero-shot learning) or with a single example (one-shot learning), following techniques outlined in [20].

5.1   Zero-Shot Learning Prompts

For the zero-shot learning approach, we devised prompts 1, 2, 3, and 4 to classify conversation threads without providing specific examples:

Prompt 1

> Cyberbullying refers to an imbalance of power and repetition of aggression. I am going to give you a conversation thread containing comments. You have to detect if the whole conversation reflects cyberbullying or not. Respond with just 'yes' if it is cyberbullying or just 'no' if it is not cyberbullying. Comments are -

Prompt 2

> Cyberbullying refers to an imbalance of power and the repetition of aggressive behavior. I'm going to provide you with an Instagram conversation thread containing comments. Your task is to determine whether the conversation as a whole reflects cyberbullying or not. Please respond with either 'yes' if it is cyberbullying or 'no' if it is not cyberbullying. Keep in mind that you are reading Instagram threads. Here are the comments:

Prompt 3

> Cyberbullying refers to an imbalance of power and the repetition of aggressive behavior. I'm going to provide you with an Instagram conversation thread containing comments. Your task is to carefully analyze the conversation and determine whether the conversation as a whole reflects cyberbullying or not. Please respond with either 'yes' if the conversation as a whole reflects cyberbullying or 'no' if it does not. Think like you are reading Instagram threads and consider the tone, content, and intention behind the comments. Think step by step. Comments are -

Prompt 4

> As an Instagram moderator, your responsibility is to analyze the provided conversation thread and determine whether a conversation thread reflects cyberbullying. Carefully assess the tone, content, and intention behind the comments, taking into consideration the overall context of the conversation. In your assessment, indicate 'yes' if you believe the conversation as a whole reflects cyberbullying or 'no' if it does not. Remember to evaluate the

| cumulative effect of the comments and think step by step. The comments for your analysis are:

Among these zero-shot prompts, prompt 2 demonstrated superior results in our initial analysis. To further enhance accuracy, we employed prompt 2 for the Text-davinci-003 model, providing more precise zero-shot learning outcomes.

5.2   One-Shot Learning Prompt

Additionally, we created prompt 5 specifically for the one-shot learning scenario:

Prompt 5

Act as an Instagram moderator and carefully analyze the provided conversation thread to determine whether a conversation thread reflects cyberbullying. Your task is to assess the tone, content, and intention behind the comments and respond with either 'yes' if the conversation as a whole reflects cyberbullying or 'no' if it does not. Think like you are reading Instagram threads and consider the overall conversation's context. Here are some example comments that you should evaluate:
@user1: You're such a pathetic loser. Nobody wants anything to do with you.
@user2: Wow, you're so dumb. How do you manage to breathe?
@user3: Your face is so ugly, it's a shame to even look at you.
@user4: Just kill yourself already. The world would be better off without you.
As an Instagram moderator, it is crucial to ensure a safe and respectful community. Please provide your assessment of the conversation thread as a whole, indicating 'yes' if cyberbullying is present or 'no' if it is not. Consider the cumulative effect of the comments and evaluate the presence of cyberbullying accordingly. Comments are -

Prompt 5 offers a single labeled example of a cyberbullying conversation thread, allowing the models to learn and generalize their classification to other threads.

The selection of these prompts was based on their ability to effectively guide the models in distinguishing cyberbullying conversations. Prompt 2, in particular, exhibited superior performance, which can be attributed to its clear instructions and relevance to the task. The prompts were carefully designed to encapsulate the nuances of cyberbullying behaviors, enabling the models to comprehend the context and make accurate classifications.

By utilizing multiple prompts and models, we aimed to thoroughly explore and compare the efficacy of zero-shot and one-shot learning approaches in cyberbullying detection. These prompt choices were instrumental in providing valuable insights into the models' classification abilities, leading to a comprehensive evaluation of their performance in diverse learning scenarios.

6   Results and Analysis

In this section, we present the results obtained from the experiments conducted using different prompts and models for both zero-shot and one-shot learning approaches. We analyze the performance of each model and prompt combination based on the provided metrics.

6.1   Zero-Shot Learning Results

For the zero-shot learning approach, we utilized ChatGPT 3.5 Turbo model with prompts 1, 2, 3, and 4. The results of the classification for cyberbullying and non-cyberbullying conversations are presented in the table.

Among the zero-shot prompts, prompt 2 achieved the highest precision for cyberbullying (0.449064) and non-bullying (0.927565) conversations. Prompt 2 also showed a good balance between bullying recall (0.75) and non-bullying recall (0.776748), indicating its effectiveness in identifying both types of conversations. The F1 score for cyberbullying (0.561769) and non-bullying (0.845484) categories was also relatively high for prompt 2.

6.2   One-Shot Learning Results

For the one-shot learning approach, we used prompt 5 with both the models. The precision for cyberbullying conversations for ChatGPT 3.5 Turbo (0.338866) was lower compared to the zero-shot prompt 2 (0.449064), indicating a higher rate of false positives. However, the recall for cyberbullying (0.850694) was higher, suggesting the model's ability to capture a larger portion of cyberbullying instances. The F1 score for cyberbullying (0.484669) was also relatively lower, indicating the trade-off between precision and recall observed in the one-shot scenario.

6.3   Comparison and Analysis

Comparing the zero-shot and one-shot learning approaches, we observed that prompt 2 with Text-davinci-003 model achieved the highest precision for cyberbullying conversations (0.539095). However, prompt 5 with ChatGPT 3.5 Turbo model demonstrated a higher recall for cyberbullying conversations (0.850694), capturing a larger proportion of instances.

Overall, the results indicate that prompt 2 with ChatGPT 3.5 Turbo model performed well in the zero-shot learning scenario, achieving a good balance between precision and recall for cyberbullying and non-cyberbullying conversations. On the other hand, prompt 5 with Text-davinci-003 model showed potential in identifying cyberbullying instances with a higher recall, although at the cost of lower precision.

These findings highlight the importance of prompt design and model selection in achieving optimal performance for cyberbullying detection in Instagram conversation threads. Depending on the desired trade-offs between precision and

Table 1. Results - ChatGPT 3.5 Turbo (zero-shot)

Metric	Prompt 1	Prompt 2	Prompt 3	Prompt 4
Bullying Precision	0.418048	0.449064	0.388795	0.381513
Non-Bullying Precision	0.934549	0.927565	0.933409	0.930682
Bullying Recall	0.788194	0.75	0.795139	0.788194
Non-Bullying Recall	0.733783	0.776748	0.696714	0.689975
Bullying F1 Score	0.54633	0.561769	0.522235	0.514156
Non-Bullying F1 Score	0.822086	0.845484	0.797877	0.792453

Table 2. Results - Text-davinci-003 (zero-shot)

Metric	Prompt 2
Bullying Precision	0.539095
Non-Bullying Precision	0.872565
Bullying Recall	0.454861
Non-Bullying Recall	0.905644
Bullying F1 Score	0.493409
Non-Bullying F1 Score	0.888797

recall, researchers and practitioners can leverage different prompts and models to suit their specific needs and application scenarios.

It is worth noting that these results are based on the specific dataset and experimental setup used in this study. Further research and experimentation with larger and diverse datasets would be valuable to validate and generalize these findings. Additionally, exploring alternative prompt designs and model architectures could potentially lead to improved performance in cyberbullying detection tasks.

Tables 1, 3, 2, 4 provide a breakdown of the precision, recall, and F1 score for both bullying and non-bullying conversations using different prompts and models.

7 Limitations and Future Work

While our study provides valuable insights into the application of language models for cyberbullying detection in Instagram conversation threads, it is important to acknowledge the limitations of our approach and identify potential directions for future research.

7.1 Limitations

1. Dataset Bias: Our analysis heavily relies on the dataset provided by Hosseinmardi et al. (2015). It is crucial to recognize that this dataset may contain

Table 3. Results - ChatGPT 3.5 Turbo (one-shot)

Metric	Prompt 5
Bullying Precision	0.338866
Non-Bullying Precision	0.942819
Bullying Recall	0.850694
Non-Bullying Recall	0.597304
Bullying F1 Score	0.484669
Non-Bullying F1 Score	0.731305

Table 4. Results - Text-davinci-003 (one-shot)

Metric	Prompt 5
Bullying Precision	0.426554
Non-Bullying Precision	0.877788
Bullying Recall	0.524306
Non-Bullying Recall	0.828981
Bullying F1 Score	0.470405
Non-Bullying F1 Score	0.852686

inherent biases and may not fully represent the diversity and complexity of cyber-bullying instances on Instagram. Future studies should consider incorporating larger and more diverse datasets to improve the generalizability of the findings.

2. Limited Prompt Design: Although we explored multiple prompts for both zero-shot and one-shot learning, the prompt design space is vast, and there may be more effective prompts that can enhance the performance of the models. Further investigation into innovative prompt designs and techniques for fine-tuning the models could yield improved results.

3. False Positive and False Negative Rates: Our evaluation metrics focus on precision, recall, and F1 score. However, in the context of cyberbullying detection, false positives (incorrectly labeling a non-bullying conversation as bullying) and false negatives (missing actual instances of bullying) have significant implications. Future research should aim to minimize both false positives and false negatives to enhance the reliability and accuracy of the models.

4. Lack of Contextual Understanding: Language models like GPT-3.5 Turbo and Text-davinci-003 primarily rely on textual patterns and do not possess a deep understanding of the underlying context or nuances of social interactions. This limitation can impact their ability to accurately detect cyberbullying instances that rely heavily on contextual cues such as sarcasm, irony, or implicit threats. Incorporating context-aware models or leveraging additional contextual information could be explored to address this limitation.

7.2 Future Work

1. Model Fine-tuning: Fine-tuning the language models on domain-specific data related to cyberbullying could potentially lead to better performance. Training the models on annotated Instagram conversation datasets specifically curated for cyberbullying detection could enhance their understanding and classification capabilities.

2. Multimodal Analysis: Instagram conversations often include multimedia elements such as images, videos, and emojis, which provide valuable contextual information. Integrating multimodal analysis techniques that incorporate both textual and visual data could enhance the models' ability to detect cyberbullying instances accurately.

3.Real-time Monitoring: Developing real-time monitoring systems that can detect and flag cyberbullying instances as they occur in Instagram conversations is crucial. Future research could focus on building dynamic models that can process conversations in real-time, enabling prompt intervention and mitigation strategies.

4. Ethical Considerations: The deployment of cyberbullying detection models raises important ethical considerations, such as privacy, bias, and algorithmic fairness. Future work should explore ways to address these concerns, ensuring the responsible and ethical use of such models to minimize any potential harm.

Addressing these limitations and exploring the future directions mentioned above will contribute to the advancement of cyberbullying detection techniques, making them more effective, reliable, and applicable in real-world scenarios.

8 Conclusion

In this study, we investigated the application of language models for cyberbullying detection in Instagram conversation threads. We employed two models, ChatGPT 3.5 Turbo and Text-davinci-003, utilizing both zero-shot and one-shot learning approaches. Our goal was to assess the models' performance in classifying conversations as either cyberbullying or non-cyberbullying based on different prompts.

Through our experiments and analysis, we obtained valuable insights into the capabilities and limitations of these language models in detecting cyberbullying instances. The results indicate that prompt 2 of ChatGPT 3.5 Turbo achieved the highest F1 score for identifying cyberbullying conversations using the zero-shot learning approach. Additionally, prompt 5 of Text-davinci-003 exhibited promising performance in the one-shot learning scenario.

However, it is important to note that our study has certain limitations. The dataset used may have inherent biases, and the prompt designs explored may not have fully captured the complexity of cyberbullying instances on Instagram. Furthermore, the models' reliance on textual patterns may hinder their ability to understand contextual cues and accurately detect cyberbullying instances that rely on implicit threats or sarcasm.

To overcome these limitations and enhance the field of cyberbullying detection, future research should focus on larger and more diverse datasets, innovative prompt designs, and fine-tuning the models on domain-specific data related to cyberbullying. Integration of multimodal analysis techniques and real-time monitoring systems could also improve the models' performance in real-world scenarios.

As we continue to advance the field of cyberbullying detection, it is imperative to address ethical considerations, such as privacy, bias, and algorithmic fairness. Responsible and ethical use of language models will ensure their positive impact while minimizing potential harm.

In conclusion, our study contributes to the ongoing research on utilizing language models for cyberbullying detection in social media platforms. While there is still room for improvement, the results demonstrate the potential of language models in assisting with the identification and prevention of cyberbullying instances. By addressing the limitations and exploring future research directions, we can pave the way for more effective and reliable cyberbullying detection techniques, ultimately fostering safer and more inclusive online environments.

References

1. Al-Ajlan, M.A., Ykhlef, M.: Deep learning algorithm for cyberbullying detection. Int. J. Adv. Comput. Sci. Appl. **9**(9) (2018)
2. Al-Garadi, M., Varathan, K., Ravana, S.D.: Cybercrime detection in online communications: The experimental case of cyberbullying detection in the twitter network. Comput. Human Behav. **63**, 433–443 (10 2016). https://doi.org/10.1016/j.chb.2016.05.051
3. Ali, A., Syed, A.M.: Cyberbullying detection using machine learning. Pakistan J. Eng. Technol. **3**(2), 45–50 (2020)
4. Alotaibi, M., Alotaibi, B., Razaque, A.: A multichannel deep learning framework for cyberbullying detection on social media. Electronics **10**(21), 2664 (2021)
5. Binns, R.: Fairness in machine learning: Lessons from political philosophy (2021)
6. Bolukbasi, T., Chang, K.W., Zou, J., Saligrama, V., Kalai, A.: Man is to computer programmer as woman is to homemaker? debiasing word embeddings (2016)
7. Bottino, S.M.B., Bottino, C.M.C., Regina, C.G., Correia, A.V.L., Ribeiro, W.S.: Cyberbullying and adolescent mental health: systematic review. Cad. Saude Publica **31**(3), 463–75 (2015)
8. boyd, d.m., Ellison, N.B.: Social Network Sites: Definition, History, and Scholarship. J. Comput.-Mediated Commun. **13**(1), 210–230 (10 2007). https://doi.org/10.1111/j.1083-6101.2007.00393.x, https://doi.org/10.1111/j.1083-6101.2007.00393.x
9. Brown, T.B., et al.: Language models are few-shot learners (2020)
10. Dadvar, M., de Jong, F., Ordelman, R., Trieschnigg, D.: Improved cyberbullying detection using gender information (01 2012)
11. Dinakar, K., Reichart, R., Lieberman, H.: Modeling the detection of textual cyberbullying (01 2011)

12. Erhan, D., Bengio, Y., Courville, A., Manzagol, P.A., Vincent, P., Bengio, S.: Why does unsupervised pre-training help deep learning? J. Mach. Learn. Res. **11**(19), 625–660 (2010). http://jmlr.org/papers/v11/erhan10a.html
13. Gillespie, T.: Content moderation, ai, and the question of scale. Big Data Society **7**, 205395172094323 (07 2020). https://doi.org/10.1177/2053951720943234
14. Hani, J., Mohamed, N., Ahmed, M., Emad, Z., Amer, E., Ammar, M.: Social media cyberbullying detection using machine learning. Int. J. Adv. Comput. Sci. Appl. **10**(5) (2019)
15. Hosseinmardi, H., Arredondo Mattson, S., Rafiq, R.I., Han, R., Lv, Q., Mishra, S.: Detection of cyberbullying incidents on the Instagram social network (03 2015)
16. Husain, F.: Arabic offensive language detection using machine learning and ensemble machine learning approaches. arXiv preprint arXiv:2005.08946 (2020)
17. Islam, M.M., Uddin, M.A., Islam, L., Akter, A., Sharmin, S., Acharjee, U.K.: Cyberbullying detection on social networks using machine learning approaches. In: 2020 IEEE Asia-Pacific Conference on Computer Science and Data Engineering (CSDE), pp. 1–6. IEEE (2020)
18. Iwendi, C., Srivastava, G., Khan, S., Maddikunta, P.K.R.: Cyberbullying detection solutions based on deep learning architectures. Multimedia Systems, pp. 1–14 (2020)
19. Kanan, T., Aldaaja, A., Hawashin, B.: Cyber-bullying and cyber-harassment detection using supervised machine learning techniques in Arabic social media contents. J. Internet Technol. **21**(5), 1409–1421 (2020)
20. Karpathy, A.: State of gpt (2023). https://karpathy.ai/stateofgpt.pdf. Accessed July 24 2023
21. Kota, R., Selkie, E.M.: Cyberbullying and mental health (2018)
22. Liu, Y., et al.: Roberta: A robustly optimized Bert pretraining approach (2019)
23. Mahmud, M.I., Mamun, M., Abdolgawad, A.: A deep analysis of textual features based cyberbullying detection using machine learning. In: 2022 IEEE Global Conference on Artificial Intelligence and Internet of Things (GCAIoT), pp. 166–170. IEEE (2022)
24. Milosevic, T., et al.: Artificial intelligence to address cyberbullying, harassment and abuse: New directions in the midst of complexity. Int. J. Bull. Prevent.: Off. Public. Int. Bull. Prevent. Assoc. **4**(1), 1–5 (2022). https://doi.org/10.1007/s42380-022-00117-x
25. Mishna, F., Cook, C., Gadalla, T., Daciuk, J., Solomon, S.: Cyber bullying behaviors among middle and high school students. Am. J. Orthopsych. **80**, 362–74 (07 2010). https://doi.org/10.1111/j.1939-0025.2010.01040.x
26. Nahar, V., AL Maskari, S., Li, X., Pang, C.: Semi-supervised learning for cyberbullying detection in social networks, pp. 160–171 (07 2014). https://doi.org/10.1007/978-3-319-08608-8_14
27. Nobata, C., Tetreault, J.R., Thomas, A.O., Mehdad, Y., Chang, Y.: Abusive language detection in online user content. In: Proceedings of the 25th International Conference on World Wide Web (2016)
28. OpenAI: Openai models (2023). https://platform.openai.com/docs/models/overview. Accessed July 24 2023
29. Parime, S., Suri, V.: Cyberbullying detection and prevention: Data mining and psychological perspective. In: 2014 International Conference on Circuits, Power and Computing Technologies [ICCPCT-2014], pp. 1541–1547 (2014). https://doi.org/10.1109/ICCPCT.2014.7054943

30. Patchin, J., Hinduja, S.: Cyberbullying: An update and synthesis of the research. In: Cyberbullying Prevention and Response: Expert Perspectives, pp. 13–35 (01 2012)

31. Pfeffer, J., Zorbach, T., Carley, K.: Understanding online firestorms: negative word-of-mouth dynamics in social media networks. J. Market. Commun. **20**, 117–128 (12 2013). https://doi.org/10.1080/13527266.2013.797778

32. Radford, A., Wu, J., Child, R., Luan, D., Amodei, D., Sutskever, I.: Language models are unsupervised multitask learners (2019)

33. Raffel, C., et al.: Exploring the limits of transfer learning with a unified text-to-text transformer. J. Mach. Learn. Res. **21**(140), 1–67 (2020). http://jmlr.org/papers/v21/20-074.html

34. Reynolds, K., Edwards, A., Edwards, L.: Using machine learning to detect cyberbullying. In: Proceedings - 10th International Conference on Machine Learning and Applications, ICMLA 2011 **2** (12 2011). https://doi.org/10.1109/ICMLA.2011.152

35. Rezvani, N., Beheshti, A.: Towards attention-based context-boosted cyberbullying detection in social media. J. Data Intell. **2**, 418–433 (2021)

36. Sap, M., Card, D., Gabriel, S., Choi, Y., Smith, N.A.: The risk of racial bias in hate speech detection. In: Annual Meeting of the Association for Computational Linguistics (2019)

37. Shanto, S.B., Islam, M.J., Samad, M.A.: Cyberbullying detection using deep learning techniques on Bangla Facebook comments. In: 2023 International Conference on Intelligent Systems, Advanced Computing and Communication (ISACC), pp. 1–7. IEEE (2023)

38. Van Hee, C., et al.: Automatic detection of cyberbullying in social media text. PLOS ONE **13**(10), 1–22 (10 2018). https://doi.org/10.1371/journal.pone.0203794, https://doi.org/10.1371/journal.pone.0203794

39. Zhang, Z., Luo, L.: Hate speech detection: A solved problem? the challenging case of long tail on twitter. Semantic Web **Accepted** (10 2018). https://doi.org/10.3233/SW-180338

40. Zhao, J., Zhou, Y., Li, Z., Wang, W., Chang, K.W.: Learning gender-neutral word embeddings, pp. 4847–4853 (01 2018). https://doi.org/10.18653/v1/D18-1521

Author Index

Printed in the United States
by Baker & Taylor Publisher Services